# Mathematics and Statistics for Financial Risk Management

# Mathematics and Statistics for Financial Risk Management

**Second Edition**

MICHAEL B. MILLER

WILEY

Published by John Wiley & Sons, Inc., Hoboken, New Jersey.
Published simultaneously in Canada.

*Library of Congress Cataloging-in-Publication Data:*

Miller, Michael B. (Michael Bernard), 1973–
    Mathematics and statistics for financial risk management / Michael B. Miller. —
2nd Edition.
        pages cm. — (Wiley finance)
    Includes bibliographical references and index.
    ISBN 978-1-118-75029-2 (hardback); ISBN 978-1-118-757555-0 (ebk); ISBN
978-1-118-75764-2 (ebk)    1. Risk management—Mathematical models.   2. Risk
management—Statistical methods.   I. Title.
    HD61.M537 2013
    332.01'5195—dc23
                                                                    2013027322

Printed in the United States of America

10 9 8 7 6 5 4 3 2 1

# Contents

# Preface

The recent financial crisis and its impact on the broader economy underscores the importance of financial risk management in today's world. At the same time, financial products and investment strategies are becoming increasingly complex. It is more important than ever that risk managers possess a sound understanding of mathematics and statistics.

*Mathematics and Statistics for Financial Risk Management* is a guide to modern financial risk management for both practitioners and academics. Risk management has made great strides in recent years. Many of the mathematical and statistical tools used in risk management today were originally adapted from other fields. As the field has matured, risk managers have refined these tools and developed their own vocabulary for characterizing risk. As the field continues to mature, these tools and vocabulary are becoming increasingly standardized. By focusing on the application of mathematics and statistics to actual risk management problems, this book helps bridge the gap between mathematics and statistics in theory and risk management in practice.

Each chapter in this book introduces a different topic in mathematics or statistics. As different techniques are introduced, sample problems and application sections demonstrate how these techniques can be applied to actual risk management problems. Exercises at the end of each chapter, and the accompanying solutions at the end of the book, allow readers to practice the techniques learned and to monitor their progress.

This book assumes that readers have a solid grasp of algebra and at least a basic understanding of calculus. Even though most chapters start out at a very basic level, the pace is necessarily fast. For those who are already familiar with the topic, the beginning of each chapter serves as a quick review and as an introduction to selected vocabulary terms and conventions. Readers who are new to these topics may find they need to spend more time in the initial sections.

Risk management in practice often requires building models using spreadsheets or other financial software. Many of the topics in this book are accompanied by an icon, as shown here.

These icons indicate that Excel examples can be found at John Wiley & Sons' companion website for *Mathematics and Statistics for Financial Risk Management, Second edition* at www.wiley.com/go/millerfinance2e.

You can also visit the author's website, www.risk256.com, for the latest financial risk management articles, code samples, and more. To provide feedback, contact the author at mike@risk256.com.

# What's New in the Second Edition

The biggest change to the second edition is the addition of two new chapters. The first new chapter, Chapter 5: Multivariate Distributions, explores important concepts for measuring the risk of portfolios, including joint distributions and copulas. The other new chapter, Chapter 6: Bayesian Analysis, expands on what was a short section in the first edition. The breadth and depth of this new chapter more accurately reflect the importance of Bayesian statistics in risk management today. Finally, the second edition includes many new problems, corrections, and small improvements to topics covered in the first edition. These included expanded sections on value at risk model validation, and generalized auto-regressive conditional heteroscedasticity (GARCH).

# What's New in the Second Edition

# Acknowledgments

This book would not have been possible without the help of many individuals. I would like to thank Jeffrey Garnett, Steve Lerit, Riyad Maznavi, Hyunsuk Moon, Elliot Noma, Eldar Radovici, and Barry Schachter for taking the time to read early drafts. The book is certainly better for their comments and feedback.

I would also like to thank everybody at John Wiley & Sons for their help in bringing this book together.

Finally, and most importantly, I would like to thank my wife, Amy, who not only read over early drafts and talked me through a number of decisions, but also put up with countless nights and weekends of typing and editing. For this and much, much more, thank you.

## CHAPTER 1

# Some Basic Math

In this chapter we review three math topics—logarithms, combinatorics, and geometric series—and one financial topic, discount factors. Emphasis is given to the specific aspects of these topics that are most relevant to risk management.

## LOGARITHMS

In mathematics, logarithms, or logs, are related to exponents, as follows:

$$\log_b a = x \Leftrightarrow a = b^x \qquad (1.1)$$

We say, "The log of $a$, base $b$, equals $x$, which implies that $a$ equals $b$ to the $x$ and vice versa." If we take the log of the right-hand side of Equation 1.1 and use the identity from the left-hand side of the equation, we can show that:

$$\log_b(b^x) = \log_b a = x$$
$$\log_b(b^x) = x \qquad (1.2)$$

Taking the log of $b^x$ effectively cancels out the exponentiation, leaving us with $x$.

An important property of logarithms is that the logarithm of the product of two variables is equal to the sum of the logarithms of those two variables. For two variables, $X$ and $Y$:

$$\log_b(XY) = \log_b X + \log_b Y \qquad (1.3)$$

Similarly, the logarithm of the ratio of two variables is equal to the difference of their logarithms:

$$\log_b\left(\frac{X}{Y}\right) = \log_b X - \log_b Y \qquad (1.4)$$

If we replace $Y$ with $X$ in Equation 1.3, we get:

$$\log_b(X^2) = 2\log_b X \qquad (1.5)$$

We can generalize this result to get the following power rule:

$$\log_b(X^n) = n\log_b X \qquad (1.6)$$

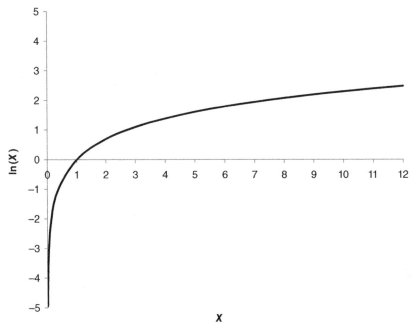

**EXHIBIT 1.1**    Natural Logarithm

In general, the base of the logarithm, $b$, can have any value. Base 10 and base 2 are popular bases in certain fields, but in many fields, and especially in finance, $e$, Euler's number, is by far the most popular. Base $e$ is so popular that mathematicians have given it its own name and notation. When the base of a logarithm is $e$, we refer to it as a *natural logarithm*. In formulas, we write:

$$\ln(a) = x \Leftrightarrow a = e^x \tag{1.7}$$

From this point on, unless noted otherwise, assume that any mention of logarithms refers to natural logarithms.

Logarithms are defined for all real numbers greater than or equal to zero. Exhibit 1.1 shows a plot of the logarithm function. The logarithm of zero is negative infinity, and the logarithm of one is zero. The function grows without bound; that is, as $X$ approaches infinity, the $\ln(X)$ approaches infinity as well.

## LOG RETURNS

One of the most common applications of logarithms in finance is computing log returns. Log returns are defined as follows:

$$r_t \equiv \ln(1 + R_t) \quad \text{where} \quad R_t = \frac{P_t - P_{t-1}}{P_{t-1}} \tag{1.8}$$

**EXHIBIT 1.2**   Log Returns and Simple Returns

| $R$ | $\ln(1 + R)$ |
|---|---|
| 1.00% | 1.00% |
| 5.00% | 4.88% |
| 10.00% | 9.53% |
| 20.00% | 18.23% |

Here $r_t$ is the log return at time $t$, $R_t$ is the standard or simple return, and $P_t$ is the price of the security at time $t$. We use this convention of capital $R$ for simple returns and lowercase $r$ for log returns throughout the rest of the book. This convention is popular, but by no means universal. Also, be careful: Despite the name, the log return is not the log of $R_t$, but the log of $(1 + R_t)$.

For small values, log returns and simple returns will be very close in size. A simple return of 0% translates exactly to a log return of 0%. A simple return of 10% translates to a log return of 9.53%. That the values are so close is convenient for checking data and preventing operational errors. Exhibit 1.2 shows some additional simple returns along with their corresponding log returns.

To get a more precise estimate of the relationship between standard returns and log returns, we can use the following approximation:[1]

$$r \approx R - \frac{1}{2}R^2 \tag{1.9}$$

As long as $R$ is small, the second term on the right-hand side of Equation 1.9 will be negligible, and the log return and the simple return will have very similar values.

## COMPOUNDING

Log returns might seem more complex than simple returns, but they have a number of advantages over simple returns in financial applications. One of the most useful features of log returns has to do with compounding returns. To get the return of a security for two periods using simple returns, we have to do something that is not very intuitive, namely adding one to each of the returns, multiplying, and then subtracting one:

$$R_{2,t} = \frac{P_t - P_{t-2}}{P_{t-2}} = (1 + R_{1,t})(1 + R_{1,t-1}) - 1 \tag{1.10}$$

Here the first subscript on $R$ denotes the length of the return, and the second subscript is the traditional time subscript. With log returns, calculating multiperiod returns is much simpler; we simply add:

$$r_{2,t} = r_{1,t} + r_{1,t-1} \tag{1.11}$$

---

[1]This approximation can be derived by taking the Taylor expansion of Equation 1.8 around zero. Though we have not yet covered the topic, for the interested reader a brief review of Taylor expansions can be found in Appendix B.

By substituting Equation 1.8 into Equation 1.10 and Equation 1.11, you can see that these definitions are equivalent. It is also fairly straightforward to generalize this notation to any return length.

---

**SAMPLE PROBLEM**

*Question:*

Using Equation 1.8 and Equation 1.10, generalize Equation 1.11 to returns of any length.

*Answer:*

$$R_{n,t} = \frac{P_t - P_{t-n}}{P_{t-n}} = \frac{P_t}{P_{t-n}} - 1 = \frac{P_t}{P_{t-1}} \frac{P_{t-1}}{P_{t-2}} \cdots \frac{P_{t-n+1}}{P_{t-n}} - 1$$

$$R_{n,t} = (1 + R_{1,t})(1 + R_{1,t-1}) \cdots (1 + R_{1,t-n+1}) - 1$$

$$(1 + R_{n,t}) = (1 + R_{1,t})(1 + R_{1,t-1}) \cdots (1 + R_{1,t-n+1})$$

$$r_{n,t} = r_{1,t} + r_{1,t-1} + \cdots + r_{1,t-n+1}$$

To get to the last line, we took the logs of both sides of the previous equation, using the fact that the log of the product of any two variables is equal to the sum of their logs, as given in Equation 1.3.

---

## LIMITED LIABILITY

Another useful feature of log returns relates to limited liability. For many financial assets, including equities and bonds, the most that you can lose is the amount that you've put into them. For example, if you purchase a share of XYZ Corporation for $100, the most you can lose is that $100. This is known as limited liability. Today, limited liability is such a common feature of financial instruments that it is easy to take it for granted, but this was not always the case. Indeed, the widespread adoption of limited liability in the nineteenth century made possible the large publicly traded companies that are so important to our modern economy, and the vast financial markets that accompany them.

That you can lose only your initial investment is equivalent to saying that the minimum possible return on your investment is −100%. At the other end of the spectrum, there is no upper limit to the amount you can make in an investment. The maximum possible return is, in theory, infinite. This range for simple returns, −100% to infinity, translates to a range of negative infinity to positive infinity for log returns.

$$R_{min} = -100\% \Rightarrow r_{min} = -\infty$$
$$R_{max} = +\infty \Rightarrow r_{max} = +\infty$$
(1.12)

As we will see in the following chapters, when it comes to mathematical and computer models in finance it is often much easier to work with variables that are unbounded—that is, variables that can range from negative infinity to positive infinity. This makes log returns a natural choice for many financial models.

## GRAPHING LOG RETURNS

Another useful feature of log returns is how they relate to log prices. By rearranging Equation 1.10 and taking logs, it is easy to see that:

$$r_t = p_t - p_{t-1} \qquad (1.13)$$

where $p_t$ is the log of $P_t$, the price at time $t$. To calculate log returns, rather than taking the log of one plus the simple return, we can simply calculate the logs of the prices and subtract.

Logarithms are also useful for charting time series that grow exponentially. Many computer applications allow you to chart data on a logarithmic scale. For an asset whose price grows exponentially, a logarithmic scale prevents the compression of data at low levels. Also, by rearranging Equation 1.13, we can easily see that the change in the log price over time is equal to the log return:

$$\Delta p_t = p_t - p_{t-1} = r_t \qquad (1.14)$$

It follows that, for an asset whose return is constant, the change in the log price will also be constant over time. On a chart, this constant rate of change over time will translate into a constant slope. Exhibits 1.3 and 1.4 both show an asset whose

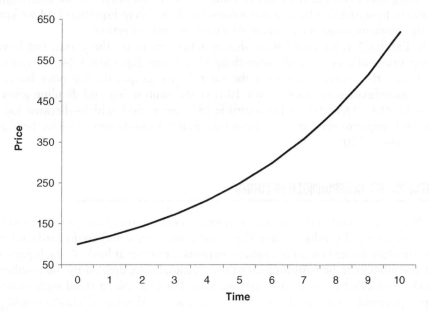

**EXHIBIT 1.3**  Normal Prices

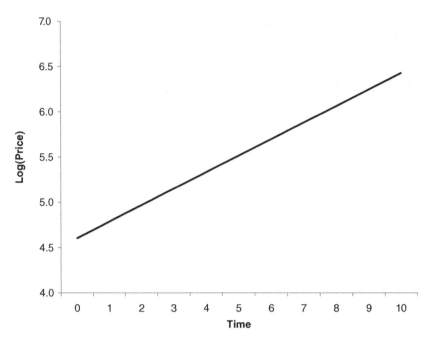

**EXHIBIT 1.4**   Log Prices

price is increasing by 20% each year. The y-axis for the first chart shows the price; the y-axis for the second chart displays the log price.

For the chart in Exhibit 1.3, it is hard to tell if the rate of return is increasing or decreasing over time. For the chart in Exhibit 1.4, the fact that the line is straight is equivalent to saying that the line has a constant slope. From Equation 1.14 we know that this constant slope is equivalent to a constant rate of return.

In Exhibit 1.4, we could have shown actual prices on the y-axis, but having the log prices allows us to do something else. Using Equation 1.14, we can easily estimate the average return for the asset. In the graph, the log price increases from approximately 4.6 to 6.4 over 10 periods. Subtracting and dividing gives us $(6.4 - 4.6)/10 = 18\%$. So the log return is 18% per period, which—because log returns and simple returns are very close for small values—is very close to the actual simple return of 20%.

## CONTINUOUSLY COMPOUNDED RETURNS

Another topic related to the idea of log returns is continuously compounded returns. For many financial products, including bonds, mortgages, and credit cards, interest rates are often quoted on an annualized periodic or nominal basis. At each payment date, the amount to be paid is equal to this nominal rate, divided by the number of periods, multiplied by some notional amount. For example, a bond with monthly coupon payments, a nominal rate of 6%, and a notional value of $1,000 would pay a coupon of $5 each month: $(6\% \times \$1,000)/12 = \$5$.

How do we compare two instruments with different payment frequencies? Are you better off paying 5% on an annual basis or 4.5% on a monthly basis? One solution is to turn the nominal rate into an annualized rate:

$$R_{\text{Annual}} = \left(1 + \frac{R_{\text{Nominal}}}{n}\right)^n - 1 \qquad (1.15)$$

where $n$ is the number of periods per year for the instrument.

If we hold $R_{\text{Annual}}$ constant as $n$ increases, $R_{\text{Nominal}}$ gets smaller, but at a decreasing rate. Though the proof is omitted here, using L'Hôpital's rule, we can prove that, at the limit, as $n$ approaches infinity, $R_{\text{Nominal}}$ converges to the log rate. As $n$ approaches infinity, it is as if the instrument is making infinitesimal payments on a continuous basis. Because of this, when used to define interest rates the log rate is often referred to as the continuously compounded rate, or simply the continuous rate. We can also compare two financial products with different payment periods by comparing their continuous rates.

## SAMPLE PROBLEM

*Question:*

You are presented with two bonds. The first has a nominal rate of 20% paid on a semiannual basis. The second has a nominal rate of 19% paid on a monthly basis. Calculate the equivalent continuously compounded rate for each bond. Assuming both bonds can be purchased at the same price, have the same credit quality, and are the same in all other respects, which is the better investment?

*Answer:*

First, we compute the annual yield for both bonds:

$$R_{1,\text{ Annual}} = \left(1 + \frac{20\%}{2}\right)^2 - 1 = 21.00\%$$

$$R_{2,\text{ Annual}} = \left(1 + \frac{19\%}{12}\right)^{12} - 1 = 20.75\%$$

Next, we convert these annualized returns into continuously compounded returns:

$$r_1 = \ln(1 + R_{1,\text{ Annual}}) = 19.06\%$$

$$r_2 = \ln(1 + R_{2,\text{ Annual}}) = 18.85\%$$

All other things being equal, the first bond is a better investment. We could base this on a comparison of either the annual rates or the continuously compounded rates.

## COMBINATORICS

In elementary combinatorics, one typically learns about combinations and permutations. Combinations tell us how many ways we can arrange a number of objects, regardless of the order, whereas permutations tell us how many ways we can arrange a number of objects, taking into account the order.

As an example, assume we have three hedge funds, denoted X, Y, and Z. We want to invest in two of the funds. How many different ways can we invest? We can invest in X and Y, X and Z, or Y and Z. That's it.

In general, if we have $n$ objects and we want to choose $k$ of those objects, the number of combinations, $C(n, k)$, can be expressed as:

$$C(n,k) = \binom{n}{k} = \frac{n!}{k!(n-k)!} \tag{1.16}$$

where $n!$ is $n$ factorial, such that:

$$n! = \begin{cases} 1 & n = 0 \\ n(n-1)(n-2)\cdots 1 & n > 0 \end{cases} \tag{1.17}$$

In our example with the three hedge funds, we would substitute $n = 3$ and $k = 2$ to get three possible combinations.

What if the order mattered? What if instead of just choosing two funds, we needed to choose a first-place fund and a second-place fund? How many ways could we do that? The answer is the number of permutations, which we express as:

$$P(n,k) = \frac{n!}{(n-k)!} \tag{1.18}$$

For each combination, there are $k!$ ways in which the elements of that combination can be arranged. In our example, each time we choose two funds, there are two ways that we can order them, so we would expect twice as many permutations. This is indeed the case. Substituting $n = 3$ and $k = 2$ into Equation 1.18, we get six permutations, which is twice the number of combinations computed previously.

Combinations arise in a number of risk management applications. The binomial distribution, which we will introduce in Chapter 4, is defined using combinations. The binomial distribution, in turn, can be used to model defaults in simple bond portfolios or to backtest value at risk (VaR) models, as we will see in Chapter 7.

Combinations are also central to the binomial theorem. Given two variables, $x$ and $y$, and a positive integer, $n$, the binomial theorem states:

$$(x+y)^n = \sum_{k=0}^{n} \binom{n}{k} x^{n-k} y^k \tag{1.19}$$

For example:

$$(x+y)^3 = x^3 + 3x^2y + 3xy^2 + y^3 \tag{1.20}$$

The binomial theorem can be useful when computing statistics such as variance, skewness, and kurtosis, which will be discussed in Chapter 3.

## DISCOUNT FACTORS

Most people have a preference for present income over future income. They would rather have a dollar today than a dollar one year from now. This is why banks charge interest on loans, and why investors expect positive returns on their investments. Even in the absence of inflation, a rational person should prefer a dollar today to a dollar tomorrow. Looked at another way, we should require more than one dollar in the future to replace one dollar today.

In finance we often talk of discounting cash flows or future values. If we are discounting at a fixed rate, $R$, then the present value and future value are related as follows:

$$V_t = \frac{V_{t+n}}{(1+R)^n} \qquad (1.21)$$

where $V_t$ is the value of the asset at time $t$ and $V_{t+n}$ is the value of the asset at time $t + n$. Because $R$ is positive, $V_t$ will necessarily be less than $V_{t+n}$. All else being equal, a higher discount rate will lead to a lower present value. Similarly, if the cash flow is further in the future—that is, $n$ is greater—then the present value will also be lower.

Rather than work with the discount rate, $R$, it is sometimes easier to work with a discount factor. In order to obtain the present value, we simply multiply the future value by the discount factor:

$$V_t = \left(\frac{1}{1+R}\right)^n V_{t+n} = \delta^n V_{t+n} \qquad (1.22)$$

Because the discount factor $\delta$ is less than one, $V_t$ will necessarily be less than $V_{t+n}$. Different authors refer to $\delta$ or $\delta^n$ as the discount factor. The concept is the same, and which convention to use should be clear from the context.

## GEOMETRIC SERIES

In the following two subsections we introduce geometric series. We start with series of infinite length. It may seem counterintuitive, but it is often easier to work with series of infinite length. With results in hand, we then move on to series of finite length in the second subsection.

### Infinite Series

The ancient Greek philosopher Zeno, in one of his famous paradoxes, tried to prove that motion was an illusion. He reasoned that in order to get anywhere, you first had to travel half the distance to your ultimate destination. Once you made it to the halfway point, though, you would still have to travel half the remaining distance. No matter how many of these half journeys you completed, there would always be another half journey left. You could never possibly reach your destination.

While Zeno's reasoning turned out to be wrong, he was wrong in a very profound way. The infinitely decreasing distances that Zeno struggled with foreshadowed calculus, with its concept of change on an infinitesimal scale. Also, infinite series of a variety of types turn up in any number of fields. In finance, we are often faced with series that can be treated as infinite. Even when the series is long but clearly finite, the same basic tools that we develop to handle infinite series can be deployed.

In the case of the original paradox, we are basically trying to calculate the following summation:

$$S = \frac{1}{2} + \frac{1}{4} + \frac{1}{8} + \cdots \tag{1.23}$$

What is $S$ equal to? If we tried the brute force approach, adding up all the terms, we would literally be working on the problem forever. Luckily, there is an easier way. The trick is to notice that multiplying both sides of the equation by ½ has the exact same effect as subtracting ½ from both sides:

| Multiply both sides by ½: | Subtract ½ from both sides: |
|---|---|
| $S = \dfrac{1}{2} + \dfrac{1}{4} + \dfrac{1}{8} + \cdots$ | $S = \dfrac{1}{2} + \dfrac{1}{4} + \dfrac{1}{8} + \cdots$ |
| $\dfrac{1}{2}S = \dfrac{1}{4} + \dfrac{1}{8} + \dfrac{1}{16} + \cdots$ | $S - \dfrac{1}{2} = \dfrac{1}{4} + \dfrac{1}{8} + \dfrac{1}{16} + \cdots$ |

The right-hand sides of the final line of both equations are the same, so the left-hand sides of both equations must also be equal. Taking the left-hand sides of both equations, and solving:

$$
\begin{aligned}
S - \frac{1}{2} &= \frac{1}{2}S \\
S - \frac{1}{2}S &= \frac{1}{2} \\
\frac{1}{2}S &= \frac{1}{2} \\
S &= 1
\end{aligned}
\tag{1.24}
$$

The fact that the infinite series adds up to one tells us that Zeno was wrong. If we keep covering half the distance but do it an infinite number of times, eventually we will cover the entire distance. The sum of all the half trips equals one full trip.

To generalize Zeno's paradox, assume we have the following series:

$$S = \sum_{i=1}^{\infty} \delta^i \tag{1.25}$$

In Zeno's case, $\delta$ was ½. Because the members of the series are all powers of the same constant, we refer to these types of series as geometric series. As long as $|\delta|$ is less than one, the sum will be finite and we can employ the same basic strategy as before, this time multiplying both sides by $\delta$.

$$
\begin{aligned}
\delta S &= \sum_{i=1}^{\infty} \delta^{i+1} \\
\delta S &= S - \delta \\
\delta &= S(1 - \delta) \\
S &= \frac{\delta}{1 - \delta}
\end{aligned}
\tag{1.26}
$$

Substituting ½ for $\delta$, we see that the general equation agrees with our previously obtained result for Zeno's paradox.

Before deriving Equation 1.26, we stipulated that $|\delta|$ had to be less than one. The reason that $|\delta|$ has to be less than one may not be obvious. If $\delta$ is equal to one, we are simply adding together an infinite number of ones, and the sum is infinite. In this case, even though it requires us to divide by zero, Equation 1.26 will produce the correct answer.

If $\delta$ is greater than one, the sum is also infinite, but Equation 1.26 will give you the wrong answer. The reason is subtle. If $\delta$ is less than one, then $\delta^{\infty}$ converges to zero. When we multiplied both sides of the original equation by $\delta$, in effect we added a $\delta^{\infty+1}$ term to the end of the original equation. If $|\delta|$ is less than one, this term is zero, and the sum is unaltered. If $|\delta|$ is greater than one, however, this final term is itself infinitely large, and we can no longer assume that the sum is unaltered. If this is at all unclear, wait until the end of the following section on finite series, where we will revisit the issue. If $\delta$ is less than $-1$, the series will oscillate between increasingly large negative and positive values and will not converge. Finally, if $\delta$ equals $-1$, the series will flip back and forth between $-1$ and $+1$, and the sum will oscillate between $-1$ and $0$.

One note of caution: In certain financial problems, you will come across geometric series that are very similar to Equation 1.25 except the first term is one, not $\delta$. This is equivalent to setting the starting index of the summation to zero ($\delta^0 = 1$). Adding one to our previous result, we obtain the following equation:

$$
S = \sum_{i=0}^{\infty} \delta^i = \frac{1}{1 - \delta}
\tag{1.27}
$$

As you can see, the change from $i = 0$ to $i = 1$ is very subtle, but has a very real impact on the sum.

## SAMPLE PROBLEM

*Question:*
    A perpetuity is a security that pays a fixed coupon for eternity. Determine the present value of a perpetuity that pays a \$5 coupon annually. Assume a constant 4% discount rate.

*Answer:*

$$V = \sum_{i=1}^{\infty} \frac{\$5}{(1.04)^i}$$

$$V = \$5 \sum_{i=1}^{\infty} \left(\frac{1}{1.04}\right)^i = \$5 \frac{\frac{1}{1.04}}{1 - \frac{1}{1.04}} = \$5 \frac{1}{1.04 - 1} = \$5 \cdot 25$$

$$V = \$125$$

### Finite Series

In many financial scenarios—including perpetuities and discount models for stocks and real estate—it is often convenient to treat an extremely long series of payments as if it were infinite. In other circumstances we are faced with very long but clearly finite series. In these circumstances the infinite series solution might provide us with a good approximation, but ultimately we will want a more precise answer.

The basic technique for summing a long but finite geometric series is the same as for an infinite geometric series. The only difference is that the terminal terms no longer converge to zero.

$$S = \sum_{i=0}^{n-1} \delta^i$$

$$\delta S = \sum_{i=0}^{n-1} \delta^{i+1} = S - \delta^0 + \delta^n \qquad (1.28)$$

$$S = \frac{1 - \delta^n}{1 - \delta}$$

We can see that for $|\delta|$ less than one, as $n$ approaches infinity $\delta^n$ goes to zero, and Equation 1.28 converges to Equation 1.27.

In finance, we will mostly be interested in situations where $|\delta|$ is less than one, but Equation 1.28, unlike Equation 1.27, is still valid for values of $|\delta|$ greater than one (check this for yourself). We did not need to rely on the final term converging to zero this time. If $\delta$ is greater than one, and we substitute infinity for $n$, we get:

$$S = \frac{1 - \delta^{\infty}}{1 - \delta} = \frac{1 - \infty}{1 - \delta} = \frac{-\infty}{1 - \delta} = \infty \qquad (1.29)$$

For the last step, we rely on the fact that $(1 - \delta)$ is negative for $\delta$ greater than one. As promised in the preceding subsection, for $\delta$ greater than one, the sum of the infinite geometric series is indeed infinite.

## SAMPLE PROBLEM

*Question:*

What is the present value of a newly issued 20-year bond with a notional value of $100 and a 5% annual coupon? Assume a constant 4% discount rate and no risk of default.

*Answer:*

This question utilizes discount factors and finite geometric series.

The bond will pay 20 coupons of $5, starting in a year's time. In addition, the notional value of the bond will be returned with the final coupon payment in 20 years. The present value, $V$, is then:

$$V = \sum_{i=1}^{20} \frac{\$5}{(1.04)^i} + \frac{\$100}{(1.04)^{20}} = \$5 \sum_{i=1}^{20} \frac{1}{(1.04)^i} + \frac{\$100}{(1.04)^{20}}$$

We start by evaluating the summation, using a discount factor of $\delta = 1/1.04 \approx 0.96$:

$$S = \sum_{i=1}^{20} \frac{1}{(1.04)^i} = \sum_{i=1}^{20} \left(\frac{1}{1.04}\right)^i = \sum_{i-1}^{20} \delta^i = \delta + \delta^2 + \cdots + \delta^{19} + \delta^{20}$$

$$\delta S = \delta^2 + \delta^3 + \cdots + \delta^{20} + \delta^{21}$$

$$\delta S = S - \delta + \delta^{21}$$

$$\delta - \delta^{21} = S(1 - \delta)$$

$$S = \frac{\delta - \delta^{21}}{1 - \delta}$$

$$S = 13.59$$

Inserting this result into the initial equation, we obtain our final result:

$$V = \$5 \times 13.59 + \frac{\$100}{(1.04)^{20}} = \$113.59$$

Note that the present value of the bond, $113.59, is greater than the notional value of the bond, $100. In general, if there is no risk of default and the coupon rate on the bond is higher than the discount rate, then the present value of the bond will be greater than the notional value of the bond.

When the price of a bond is less than the notional value of the bond, we say that the bond is selling at a discount. When the price of the bond is greater than the notional value, as in this example, we say that it is selling at a premium. When the price is exactly the same as the notional value we say that it is selling at par.

## PROBLEMS

1. Solve for $y$, where:
   a. $y = \ln(e^5)$
   b. $y = \ln(1/e)$
   c. $y = \ln(10e)$

2. The nominal monthly rate for a loan is quoted at 5%. What is the equivalent annual rate? Semiannual rate? Continuous rate?

3. Over the course of a year, the log return on a stock market index is 11.2%. The starting value of the index is 100. What is the value at the end of the year?

4. You have a portfolio of 10 bonds. In how many different ways can exactly two bonds default? Assume the order in which the bonds default is unimportant.

5. What is the present value of a perpetuity that pays $100 per year? Use an annual discount rate of 4%, and assume the first payment will be made in exactly one year.

6. ABC stock will pay a $1 dividend in one year. Assume the dividend will continue to be paid annually forever and the dividend payments will increase in size at a rate of 5%. Value this stream of dividends using a 6% annual discount rate.

7. What is the present value of a 10-year bond with a $100 face value, which pays a 6% coupon annually? Use an 8% annual discount rate.

8. Solve for $x$, where $e^{e^x} = 10$.

9. Calculate the value of the following summation: $\sum_{i=0}^{9}(-0.5)^i$

10. The risk department of your firm has 10 analysts. You need to select four analysts to serve on a special audit committee. How many possible groupings of four analysts can be put together?

11. What is the present value of a newly issued 10-year bond with a notional value of $100 and a 2% annual coupon? Assume a constant 5% annual discount rate and no risk of default.

## CHAPTER 2

# Probabilities

In this chapter we explore the application of probabilities to risk management. We also introduce basic terminology and notations that will be used throughout the rest of this book.

## DISCRETE RANDOM VARIABLES

The concept of probability is central to risk management. Many concepts associated with probability are deceptively simple. The basics are easy, but there are many potential pitfalls.

In this chapter, we will be working with both discrete and continuous random variables. Discrete random variables can take on only a countable number of values—for example, a coin, which can be only heads or tails, or a bond, which can have only one of several letter ratings (AAA, AA, A, BBB, etc.). Assume we have a discrete random variable $X$, which can take various values, $x_i$. Further assume that the probability of any given $x_i$ occurring is $p_i$. We write:

$$P[X = x_i] = p_i \text{ s.t. } x_i \in \{x_1, x_2, \ldots, x_n\} \tag{2.1}$$

where $P[\cdot]$ is our probability operator.[1]

An important property of a random variable is that the sum of all the probabilities must equal one. In other words, the probability of any event occurring must equal one. Something has to happen. Using our current notation, we have:

$$\sum_{i=i}^{n} p_i = 1 \tag{2.2}$$

## CONTINUOUS RANDOM VARIABLES

In contrast to a discrete random variable, a continuous random variable can take on any value within a given range. A good example of a continuous random

---

[1] "s.t." is shorthand for "such that". The final term indicates that $x_i$ is a member of a set that includes $n$ possible values, $x_1, x_2, \ldots, x_n$. You could read the full equation as: "The probability that $X$ equals $x_i$ is equal to $p_i$, such that $x_i$ is a member of the set $x_1, x_2$, to $x_n$."

variable is the return of a stock index. If the level of the index can be any real number between zero and infinity, then the return of the index can be any real number greater than −1.

Even if the range that the continuous variable occupies is finite, the number of values that it can take is infinite. For this reason, for a continuous variable, the probability of any *specific* value occurring is zero.

Even though we cannot talk about the probability of a specific value occurring, we can talk about the probability of a variable being within a certain range. Take, for example, the return on a stock market index over the next year. We can talk about the probability of the index return being between 6% and 7%, but talking about the probability of the return being exactly 6.001% is meaningless. Between 6% and 7% there are an infinite number of possible values. The probability of any one of those infinite values occurring is zero.

For a continuous random variable $X$, then, we can write:

$$P[r_1 < X < r_2] = p \tag{2.3}$$

which states that the probability of our random variable, $X$, being between $r_1$ and $r_2$ is equal to $p$.

## Probability Density Functions

For a continuous random variable, the probability of a specific event occurring is not well defined, but some events are still more likely to occur than others. Using annual stock market returns as an example, if we look at 50 years of data, we might notice that there are more data points between 0% and 10% than there are between 10% and 20%. That is, the density of points between 0% and 10% is higher than the density of points between 10% and 20%.

For a continuous random variable we can define a probability density function (PDF), which tells us the likelihood of outcomes occurring between any two points. Given our random variable, $X$, with a probability $p$ of being between $r_1$ and $r_2$, we can define our density function, $f(x)$, such that:

$$\int_{r_1}^{r_2} f(x)dx = p \tag{2.4}$$

The probability density function is often referred to as the probability distribution function. Both terms are correct, and, conveniently, both can be abbreviated PDF.

As with discrete random variables, the probability of any value occurring must be one:

$$\int_{r_{\min}}^{r_{\max}} f(x)dx = 1 \tag{2.5}$$

where $r_{\min}$ and $r_{\max}$ define the lower and upper bounds of $f(x)$.

## SAMPLE PROBLEM

*Question:*

Define the probability density function for the price of a zero coupon bond with a notional value of $10 as:

$$f(x) = \frac{x}{50} \text{ s.t. } 0 \leq x \leq 10$$

where $x$ is the price of the bond. What is the probability that the price of the bond is between $8 and $9?

*Answer:*

First, note that this is a legitimate probability function. By integrating the PDF from its minimum to its maximum, we can show that the probability of any value occurring is indeed one:

$$\int_0^{10} \frac{x}{50} dx = \frac{1}{50} \int_0^{10} x dx = \frac{1}{50} \left[ \frac{1}{2} x^2 \right]_0^{10} = \frac{1}{100} (10^2 - 0^2) = 1$$

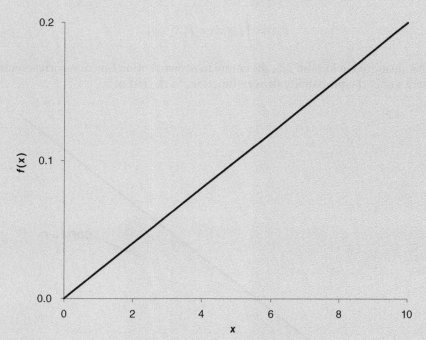

**EXHIBIT 2.1** Probability Density Function

If we graph the function, as in Exhibit 2.1, we can also see that the area under the curve is one. Using simple geometry:

$$\text{Area of triangle} = \frac{1}{2} \cdot \text{Base} \cdot \text{Height} = \frac{1}{2} \cdot 10 \cdot 0.2 = 1$$

To answer the question, we simply integrate the probability density function between 8 and 9:

$$\int_{8}^{9} \frac{x}{50} dx = \left[ \frac{1}{100} x^2 \right]_{8}^{9} = \frac{1}{100}(9^2 - 8^2) = \frac{17}{100} = 17\%$$

The probability of the price ending up between $8 and $9 is 17%.

### Cumulative Distribution Functions

Closely related to the concept of a probability density function is the concept of a cumulative distribution function or cumulative density function (both abbreviated CDF). A cumulative distribution function tells us the probability of a random variable being less than a certain value. The CDF can be found by integrating the probability density function from its lower bound. Traditionally, the cumulative distribution function is denoted by the capital letter of the corresponding density function. For a random variable $X$ with a probability density function $f(x)$, then, the cumulative distribution function, $F(x)$, could be calculated as follows:

$$F(a) = \int_{-\infty}^{a} f(x)dx = P[X \leq a] \tag{2.6}$$

As illustrated in Exhibit 2.2, the cumulative distribution function corresponds to the area under the probability density function, to the left of $a$.

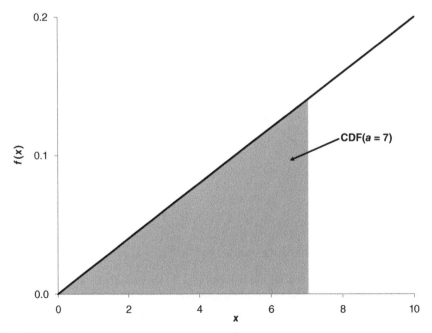

**EXHIBIT 2.2**   Relationship between Cumulative Distribution Function and Probability Density Function

By definition, the cumulative distribution function varies from 0 to 1 and is nondecreasing. At the minimum value of the probability density function, the CDF must be zero. There is no probability of the variable being less than the minimum. At the other end, all values are less than the maximum of the PDF. The probability is 100% (CDF = 1) that the random variable will be less than or equal to the maximum. In between, the function is nondecreasing. The reason that the CDF is nondecreasing is that, at a minimum, the probability of a random variable being between two points is zero. If the CDF of a random variable at 5 is 50%, then the lowest it could be at 6 is 50%, which would imply 0% probability of finding the variable between 5 and 6. There is no way the CDF at 6 could be less than the CDF at 5.

Just as we can get the cumulative distribution from the probability density function by integrating, we can get the PDF from the CDF by taking the first derivative of the CDF:

$$f(x) = \frac{dF(x)}{dx} \tag{2.7}$$

That the CDF is nondecreasing is another way of saying that the PDF cannot be negative.

If instead of wanting to know the probability that a random variable is less than a certain value, what if we want to know the probability that it is greater than a certain value, or between two values? We can handle both cases by adding and subtracting cumulative distribution functions. To find the probability that a variable is between two values, $a$ and $b$, assuming $b$ is greater than $a$, we subtract:

$$P[a < X \leq b] = \int_a^b f(x)dx = F(b) - F(a) \tag{2.8}$$

To get the probability that a variable is greater than a certain value, we simply subtract from 1:

$$P[X > a] = 1 - F(a) \tag{2.9}$$

This result can be obtained by substituting infinity for $b$ in the previous equation, remembering that the CDF at infinity must be 1.

## SAMPLE PROBLEM

*Question:*
Calculate the cumulative distribution function for the probability density function from the previous problem:

$$f(x) = \frac{x}{50} \text{ s.t. } 0 \leq x \leq 10 \tag{2.10}$$

Then answer the previous problem: What is the probability that the price of the bond is between $8 and $9?

*Answer:*
The CDF can be found by integrating the PDF:

$$F(a) = \int_0^a f(x)\,dx = \int_0^a \frac{x}{50}\,dx = \frac{1}{50}\int_0^a x\,dx = \frac{1}{50}\left[\frac{1}{2}x^2\right]_0^a = \frac{a^2}{100}$$

To get the answer to the question, we simply evaluate the CDF at $8 and $9 and subtract:

$$P[\$8 < x \le \$9] = F(9) - F(8) = \frac{9^2}{100} - \frac{8^2}{100} = \frac{81}{100} - \frac{64}{100} = \frac{17}{100} = 17\%$$

As before, the probability of the price ending up between $8 and $9 is 17%.

## Inverse Cumulative Distribution Functions

The inverse of the cumulative distribution can also be useful. For example, we might want to know that there is a 5% probability that a given equity index will return less than −10.6%, or that there is a 1% probability of interest rates increasing by more than 2% over a month.

More formally, if $F(a)$ is a cumulative distribution function, then we define $F^{-1}(p)$, the inverse cumulative distribution, as follows:

$$F(a) = p \Leftrightarrow F^{-1}(p) = a \text{ s.t. } 0 \le p \le 1 \tag{2.11}$$

As we will see in Chapter 4, while some popular distributions have very simple inverse cumulative distribution functions, for other distributions no explicit inverse exists.

## SAMPLE PROBLEM

*Question:*
Given the cumulative distribution from the previous sample problem:

$$F(a) = \frac{a^2}{100} \text{ s.t. } 0 \le a \le 10$$

Calculate the inverse cumulative distribution function. Find the value of $a$ such that 25% of the distribution is less than or equal to $a$.

*Answer:*
We have:

$$F(a) = p = \frac{a^2}{100}$$

Solving for $p$:

$$a = 10\sqrt{p}$$

Therefore, the inverse CDF is:

$$F^{-1}(p) = 10\sqrt{p}$$

We can quickly check that $p = 0$ and $p = 1$, return 0 and 10, the minimum and maximum of the distribution. For $p = 25\%$ we have:

$$F^{-1}(0.25) = 10\sqrt{0.25} = 10 \cdot 0.5 = 5$$

So 25% of the distribution is less than or equal to 5.

## MUTUALLY EXCLUSIVE EVENTS

For a given random variable, the probability of any of two mutually exclusive events occurring is just the sum of their individual probabilities. In statistics notation, we can write:

$$P[A \cup B] = P[A] + P[B] \tag{2.12}$$

where $[A \cup B]$ is the union of $A$ and $B$. This is the probability of either $A$ *or* $B$ occurring. This is true only of mutually exclusive events.

This is a very simple rule, but, as mentioned at the beginning of the chapter, probability can be deceptively simple, and this property is easy to confuse. The confusion stems from the fact that *and* is synonymous with addition. If you say it this way, then the probability that $A$ or $B$ occurs is equal to the probability of $A$ *and* the probability of $B$. It is not terribly difficult, but you can see where this could lead to a mistake.

This property of mutually exclusive events can be extended to any number of events. The probability that any of $n$ mutually exclusive events occurs is simply the sum of the probabilities of those $n$ events.

## SAMPLE PROBLEM

*Question:*
   Calculate the probability that a stock return is either below −10% or above 10%, given:

$$P[R < -10\%] = 14\%$$
$$P[R > +10\%] = 17\%$$

*Answer:*
   Note that the two events are mutually exclusive; the return cannot be below −10% and above 10% at the same time. The answer is: 14% + 17% = 31%.

## INDEPENDENT EVENTS

In the preceding example, we were talking about one random variable and two mutually exclusive events, but what happens when we have more than one random variable? What is the probability that it rains tomorrow *and* the return on stock XYZ is greater than 5%? The answer depends crucially on whether the two random variables influence each other. If the outcome of one random variable is not influenced by the outcome of the other random variable, then we say those variables are independent. *If* stock market returns are independent of the weather, then the stock market should be just as likely to be up on rainy days as it is on sunny days.

Assuming that the stock market and the weather are independent random variables, then the probability of the market being up and rain is just the product of the probabilities of the two events occurring individually. We can write this as follows:

$$P[\text{rain and market up}] = P[\text{rain} \cap \text{market up}] = P[\text{rain}] \cdot P[\text{market up}] \quad (2.13)$$

We often refer to the probability of two events occurring together as their joint probability.

---

### SAMPLE PROBLEM

*Question:*
According to the most recent weather forecast, there is a 20% chance of rain tomorrow. The probability that stock XYZ returns more than 5% on any given day is 40%. The two events are independent. What is the probability that it rains and stock XYZ returns more than 5% tomorrow?

*Answer:*
Since the two events are independent, the probability that it rains and stock XYZ returns more than 5% is just the product of the two probabilities. The answer is: 20% × 40% = 8%.

---

## PROBABILITY MATRICES

When dealing with the joint probabilities of two variables, it is often convenient to summarize the various probabilities in a probability matrix or probability table. For example, pretend we are investigating a company that has issued both bonds and stock. The bonds can be downgraded, upgraded, or have no change in rating. The stock can either outperform the market or underperform the market.

In Exhibit 2.3, the probability of both the company's stock outperforming the market and the bonds being upgraded is 15%. Similarly, the probability of the stock underperforming the market and the bonds having no change in rating is 25%. We can also see the unconditional probabilities, by adding across a row or down a

**EXHIBIT 2.3**  Bonds versus Stock Matrix

|  |  | Stock | | |
|---|---|---|---|---|
|  |  | Outperform | Underperform | |
| Bonds | Upgrade | 15% | 5% | 20% |
|  | No Change | 30% | 25% | 55% |
|  | Downgrade | 5% | 20% | 25% |
|  |  | 50% | 50% | 100% |

column. The probability of the bonds being upgraded, irrespective of the stock's performance, is: 15% + 5% = 20%. Similarly, the probability of the equity outperforming the market is: 15% + 30% + 5% = 50%. Importantly, all of the joint probabilities add to 100%. Given all the possible events, one of them must happen.

## SAMPLE PROBLEM

*Question:*

You are investigating a second company. As with our previous example, the company has issued both bonds and stock. The bonds can be downgraded, upgraded, or have no change in rating. The stock can either outperform the market or underperform the market. You are given the probability matrix shown in Exhibit 2.4, which is missing three probabilities, X, Y, and Z. Calculate values for the missing probabilities.

**EXHIBIT 2.4**  Bonds versus Stock Matrix

|  |  | Stock | | |
|---|---|---|---|---|
|  |  | Outperform | Underperform | |
| Bonds | Upgrade | 5% | 0% | 5% |
|  | No Change | 40% | Y | Z |
|  | Downgrade | X | 30% | 35% |
|  |  | 50% | 50% | 100% |

*Answer:*

All of the values in the first column must add to 50%, the probability of the stock outperforming the market; therefore, we have:

$$5\% + 40\% + X = 50\%$$
$$X = 5\%$$

We can check our answer for X by summing across the third row: 5% + 30% = 35%.

Looking down the second column, we see that $Y$ is equal to 20%:

$$0\% + Y + 30\% = 50\%$$
$$Y = 20\%$$

Finally, knowing that $Y = 20\%$, we can sum across the second row to get $Z$:

$$40\% + Y = 40\% + 20\% = Z$$
$$Z = 60\%$$

## CONDITIONAL PROBABILITY

The concept of independence is closely related to the concept of conditional probability. Rather than trying to determine the probability of the market being up *and* having rain, we can ask, "What is the probability that the stock market is up *given* that it is raining?" We can write this as a conditional probability:

$$P[\text{market up} \mid \text{rain}] = p \tag{2.14}$$

The vertical bar signals that the probability of the first argument is conditional on the second. You would read Equation 2.14 as "The probability of 'market up' given 'rain' is equal to $p$."

Using the conditional probability, we can calculate the probability that it will rain *and* that the market will be up.

$$P[\text{market up and rain}] = P[\text{market up} \mid \text{rain}] \cdot P[\text{rain}] \tag{2.15}$$

For example, if there is a 10% probability that it will rain tomorrow and the probability that the market will be up *given* that it is raining is 40%, then the probability of rain and the market being up is 4%: $40\% \times 10\% = 4\%$.

From a statistics standpoint, it is just as valid to calculate the probability that it will rain and that the market will be up as follows:

$$P[\text{market up and rain}] = P[\text{rain} \mid \text{market up}] \cdot P[\text{market up}] \tag{2.16}$$

As we will see in Chapter 6 when we discuss Bayesian analysis, even though the right-hand sides of Equations 2.15 and 2.16 are mathematically equivalent, how we interpret them can often be different.

We can also use conditional probabilities to calculate unconditional probabilities. On any given day, either it rains or it does not rain. The probability that the market will be up, then, is simply the probability of the market being up when it is raining plus the probability of the market being up when it is not raining. We have:

$$P[\text{market up}] = P[\text{market up and rain}] + P[\text{market up and } \overline{\text{rain}}]$$

$$P[\text{market up}] = P[\text{market up} \mid \text{rain}] \cdot P[\text{rain}] + P[\text{market up} \mid \overline{\text{rain}}] \cdot P[\overline{\text{rain}}] \tag{2.17}$$

Here we have used a line over *rain* to signify logical negation; $\overline{\text{rain}}$ can be read as "not rain."

In general, if a random variable $X$ has $n$ possible values, $x_1, x_2, \ldots, x_n$, then the unconditional probability of $Y$ can be calculated as:

$$P[Y] = \sum_{i=1}^{n} P[Y \mid x_i]\, P[x_i] \tag{2.18}$$

If the probability of the market being up on a rainy day is the same as the probability of the market being up on a day with no rain, then we say that the market is conditionally independent of rain. If the market is conditionally independent of rain, then the probability that the market is up given that it is raining must be equal to the unconditional probability of the market being up. To see why this is true, we replace the conditional probability of the market being up given no rain with the conditional probability of the market being up given rain in Equation 2.17 (we can do this because we are assuming that these two conditional probabilities are equal).

$$P[\text{market up}] = P[\text{market up} \mid \text{rain}] \cdot P[\text{rain}] + P[\text{market up} \mid \text{rain}] \cdot P[\overline{\text{rain}}]$$

$$P[\text{market up}] = P[\text{market up} \mid \text{rain}] \cdot (P[\text{rain}] + P[\overline{\text{rain}}]) \tag{2.19}$$

$$P[\text{market up}] = P[\text{market up} \mid \text{rain}]$$

In the last line of Equation 2.19, we rely on the fact that the probability of rain plus the probability of no rain is equal to one. Either it rains or it does not rain.

In Equation 2.19 we could just have easily replaced the conditional probability of the market being up given rain with the conditional probability of the market being up given no rain. If the market is conditionally independent of rain, then it is also true that the probability that the market is up given that it is not raining must be equal to the unconditional probability of the market being up:

$$P[\text{market up}] = P[\text{market up} \mid \overline{\text{rain}}] \tag{2.20}$$

In the previous section, we noted that if the market is independent of rain, then the probability that the market will be up and that it will rain must be equal to the probability of the market being up multiplied by the probability of rain. To see why this must be true, we simply substitute the last line of Equation 2.19 into Equation 2.15:

$$P[\text{market up and rain}] = P[\text{market up} \mid \text{rain}] \cdot P[\text{rain}]$$

$$P[\text{market up and rain}] = P[\text{market up}] \cdot P[\text{rain}] \tag{2.21}$$

Remember that Equation 2.21 is true only if the market being up and rain are independent. If the weather somehow affects the stock market, however, then the conditional probabilities might not be equal. We could have a situation where:

$$P[\text{market up} \mid \text{rain}] \neq P[\text{market up} \mid \overline{\text{rain}}] \tag{2.22}$$

In this case, the weather and the stock market are no longer independent. We can no longer multiply their probabilities together to get their joint probability.

## PROBLEMS

1. You are invested in two hedge funds. The probability that hedge fund Alpha generates positive returns in any given year is 60%. The probability that hedge fund Omega generates positive returns in any given year is 70%. Assume the returns are independent. What is the probability that both funds generate positive returns in a given year? What is the probability that both funds lose money?

2. Corporation ABC issues $100 million of bonds. The bonds are rated BBB. The probability that the rating on the bonds is upgraded within the year is 8%. The probability of a downgrade is 4%. What is the probability that the rating remains unchanged?

3. Stock XYZ has a 20% chance of losing more than 10% in a given month. There is also a 30% probability that XYZ gains more than 10%. What is the probability that stock XYZ either loses more than 10% or gains more than 10%?

4. There is a 30% chance that oil prices will increase over the next six months. If oil prices increase, there is a 60% chance that the stock market will be down. What is the probability that oil prices increase and the stock market is down over the next six months?

5. Given the following density function:

$$f(x) = \begin{cases} c(100 - x^2) & \text{for} -10 \leq x \leq 10 \\ 0 & \text{otherwise} \end{cases}$$

Calculate the value of $c$.

6. Given the following cumulative distribution function, $F(x)$, for $0 \leq x \leq 10$:

$$F(x) = \frac{x}{100}(20 - x)$$

Check that this is a valid CDF; that is, show that $F(0) = 0$ and $F(10) = 1$. Calculate the probability density function, $f(x)$.

7. Given the probability density function, $f(x)$:

$$f(x) = \frac{c}{x}$$

where $1 \leq x \leq e$. Calculate the cumulative distribution function, $F(x)$, and solve for the constant $c$.

8. You own two bonds. Both bonds have a 30% probability of defaulting. Their default probabilities are statistically independent. What is the probability that both bonds default? What is the probability that only one bond defaults? What is the probability that neither bond defaults?

9. The following table is a one-year ratings transition matrix. Given a bond's rating now, the matrix gives the probability associated with the bond having a given rating in a year's time. For example, a bond that starts the year with an A rating has a 90% chance of maintaining that rating and an 8% chance of migrating to a B rating. Given a B-rated bond, what is the probability that the bond defaults (D rating) over one year? What is the probability that the bond defaults over two years?

|  |  | To a rating of: | | | |
|---|---|---|---|---|---|
|  |  | **A** | **B** | **C** | **D** |
| **From a rating of:** | **A** | 90% | 8% | 2% | 0% |
|  | **B** | 10% | 80% | 8% | 2% |
|  | **C** | 0% | 25% | 60% | 15% |
|  | **D** | 0% | 0% | 0% | 100% |

10. Your firm forecasts that there is a 50% probability that the market will be up significantly next year, a 20% probability that the market will be down significantly next year, and a 30% probability that the market will be flat, neither up or down significantly. You are asked to evaluate the prospects of a new portfolio manager. The manager has a long bias and is likely to perform better in an up market. Based on past data, you believe that the probability that the manager will be up if the market is up significantly is 80%, and that the probability that the manager will be up if the market is down significantly is only 10%. If the market is flat, the manager is just as likely to be up as to be down. What is the unconditional probability that the manager is up next year?

## CHAPTER 3

# Basic Statistics

In this chapter we will learn how to describe a collection of data in precise statistical terms. Many of the concepts will be familiar, but the notation and terminology might be new. This notation and terminology will be used throughout the rest of the book.

## AVERAGES

Everybody knows what an average is. We come across averages every day, whether they are earned run averages in baseball or grade point averages in school. In statistics there are actually three different types of averages: means, modes, and medians. By far the most commonly used average in risk management is the mean.

### Population and Sample Data

If you wanted to know the mean age of people working in your firm, you would simply ask every person in the firm his or her age, add the ages together, and divide by the number of people in the firm. Assuming there are $n$ employees and $a_i$ is the age of the $i$th employee, then the mean, $\mu$, is simply:

$$\mu = \frac{1}{n} \sum_{i=1}^{n} a_i = \frac{1}{n}(a_1 + a_2 + \cdots + a_{n-1} + a_n) \tag{3.1}$$

It is important at this stage to differentiate between population statistics and sample statistics. In this example, $\mu$ is the population mean. Assuming nobody lied about his or her age, and forgetting about rounding errors and other trivial details, we know the mean age of the people in your firm *exactly*. We have a complete data set of everybody in your firm; we've surveyed the entire population.

This state of absolute certainty is, unfortunately, quite rare in finance. More often, we are faced with a situation such as this: estimate the mean return of stock ABC, given the most recent year of daily returns. In a situation like this, we assume there is some underlying data-generating process, whose statistical properties are constant over time. The underlying process has a true mean, but we cannot observe it directly. We can only estimate the true mean based on our limited data sample. In our example, assuming $n$ returns, we estimate the mean using the same formula as before:

$$\hat{\mu} = \frac{1}{n}\sum_{i=1}^{n} r_i = \frac{1}{n}\left(r_1 + r_2 + \cdots + r_{n-1} + r_n\right) \tag{3.2}$$

where $\hat{\mu}$ (pronounced "mu hat") is our *estimate* of the true mean, $\mu$, based on our sample of $n$ returns. We call this the sample mean.

The median and mode are also types of averages. They are used less frequently in finance, but both can be useful. The median represents the center of a group of data; within the group, half the data points will be less than the median, and half will be greater. The mode is the value that occurs most frequently.

---

**SAMPLE PROBLEM**

*Question:*
Calculate the mean, median, and mode of the following data set:

$$-20\%, -10\%, -5\%, -5\%, 0\%, 10\%, 10\%, 10\%, 19\%$$

*Answer:*

$$\text{Mean} = \frac{1}{9}(-20\% - 10\% - 5\% - 5\% + 0\% + 10\% + 10\% + 10\% + 19\%) = 1\%$$

$$\text{Mode} = 10\%$$

$$\text{Median} = 0\%$$

---

If there is an even number of data points, the median is found by averaging the two centermost points. In the following series:

$$5\%, 10\%, 20\%, 25\%$$

the median is 15%. The median can be useful for summarizing data that is asymmetrical or contains significant outliers.

A data set can also have more than one mode. If the maximum frequency is shared by two or more values, all of those values are considered modes. In the following example, the modes are 10% and 20%:

$$5\%, 10\%, 10\%, 10\%, 14\%, 16\%, 20\%, 20\%, 20\%, 24\%$$

In calculating the mean in Equation 3.1 and Equation 3.2, each data point was counted exactly once. In certain situations, we might want to give more or less weight to certain data points. In calculating the average return of stocks in an equity index, we might want to give more weight to larger firms, perhaps weighting their returns in proportion to their market capitalizations. Given $n$ data points, $x_i = x_1, x_2,\ldots, x_n$, with corresponding weights, $w_i$, we can define the weighted mean, $\mu_w$, as:

$$\mu_w = \frac{\sum_{i=1}^{n} w_i x_i}{\sum_{i=1}^{n} w_i} \tag{3.3}$$

The standard mean from Equation 3.1 can be viewed as a special case of the weighted mean, where all the values have equal weight.

## Discrete Random Variables

For a discrete random variable, we can also calculate the mean, median, and mode. For a random variable, $X$, with possible values, $x_i$, and corresponding probabilities, $p_i$, we define the mean, $\mu$, as:

$$\mu = \sum_{i=1}^{n} p_i x_i \tag{3.4}$$

The equation for the mean of a discrete random variable is a special case of the weighted mean, where the outcomes are weighted by their probabilities, and the sum of the weights is equal to one.

The median of a discrete random variable is the value such that the probability that a value is less than or equal to the median is equal to 50%. Working from the other end of the distribution, we can also define the median such that 50% of the values are greater than or equal to the median. For a random variable, $X$, if we denote the median as $m$, we have:

$$P[X \geq m] = P[X \leq m] = 0.50 \tag{3.5}$$

For a discrete random variable, the mode is the value associated with the highest probability. As with population and sample data sets, the mode of a discrete random variable need not be unique.

## SAMPLE PROBLEM

*Question:*
   At the start of the year, a bond portfolio consists of two bonds, each worth $100. At the end of the year, if a bond defaults, it will be worth $20. If it does not default, the bond will be worth $100. The probability that both bonds default is 20%. The probability that neither bond defaults is 45%. What are the mean, median, and mode of the year-end portfolio value?

*Answer:*

We are given the probability for two outcomes:

$$P[V = \$40] = 20\%$$

$$P[V = \$200] = 45\%$$

At year-end, the value of the portfolio, $V$, can have only one of three values, and the sum of all the probabilities must sum to 100%. This allows us to calculate the final probability:

$$P[V = \$120] = 100\% - 20\% - 45\% = 35\%$$

The mean of $V$ is then $140:

$$\mu = 0.20 \cdot \$40 + 0.35 \cdot \$120 + 0.45 \cdot \$200 = \$140$$

The mode of the distribution is $200; this is the most likely single outcome. The median of the distribution is $120; half of the outcomes are less than or equal to $120.

### Continuous Random Variables

We can also define the mean, median, and mode for a continuous random variable. To find the mean of a continuous random variable, we simply integrate the product of the variable and its probability density function (PDF). In the limit, this is equivalent to our approach to calculating the mean of a discrete random variable. For a continuous random variable, $X$, with a PDF, $f(x)$, the mean, $\mu$, is then:

$$\mu = \int_{x_{min}}^{x_{max}} xf(x)dx \tag{3.6}$$

The median of a continuous random variable is defined exactly as it is for a discrete random variable, such that there is a 50% probability that values are less than or equal to, or greater than or equal to, the median. If we define the median as $m$, then:

$$\int_{x_{min}}^{m} f(x)dx = \int_{m}^{x_{max}} f(x)dx = 0.50 \tag{3.7}$$

Alternatively, we can define the median in terms of the cumulative distribution function. Given the cumulative distribution function, $F(x)$, and the median, $m$, we have:

$$F(m) = 0.50 \tag{3.8}$$

The mode of a continuous random variable corresponds to the maximum of the density function. As before, the mode need not be unique.

## SAMPLE PROBLEM

*Question:*

Using the now-familiar probability density function from Chapter 2,

$$f(x) = \frac{x}{50} \text{ s.t. } 0 \le x \le 10$$

what are the mean, median, and mode of $x$?

*Answer:*

As we saw in a previous example, this probability density function is a triangle, between $x = 0$ and $x = 10$, and zero everywhere else. See Exhibit 3.1.

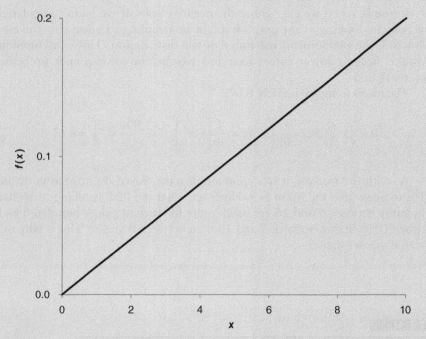

**EXHIBIT 3.1**   Probability Density Function

For a continuous distribution, the mode corresponds to the maximum of the PDF. By inspection of the graph, we can see that the mode of $f(x)$ is equal to 10.

To calculate the median, we need to find $m$, such that the integral of $f(x)$ from the lower bound of $f(x)$, zero, to $m$ is equal to 0.50. That is, we need to find:

$$\int_0^m \frac{x}{50} dx = 0.50$$

First we solve the left-hand side of the equation:

$$\int_0^m \frac{x}{50} dx = \frac{1}{50} \int_0^m x\, dx = \frac{1}{50}\left[\frac{1}{2}x^2\right]_0^m = \frac{1}{100}(m^2 - 0) = \frac{m^2}{100}$$

Setting this result equal to 0.50 and solving for $m$, we obtain our final answer:

$$\frac{m^2}{100} = 0.50$$

$$m^2 = 50$$

$$m = \sqrt{50} = 7.07$$

In the last step we can ignore the negative root. If we hadn't calculated the median, looking at the graph it might be tempting to guess that the median is 5, the midpoint of the range of the distribution. This is a common mistake. Because lower values have less weight, the median ends up being greater than 5.

The mean is approximately 6.67:

$$\mu = \int_0^{10} x\frac{x}{50} dx = \frac{1}{50}\int_0^{10} x^2 dx = \frac{1}{50}\left[\frac{1}{3}x^3\right]_0^{10} = \frac{1,000}{150} = \frac{20}{3} = 6.67$$

As with the median, it is a common mistake, based on inspection of the PDF, to guess that the mean is 5. However, what the PDF is telling us is that outcomes between 5 and 10 are much more likely than values between 0 and 5 (the PDF is higher between 5 and 10 than between 0 and 5). This is why the mean is greater than 5.

## EXPECTATIONS

On January 15, 2005, the Huygens space probe landed on the surface of Titan, the largest moon of Saturn. This was the culmination of a seven-year-long mission. During its descent and for over an hour after touching down on the surface, Huygens sent back detailed images, scientific readings, and even sounds from a strange world. There are liquid oceans on Titan, the landing site was littered with "rocks" composed of water ice, and weather on the moon includes methane rain. The Huygens probe was named after Christiaan Huygens, a Dutch polymath who first discovered Titan in 1655. In addition to astronomy and physics, Huygens had more prosaic interests, including probability theory. Originally published in Latin in 1657, *De Ratiociniis in Ludo Aleae*, or *On the Logic of Games of Chance*, was one of the first texts to formally explore one of the most important concepts in probability theory, namely expectations.

Like many of his contemporaries, Huygens was interested in games of chance. As he described it, if a game has a 50% probability of paying $3 and a 50% probability of paying $7, then this is, in a way, equivalent to having $5 with certainty. This is because we *expect*, on average, to win $5 in this game:

$$50\% \cdot \$3 + 50\% \cdot \$7 = \$5 \tag{3.9}$$

As one can already see, the concepts of expectations and averages are very closely linked. In the current example, if we play the game only once, there is no chance of winning exactly $5; we can win only $3 or $7. Still, even if we play the game only once, we say that the expected value of the game is $5. That we are talking about the mean of all the potential payouts is understood.

We can express the concept of expectations more formally using the expectation operator. We could state that the random variable, $X$, has an expected value of $5 as follows:

$$E[X] = 0.50 \cdot \$3 + 0.50 \cdot \$7 = \$5 \tag{3.10}$$

where $E[\cdot]$ is the expectation operator.[1]

In this example, the mean and the expected value have the same numeric value, $5. The same is true for discrete and continuous random variables. The expected value of a random variable is equal to the mean of the random variable.

While the value of the mean and the expected value may be the same in many situations, the two concepts are not exactly the same. In many situations in finance and risk management, the terms can be used interchangeably. The difference is often subtle.

As the name suggests, expectations are often thought of as being forward-looking. Pretend we have a financial asset for which next year's mean annual return is known and equal to 15%. This is not an estimate; in this hypothetical scenario, we actually know that the mean *is* 15%. We say that the expected value of the return next year is 15%. We expect the return to be 15%, because the probability-weighted mean of all the possible outcomes is 15%.

Now pretend that we don't actually *know* what the mean return of the asset is, but we have 10 years' worth of historical data for which the mean is 15%. In this case the expected value may or may not be 15%. *If* we decide that the expected value is equal to 15%, based on the data, then we are making two assumptions: first, we are assuming that the returns in our sample were generated by the same random process over the entire sample period; second, we are assuming that the returns will continue to be generated by this same process in the future. These are very strong assumptions. *If* we have other information that leads us to believe that one or both of these assumptions are false, then we may decide that the expected value is something other than 15%. In finance and risk management, we often assume that the data we are interested in are being generated by a consistent, unchanging process. Testing the validity of this assumption can be an important part of risk management in practice.

---

[1]Those of you with a background in physics might be more familiar with the term *expectation value* and the notation $\langle X \rangle$ rather than $E[X]$. This is a matter of convention. Throughout this book we use the term *expected value* and $E[\ ]$, which are currently more popular in finance and econometrics. Risk managers should be familiar with both conventions.

The concept of expectations is also a much more general concept than the concept of the mean. Using the expectation operator, we can derive the expected value of functions of random variables. As we will see in subsequent sections, the concept of expectations underpins the definitions of other population statistics (variance, skewness, kurtosis), and is important in understanding regression analysis and time series analysis. In these cases, even when we could use the mean to describe a calculation, in practice we tend to talk exclusively in terms of expectations.

## SAMPLE PROBLEM

*Question:*
At the start of the year, you are asked to price a newly issued zero coupon bond. The bond has a notional of $100. You believe there is a 20% chance that the bond will default, in which case it will be worth $40 at the end of the year. There is also a 30% chance that the bond will be downgraded, in which case it will be worth $90 in a year's time. If the bond does not default and is not downgraded, it will be worth $100. Use a continuous interest rate of 5% to determine the current price of the bond.

*Answer:*
We first need to determine the expected future value of the bond—that is, the expected value of the bond in one year's time. We are given the following:

$$P[V_{t+1} = \$40] = 0.20$$
$$P[V_{t+1} = \$90] = 0.30$$

Because there are only three possible outcomes, the probability of no downgrade and no default must be 50%:

$$P[V_{t+1} = \$100] = 1 - 0.20 - 0.30 = 0.50$$

The expected value of the bond in one year is then:

$$E[V_{t+1}] = 0.20 \cdot \$40 + 0.30 \cdot \$90 + 0.50 \cdot \$100 = \$85$$

To get the current price of the bond we then discount this expected future value:

$$E[V_t] = e^{-0.05}E[V_{t+1}] = e^{-0.05}\$85 = \$80.85$$

The current price of the bond, in this case $80.85, is often referred to as the present value or fair value of the bond. The price is considered fair because the discounted expected value of the bond is the price that a risk-neutral investor would pay for the bond.

The expectation operator is linear. That is, for two random variables, $X$ and $Y$, and a constant, $c$, the following two equations are true:

$$E[X + Y] = E[X] + E[Y]$$

$$E[cX] = cE[X]$$

(3.11)

If the expected value of one option, A, is \$10, and the expected value of option B is \$20, then the expected value of a portfolio containing A and B is \$30, and the expected value of a portfolio containing five contracts of option A is \$50.

Be very careful, though; the expectation operator is not multiplicative. The expected value of the product of two random variables is not necessarily the same as the product of their expected values:

$$E[XY] \neq E[X]E[Y]$$

(3.12)

Imagine we have two binary options. Each pays either \$100 or nothing, depending on the value of some underlying asset at expiration. The probability of receiving \$100 is 50% for both options. Further, assume that it is always the case that if the first option pays \$100, the second pays \$0, and vice versa. The expected value of each option separately is clearly \$50. If we denote the payout of the first option as $X$ and the payout of the second as $Y$, we have:

$$E[X] = E[Y] = 0.50 \cdot \$100 + 0.50 \cdot \$0 = \$50$$

(3.13)

It follows that $E[X]E[Y] = \$50 \times \$50 = \$2,500$. In each scenario, though, one option is valued at zero, so the product of the payouts is always zero: $\$100 \cdot \$0 = \$0 \cdot \$100 = \$0$. The expected value of the product of the two option payouts is:

$$E[XY] = 0.50 \cdot \$100 \cdot \$0 + 0.50 \cdot \$0 \cdot \$100 = \$0$$

(3.14)

In this case, the product of the expected values and the expected value of the product are clearly not equal. In the special case where $E[XY] = E[X]E[Y]$, we say that $X$ and $Y$ are independent.

If the expected value of the product of two variables does not necessarily equal the product of the expectations of those variables, it follows that the expected value of the product of a variable with itself does not necessarily equal the product of the expectation of that variable with itself; that is:

$$E[X^2] \neq E[X]^2$$

(3.15)

Imagine we have a fair coin. Assign heads a value of +1 and tails a value of –1. We can write the probabilities of the outcomes as follows:

$$P[X = +1] = P[X = -1] = 0.50$$

(3.16)

The expected value of any coin flip is zero, but the expected value of $X^2$ is +1, not zero:

$$E[X] = 0.50 \cdot (+1) + 0.50 \cdot (-1) = 0$$

$$E[X]^2 = 0^2 = 0 \tag{3.17}$$

$$E[X^2] = 0.50 \cdot (+1^2) + 0.50 \cdot (-1^2) = 1$$

As simple as this example is, this distinction is very important. As we will see, the difference between $E[X^2]$ and $E[X]^2$ is central to our definition of variance and standard deviation.

---

## SAMPLE PROBLEM

*Question:*
   Given the following equation,

$$y = (x + 5)^3 + x^2 + 10x$$

what is the expected value of $y$? Assume the following:

$$E[x] = 4$$

$$E[x^2] = 9$$

$$E[x^3] = 12$$

*Answer:*
   Note that $E[x^2]$ and $E[x^3]$ cannot be derived from knowledge of $E[x]$. In this problem, $E[x^2] \neq E[x]^2$ and $E[x^3] \neq E[x]^3$.
   To find the expected value of $y$, then, we first expand the term $(x + 5)^3$ within the expectation operator:

$$E[y] = E[(x + 5)^3 + x^2 + 10x] = E[x^3 + 16x^2 + 85x + 125]$$

Because the expectation operator is linear, we can separate the terms in the summation and move the constants outside the expectation operator:

$$E[y] = E[x^3] + E[16x^2] + E[85x] + E[125]$$

$$= E[x^3] + 16E[x^2] + 85E[x] + 125$$

At this point, we can substitute in the values for $E[x]$, $E[x^2]$, and $E[x^3]$, which were given at the start of the exercise:

$$E[Y] = 12 + 16 \cdot 9 + 85 \cdot 4 + 125 = 621$$

This gives us the final answer, 621.

## VARIANCE AND STANDARD DEVIATION

The variance of a random variable measures how noisy or unpredictable that random variable is. Variance is defined as the expected value of the difference between the variable and its mean squared:

$$\sigma^2 = E[(X - \mu)^2] \tag{3.18}$$

where $\sigma^2$ is the variance of the random variable $X$ with mean $\mu$.

The square root of variance, typically denoted by $\sigma$, is called standard deviation. In finance we often refer to standard deviation as volatility. This is analogous to referring to the mean as the average. Standard deviation is a mathematically precise term, whereas volatility is a more general concept.

### SAMPLE PROBLEM

*Question:*
A derivative has a 50/50 chance of being worth either +10 or −10 at expiry. What is the standard deviation of the derivative's value?

*Answer:*

$$\mu = 0.50 \cdot 10 + 0.50 \cdot (-10) = 0$$

$$\sigma^2 = 0.50 \cdot (10 - 0)^2 + 0.50 \cdot (-10 - 0)^2 = 0.5 \cdot 100 + 0.5 \cdot 100 = 100$$

$$\sigma = 10$$

In the previous example, we were calculating the population variance and standard deviation. *All* of the possible outcomes for the derivative were known.

To calculate the sample variance of a random variable $X$ based on $n$ observations, $x_1, x_2, \ldots, x_n$, we can use the following formula:

$$\hat{\sigma}_x^2 = \frac{1}{n-1} \sum_{i=1}^{n} (x_i - \hat{\mu}_x)$$

$$E[\hat{\sigma}_x^2] = \sigma_x^2 \tag{3.19}$$

where $\hat{\mu}_x$ is the sample mean as in Equation 3.2. Given that we have $n$ data points, it might seem odd that we are dividing the sum by $(n - 1)$ and not $n$. The reason has to do with the fact that $\hat{\mu}_x$ itself is an estimate of the true mean, which also contains a fraction of each $x_i$. We leave the proof for a problem at the end of the chapter, but it turns out that dividing by $(n - 1)$, not $n$, produces an unbiased estimate of $\sigma^2$. If the mean is known or we are calculating the population variance, then we divide by $n$. If instead the mean is also being estimated, then we divide by $n - 1$.

Equation 3.18 can easily be rearranged as follows (the proof of this equation is also left as an exercise):

$$\sigma^2 = E[X^2] - \mu^2 = E[X^2] - E[X]^2 \tag{3.20}$$

Note that variance can be nonzero only if $E[X]^2 \neq E[X]^2$.

When writing computer programs, this last version of the variance formula is often useful, since it allows us to calculate the mean and the variance in the same loop.

In finance it is often convenient to assume that the mean of a random variable is equal to zero. For example, based on theory, we might expect the spread between two equity indexes to have a mean of zero in the long run. In this case, the variance is simply the mean of the squared returns.

---

### SAMPLE PROBLEM

*Question:*
Assume that the mean of daily Standard & Poor's (S&P) 500 Index returns is zero. You observe the following returns over the course of 10 days:

| 7% | –4% | 11% | 8% | 3% | 9% | –21% | 10% | –9% | –1% |
|----|-----|-----|----|----|----|------|-----|-----|-----|

Estimate the standard deviation of daily S&P 500 Index returns.

*Answer:*
The sample mean is not exactly zero, but we are told to assume that the population mean *is* zero; therefore:

$$\hat{\sigma}_r^2 = \frac{1}{n}\sum_{i=1}^{n}(r_i^2 - 0^2) = \frac{1}{n}\sum_{i=1}^{n}r_i^2$$

$$\hat{\sigma}_r^2 = \frac{1}{10}0.0963 = 0.00963$$

$$\hat{\sigma}_r = 9.8\%$$

Note, because we were told to assume the mean was known, we divide by $n = 10$, not $(n - 1) = 9$.

---

As with the mean, for a continuous random variable we can calculate the variance by integrating with the probability density function. For a continuous random variable, $X$, with a probability density function, $f(x)$, the variance can be calculated as:

$$\sigma^2 = \int_{x_{min}}^{x_{max}} (x - \mu)^2 f(x)dx \tag{3.21}$$

It is not difficult to prove that, for either a discrete or a continuous random variable, multiplying by a constant will increase the standard deviation by the same factor:

$$\sigma[cX] = c\sigma[X] \tag{3.22}$$

In other words, if you own \$10 of an equity with a standard deviation of \$2, then \$100 of the same equity will have a standard deviation of \$20.

Adding a constant to a random variable, however, does not alter the standard deviation or the variance:

$$\sigma[X + c] = \sigma[X] \tag{3.23}$$

This is because the impact of $c$ on the mean is the same as the impact of $c$ on any draw of the random variable, leaving the deviation from the mean for any draw unchanged. In theory, a risk-free asset should have zero variance and standard deviation. If you own a portfolio with a standard deviation of \$20, and then you add \$1,000 of cash to that portfolio, the standard deviation of the portfolio should still be \$20.

## STANDARDIZED VARIABLES

It is often convenient to work with variables where the mean is zero and the standard deviation is one. From the preceding section it is not difficult to prove that, given a random variable $X$ with mean $\mu$ and standard deviation $\sigma$, we can define a second random variable $Y$:

$$Y = \frac{X - \mu}{\sigma} \tag{3.24}$$

such that $Y$ will have a mean of zero and a standard deviation of one. We say that $X$ has been standardized, or that $Y$ is a standard random variable. In practice, if we have a data set and we want to standardize it, we first compute the sample mean and the standard deviation. Then, for each data point, we subtract the mean and divide by the standard deviation.

The inverse transformation can also be very useful when it comes to creating computer simulations. Simulations often begin with standardized variables, which need to be transformed into variables with a specific mean and standard deviation. In this case, we simply take the output from the standardized variable, multiply by the desired standard deviation, and then add the desired mean. The order is important. Adding a constant to a random variable will not change the standard deviation, but multiplying a non-mean-zero variable by a constant will change the mean.

**SAMPLE PROBLEM**

*Question:*
Assume that a random variable $Y$ has a mean of zero and a standard deviation of one. Given two constants, $\mu$ and $\sigma$, calculate the expected values of $X_1$ and $X_2$, where $X_1$ and $X_2$ are defined as:

$$X_1 = \sigma Y + \mu$$
$$X_2 = \sigma(Y + \mu)$$

*Answer:*
The expected value of $X_1$ is $\mu$:

$$E[X_1] = E[\sigma Y + \mu] = \sigma E[Y] + E[\mu] = \sigma \cdot 0 + \mu = \mu$$

The expected value of $X_2$ is $\sigma\mu$:

$$E[X_2] = E[\sigma(Y + \mu)] = E[\sigma Y + \sigma\mu] = \sigma E[Y] + \sigma\mu = \sigma \cdot 0 + \sigma\mu = \sigma\mu$$

As warned in the previous section, multiplying a standard normal variable by a constant and then adding another constant produces a different result than if we first add and then multiply.

## COVARIANCE

Up until now we have mostly been looking at statistics that summarize one variable. In risk management, we often want to describe the relationship between two random variables. For example, is there a relationship between the returns of an equity and the returns of a market index?

Covariance is analogous to variance, but instead of looking at the deviation from the mean of one variable, we are going to look at the relationship between the deviations of two variables:

$$\sigma_{XY} = E[(X - \mu_X)(Y - \mu_Y)] \tag{3.25}$$

where $\sigma_{XY}$ is the covariance between two random variables, $X$ and $Y$, with means $\mu_X$ and $\mu_Y$, respectively. As you can see from the definition, variance is just a special case of covariance. Variance is the covariance of a variable with itself.

If $X$ tends to be above $\mu_X$ when $Y$ is above $\mu_Y$ (both deviations are positive) and $X$ tends to be below $\mu_X$ when $Y$ is below $\mu_Y$ (both deviations are negative), then the covariance will be positive (a positive number multiplied by a positive number is positive; likewise, for two negative numbers). If the opposite is true and the deviations tend to be of opposite sign, then the covariance will be negative. If the deviations have no discernible relationship, then the covariance will be zero.

Earlier in this chapter, we cautioned that the expectation operator is not generally multiplicative. This fact turns out to be closely related to the concept of covariance. Just as we rewrote our variance equation earlier, we can rewrite Equation 3.25 as follows:

$$\sigma_{XY} = E[(X - \mu_X)(Y - \mu_Y)] = E[XY] - \mu_X\mu_Y = E[XY] - E[X]E[Y] \qquad (3.26)$$

In the special case where the covariance between $X$ and $Y$ is zero, the expected value of $XY$ is equal to the expected value of $X$ multiplied by the expected value of $Y$:

$$\sigma_{XY} = 0 \Rightarrow E[XY] = E[X]E[Y] \qquad (3.27)$$

If the covariance is anything other than zero, then the two sides of this equation cannot be equal. Unless we know that the covariance between two variables is zero, we cannot assume that the expectation operator is multiplicative.

In order to calculate the covariance between two random variables, $X$ and $Y$, assuming the means of both variables are known, we can use the following formula:

$$\hat{\sigma}_{X,Y} = \frac{1}{n} \sum_{i=1}^{n} (x_i - \mu_X)(y_i - \mu_Y) \qquad (3.28)$$

If the means are unknown and must also be estimated, we replace $n$ with $(n - 1)$:

$$\hat{\sigma}_{X,Y} = \frac{1}{n-1} \sum_{i=1}^{n} (x_i - \hat{\mu}_X)(y_i - \hat{\mu}_Y) \qquad (3.29)$$

If we replaced $y_i$ in these formulas with $x_i$, calculating the covariance of $X$ with itself, the resulting equations would be the same as the equations for calculating variance from the previous section.

## CORRELATION

Closely related to the concept of covariance is correlation. To get the correlation of two variables, we simply divide their covariance by their respective standard deviations:

$$\rho_{XY} = \frac{\sigma_{XY}}{\sigma_X \sigma_Y} \qquad (3.30)$$

Correlation has the nice property that it varies between −1 and +1. If two variables have a correlation of +1, then we say they are perfectly correlated. If the ratio of one variable to another is always the same and positive, then the two variables will be perfectly correlated.

If two variables are highly correlated, it is often the case that one variable *causes* the other variable, or that both variables share a common underlying driver. We will see in later chapters, though, that it is very easy for two random variables with no causal link to be highly correlated. *Correlation does not prove causation*. Similarly, if two variables are uncorrelated, it does not necessarily follow that they are unrelated. For example, a random variable that is symmetrical around zero and the square of that variable will have zero correlation.

## SAMPLE PROBLEM

*Question:*
    $X$ is a random variable. $X$ has an equal probability of being −1, 0, or +1. What is the correlation between $X$ and $Y$ if $Y = X^2$?

*Answer:*
    We have:

$$P[X = -1] = P[X = 0] = P[X = 1] = \frac{1}{3}$$

$$Y = X^2$$

First, we calculate the mean of both variables:

$$E[X] = \frac{1}{3}(-1) + \frac{1}{3}(0) + \frac{1}{3}(1) = 0$$

$$E[Y] = \frac{1}{3}(-1^2) + \frac{1}{3}(0^2) + \frac{1}{3}(1^2) = \frac{1}{3}(1) + \frac{1}{3}(0) + \frac{1}{3}(1) = \frac{2}{3}$$

The covariance can be found as:

$$\text{Cov}[X,Y] = E[(X - E[X])(Y - E[Y])]$$

$$\text{Cov}[X,Y] = \frac{1}{3}(-1-0)\left(1 - \frac{2}{3}\right) + \frac{1}{3}(0-0)\left(0 - \frac{2}{3}\right)$$

$$+ \frac{1}{3}(1-0)\left(1 - \frac{2}{3}\right) = 0$$

Because the covariance is zero, the correlation is also zero. There is no need to calculate the variances or standard deviations.

As forewarned, even though $X$ and $Y$ are clearly related, their correlation is zero.

## APPLICATION: PORTFOLIO VARIANCE AND HEDGING

If we have a portfolio of securities and we wish to determine the variance of that portfolio, all we need to know is the variance of the underlying securities and their respective correlations.

For example, if we have two securities with random returns $X_A$ and $X_B$, with means $\mu_A$ and $\mu_B$ and standard deviations $\sigma_A$ and $\sigma_B$, respectively, we can calculate the variance of $X_A$ plus $X_B$ as follows:

$$\sigma_{A+B}^2 = \sigma_A^2 + \sigma_B^2 + 2\rho_{AB}\sigma_A\sigma_B \tag{3.31}$$

where $\rho_{AB}$ is the correlation between $X_A$ and $X_B$. The proof is left as an exercise. Notice that the last term can either increase or decrease the total variance. Both standard deviations must be positive; therefore, if the correlation is positive, the overall variance will be higher than in the case where the correlation is negative.

If the variance of both securities is equal, then Equation 3.31 simplifies to:

$$\sigma_{A+B}^2 = 2\sigma^2(1+\rho_{AB}) \quad \text{where } \sigma_A^2 = \sigma_B^2 = \sigma^2 \tag{3.32}$$

We know that the correlation can vary between −1 and +1, so, substituting into our new equation, the portfolio variance must be bound by 0 and $4\sigma^2$. If we take the square root of both sides of the equation, we see that the standard deviation is bound by 0 and $2\sigma$. Intuitively, this should make sense. If, on the one hand, we own one share of an equity with a standard deviation of \$10 and then purchase another share of the *same* equity, then the standard deviation of our two-share portfolio must be \$20 (trivially, the correlation of a random variable with itself must be one). On the other hand, if we own one share of this equity and then purchase another security that always generates the exact opposite return, the portfolio is perfectly balanced. The returns are always zero, which implies a standard deviation of zero.

In the special case where the correlation between the two securities is zero, we can further simplify our equation. For the standard deviation:

$$\rho_{AB} = 0 \Rightarrow \sigma_{A+B} = \sqrt{2}\sigma \tag{3.33}$$

We can extend Equation 3.31 to any number of variables:

$$Y = \sum_{i=1}^{n} X_i$$

$$\sigma_Y^2 = \sum_{i=1}^{n}\sum_{j=1}^{n} \rho_{ij}\sigma_i\sigma_j \tag{3.34}$$

In the case where all of the $X_i$'s are uncorrelated and all the variances are equal to $\sigma$, Equation 3.32 simplifies to:

$$\sigma_Y = \sqrt{n}\sigma \quad \text{iff } \rho_{ij} = 0 \ \forall \ i \neq j \tag{3.35}$$

This is the famous square root rule for the addition of uncorrelated variables. There are many situations in statistics in which we come across collections of random variables that are independent and have the same statistical properties. We term these variables independent and identically distributed (i.i.d.). In risk management we might have a large portfolio of securities, which can be approximated as a collection of i.i.d. variables. As we will see in subsequent chapters, this i.i.d. assumption also plays an important role in estimating the uncertainty inherent in statistics derived from sampling, and in the analysis of time series. In each of these situations, we will come back to this square root rule.

By combining Equation 3.31 with Equation 3.22, we arrive at an equation for calculating the variance of a linear combination of variables. If $Y$ is a linear combination of $X_A$ and $X_B$, such that:

$$Y = aX_A + bX_B \tag{3.36}$$

then, using our standard notation, we have:

$$\sigma_Y^2 = a^2\sigma_A^2 + b^2\sigma_B^2 + 2ab\rho_{AB}\sigma_A\sigma_B \tag{3.37}$$

Correlation is central to the problem of hedging. Using the same notation as before, imagine we have \$1 of Security A, and we wish to hedge it with \$$h$ of Security B (if $h$ is positive, we are buying the security; if $h$ is negative, we are shorting the security). In other words, $h$ is the hedge ratio. We introduce the random variable $P$ for our hedged portfolio. We can easily compute the variance of the hedged portfolio using Equation 3.37:

$$P = X_A + hX_B$$
$$\sigma_P^2 = \sigma_A^2 + h^2\sigma_B^2 + 2h\rho_{AB}\sigma_A\sigma_B \tag{3.38}$$

As a risk manager, we might be interested to know what hedge ratio would achieve the portfolio with the least variance. To find this minimum variance hedge ratio, we simply take the derivative of our equation for the portfolio variance with respect to $h$, and set it equal to zero:

$$\frac{d\sigma_P^2}{dh} = 2h\sigma_B^2 + 2\rho_{AB}\sigma_A\sigma_B$$
$$h^* = -\rho_{AB}\frac{\sigma_A}{\sigma_B} \tag{3.39}$$

You can check that this is indeed a minimum by calculating the second derivative.

Substituting $h^*$ back into our original equation, we see that the smallest variance we can achieve is:

$$\min[\sigma_P^2] = \sigma_A^2(1 - \rho_{AB}^2) \tag{3.40}$$

At the extremes, where $\rho_{AB}$ equals −1 or +1, we can reduce the portfolio volatility to zero by buying or selling the hedge asset in proportion to the standard deviation of the assets. In between these two extremes we will always be left with some positive portfolio variance. This risk that we cannot hedge is referred to as idiosyncratic risk.

If the two securities in the portfolio are positively correlated, then selling $$h$ of Security B will reduce the portfolio's variance to the minimum possible level. Sell any less and the portfolio will be underhedged. Sell any more and the portfolio will be over hedged. In risk management it is possible to have too much of a good thing. A common mistake made by portfolio managers is to over hedge with a low-correlation instrument.

Notice that when $\rho_{AB}$ equals zero (i.e., when the two securities are uncorrelated), the optimal hedge ratio is zero. You cannot hedge one security with another security if they are uncorrelated. Adding an uncorrelated security to a portfolio will always increase its variance.

This last statement is not an argument against diversification. If your entire portfolio consists of $100 invested in Security A and you *add* any amount of an uncorrelated Security B to the portfolio, the dollar standard deviation of the portfolio will increase. Alternatively, if Security A and Security B are uncorrelated and have the same standard deviation, then *replacing* some of Security A with Security B will decrease the dollar standard deviation of the portfolio. For example, $80 of Security A plus $20 of Security B will have a lower standard deviation than $100 of Security A, but $100 of Security A *plus* $20 of Security B will have a higher standard deviation—again, assuming Security A and Security B are uncorrelated and have the same standard deviation.

## MOMENTS

Previously, we defined the mean of a variable $X$ as:

$$\mu = E[X]$$

It turns out that we can generalize this concept as follows:

$$m_k = E[X^k] \tag{3.41}$$

We refer to $m_k$ as the $k$th moment of $X$. The mean of $X$ is also the first moment of $X$.

Similarly, we can generalize the concept of variance as follows:

$$\mu_k = E[(X - \mu)^k] \tag{3.42}$$

We refer to $\mu_k$ as the $k$th central moment of $X$. We say that the moment is central because it is centered on the mean. Variance is simply the second central moment.

While we can easily calculate any central moment, in risk management it is very rare that we are interested in anything beyond the fourth central moment.

## SKEWNESS

The second central moment, variance, tells us how spread out a random variable is around the mean. The third central moment tells us how symmetrical the distribution is around the mean. Rather than working with the third central moment directly, by convention we first standardize the statistic. This standardized third central moment is known as skewness:

$$\text{Skewness} = \frac{E[(X - \mu)^3]}{\sigma^3} \qquad (3.43)$$

where $\sigma$ is the standard deviation of $X$, and $\mu$ is the mean of $X$.

By standardizing the central moment, it is much easier to compare two random variables. Multiplying a random variable by a constant will not change the skewness.

A random variable that is symmetrical about its mean will have zero skewness. If the skewness of the random variable is positive, we say that the random variable exhibits positive skew. Exhibits 3.2 and 3.3 show examples of positive and negative skewness.

Skewness is a very important concept in risk management. If the distributions of returns of two investments are the same in all respects, with the same mean and standard deviation, but different skews, then the investment with more negative skew is generally considered to be more risky. Historical data suggest that many financial assets exhibit negative skew.

As with variance, the equation for skewness differs depending on whether we are calculating the population skewness or the sample skewness. For the population

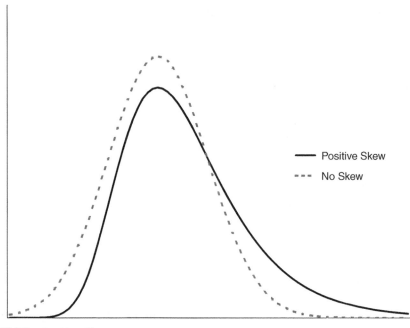

**EXHIBIT 3.2**   Positive Skew

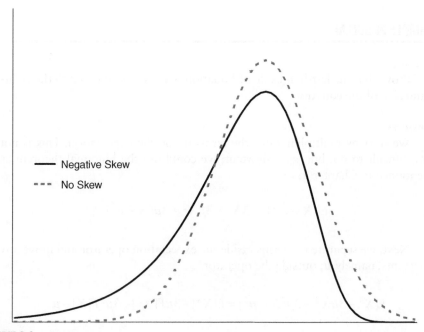

**EXHIBIT 3.3** Negative Skew

statistic, the skewness of a random variable $X$, based on $n$ observations, $x_1, x_2, \ldots,$ $x_n$, can be calculated as:

$$\hat{s} = \frac{1}{n} \sum_{i=1}^{n} \left( \frac{x_i - \mu}{\sigma} \right)^3 \tag{3.44}$$

where $\mu$ is the population mean and $\sigma$ is the population standard deviation. Similar to our calculation of sample variance, if we are calculating the sample skewness there is going to be an overlap with the calculation of the sample mean and sample standard deviation. We need to correct for that. The sample skewness can be calculated as:

$$\tilde{s} = \frac{n}{(n-1)(n-2)} \sum_{i=1}^{n} \left( \frac{x_i - \hat{\mu}}{\hat{\sigma}} \right)^3 \tag{3.45}$$

Based on Equation 3.20, for variance, it is tempting to guess that the formula for the third central moment can be written simply in terms of $E[X^3]$ and $\mu$. Be careful, as the two sides of this equation are not equal:

$$E[(X - \mu)^k] \neq E[X^3] - \mu^3 \tag{3.46}$$

The correct equation is:

$$E[(X - \mu)^3] = E[X^3] - 3\mu\sigma^2 - \mu^3 \tag{3.47}$$

## SAMPLE PROBLEM

*Question:*

Prove that the left-hand side of Equation 3.47 is indeed equal to the right-hand side of the equation.

*Answer:*

We start by multiplying out the terms inside the expectation. This is not too difficult to do, but, as a shortcut, we could use the binomial theorem as mentioned in Chapter 1:

$$E[(X - \mu)^3] = E[X^3 - 3\mu X^2 + 3\mu^2 X - \mu^3]$$

Next, we separate the terms inside the expectation operator and move any constants, namely $\mu$, outside the operator:

$$E[X^3 - 3\mu X^2 + 3\mu^2 X - \mu^3] = E[X^3] - 3\mu E[X^2] + 3\mu^2 E[X] - \mu^3$$

$E[X]$ is simply the mean, $\mu$. For $E[X^2]$, we reorganize our equation for variance, Equation 3.20, as follows:

$$\sigma^2 = E[X^2] - \mu^2$$
$$E[X^2] = \sigma^2 + \mu^2$$

Substituting these results into our equation and collecting terms, we arrive at the final equation:

$$E[(X - \mu)^3] = E[X^3] - 3\mu(\sigma^2 + \mu^2) + 3\mu^2\mu - \mu^3$$
$$E[(X - \mu)^3] = E[X^3] - 3\mu\sigma^2 - \mu^3$$

For many symmetrical continuous distributions, the mean, median, and mode all have the same value. Many continuous distributions with negative skew have a mean that is less than the median, which is less than the mode. For example, it might be that a certain derivative is just as likely to produce positive returns as it is to produce negative returns (the median is zero), but there are more big negative returns than big positive returns (the distribution is skewed), so the mean is less than zero. As a risk manager, understanding the impact of skew on the mean relative to the median and mode can be useful. Be careful, though, as this rule of thumb does not always work. Many practitioners mistakenly believe that this rule of thumb is in fact always true. It is not, and it is very easy to produce a distribution that violates this rule.

## KURTOSIS

The fourth central moment is similar to the second central moment, in that it tells us how spread out a random variable is, but it puts more weight on extreme points. As with skewness, rather than working with the central moment directly, we typically work with a standardized statistic. This standardized fourth central moment is known as kurtosis. For a random variable $X$, we can define the kurtosis as $K$, where:

$$K = \frac{E[(X - \mu)^4]}{\sigma^4} \tag{3.48}$$

where $\sigma$ is the standard deviation of $X$, and $\mu$ is its mean.

By standardizing the central moment, it is much easier to compare two random variables. As with skewness, multiplying a random variable by a constant will not change the kurtosis.

The following two populations have the same mean, variance, and skewness. The second population has a higher kurtosis.

Population 1: {−17, −17, 17, 17}
Population 2: {−23, −7, 7, 23}

Notice, to balance out the variance, when we moved the outer two points out six units, we had to move the inner two points in 10 units. Because the random variable with higher kurtosis has points further from the mean, we often refer to distribution with high kurtosis as fat-tailed. Exhibits 3.4 and 3.5 show examples of continuous distributions with high and low kurtosis.

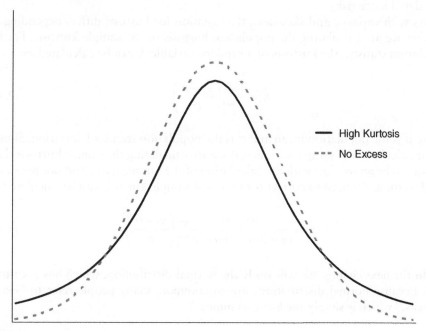

**EXHIBIT 3.4**   High Kurtosis

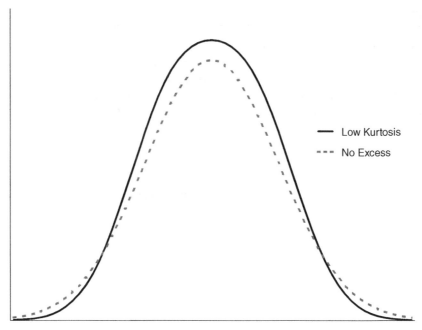

**EXHIBIT 3.5** Low Kurtosis

Like skewness, kurtosis is an important concept in risk management. Many financial assets exhibit high levels of kurtosis. If the distribution of returns of two assets have the same mean, variance, and skewness but different kurtosis, then the distribution with the higher kurtosis will tend to have more extreme points, and be considered more risky.

As with variance and skewness, the equation for kurtosis differs depending on whether we are calculating the population kurtosis or the sample kurtosis. For the population statistic, the kurtosis of a random variable $X$ can be calculated as:

$$\hat{K} = \frac{1}{n}\sum_{i=1}^{n}\left(\frac{x_i - \mu}{\sigma}\right)^4 \tag{3.49}$$

where $\mu$ is the population mean and $\sigma$ is the population standard deviation. Similar to our calculation of sample variance, if we are calculating the sample kurtosis there is going to be an overlap with the calculation of the sample mean and sample standard deviation. We need to correct for that. The sample kurtosis can be calculated as:

$$\tilde{K} = \frac{n(n+1)}{(n-1)(n-2)(n-3)}\sum_{i=1}^{n}\left(\frac{x_i - \hat{\mu}}{\hat{\sigma}}\right)^4 \tag{3.50}$$

In the next chapter we will study the normal distribution, which has a kurtosis of 3. Because normal distributions are so common, many people refer to "excess kurtosis," which is simply the kurtosis minus 3.

$$K_{\text{excess}} = K - 3 \tag{3.51}$$

In this way, the normal distribution has an excess kurtosis of 0. Distributions with positive excess kurtosis are termed leptokurtotic. Distributions with negative excess kurtosis are termed platykurtotic. Be careful; by default, many applications calculate excess kurtosis, not kurtosis.

When we are also estimating the mean and variance, calculating the sample excess kurtosis is somewhat more complicated than just subtracting 3. If we have $n$ points, then the correct formula is:

$$\tilde{K}_{\text{excess}} = \tilde{K} - 3\frac{(n-1)^2}{(n-2)(n-3)} \tag{3.52}$$

where $\tilde{K}$ is the sample kurtosis from Equation 3.50. As $n$ increases, the last term on the right-hand side converges to 3.

## COSKEWNESS AND COKURTOSIS

Just as we generalized the concept of mean and variance to moments and central moments, we can generalize the concept of covariance to cross central moments. The third and fourth standardized cross central moments are referred to as coskewness and cokurtosis, respectively. Though used less frequently, higher-order cross moments can be very important in risk management.

As an example of how higher-order cross moments can impact risk assessment, take the series of returns shown in Exhibit 3.6 for four fund managers, A, B, C, and D.

In this admittedly contrived setup, each manager has produced exactly the same set of returns; only the order in which the returns were produced is different. It follows that the mean, standard deviation, skew, and kurtosis of the returns are exactly the same for each manager. In this example it is also the case that the covariance between managers A and B is the same as the covariance between managers C and D.

If we combine A and B in an equally weighted portfolio and combine C and D in a separate equally weighted portfolio, we get the returns shown in Exhibit 3.7.

**EXHIBIT 3.6**  Fund Returns

| Time | A | B | C | D |
|------|-------|--------|--------|--------|
| 1 | 0.0% | −3.8% | −15.3% | −15.3% |
| 2 | −3.8% | −15.3% | −7.2% | −7.2% |
| 3 | −15.3% | 3.8% | 0.0% | −3.8% |
| 4 | −7.2% | −7.2% | −3.8% | 15.3% |
| 5 | 3.8% | 0.0% | 3.8% | 0.0% |
| 6 | 7.2% | 7.2% | 7.2% | 7.2% |
| 7 | 15.3% | 15.3% | 15.3% | 3.8% |

**EXHIBIT 3.7**   Combined Fund Returns

| Time | A + B | C + D |
|------|-------|-------|
| 1 | −1.9% | −15.3% |
| 2 | −9.5% | −7.2% |
| 3 | −5.8% | −1.9% |
| 4 | −7.2% | 5.8% |
| 5 | 1.9% | 1.9% |
| 6 | 7.2% | 7.2% |
| 7 | 15.3% | 9.5% |

The two portfolios have the same mean and standard deviation, but the skews of the portfolios are different. Whereas the worst return for A + B is −9.5%, the worst return for C + D is −15.3%. As a risk manager, knowing that the worst outcome for portfolio C + D is more than 1.6 times as bad as the worst outcome for A + B could be very important.

So how did two portfolios whose constituents seemed so similar end up being so different? One way to understand what is happening is to graph the two sets of returns for each portfolio against each other, as shown in Exhibits 3.8 and 3.9.

The two charts share a certain symmetry, but are clearly different. In the first portfolio, A + B, the two managers' best positive returns occur during the same time period, but their worst negative returns occur in different periods. This causes the distribution of points to be skewed toward the top-right of the chart. The situation

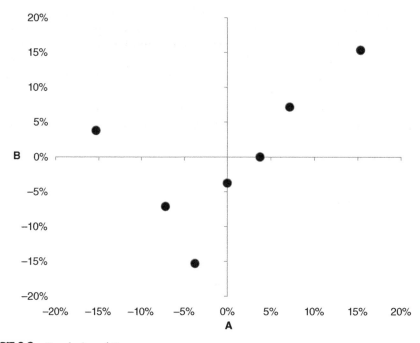

**EXHIBIT 3.8**   Funds A and B

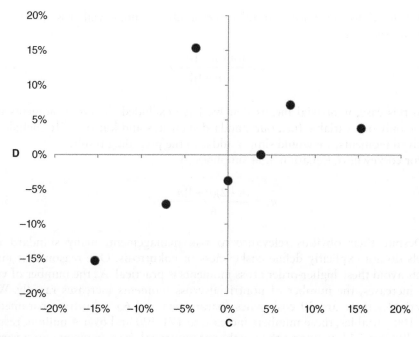

**EXHIBIT 3.9** Funds C and D

is reversed for managers C and D: their worst negative returns occur in the same period, but their best positive returns occur in different periods. In the second chart, the points are skewed toward the bottom-left of the chart.

The reason the charts look different, and the reason the returns of the two portfolios are different, is because the coskewness between the managers in each of the portfolios is different. For two random variables, there are actually two nontrivial coskewness statistics. For example, for managers A and B, we have:

$$S_{AAB} = E[(A - \mu_A)^2 (B - \mu_B)] / \sigma_A^2 \sigma_B$$
$$S_{ABB} = E[(A - \mu_A)(B - \mu_B)^2] / \sigma_A \sigma_B^2$$

(3.53)

The complete set of sample coskewness statistics for the sets of managers is shown in Exhibit 3.10.

Both coskewness values for A and B are positive, whereas they are both negative for C and D. Just as with skewness, negative values of coskewness tend to be associated with greater risk.

**EXHIBIT 3.10** Sample Coskewness

|  | A + B | C + D |
|---|---|---|
| $S_{XXY}$ | 0.99 | −0.58 |
| $S_{XYY}$ | 0.58 | −0.99 |

In general, for $n$ random variables, the number of nontrivial cross central moments of order $m$ is:

$$k = \frac{(m+n-1)!}{m!(n-1)!} - n \tag{3.54}$$

In this case, nontrivial means that we have excluded the cross moments that involve only one variable (i.e., our standard skewness and kurtosis). To include the nontrivial moments, we would simply add $n$ to the preceding result.

For coskewness, Equation 3.54 simplifies to:

$$k_3 = \frac{(n+2)(n+1)n}{6} - n \tag{3.55}$$

Despite their obvious relevance to risk management, many standard risk models do not explicitly define coskewness or cokurtosis. One reason that many models avoid these higher-order cross moments is practical. As the number of variables increases, the number of nontrivial cross moments increases rapidly. With 10 variables there are 30 coskewness parameters and 65 cokurtosis parameters. With 100 variables, these numbers increase to 171,600 and over 4 million, respectively. Exhibit 3.11 compares the number of nontrivial cross moments for a variety of sample sizes. In most cases there is simply not enough data to calculate all of these cross moments.

Risk models with time-varying volatility (e.g., GARCH; see Chapter 11) or time-varying correlation can display a wide range of behaviors with very few free parameters. Copulas (see Chapter 5) can also be used to describe complex interactions between variables that go beyond covariances, and have become popular in risk management in recent years. All of these approaches capture the essence of coskewness and cokurtosis, but in a more tractable framework. As a risk manager, it is important to differentiate between these models—which address the higher-order cross moments indirectly—and models that simply omit these risk factors altogether.

**EXHIBIT 3.11**   Number of Nontrivial Cross Moments

| $n$ | Covariance | Coskewness | Cokurtosis |
|-----|-----------|-----------|-----------|
| 2   | 1         | 2         | 3         |
| 5   | 10        | 30        | 65        |
| 10  | 45        | 210       | 705       |
| 20  | 190       | 1,520     | 8,835     |
| 30  | 435       | 4,930     | 40,890    |
| 100 | 4,950     | 171,600   | 4,421,175 |

## BEST LINEAR UNBIASED ESTIMATOR (BLUE)

In this chapter we have been careful to differentiate between the true parameters of a distribution and estimates of those parameters based on a sample of population data. In statistics we refer to these parameter estimates, or to the method of obtaining the estimate, as an estimator. For example, at the start of the chapter, we introduced an estimator for the sample mean:

$$\hat{\mu} = \frac{1}{n}\sum_{i=1}^{n} x_i \qquad (3.56)$$

This formula for computing the mean is so popular that we're likely to take it for granted. Why this equation, though? One justification that we gave earlier is that this particular estimator provides an unbiased estimate of the true mean. That is:

$$E[\hat{\mu}] = \mu \qquad (3.57)$$

Clearly, a good estimator should be unbiased. That said, for a given data set, we could imagine any number of unbiased estimators of the mean. For example, assuming there are three data points in our sample, $x_1$, $x_2$, and $x_3$, the following equation:

$$\tilde{\mu} = 0.75x_1 + 0.25x_2 + 0.00x_3 \qquad (3.58)$$

is also an unbiased estimator of the mean. Intuitively, this new estimator seems strange; we have put three times as much weight on $x_1$ as on $x_2$, and we have put no weight on $x_3$. There is no reason, as we have described the problem, to believe that any one data point is better than any other, so distributing the weight equally might seem more logical. Still, the estimator in Equation 3.58 is unbiased, and our criterion for judging this estimator to be strange seems rather subjective. What we need is an objective measure for comparing different unbiased estimators.

As we will see in coming chapters, just as we can measure the variance of random variables, we can measure the variance of parameter estimators as well. For example, if we measure the sample mean of a random variable several times, we can get a different answer each time. Imagine rolling a die 10 times and taking the average of all the rolls. Then repeat this process again and again. The sample mean is potentially different for each sample of 10 rolls. It turns out that this variability of the sample mean, or any other distribution parameter, is a function not only of the underlying variable, but of the form of the estimator as well.

When choosing among all the unbiased estimators, statisticians typically try to come up with the estimator with the minimum variance. In other words, we want to choose a formula that produces estimates for the parameter that are consistently close to the true value of the parameter. If we limit ourselves to estimators that can be written as a linear combination of the data, we can often prove that a particular candidate has the minimum variance among all the potential unbiased estimators. We call an estimator with these properties the best linear unbiased estimator, or BLUE. All of the estimators that we produced in this chapter for the mean, variance, covariance, skewness, and kurtosis are either BLUE or the ratio of BLUE estimators.

## PROBLEMS

1. Compute the mean and the median of the following series of returns:

| 12% | 5% | −8% | 20% | 4% | 10% | 2% |
|-----|-----|-----|-----|-----|-----|-----|

2. Compute the sample mean and the standard deviation of the following returns:

| 7% | 2% | 6% | −4% | −4% | 3% | 0% | 18% | −1% |
|-----|-----|-----|-----|-----|-----|-----|-----|-----|

3. Prove that Equation 3.2 is an unbiased estimator of the mean. That is, show that $E[\hat{\mu}] = \mu$ .

4. What is the standard deviation of the estimator in Equation 3.2? Assume the various data points are i.i.d.

5. Calculate the population covariance and correlation of the following series:

| Series #1 | 21% | 53% | 83% | 19% |
|-----------|-----|-----|-----|-----|
| Series #2 | 20% | 32% | 80% | 40% |

6. Calculate the population mean, standard deviation, and skewness of each of the following two series:

| Series #1 | −51 | −21 | 21 | 51 |
|-----------|-----|-----|-----|-----|
| Series #2 | −61 | −7 | 33 | 35 |

7. Calculate the population mean, standard deviation, and kurtosis for each of the following two series:

| Series #1 | −23 | −7 | 7 | 23 |
|-----------|-----|-----|-----|-----|
| Series #2 | −17 | −17 | 17 | 17 |

8. Given the probability density function for a random variable $X$,

$$f(x) = \frac{x}{18} \quad \text{for } 0 \leq x \leq 6$$

find the variance of $X$.

9. Prove that Equation 3.19, reproduced here, is an unbiased estimator of variance.

$$\hat{\sigma}_x^2 = \frac{1}{n-1} \sum_{i=1}^{n} (x_i - \hat{\mu}_x)$$

$$E[\hat{\sigma}_x^2] = \sigma^2{}_x$$

10. Given two random variables, $X_A$ and $X_B$, with corresponding means $\mu_A$ and $\mu_B$ and standard deviations $\sigma_A$ and $\sigma_B$, prove that the variance of $X_A$ plus $X_B$ is:

$$\text{Var}[X_A + X_B] = \sigma_A^2 + \sigma_B^2 + 2\rho_{AB}\sigma_A\sigma_B$$

where $\rho_{AB}$ is the correlation between $X_A$ and $X_B$.

11. A \$100 notional, zero coupon bond has one year to expiry. The probability of default is 10%. In the event of default, assume that the recovery rate is 40%. The continuously compounded discount rate is 5%. What is the present value of this bond?

## CHAPTER 4

# Distributions

In Chapter 2, we were introduced to random variables. In nature and in finance, random variables tend to follow certain patterns, or distributions. In this chapter we will learn about some of the most widely used probability distributions in risk management.

## PARAMETRIC DISTRIBUTIONS

Distributions can be divided into two broad categories: parametric distributions and nonparametric distributions. A parametric distribution can be described by a mathematical function. In the following sections we explore a number of parametric distributions, including the uniform distribution and the normal distribution. A nonparametric distribution cannot be summarized by a mathematical formula. In its simplest form, a nonparametric distribution is just a collection of data. An example of a nonparametric distribution would be a collection of historical returns for a security.

Parametric distributions are often easier to work with, but they force us to make assumptions, which may not be supported by real-world data. Nonparametric distributions can fit the observed data perfectly. The drawback of nonparametric distributions is that they are potentially too specific, which can make it difficult to draw any general conclusions.

## UNIFORM DISTRIBUTION

For a continuous random variable, $X$, recall that the probability of an outcome occurring between $b_1$ and $b_2$ can be found by integrating as follows:

$$P[b_1 \leq X \leq b_2] = \int_{b_1}^{b_2} f(x)dx$$

where $f(x)$ is the probability density function (PDF) of $X$.

The uniform distribution is one of the most fundamental distributions in statistics. The probability density function is given by the following formula:

$$u(b_1,b_2) = \begin{cases} c & \forall\, b_1 \le x \le b_2 \\ 0 & \forall\, b_1 > x > b_2 \end{cases} \quad \text{s.t. } b_2 > b_1 \tag{4.1}$$

In other words, the probability density is constant and equal to $c$ between $b_1$ and $b_2$, and zero everywhere else. Exhibit 4.1 shows the plot of a uniform distribution's probability density function.

Because the probability of any outcome occurring must be one, we can find the value of $c$ as follows:

$$\int_{-\infty}^{+\infty} u(b_1,b_2)dx = 1$$

$$\int_{-\infty}^{+\infty} u(b_1,b_2)dx = \int_{-\infty}^{b_1} 0\,dx + \int_{b_1}^{b_2} c\,dx + \int_{b_2}^{+\infty} 0\,dx = \int_{b_1}^{b_2} c\,dx$$

$$\int_{b_1}^{b_2} c\,dx = [cx]_{b_1}^{b_2} = c(b_2 - b_1) = 1 \tag{4.2}$$

$$c = \frac{1}{b_2 - b_1}$$

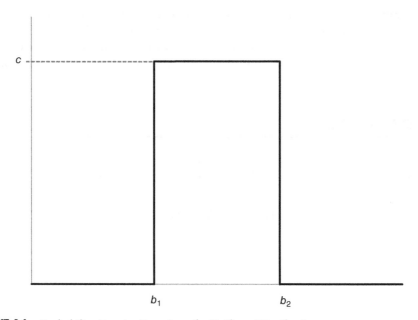

**EXHIBIT 4.1**  Probability Density Function of a Uniform Distribution

On reflection, this result should be obvious from the graph of the density function. That the probability of any outcome occurring must be one is equivalent to saying that the area under the probability density function must be equal to one. In Exhibit 4.1, we only need to know that the area of a rectangle is equal to the product of its width and its height to determine that $c$ is equal to $1/(b_2 - b_1)$.

With the probability density function in hand, we can proceed to calculate the mean and the variance. For the mean:

$$\mu = \int_{b_1}^{b_2} cx\, dx = \frac{1}{2}(b_2 + b_1) \tag{4.3}$$

In other words, the mean is just the average of the start and end values of the distribution.

Similarly, for the variance, we have:

$$\sigma^2 = \int_{b_1}^{b_2} c(x - \mu)^2\, dx = \frac{1}{12}(b_2 - b_1)^2 \tag{4.4}$$

This result is not as intuitive. The proof of both results is left as an exercise at the end of the chapter.

For the special case where $b_1 = 0$ and $b_2 = 1$, we refer to the distribution as a standard uniform distribution. Standard uniform distributions are extremely common. The default random number generator in most computer programs (technically a pseudo random number generator) is typically a standard uniform random variable. Because these random number generators are so ubiquitous, uniform distributions often serve as the building blocks for computer models in finance.

To calculate the cumulative distribution function (CDF) of the uniform distribution, we simply integrate the PDF. Again, assuming a lower bound of $b_1$ and an upper bound of $b_2$, we have:

$$P[X \le a] = \int_{b_1}^{a} c\, dz = c[z]_{b_1}^{a} = \frac{a - b_1}{b_2 - b_1} \tag{4.5}$$

As required, when $a$ equals $b_1$, we are at the minimum, and the CDF is zero. Similarly, when $a$ equals $b_2$, we are at the maximum, and the CDF equals one.

As we will see later, we can use combinations of uniform distributions to approximate other more complex distributions. As we will see in the next section, uniform distributions can also serve as the basis of other simple distributions, including the Bernoulli distribution.

## BERNOULLI DISTRIBUTION

Bernoulli's principle explains how the flow of fluids or gases leads to changes in pressure. It can be used to explain a number of phenomena, including how the wings of airplanes provide lift. Without it, modern aviation would be impossible. Bernoulli's principle is named after Daniel Bernoulli, an eighteenth-century Dutch-Swiss mathematician and scientist. Daniel came from a family of accomplished mathematicians. Daniel and his cousin Nicolas Bernoulli first described and presented a proof for the St. Petersburg paradox. But it is not Daniel or Nicolas, but rather their uncle, Jacob Bernoulli, for whom the Bernoulli distribution is named. In addition to the Bernoulli distribution, Jacob is credited with first describing the concept of continuously compounded returns, and, along the way, discovering Euler's number, $e$, both of which we explored in Chapter 1.

The Bernoulli distribution is incredibly simple. A Bernoulli random variable is equal to either zero or one. If we define $p$ as the probability that $X$ equals one, we have:

$$P[X = 1] = p \text{ and } P[X = 0] = 1 - p \tag{4.6}$$

We can easily calculate the mean and variance of a Bernoulli variable:

$$\mu = p \cdot 1 + (1 - p) \cdot 0 = p$$
$$\sigma^2 = p \cdot (1 - p)^2 + (1 - p) \cdot (0 - p)^2 = p(1 - p) \tag{4.7}$$

Binary outcomes are quite common in finance: a bond can default or not default; the return of a stock can be positive or negative; a central bank can decide to raise rates or not to raise rates.

In a computer simulation, one way to model a Bernoulli variable is to start with a standard uniform variable. Conveniently, both the standard uniform variable and our Bernoulli probability, $p$, range between zero and one. If the draw from the standard uniform variable is less than $p$, we set our Bernoulli variable equal to one; likewise, if the draw is greater than or equal to $p$, we set the Bernoulli variable to zero (see Exhibit 4.2).

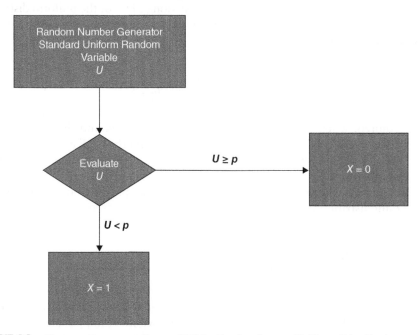

**EXHIBIT 4.2** How to Generate a Bernoulli Distribution from a Uniform Distribution

## BINOMIAL DISTRIBUTION

A binomial distribution can be thought of as a collection of Bernoulli random variables. If we have two independent bonds and the probability of default for both is 10%, then there are three possible outcomes: no bond defaults, one bond defaults, or both bonds default. Labeling the number of defaults $K$:

$$P[K = 0] = (1 - 10\%)^2 = 81\%$$
$$P[K = 1] = 2 \cdot 10\% \cdot (1 - 10\%) = 18\%$$
$$P[K = 2] = 10\%^2 = 1\%$$

Notice that for $K = 1$ we have multiplied the probability of a bond defaulting, 10%, and the probability of a bond not defaulting, 1 – 10%, by 2. This is because there are two ways in which exactly one bond can default: The first bond defaults and the second does not, or the second bond defaults and the first does not.

If we now have three bonds, still independent and with a 10% chance of defaulting, then:

$$P[K = 0] = (1 - 10\%)^3 = 72.9\%$$
$$P[K = 1] = 3 \cdot 10\% \cdot (1 - 10\%)^2 = 24.3\%$$
$$P[K = 2] = 3 \cdot 10\%^2 \cdot (1 - 10\%) = 2.7\%$$
$$P[K = 3] = 10\%^3 = 0.1\%$$

Notice that there are three ways in which we can get exactly one default and three ways in which we can get exactly two defaults.

We can extend this logic to any number of bonds. If we have $n$ bonds, the number of ways in which $k$ of those bonds can default is given by the number of combinations:

$$\binom{n}{k} = \frac{n!}{k!(n-k)!} \tag{4.8}$$

Similarly, if the probability of one bond defaulting is $p$, then the probability of any *particular* $k$ bonds defaulting is simply $p^k(1-p)^{n-k}$. Putting these two together, we can calculate the probability of any $k$ bonds defaulting as:

$$P[K = k] = \binom{n}{k} p^k (1 - p)^{n-k} \tag{4.9}$$

This is the probability density function for the binomial distribution. You should check that this equation produces the same result as our examples with two and three bonds. While the general proof is somewhat complicated, it is not difficult to prove that the probabilities sum to one for $n = 2$ or $n = 3$, no matter what value $p$ takes. It is a common mistake when calculating these probabilities to leave out the combinatorial term.

For the formulation in Equation 4.9, the mean of random variable $K$ is equal to $np$. So for a bond portfolio with 40 bonds, each with a 20% chance of defaulting, we would expect eight bonds ($8 = 20 \times 0.40$) to default on average. The variance of a binomial distribution is $np(1 - p)$.

---

**SAMPLE PROBLEM**

*Question:*
Assume we have four bonds, each with a 10% probability of defaulting over the next year. The event of default for any given bond is independent of the other bonds defaulting. What is the probability that zero, one, two, three, or all of the bonds default? What is the mean number of defaults? The standard deviation?

*Answer:*
We can calculate the probability of each possible outcome as follows:

| # of Defaults | $\binom{n}{k}$ | $p^k(1-p)^{n-k}$ | Probability |
|---|---|---|---|
| 0 | 1 | 65.61% | 65.61% |
| 1 | 4 | 7.29% | 29.16% |
| 2 | 6 | 0.81% | 4.86% |
| 3 | 4 | 0.09% | 0.36% |
| 4 | 1 | 0.01% | 0.01% |
| | | | 100.00% |

We can calculate the mean number of defaults two ways. The first is to use our formula for the mean:

$$\mu = np = 4 \cdot 10\% = 0.40$$

On average there are 0.40 defaults. The other way we could arrive at this result is to use the probabilities from the table. We get:

$$\mu = \sum_{i=0}^{4} p_i x_i = 65.61\% \cdot 0 + 29.16\% \cdot 1 + 4.86\% \cdot 2 + 0.36\% \cdot 3$$
$$+ 0.01\% \cdot 4 = 0.40$$

This is consistent with our earlier result.

To calculate the standard deviation, we also have two choices. Using our formula for variance, we have:

$$\sigma^2 = np(1-p) = 4 \cdot 10\%(1-10\%) = 0.36$$
$$\sigma = 0.60$$

As with the mean, we could also use the probabilities from the table:

$$\sigma^2 = \sum_{i=0}^{4} p_i (x_i - \mu)^2$$
$$\sigma^2 = 65.61\% \cdot 0.16 + 29.16\% \cdot 0.36 + 4.86\% \cdot 2.56 + 0.36\% \cdot 6.76$$
$$+ 0.01\% \cdot 12.96 = 0.36$$
$$\sigma = 0.60$$

Again, this is consistent with our earlier result.

Exhibit 4.3 shows binomial distributions with $p = 0.50$, for $n = 4$, 16, and 64. The highest point of each distribution occurs in the middle. In other words, when $p = 0.50$, the most likely outcome for a binomial random variable, the mode, is $n/2$ when $n$ is even, or the whole numbers either side of $n/2$ when $n$ is odd.

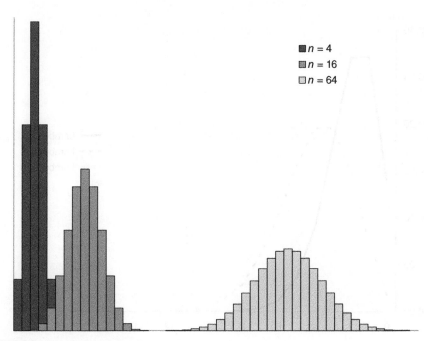

■ $n = 4$
■ $n = 16$
□ $n = 64$

**EXHIBIT 4.3**　Binomial Probability Density Functions

## POISSON DISTRIBUTION

Another useful discrete distribution is the Poisson distribution, named for the French mathematician Simeon Denis Poisson.

For a Poisson random variable $X$,

$$P[X = n] = \frac{\lambda^n}{n!} e^{-\lambda} \qquad (4.10)$$

for some constant $\lambda$, it turns out that both the mean and variance of $X$ are equal to $\lambda$. Exhibit 4.4 shows the probability density functions for three Poisson distributions.

The Poisson distribution is often used to model the occurrence of events over time—for example, the number of bond defaults in a portfolio or the number of crashes in equity markets. In this case, $n$ is the number of events that occur in an interval, and $\lambda$ is the expected number of events in the interval. Poisson distributions are often used to model jumps in jump-diffusion models.

If the rate at which events occur over time is constant, and the probability of any one event occurring is independent of all other events, then we say that the events follow a Poisson process, where:

$$P[X = n] = \frac{(\lambda t)^n}{n!} e^{-\lambda t} \qquad (4.11)$$

where $t$ is the amount of time elapsed. In other words, the expected number of events before time $t$ is equal to $\lambda t$.

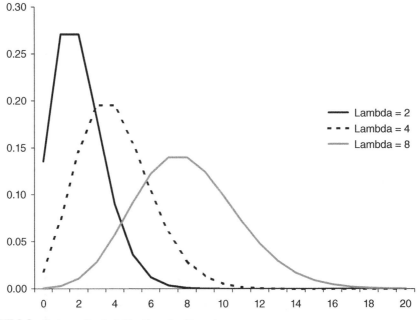

**EXHIBIT 4.4**   Poisson Probability Density Functions

---

**SAMPLE PROBLEM**

*Question:*
Assume that defaults in a large bond portfolio follow a Poisson process. The expected number of defaults each month is four. What is the probability that there are exactly three defaults over the course of one month? Over two months?

*Answer:*
For the first question, we solve the following:

$$P[X = 3] = \frac{(\lambda t)^n}{n!} e^{-\lambda t} = \frac{(4 \cdot 1)^3}{3!} e^{-4 \cdot 1} = 19.5\%$$

Over two months, the answer is:

$$P[X = 3] = \frac{(\lambda t)^n}{n!} e^{-\lambda t} = \frac{(4 \cdot 2)^3}{3!} e^{-4 \cdot 2} = 2.9\%$$

---

## NORMAL DISTRIBUTION

The normal distribution is probably the most widely used distribution in statistics, and is extremely popular in finance. The normal distribution occurs in a large number of settings, and is extremely easy to work with.

In popular literature, the normal distribution is often referred to as the bell curve because of the shape of its probability density function (see Exhibit 4.5).

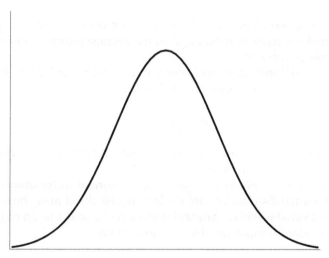

**EXHIBIT 4.5**   Normal Distribution Probability Density Function

The probability density function of the normal distribution is symmetrical, with the mean and median coinciding with the highest point of the PDF. Because it is symmetrical, the skew of a normal distribution is always zero. The kurtosis of a normal distribution is always 3. By definition, the excess kurtosis of a normal distribution is zero.

In some fields it is more common to refer to the normal distribution as the Gaussian distribution, after the famous German mathematician Johann Gauss, who is credited with some of the earliest work with the distribution. It is not the case that one name is more precise than the other as is the case with mean and average. Both normal distribution and Gaussian distribution are acceptable terms.

For a random variable $X$, the probability density function for the normal distribution is:

$$f(x) = \frac{1}{\sigma\sqrt{2\pi}} e^{-\frac{1}{2}\left(\frac{x-\mu}{\sigma}\right)^2} \tag{4.12}$$

The distribution is described by two parameters, $\mu$ and $\sigma$; $\mu$ is the mean of the distribution and $\sigma$ is the standard deviation. We leave the proofs of these statements for the exercises at the end of the chapter.

Rather than writing out the entire density function, when a variable is normally distributed it is the convention to write:

$$X \sim N(\mu, \sigma^2) \tag{4.13}$$

This would be read "$X$ is normally distributed with a mean of $\mu$ and variance of $\sigma^2$."

One reason that normal distributions are easy to work with is that any linear combination of independent normal variables is also normal. If we have two normally distributed variables, $X$ and $Y$, and two constants, $a$ and $b$, then $Z$ is also normally distributed:

$$Z = aX + bY \text{ s.t. } Z \sim N(a\mu_X + b\mu_Y, a^2\sigma_X^2 + b^2\sigma_Y^2) \tag{4.14}$$

This is very convenient. For example, if the log returns of individual stocks are independent and normally distributed, then the average return of those stocks will also be normally distributed.

When a normal distribution has a mean of zero and a standard deviation of one, it is referred to as a standard normal distribution.

$$\phi = \frac{1}{\sqrt{2\pi}} e^{-\frac{1}{2}x^2} \tag{4.15}$$

It is the convention to denote the standard normal PDF by $\phi$, and the cumulative standard normal distribution by $\Phi$.

Because a linear combination of independent normal distributions is also normal, standard normal distributions are the building blocks of many financial models. To get a normal variable with a standard deviation of $\sigma$ and a mean of $\mu$, we simply multiply the standard normal variable by $\sigma$ and add $\mu$.

$$X = \mu + \sigma\phi \Rightarrow X \sim N(\mu, \sigma^2) \tag{4.16}$$

To create two correlated normal variables, we can combine three independent standard normal variables, $X_1$, $X_2$, and $X_3$, as follows:

$$X_A = \sqrt{\rho}X_1 + \sqrt{1-\rho}X_2$$
$$X_B = \sqrt{\rho}X_1 + \sqrt{1-\rho}X_3$$

(4.17)

In this formulation, $X_A$ and $X_B$ are also standard normal variables, but with a correlation of $\rho$. The proof is left for an exercise at the end of the chapter.

Normal distributions are used throughout finance and risk management. In the first chapter, we suggested that log returns are extremely useful in financial modeling. One attribute that makes log returns particularly attractive is that they can be modeled using normal distributions. Normal distributions can generate numbers from negative infinity to positive infinity. For a particular normal distribution, the most extreme values might be extremely unlikely, but they can occur. This poses a problem for standard returns, which typically cannot be less than −100%. For log returns, though, there is no such constraint. Log returns also can range from negative to positive infinity.

Normally distributed log returns are widely used in financial simulations, and form the basis of a number of financial models, including the Black-Scholes option pricing model. As we will see in the coming chapters, while this normal assumption is often a convenient starting point, much of risk management is focused on addressing departures from this normality assumption.

There is no explicit solution for the cumulative standard normal distribution, or for its inverse. That said, most statistical packages will be able to calculate values for both functions. To calculate values for the CDF or inverse CDF for the normal distribution, there are a number of well-known numerical approximations.

Because the normal distribution is so widely used, most practitioners are expected to have at least a rough idea of how much of the distribution falls within one, two, or three standard deviations. In risk management it is also useful to know how many standard deviations are needed to encompass 95% or 99% of outcomes. Exhibit 4.6 lists some common values. Notice that for each row in the table, there is a "one-tailed" and "two-tailed" column. If we want to know how far we have to go to encompass 95% of the mass in the density function, the one-tailed value tells us

**EXHIBIT 4.6** Normal Distribution Confidence Intervals

|        | One-Tailed | Two-Tailed |
|--------|-----------|-----------|
| 1.0%   | −2.33     | −2.58     |
| 2.5%   | −1.96     | −2.24     |
| 5.0%   | −1.64     | −1.96     |
| 10.0%  | −1.28     | −1.64     |
| 90.0%  | 1.28      | 1.64      |
| 95.0%  | 1.64      | 1.96      |
| 97.5%  | 1.96      | 2.24      |
| 99.0%  | 2.33      | 2.58      |

that 95% of the values are less than 1.64 standard deviations above the mean. Because the normal distribution is symmetrical, it follows that 5% of the values are less than 1.64 standard deviations below the mean. The two-tailed value, in turn, tells us that 95% of the mass is within +/–1.96 standard deviations of the mean. It follows that 2.5% of the outcomes are less than –1.96 standard deviations from the mean, and 2.5% are greater than +1.96 standard deviations from the mean. Rather than one-tailed and two-tailed, some authors refer to "one-sided" and "two-sided" values.

## LOGNORMAL DISTRIBUTION

It's natural to ask: if we assume that log returns are normally distributed, then how are standard returns distributed? To put it another way: rather than modeling log returns with a normal distribution, can we use another distribution and model standard returns directly?

The answer to these questions lies in the lognormal distribution, whose density function is given by:

$$f(x) = \frac{1}{x\sigma\sqrt{2\pi}} e^{-\frac{1}{2}\left(\frac{\ln x - \mu}{\sigma}\right)^2} \tag{4.18}$$

If a variable has a lognormal distribution, then the log of that variable has a normal distribution. So, if log returns are assumed to be normally distributed, then one plus the standard return will be lognormally distributed.

Unlike the normal distribution, which ranges from negative infinity to positive infinity, the lognormal distribution is undefined, or zero, for negative values. Given an asset with a standard return, $R$, if we model $(1 + R)$ using the lognormal distribution, then $R$ will have a minimum value of –100%. As mentioned in Chapter 1, this feature, which we associate with limited liability, is common to most financial assets. Using the lognormal distribution provides an easy way to ensure that we avoid returns less than –100%. The probability density function for a lognormal distribution is shown in Exhibit 4.7.

Equation 4.18 looks almost exactly like the equation for the normal distribution, Equation 4.12, with $x$ replaced by $\ln(x)$. Be careful, though, as there is also the $x$ in the denominator of the leading fraction. At first it might not be clear what the $x$ is doing there. By carefully rearranging Equation 4.18, we can get something that, while slightly longer, looks more like the normal distribution in form:

$$f(x) = e^{\frac{1}{2}\sigma^2 - \mu} \frac{1}{\sigma\sqrt{2\pi}} e^{-\frac{1}{2}\left(\frac{\ln x - (\mu - \sigma^2)}{\sigma}\right)^2} \tag{4.19}$$

While not as pretty, this starts to hint at what we've actually done. Rather than being symmetrical around $\mu$, as in the normal distribution, the lognormal distribution is asymmetrical and peaks at $\exp(\mu - \sigma^2)$.

Given $\mu$ and $\sigma$, the mean is given by:

$$E[X] = e^{\mu + \frac{1}{2}\sigma^2} \tag{4.20}$$

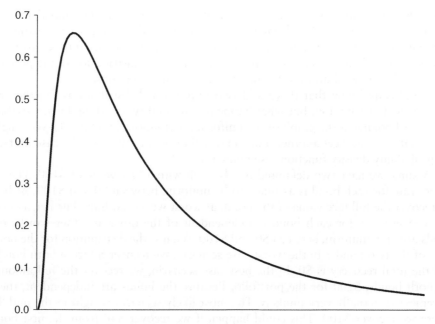

**EXHIBIT 4.7** Lognormal Probability Density Function

This result looks very similar to the Taylor expansion of the natural logarithm around one. Remember from Chapter 1, if $R$ is a standard return and $r$ the corresponding log return, then:

$$r \approx R - \frac{1}{2}R^2 \tag{4.21}$$

Be careful: Because these equations are somewhat similar, it is very easy to get the signs in front of $\sigma^2$ and $R^2$ backward.

The variance of the lognormal distribution is given by:

$$E[(X - E[X])^2] = (e^{\sigma^2} - 1)e^{2\mu + \sigma^2} \tag{4.22}$$

The equations for the mean and the variance hint at the difficulty of working with lognormal distributions directly. It is convenient to be able to describe the returns of a financial instrument as being lognormally distributed, rather than having to say the log returns of that instrument are normally distributed. When it comes to modeling, though, even though they are equivalent, it is often easier to work with log returns and normal distributions than with standard returns and lognormal distributions.

## CENTRAL LIMIT THEOREM

Assume we have an index made up of a large number of equities, or a bond portfolio that contains a large number of similar bonds. In these situations and many more, it is often convenient to assume that the constituent elements—the equities or bonds—are made up of statistically identical random variables, and that these variables are uncorrelated with each other. As mentioned previously, in statistics we term these variables independent and identically distributed (i.i.d.). If the constituent elements are i.i.d., it turns out we can say a lot about the distribution of the population, even if the distribution of the individual elements is unknown.

We already know that if we add two i.i.d. normal distributions together we get a normal distribution, but what happens if we add two i.i.d. uniform variables together? Looking at the graph of the uniform distribution (Exhibit 4.1), you might think that we would get another uniform distribution, but this isn't the case. In fact, the probability density function resembles a triangle.

Assume we have two defaulted bonds, each with a face value of $100. The recovery rate for each bond is assumed to be uniform, between $0 and $100. At best we recover the full face value of the bond; at worst we get nothing. Further, assume the recovery rate for each bond is independent of the other. In other words, the bonds are i.i.d. uniform, between $0 and $100. What is the distribution for the portfolio of the two bonds? In the worst-case scenario, we recover $0 from both bonds, and the total recovery is $0. In the best-case scenario, we recover the full amount for both bonds, $200 for the portfolio. Because the bonds are independent, these extremes are actually very unlikely. The most likely scenario is right in the middle, where we recover $100. This could happen if we recover $40 from the first bond and $60 from the second, $90 from the first and $10 from the second, or any of an infinite number of combinations. Exhibit 4.8 shows the distribution of values for the portfolio of two i.i.d. bonds.

With three bonds, the distribution ranges from $0 to $300, with the mode at $150. With four bonds, the distribution ranges from $0 to $400, with the mode at

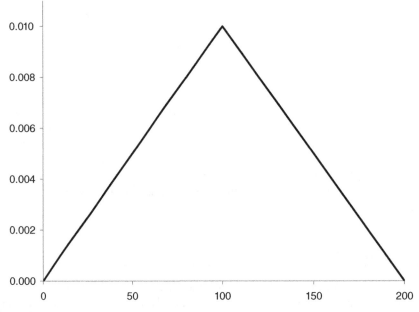

**EXHIBIT 4.8**   Sum of Two i.i.d. Uniform Distributions

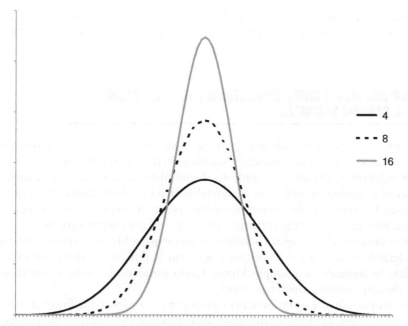

**EXHIBIT 4.9**  Sums of Various i.i.d. Uniform Distributions

$200. As we continue to add more bonds, the shape of the distribution function continues to change. Exhibit 4.9 shows the density functions for the sums of 4, 8, and 16 i.i.d. uniform variables, scaled to have the same range.

Oddly enough, even though we started with uniform variables, the distribution is starting to look increasingly like a normal distribution. The resemblance is not just superficial; it turns out that as we add more and more variables, the distribution actually converges to a normal distribution. What's more, this is not just true if we start out with uniform distributions; it applies to any distributions with finite variance.[1] This result is known as the central limit theorem.

More formally, if we have $n$ i.i.d. random variables, $X_1, X_2, \ldots, X_n$, each with mean $\mu$ and standard deviation $\sigma$, and we define $S_n$ as the sum of those $n$ variables, then:

$$\lim_{n \to \infty} S_n \sim N(n\mu, n\sigma^2) \tag{4.23}$$

In other words, as $n$ approaches infinity, the sum converges to a normal distribution. This result is one of the most important results in statistics and is the reason why the normal distribution is so ubiquitous. In risk, as in a number of other fields, we are often presented with data that either is i.i.d. by construction or is assumed to be i.i.d. Even when the underlying variables are not normal—which is rare in practice—the i.i.d. assumption, combined with the central limit theorem, allows us

---

[1]Even though we have not yet encountered any distributions with infinite variance, they can exist. The Cauchy distribution is an example of a parametric distribution with infinite variance. While rare in finance, it's good to know that these distributions can exist.

to approximate a large collection of data using a normal distribution. The central limit theorem is often used to justify the approximation of financial variables by a normal distribution.

## APPLICATION: MONTE CARLO SIMULATIONS PART I: CREATING NORMAL RANDOM VARIABLES

While some problems in risk management have explicit analytic solutions, many problems have no exact mathematical solution. In these cases, we can often approximate a solution by creating a Monte Carlo simulation. A Monte Carlo simulation consists of a number of trials. For each trial we feed random inputs into a system of equations. By collecting the outputs from the system of equations for a large number of trials, we can estimate the statistical properties of the output variables.

Even in cases where explicit solutions might exist, a Monte Carlo solution might be preferable in practice if the explicit solution is difficult to derive or extremely complex. In some cases a simple Monte Carlo simulation can be easier to understand, thereby reducing operational risk.

As an example of a situation where we might use a Monte Carlo simulation, pretend we are asked to evaluate the mean and standard deviation of the profits from a fixed-strike arithmetic Asian option, where the value of the option, $V$, at expiry is:

$$V = \max\left[\frac{1}{T}\sum_{t=1}^{T} S_t - X, 0\right] \qquad (4.24)$$

Here $X$ is the strike price, $S_t$ is the closing price of the underlying asset at time $t$, and $T$ is the number of periods in the life of the option. In other words, the value of the option at expiry is the greater of zero or the average price of the underlying asset less the strike price.

Assume there are 200 days until expiry. Further, we are told that the returns of the underlying asset are lognormal, with a mean of 10% and a standard deviation of 20%. The input to our Monte Carlo simulation would be lognormal variables with the appropriate mean and standard deviation. For each trial, we would generate 200 random daily returns, use the returns to calculate a series of random prices, calculate the average of the price series, and use the average to calculate the value of the option. We would repeat this process again and again, using a different realization of the random returns each time, and each time calculating a new value for the option.

The initial step in the Monte Carlo simulation, generating the random inputs, can itself be very complex. In Chapter 8, we will learn how to create correlated normally distributed random variables from a set of uncorrelated normally distributed random variables. How do we create the uncorrelated normally distributed random variables to start with? Many special-purpose statistical packages contain functions that will generate random draws from normal distributions. If the application we are using does not have this feature, but does have a standard random number generator, which generates a standard uniform distribution, there are two ways we can generate random normal variables. The first is to use an inverse normal transformation. As mentioned previously, there is no explicit formula for the inverse normal transformation, but there are a number of good approximations.

The second approach takes advantage of the central limit theorem. By adding together a large number of i.i.d. uniform distributions and then multiplying and adding the correct constants, a good approximation to any normal variable can be formed. A classic approach is to simply add 12 standard uniform variables together, and subtract 6:

$$X = \sum_{i=1}^{12} U_i - 6 \tag{4.25}$$

Because the mean of a standard uniform variable is ½ and the variance is ¹⁄₁₂, this produces a good approximation to a standard normal variable, with mean zero and standard deviation of one. By utilizing a greater number of uniform variables, we could increase the accuracy of our approximation, but for most applications, this approximation is more than adequate.

## CHI-SQUARED DISTRIBUTION

If we have $k$ independent standard normal variables, $Z_1, Z_2, \ldots, Z_k$, then the sum of their squares, $S$, has a chi-squared distribution. We write:

$$S = \sum_{i=1}^{k} Z_i^2$$
$$S \sim \chi_k^2 \tag{4.26}$$

The variable $k$ is commonly referred to as the degrees of freedom. It follows that the sum of two independent chi-squared variables, with $k_1$ and $k_2$ degrees of freedom, will follow a chi-squared distribution, with $(k_1 + k_2)$ degrees of freedom.

Because the chi-squared variable is the sum of squared values, it can take on only nonnegative values and is asymmetrical. The mean of the distribution is $k$, and the variance is $2k$. As $k$ increases, the chi-squared distribution becomes increasingly symmetrical. As $k$ approaches infinity, the chi-squared distribution converges to the normal distribution. Exhibit 4.10 shows the probability density functions for some chi-squared distributions with different values for $k$.

For positive values of $x$, the probability density function for the chi-squared distribution is:

$$f(x) = \frac{1}{2^{k/2} \Gamma(k/2)} x^{\frac{k}{2}-1} e^{-\frac{x}{2}} \tag{4.27}$$

where $\Gamma$ is the gamma function:

$$\Gamma(n) = \int_0^\infty x^{n-1} e^{-x} dx \tag{4.28}$$

The chi-squared distribution is widely used in risk management, and in statistics in general, for hypothesis testing.

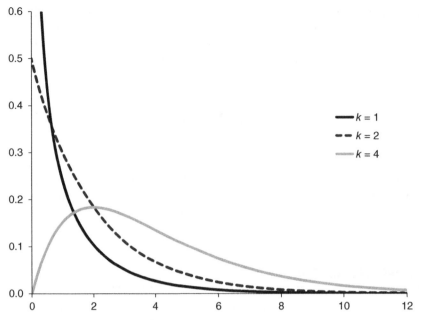

**EXHIBIT 4.10**    Chi-Squared Probability Density Functions

## STUDENT'S *t* DISTRIBUTION

Another extremely popular distribution in statistics and in risk management is Student's *t* distribution. The distribution was first described in English, in 1908, by William Sealy Gosset, an employee at the Guinness brewery in Dublin. In order to comply with his firm's policy on publishing in public journals, he submitted his work under the pseudonym Student. The distribution has been known as Student's *t* distribution ever since. In practice, it is often referred to simply as the *t* distribution.

If $Z$ is a standard normal variable and $U$ is a chi-square variable with $k$ degrees of freedom, which is independent of $Z$, then the random variable $X$,

$$X = \frac{Z}{\sqrt{U/k}} \tag{4.29}$$

follows a *t* distribution with $k$ degrees of freedom.

Mathematically, the distribution is quite complicated. The probability density function can be written:

$$f(x) = \frac{\Gamma\left(\dfrac{k+1}{2}\right)}{\sqrt{k\pi}\,\Gamma\left(\dfrac{k}{2}\right)}\left(1+\frac{x^2}{k}\right)^{-\frac{(k+1)}{2}} \tag{4.30}$$

where $k$ is the degrees of freedom and $\Gamma$ is the gamma function.

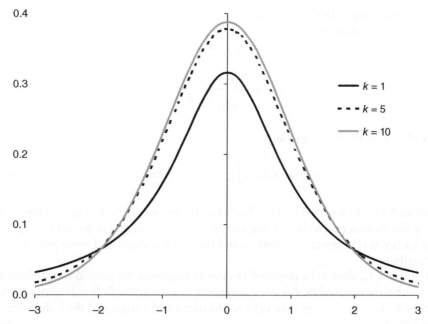

**EXHIBIT 4.11**   Student's $t$ Probability Density Functions

Very few risk managers will memorize this PDF equation, but it is important to understand the basic shape of the distribution and how it changes with $k$. Exhibit 4.11 shows the probability density function for three Student's $t$ distributions. Notice how changing the value of $k$ changes the shape of the distribution, specifically the tails.

The $t$ distribution is symmetrical around its mean, which is equal to zero. For low values of $k$, the $t$ distribution looks very similar to a standard normal distribution, except that it displays excess kurtosis. As $k$ increases, this excess kurtosis decreases. In fact, as $k$ approaches infinity, the $t$ distribution converges to a standard normal distribution.

The variance of the $t$ distribution for $k > 2$ is $k/(k - 2)$. You can see that as $k$ increases, the variance of the $t$ distribution converges to one, the variance of the standard normal distribution.

As we will see in the following chapter, the $t$ distribution's popularity derives mainly from its use in hypothesis testing. The $t$ distribution is also a popular choice for modeling the returns of financial assets, since it displays excess kurtosis.

## F-DISTRIBUTION

If $U_1$ and $U_2$ are two independent chi-squared distributions with $k_1$ and $k_2$ degrees of freedom, respectively, then $X$,

$$X = \frac{U_1 / k_1}{U_2 / k_2} \sim F(k_1, k_2) \tag{4.31}$$

follows an $F$-distribution with parameters $k_1$ and $k_2$.

The probability density function of the $F$-distribution, as with the chi-squared distribution, is rather complicated:

$$f(x) = \frac{\sqrt{\dfrac{(k_1 x)^{k_1} k_2^{k_2}}{(k_1 x + k_2)^{k_1+k_2}}}}{x B\left(\dfrac{k_1}{2}, \dfrac{k_2}{2}\right)} \tag{4.32}$$

where $B(x, y)$ is the beta function:

$$B(x, y) = \int_0^1 z^{x-1}(1-z)^{y-1} dz \tag{4.33}$$

As with the chi-squared and Student's $t$ distributions, memorizing the probability density function is probably not something most risk managers would be expected to do; rather, it is important to understand the general shape and some properties of the distribution.

Exhibit 4.12 shows the probability density functions for several $F$-distributions. Because the chi-squared PDF is zero for negative values, the $F$-distribution's density function is also zero for negative values. The mean and variance of the $F$-distribution are as follows:

$$\mu = \frac{k_2}{k_2 - 2} \text{ for } k_2 > 2$$

$$\sigma^2 = \frac{2k_2^2(k_1 + k_2 - 2)}{k_1(k_2 - 2)^2(k_2 - 4)} \text{ for } k_2 > 4 \tag{4.34}$$

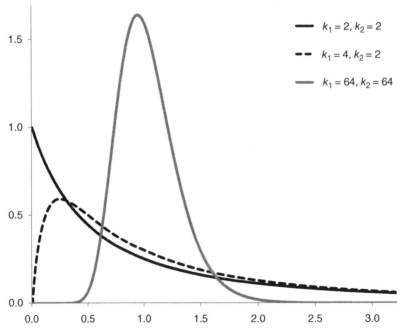

**EXHIBIT 4.12**   $F$-Distribution Probability Density Functions

As $k_1$ and $k_2$ increase, the mean and mode converge to one. As $k_1$ and $k_2$ approach infinity, the F-distribution converges to a normal distribution.

There is also a nice relationship between Student's $t$ distribution and the F-distribution. From the description of the $t$ distribution, Equation 4.29, it is easy to see that the square of a variable with a $t$ distribution has an F-distribution. More specifically, if $X$ is a random variable with a $t$ distribution with $k$ degrees of freedom, then $X^2$ has an F-distribution with 1 and $k$ degrees of freedom:

$$X^2 \sim F(1, k) \qquad (4.35)$$

## TRIANGULAR DISTRIBUTION

It is often useful in risk management to have a distribution with a fixed minimum and maximum—for example, when modeling default rates and recovery rates, which by definition cannot be less than zero or greater than one. The uniform distribution is an example of a continuous distribution with a finite range. While the uniform distribution is extremely simple to work with (it is completely described by two parameters), it is rather limited in that the probability of an event is constant over its entire range.

The triangular distribution is a distribution whose PDF is a triangle. As with the uniform distribution, it has a finite range. Mathematically, the triangular distribution is only slightly more complex than a uniform distribution, but much more flexible. The triangular distribution has a unique mode, and can be symmetric, positively skewed, or negatively skewed.

The PDF for a triangular distribution with a minimum of $a$, a maximum of $b$, and a mode of $c$ is described by the following two-part function:

$$f(x) = \begin{cases} \dfrac{2(x-a)}{(b-a)(c-a)} & a \le x \le c \\[2mm] \dfrac{2(b-x)}{(b-a)(b-c)} & c < x \le b \end{cases} \qquad (4.36)$$

Exhibit 4.13 shows a triangular distribution where $a$, $b$, and $c$ are 0.0, 1.0, and 0.8, respectively.

It is easily verified that the PDF is zero at both $a$ and $b$, and that the value of $f(x)$ reaches a maximum, $2/(b-a)$, at $c$. Because the area of a triangle is simply one half the base multiplied by the height, it is also easy to confirm that the area under the PDF is equal to one.

The mean, $\mu$, and variance, $\sigma^2$, of a triangular distribution are given by:

$$\mu = \frac{a+b+c}{3}$$
$$\sigma^2 = \frac{a^2+b^2+c^2-ab-ac-bc}{18} \qquad (4.37)$$

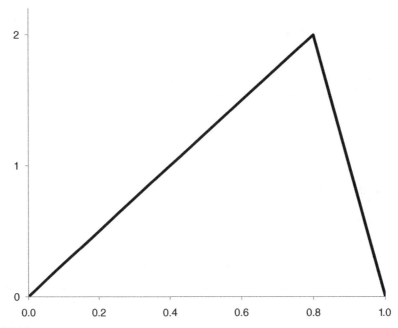

**EXHIBIT 4.13** Triangular Distribution Probability Density Function

## BETA DISTRIBUTION

The beta distribution is another distribution with a finite range. It is more complicated than the triangular distribution mathematically, but it is also much more flexible.

As with the triangular distribution, the beta distribution can be used to model default rates and recovery rates. As we will see in Chapter 6, the beta distribution is also extremely useful in Bayesian analysis.

The beta distribution is defined on the interval from zero to one. The PDF is defined as follows, where $a$ and $b$ are two positive constants:

$$f(x) = \frac{1}{B(a,b)} x^{a-1}(1-x)^{b-1} \quad 0 \le x \le 1 \tag{4.38}$$

where $B(a,b)$ is the beta function as described earlier for the $F$-distribution. The uniform distribution is a special case of the beta distribution, where both $a$ and $b$ are equal to one. Exhibit 4.14 shows four different parameterizations of the beta distribution.

The mean, $\mu$, and variance, $\sigma^2$, of a beta distribution are given by:

$$\mu = \frac{a}{a+b}$$
$$\sigma^2 = \frac{ab}{(a+b)^2(a+b+1)} \tag{4.39}$$

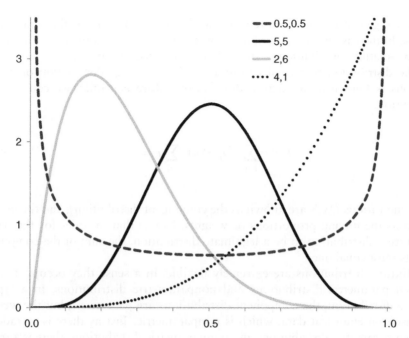

**EXHIBIT 4.14** Beta Distribution Probability Density Functions

## MIXTURE DISTRIBUTIONS

Imagine a stock whose log returns follow a normal distribution with low volatility 90% of the time, and a normal distribution with high volatility 10% of the time. Most of the time the world is relatively dull, and the stock just bounces along. Occasionally, though—maybe there is an earnings announcement or some other news event—the stock's behavior is more extreme. We could write the combined density function as:

$$f(x) = w_L f_L(x) + w_H f_H(x) \qquad (4.40)$$

where $w_L = 0.90$ is the probability of the return coming from the low-volatility distribution, $f_L(x)$, and $w_H = 0.10$ is the probability of the return coming from the high-volatility distribution $f_H(x)$. We can think of this as a two-step process. First, we randomly choose the high or low distribution, with a 90% chance of picking the low distribution. Second, we generate a random return from the chosen normal distribution. The final distribution, $f(x)$, is a legitimate probability distribution in its own right, and although it is equally valid to describe a random draw directly from this distribution, it is often helpful to think in terms of this two-step process.

Note that the two-step process is not the same as the process described in a previous section for adding two random variables together. An example of adding two random variables together is a portfolio of two stocks. At each point in time, each stock generates a random return, and the portfolio return is the sum of *both* returns. In the case we are describing now, the return appears to come from *either* the low-volatility distribution *or* the high-volatility distribution.

The distribution that results from a weighted average distribution of density functions is known as a mixture distribution. More generally, we can create a distribution:

$$f(x) = \sum_{i=1}^{n} w_i f_i(x) \text{ s.t. } \sum_{i=1}^{n} w_i = 1 \tag{4.41}$$

where the various $f_i(x)$'s are known as the component distributions, and the $w_i$'s are known as the mixing proportions or weights. Notice that in order for the resulting mixture distribution to be a legitimate distribution, the sum of the component weights must equal one.

Mixture distributions are extremely flexible. In a sense they occupy a realm between parametric distributions and nonparametric distributions. In a typical mixture distribution, the component distributions are parametric, but the weights are based on empirical data, which is nonparametric. Just as there is a trade-off between parametric distributions and nonparametric distributions, there is a trade-off between using a low number and a high number of component distributions. By adding more and more component distributions, we can approximate any data set with increasing precision. At the same time, as we add more and more component distributions, the conclusions that we can draw tend to become less general in nature.

Just by adding two normal distributions together, we can develop a large number of interesting distributions. Similar to the previous example, if we combine two normal distributions with the same mean but different variances, we can get a symmetrical mixture distribution that displays excess kurtosis. By shifting the mean of one distribution, we can also create a distribution with positive or negative skew. Exhibit 4.15 shows an example of a skewed mixture distribution created from two normal distributions.

Finally, if we move the means far enough apart, the resulting mixture distribution will be bimodal; that is, the PDF will have two distinct maxima, as shown in Exhibit 4.16.

Mixture distributions can be extremely useful in risk management. Securities whose return distributions are skewed or have excess kurtosis are often considered riskier than those with normal distributions, since extreme events can occur more frequently. Mixture distributions provide a ready method for modeling these attributes.

A bimodal distribution can be extremely risky. If one component of a security's returns has an extremely low mixing weight, we might be tempted to ignore that component. If the component has an extremely negative mean, though, ignoring it could lead us to severely underestimate the risk of the security. Equity market crashes are a perfect example of an extremely low-probability, highly negative mean event.

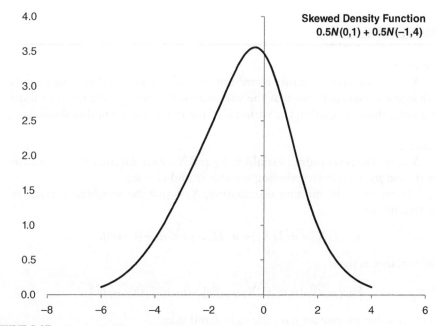

**EXHIBIT 4.15**  Skewed Mixture Distribution

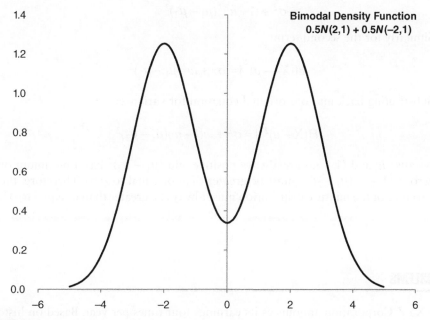

**EXHIBIT 4.16**  Bimodal Mixture Distribution

## SAMPLE PROBLEM

*Question:*

Assume we have a mixture distribution with two independent components with equal variance. Prove that the variance of the mixture distribution must be greater than or equal to the variance of the two component distributions.

*Answer:*

Assume the two random variables, $X_1$ and $X_2$, have variance $\sigma^2$. The means are $\mu_1$ and $\mu_2$, with corresponding weights $w$ and $(1-w)$.

The mean of the mixture distribution, $X$, is just the weighted average of the two means:

$$\mu = E[X] = w_1 E[X_1] + w_2 E[X_2] = w\mu_1 + (1-w)\mu_2$$

The variance is then:

$$E[(X-\mu)^2)] = w_1 E[(X_1-\mu)^2)] + (1-w)E[(X_2-\mu)^2]$$

First, we solve for one term on the right-hand side:

$$
\begin{aligned}
E[(X_1-\mu)^2] &= E[(X_1-w\mu_1-(1-w)\mu_2)^2] \\
&= E[(X_1-\mu_1-(1-w)(\mu_2-\mu_1))^2] \\
&= E[(X_1-\mu_1)^2 - 2(X_1-\mu_1)(1-w)(\mu_2-\mu_1) \\
&\quad +(1-w)^2(\mu_2-\mu_1)^2] \\
&= \sigma^2 + (1-w)^2(\mu_1-\mu_2)^2
\end{aligned}
$$

Similarly for the second term:

$$E[(X_2-\mu)^2] = \sigma^2 + w^2(\mu_1-\mu_2)^2$$

Substituting back into our original equation for variance:

$$E[(X-\mu)^2)] = \sigma^2 + w(1-w)(\mu_1-\mu_2)^2$$

Because $w$ and $(1-w)$ are always positive and $(\mu_1-\mu_2)^2$ has a minimum of zero, $w(1-w)(\mu_1-\mu_2)^2$ must be greater than or equal to zero. Therefore, the variance of the mixture distribution must always be greater than or equal to $\sigma^2$.

## PROBLEMS

1. XYZ Corporation announces its earnings four times per year. Based on historical data, you estimate that in any given quarter the probability that XYZ Corporation's earnings will exceed consensus estimates is 30%. Also, the probability

of exceeding the consensus in any one quarter is independent of the outcome in any other quarter. What is the probability that XYZ Corporation will exceed estimates three times in a given year?

2. The market risk group at your firm has developed a value at risk (VaR) model. In Chapter 7 we examine VaR models more closely. In the meantime, assume the probability of an exceedance event on any given day is 5%, and the probability of an exceedance event occurring on any given day is independent of an exceedance event having occurred on any previous day. What is the probability that there are two exceedances over 20 days?

3. Assume the annual returns of Fund A are normally distributed with a mean and standard deviation of 30%. The annual returns of Fund B are also normally distributed, but with a mean and standard deviation of 40%. The returns of both funds are independent of each other. What is the mean and standard deviation of the difference of the returns of the two funds, Fund B minus Fund A? At the end of the year, Fund B has returned 80%, and Fund A has lost 12%. How likely is it that Fund B outperforms Fund A by this much or more?

4. The number of defaults per month in a large bond portfolio follows a Poisson process. On average, there are two defaults per month. The number of defaults is independent from one month to the next. What is the probability that there are five defaults over five months? Ten defaults? Fifteen defaults?

5. The annual returns of an emerging markets bond fund have a mean return of 10% and a standard deviation of 15%. Your firm invests $200 million into the fund. What is the probability of losing more than $18.4 million? Assume the returns are normally distributed, and ignore the limited liability constraint (i.e., the impossibility of losing more than the initial $200 million investment).

6. The annual returns of an emerging markets exchange-traded fund (ETF) have an expected return of 20.60% and a standard deviation of 30.85%. You are asked to estimate the likelihood of extreme return scenarios. Assume the returns are normally distributed. What is the probability that returns are worse than −30%?

7. For a uniform distribution with a lower bound $x_1$ and an upper bound $x_2$, prove that the formulas for calculating the mean and variance are:

$$\mu = \frac{1}{2}(x_2 + x_1)$$

$$\sigma^2 = \frac{1}{12}(x_2 - x_1)^2$$

8. Prove that the normal distribution is a proper probability distribution. That is, show that:

$$\int_{-\infty}^{\infty} \frac{1}{\sqrt{2\pi\sigma^2}} e^{-\frac{(x-\mu)^2}{2\sigma^2}} dx = 1$$

You may find it necessary to use the Gaussian integral:

$$\int_{-\infty}^{\infty} e^{-x^2} dx = \sqrt{\pi}$$

9. Prove that the mean of the normal distribution, as specified in Equation 4.12, is $\mu$. That is, show that:

$$\int_{-\infty}^{\infty} x \frac{1}{\sqrt{2\pi\sigma^2}} e^{-\frac{(x-\mu)^2}{2\sigma^2}} dx = \mu$$

10. Prove that the variance of a normal distribution, as specified in Equation 4.12, is $\sigma^2$. You may find the following result useful:

$$\int_{-\infty}^{\infty} x^2 e^{-x^2} dx = \frac{1}{2}\sqrt{\pi}$$

11. Prove that the correlation between $X_A$ and $X_B$ is $\rho$, where:

$$X_A = \sqrt{\rho}X_1 + \sqrt{1-\rho}X_2$$
$$X_B = \sqrt{\rho}X_1 + \sqrt{1-\rho}X_3$$

and $X_1$, $X_2$, and $X_3$ are uncorrelated standard normal variables.

12. Imagine we have two independent uniform distributions, $A$ and $B$. $A$ ranges between $-2$ and $-1$, and is zero everywhere else. $B$ ranges between $+1$ and $+2$, and is zero everywhere else. What are the mean and standard deviation of a portfolio that consists of 50% $A$ and 50% $B$? What are the mean and standard deviation of a portfolio where the return is a 50/50 mixture distribution of $A$ and $B$?

## CHAPTER 5

# Multivariate Distributions and Copulas

In this chapter we explore distributions involving more than one variable, and provide a brief overview of copulas. Multivariate distributions are an important tool for modeling portfolios.

## MULTIVARIATE DISTRIBUTIONS

A multivariate distribution or joint distribution is a distribution involving two or more variables. We begin our exploration of multivariate distributions by examining discrete distributions, before moving on to continuous distributions.

### Discrete Distributions

A probability matrix is an example of a discrete multivariate distribution. The following probability matrix from Chapter 2 lists various probabilities for the performance of the equity and bonds of a company.

This is a discrete joint distribution with two random variables, one for the performance of the equity and one for the performance of the bonds. A joint distribution with two random variables can also be referred to as a bivariate distribution. In Exhibit 5.1 there are six distinct joint probabilities. For example, the joint probability of both equity outperforming *and* bonds being downgraded is 5%. As is required of any distribution, the sum of all the probabilities is equal to 100%.

We can easily create a joint distribution for any number of random variables, though displaying the results in a simple probability matrix would be difficult for

**EXHIBIT 5.1**   Probability Matrix

|  |  | Equity | |
| --- | --- | --- | --- |
|  |  | Outperform | Underperform |
| Bonds | Upgrade | 15% | 5% |
|  | No Change | 30% | 25% |
|  | Downgrade | 5% | 20% |

**EXHIBIT 5.2**  Joint Probabilities Table

| Fund A | Fund B | Fund C | Probability |
|--------|--------|--------|-------------|
| Under | Under | Under | 1% |
| Under | Under | Over | 2% |
| Under | Over | Under | 8% |
| Under | Over | Over | 22% |
| Over | Under | Under | 35% |
| Over | Under | Over | 22% |
| Over | Over | Under | 8% |
| Over | Over | Over | 2% |
| | | | 100% |

more than two variables. No matter how many variables there are, the basic idea is the same: To define a discrete distribution, we assign a probability to every possible joint outcome, and the sum of those probabilities must add up to 100%.

As another example, pretend we are interested in three mutual funds, Fund A, Fund B, and Fund C; furthermore, assume we are interested only in the probability of the funds generating returns that are under or over a particular benchmark. With three funds and two possible outcomes for each fund, there is a total of eight distinct outcomes, each with an associated joint probability. We could list them in a table as in Exhibit 5.2.

Rather than increasing the number of variables, we could increase the number of possible outcomes for each variable. In Exhibit 5.3 we have the joint distribution for two bonds, each of which can have one of eight possible letter ratings at the end of the year. This gives us a total of 64 possible outcomes.

In theory, we could create a matrix of any size. As the number of possible outcomes approaches infinity, the discrete multivariate distribution converges to a continuous multivariate distribution, or continuous joint distribution.

**EXHIBIT 5.3**  Joint Distribution Matrix

| | | Bond #1 | | | | | | | |
|---|---|---|---|---|---|---|---|---|---|
| | | AAA | AA | A | BBB | BB | B | C | D |
| Bond #2 | AAA | 0.0% | 0.2% | 0.2% | 0.4% | 0.2% | 0.1% | 0.0% | 0.0% |
| | AA | 0.1% | 0.6% | 1.8% | 2.9% | 1.8% | 0.4% | 0.2% | 0.1% |
| | A | 0.2% | 1.8% | 5.3% | 8.3% | 5.3% | 1.5% | 0.3% | 0.2% |
| | BBB | 0.3% | 2.9% | 8.3% | 13.0% | 8.3% | 2.6% | 0.4% | 0.0% |
| | BB | 0.2% | 1.8% | 5.0% | 8.0% | 5.3% | 1.8% | 0.1% | 0.1% |
| | B | 0.1% | 0.5% | 1.8% | 2.6% | 1.3% | 0.6% | 0.1% | 0.0% |
| | C | 0.1% | 0.1% | 0.3% | 0.6% | 0.5% | 0.3% | 0.0% | 0.0% |
| | D | 0.0% | 0.1% | 0.2% | 0.4% | 0.2% | 0.2% | 0.0% | 0.0% |

## Continuous Distributions

Just as with a single random variable, we can define a continuous joint distribution based on its probability density function (PDF). If we have two random variables, $X$ and $Y$, for example, we could define the joint PDF, $f(x,y)$, such that the probability of finding $X$ between $x_1$ and $x_2$ and at the same time finding $Y$ between $y_1$ and $y_2$ is given by:

$$P[x_1 \le X \le x_2, y_1 \le Y \le y_2] = \int_{x_1}^{x_2} \int_{y_1}^{y_2} f(x,y) dx dy \qquad (5.1)$$

where $x_1 < x_2$ and $y_1 < y_2$. As with any distribution, some event has to occur, and if we integrate over all possible values of $X$ and $Y$, the total must be 1:

$$\int_x \int_y f(x,y) dx dy = 1 \qquad (5.2)$$

For a joint distribution, we can also define a cumulative distribution function (CDF), $F(x,y)$:

$$F(x,y) = P[X \le x, Y \le Y] = \int_{-\infty}^{x} \int_{-\infty}^{y} f(t,u) dt du \qquad (5.3)$$

To go from a joint cumulative distribution to a joint probability density function, we simply take the partial derivative with respect to all the underlying variables. For our bivariate distribution, we have:

$$f(x,y) = \frac{\partial^2 F(x,y)}{\partial x \partial y} \qquad (5.4)$$

The right-hand side of Equation 5.4 is the second-order cross partial derivative of $F(x,y)$.

---

### SAMPLE PROBLEM

*Question:*
  Imagine we have two bonds, whose value can vary between \$0 and \$100. Assume the joint distribution function for the value of the bonds is a joint uniform distribution, such that $f(x,y)$ equals $c$, a constant, for all values of $X$ and $Y$ between \$0 and \$100, and is zero everywhere else. That is:

$$f(x,y) = \begin{cases} 0 & \forall\ 0 > X > 100, 0 > Y > 100 \\ c & \forall\ 0 \le X \le 100, 0 \le Y \le 100 \end{cases}$$

Find $c$.

*Answer:*
  Integrating over all possible values, it must be the case that:

$$\int_0^{100} \int_0^{100} c\, dx dy = 1$$

Solving, we have:

$$\int_0^{100} \int_0^{100} c\,dx\,dy = c[xy]\Big|_{x=0,y=0}^{x=100,y=100} = c(100 \cdot 100 - 0 \cdot 0) = 10{,}000c$$

$$10{,}000c = 1$$

$$c = \frac{1}{10{,}000}$$

We can define joint probability density functions and joint cumulative distribution functions for any number of variables. For example, with $n$ variables, $X_1$, $X_2$, ..., $X_n$, the joint cumulative distribution, $F(x_1, x_2, \ldots, x_n)$, in terms of the probability density function, $f(x_1, x_2, \ldots, x_n)$, would be:

$$F(x_1, x_2, \ldots, x_n) = P[X_1 \le x_1, X_2 \le x_2, \ldots, X_n \le x_n]$$
$$= \int_{-\infty}^{x_1} \int_{-\infty}^{x_2} \ldots \int_{-\infty}^{x_n} f(y_1, y_2, \ldots, y_n)\,dy_1\,dy_2 \ldots dy_n \tag{5.5}$$

### Visualization

Just as we can graph the probability density function for one variable in two dimensions, we can graph the probability density function for a joint distribution of two variables in three dimensions. Exhibit 5.4 shows the probability density function from the previous sample problem. Here, the value of the density function corresponds to the distance along the $z$-axis, or the height of the distribution.

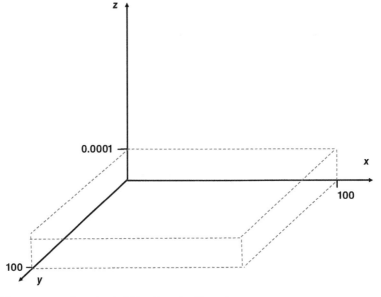

**EXHIBIT 5.4**  Joint Uniform Probability Density Function

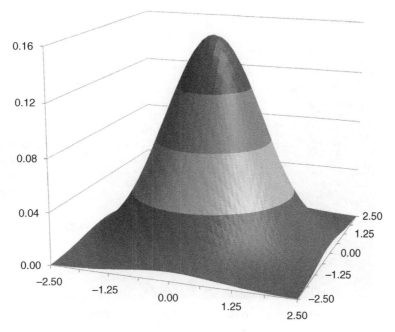

**EXHIBIT 5.5**   Bivariate Standard Normal PDF

As we might expect, the joint PDF resembles a box, whose volume is equal to one.

Exhibit 5.5 shows a bivariate normal distribution. In this case it is a joint standard normal distribution, where both variables, $X$ and $Y$, are standard normal variables.

Three-dimensional charts look nice, but the perspective can hide details. An alternative way to visualize a joint distribution of two variables is by using a contour graph. In a contour graph it is as if we are looking at the three-dimensional graph from directly overhead. Exhibit 5.6 is a contour graph corresponding to the joint normal PDF in Exhibit 5.5. Different shades of gray represent different values for the density function. The borders between different regions are called isolines or isoquants, because all of the points on one isoquant have the same value.

Beyond two variables, visualization becomes more difficult. Even when more variables are involved, starting with the two-variable case can be convenient for purposes of exposition or for gaining intuition.

### Correlation

Up until this point, we have not said anything about correlation. How would we recognize correlation in a joint distribution? One way would be to examine the contour graph of the distribution. Notice in Exhibit 5.6 how the distribution is symmetric across both axes. This tells us that, for a given value of $X$, positive values and negative values of $Y$ are equally likely, and vice versa. This suggests that $X$ and $Y$ are uncorrelated.

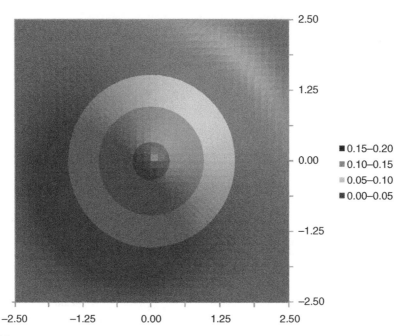

**EXHIBIT 5.6**   Bivariate Standard Normal PDF Contour Graph

Now look at Exhibit 5.7. Rather than forming concentric circles around the origin, the contour lines in this chart form ellipses. This graph is symmetric, but not about the $x$- and $y$-axes. As it turns out, this graph is also based on the PDF of a joint standard normal distribution. The only difference between this joint distribution and the previous joint distribution is the correlation between $X$ and $Y$.

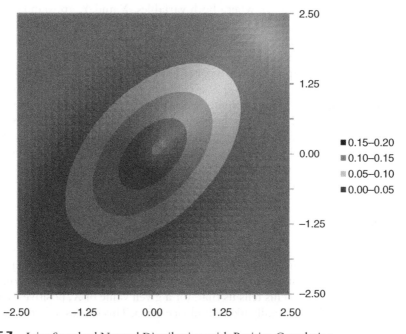

**EXHIBIT 5.7**   Joint Standard Normal Distribution with Positive Correlation

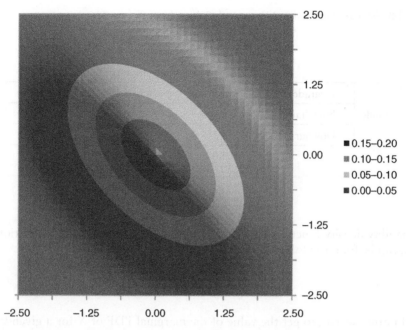

**EXHIBIT 5.8** Joint Standard Normal Distribution with Negative Correlation

In Exhibit 5.7 we can see from the contour graph that $X$ is more likely to be positive when $Y$ is positive (the density function is higher), and $X$ is more likely to be negative when $Y$ is negative. In other words, $X$ and $Y$ are positively correlated.

If $X$ and $Y$ were negatively correlated, the contour graph would be deformed in the opposite way. Exhibit 5.8 shows a contour graph of the PDF of two negatively correlated standard normal variables.

## Marginal Distributions

Given a joint distribution, we can easily recover the distribution for each of the underlying random variables. In this context the individual univariate distributions are known as marginal distributions.

We illustrate this first with discrete distributions. The probability matrix from the beginning of the chapter is reproduced here as Exhibit 5.9 with the addition of subtotals for the rows and columns. These subtotals form the marginal distributions.

By adding up the columns of the matrix, we see that there is a 50% chance that the equity outperforms the market and a 50% chance that the equity underperforms the market. This is the marginal distribution of the equity. Notice that these probabilities are unconditional; they do not depend on what happens to the bonds. Likewise, the marginal distribution of the bonds has three possible states, whose probabilities can be found by summing across each row. The probability of an upgrade is 20%, the probability of no change is 55%, and the probability of a downgrade is 25%. The marginal distributions are proper distributions in and of themselves. In both cases, the probabilities of the marginal distributions sum to one.

We can summarize this process for obtaining marginal distributions mathematically. For a discrete joint distribution of two random variables, $X$ and $Y$, with a joint

**EXHIBIT 5.9**  Probability Matrix with Subtotals

|  |  | Equity | | |
|---|---|---|---|---|
|  |  | Outperform | Underperform | |
| Bonds | Upgrade | 15% | 5% | 20% |
|  | No Change | 30% | 25% | 55% |
|  | Downgrade | 5% | 20% | 25% |
|  |  | 50% | 50% | |

probability density function, $f(x,y)$, the marginal probability density function of $X$, $f_x(x)$, can be found as follows:

$$f_x(x) = \sum_y f(x,y) \tag{5.6}$$

In other words, to get the value of the marginal PDF of $X$ for a given value of $X$, $x$, we simply sum over all values of $Y$, with $X$ set equal to $x$. To get the marginal distribution of $Y$, we simply reverse variables, summing over all possible values of $X$ for a given value of $Y$.

For a continuous joint distribution, the analogous process involves integrating over all possible values of the other variable. For a continuous joint distribution of two random variables, $X$ and $Y$, with a joint probability density function, $f(x,y)$, the marginal probability density function of $X$, $f_x(x)$, can be found as follows:

$$f_x(x) = \int_y f(x,t)dt \tag{5.7}$$

As before, we can reverse the variables to obtain the marginal distribution for $Y$.

We can also obtain the marginal distribution from the joint cumulative distribution by taking the derivative of the joint distribution. For a joint distribution of two variables, $X$ and $Y$, we can obtain the marginal distribution of $X$ by taking the derivative of the joint distribution with respect to $X$:

$$f_x(x) = \frac{\partial F(x,y)}{\partial x} \tag{5.8}$$

There is an important link between the marginal distributions and independence. If two random variables, $X$ and $Y$, are independent, then the joint PDF will be equal to the product of the marginal PDFs. The reverse is also true: If the joint PDF is equal to the product of the marginal PDFs, then $X$ and $Y$ are independent:

$$f(x,y) = f_x(x)f_y(y) \Leftrightarrow X \text{ and } Y \text{ are independent} \tag{5.9}$$

If two random variables are independent, then the product of their cumulative distribution functions is also equal to the CDF of their joint distribution.

### SAMPLE PROBLEM

*Question:*
  Given the following joint probability density function, prove that $X$ and $Y$ are independent:

$$f(x,y) = \begin{cases} 0 & \forall\ 0 > X > 100, 0 > Y > 100 \\ c & \forall\ 0 \leq X \leq 100, 0 \leq Y \leq 100 \end{cases}$$

where $c$ is equal to 1/10,000.

*Answer:*
  We start by calculating the marginal distribution of $X$:

$$f_x(x) = \int_y f(x,t)dt = \int_{-\infty}^{0} 0\,dt + \int_{0}^{100} c\,dt + \int_{110}^{\infty} 0\,dt$$

$$f_x(x) = 0 + \int_{0}^{100} c\,dt + 0$$

$$f_x(x) = \int_{0}^{100} c\,dt = c[t]_0^{100} = c(100-0) = 100c = \frac{1}{100}$$

$$f_x(x) = \frac{1}{100}$$

Because $f(x,y)$ only involves a constant, it is not surprising that we get the same answer for the marginal distribution of $Y$:

$$f_y(x) = \int_x f(t,y)dt = \int_{0}^{100} c\,dt = c[t]_0^{100} = c(100-0) = 100c = \frac{1}{100}$$

Putting the two together, we can see that the product of the marginal distributions is equal to the joint distribution.

$$f(x,y) = \frac{1}{10,000} = \frac{1}{100}\frac{1}{100} = f_x(x)f_y(y)$$

Because the joint PDF is equal to the product of the marginal PDFs, it follows that $X$ and $Y$ must be independent.

## COPULAS

In this section we introduce the concept of the copula. In statistics, copulas are used to describe various types of multivariate distributions.

### What Is a Copula?

In the previous section we showed three graphs of joint normal distributions, one where the two variables were uncorrelated, one where the two variables were positively correlated, and one where the two variables were negatively correlated. So what about Exhibit 5.10?

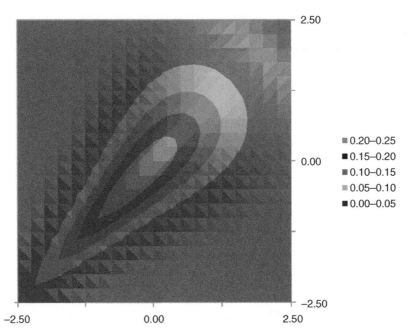

2.50

0.00

- 0.20–0.25
- 0.15–0.20
- 0.10–0.15
- 0.05–0.10
- 0.00–0.05

–2.50

−2.50          0.00          2.50

**EXHIBIT 5.10**   Bivariate Standard Normal PDF with Clayton Copula

It turns out that Exhibit 5.10 is also a joint normal distribution. Unlike the previous three examples where the contour lines were all ellipses (circles being special types of ellipses), this new chart has more of a teardrop shape. In this new graph, it appears that extreme negative-negative results are more likely than extreme positive-positive results.

The graph in Exhibit 5.10 was produced using a special function known as a copula. In everyday parlance, a copula is simply something that joins or couples. In statistics, a copula is a function used to combine two or more cumulative distribution functions in order to produce one joint cumulative distribution function.

In many fields, when it comes to joint distributions, ellipses are all that you will see. In finance, assuming a joint distribution is elliptical when in fact it is not can lead to a serious underestimation of risk. In Chapter 3, we saw how coskewness and cokurtosis could impact the risk of a portfolio. Though we did not recognize it as such at the time, the sample distributions with extreme coskewness in Chapter 3 were nonelliptical. Copulas provide us with a method for producing and describing nonelliptical joint distributions.

There is an infinite number of ways in which two distributions can be related to each other, but statisticians have found it useful to describe a few prototypical patterns. Examples include the Gaussian, $t$, Gumbel, Frank, and Clayton copulas. The last three copulas—the Gumbel, Frank, and Clayton copulas—are members of a class of copulas known as the Archimedean copulas. Each of these named copulas has a characteristic way of distorting the relationship between two variables. Exhibit 5.10 is an example of a joint distribution based on the Clayton copula. The Clayton copula exhibits greater dependence in the negative tail than in the positive tail, a not-uncommon feature of financial returns, making it a popular choice in risk management. Appendix F contains a brief summary of several popular copulas.

A copula only defines a relationship between univariate distributions. The underlying distributions themselves can be any shape or size. For instance, we can talk about a normal Gumbel copula, meaning the marginal distributions are all normal, and we can talk about a lognormal Gumbel copula, meaning the marginal distributions are lognormal. We can even talk about a normal-lognormal Gumbel copula, meaning one of the marginal distributions is normal and one is lognormal.

Mechanically, copulas take as their inputs two or more cumulative distributions and output a joint cumulative distribution. The advantage of working with cumulative distributions is that the range is always the same. No matter what the distribution is, the output of a cumulative distribution always ranges from 0% to 100%.

We typically represent cumulative distributions with capital letters, for example $F(x)$. In order to make the formulas more readable, when describing copulas we often use lowercase letters instead. For example, given two cumulative distributions, $u$ and $v$, and a constant, $\alpha$, we can write Frank's copula as:

$$C(u,v) = \frac{1}{\alpha}\ln\left[1 + \frac{(e^{\alpha u} - 1)(e^{\alpha v} - 1)}{e^{\alpha} - 1}\right] \qquad (5.10)$$

As used in Equation 5.10, $\alpha$ determines the shape of the joint cumulative distribution, $C(u,v)$. In the case of Frank's copula, it is fairly easy to see that when both $u$ and $v$ are 100%, $C(u,v)$ is also 100%. In other words, if an outcome for the first variable is certain, and another outcome is certain for the second variable, then the chance of both outcomes occurring is also certain. It's slightly more difficult to see, but in the limit, as both $u$ and $v$ go to zero, $C(u,v)$ also goes to zero.

## SAMPLE PROBLEM

*Question:*
    Assume we have two standard uniform random variables, $X$ and $Y$, whose joint distribution is defined by Frank's copula. What is the formula for the cumulative distribution of the two variables? What is the formula for the probability density function for $\alpha = 1$?

*Answer:*
    If $X$ is a standard uniform variable, then its cumulative distribution function is defined as:

$$F(x) = \begin{cases} 0 & \forall\ 0 > x > 1 \\ x & \forall\ 0 \leq x \leq 1 \end{cases}$$

$Y$ is defined similarly. Using Equation 5.10, and setting $F(x)$ equal to $u$ and $F(Y)$ equal to $v$, for values of $X$ and $Y$ less than 0 or greater than 1, we have:

$$F(x,y) = \frac{1}{\alpha}\ln\left[1 + \frac{(e^{\alpha 0} - 1)(e^{\alpha 0} - 1)}{e^{\alpha} - 1}\right] = \frac{1}{\alpha}\ln\left[1 + \frac{(1-1)(1-1)}{e^{\alpha} - 1}\right] = \frac{1}{\alpha}\ln[1] = 0$$

For values of $X$ and $Y$ between 0 and 1, we have:

$$F(x,y) = \frac{1}{\alpha}\ln\left[1 + \frac{(e^{\alpha x}-1)(e^{\alpha y}-1)}{e^{\alpha}-1}\right]$$

For $\alpha = 1$, this simplifies to:

$$F(x,y) = \ln\left[1 + \frac{(e^x-1)(e^y-1)}{e-1}\right] = \ln(e^{x+y}-e^x-e^y+e) - \ln(e-1)$$

We can quickly check that for $x = y = 0$, we have $F(x,y) = 0$; and for $x = y = 1$, we have $F(x,y) = 1$.

To get the probability density function, we need to calculate the second partial derivative with respect to $x$ and then $y$:

$$f(x,y) = \frac{\partial^2 F(x,y)}{\partial x \partial y} = \frac{\partial}{\partial y}\left[\frac{e^{x+y}-e^x}{(e^{x+y}-e^x-e^y+e)}\right]$$

$$f(x,y) = \frac{e^{x+y}}{(e^{x+y}-e^x-e^y+e)} - \frac{(e^{x+y}-e^y)(e^{x+y}-e^x)}{(e^{x+y}-e^x-e^y+e)^2}$$

$$f(x,y) = \frac{e^{x+y}(e-1)}{(e^{x+y}-e^x-e^y+e)^2}$$

The joint distribution is shown in Exhibit 5.11.

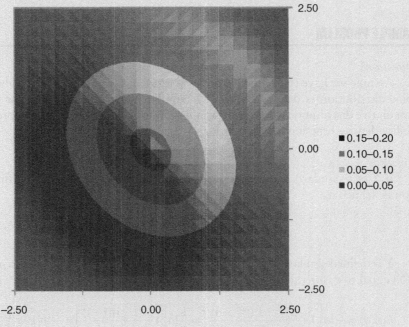

2.50

0.00

■ 0.15–0.20
■ 0.10–0.15
▨ 0.05–0.10
■ 0.00–0.05

−2.50

−2.50                    0.00                    2.50

**EXHIBIT 5.11**   Frank's Joint Standard Uniform PDF, $\alpha = 1$

In the preceding sample problem, in order to calculate the joint PDF we first calculated the joint CDF. There is another way we could proceed. Assume we have two cumulative distributions, $u = F(x)$ and $v = F(y)$; then, making use of the chain rule, we have:

$$f(x,y) = \frac{\partial^2 C(u,v)}{\partial x \partial y} = \frac{\partial^2 C(u,v)}{\partial u \partial v}\frac{\partial u}{\partial x}\frac{\partial v}{\partial y} = c(u,v)f(x)f(y) \tag{5.11}$$

Here we have denoted the second cross partial derivative of $C(u,v)$ by $c(u,v)$; $c(u,v)$ is often referred to as the density function of the copula. Because $c(u,v)$ depends on only the copula and not the marginal distributions, we can calculate $c(u,v)$ once and then apply it to many different problems.

## SAMPLE PROBLEM

*Question:*
Calculate the density function for Frank's copula when $\alpha = 1$. Use the results to calculate the joint probability density function for two standard uniform variables.

*Answer:*
We start by rearranging our formulas for Frank's copula:

$$C(u,v) = \frac{1}{\alpha}\ln\left[1 + \frac{(e^{\alpha u}-1)(e^{\alpha v}-1)}{e^{\alpha}-1}\right] = \frac{1}{\alpha}\ln(e^{\alpha} + e^{\alpha(u+v)} - e^{\alpha u} - e^{\alpha v}) - \frac{1}{\alpha}\ln(e^{\alpha}-1)$$

Next, we calculate the density function for Frank's copula by taking the partial derivative with respect to $u$ and $v$. The order is not important. We can take the derivative with respect to $u$ and then $v$, or $v$ and then $u$:

$$c(u,v) = \frac{\partial^2 C(u,v)}{\partial u \partial v}$$

$$c(u,v) = \frac{\partial}{\partial u}\left[\frac{1}{\alpha}\frac{\alpha e^{\alpha(u+v)} - \alpha e^{\alpha v}}{(e^{\alpha} + e^{\alpha(u+v)} - e^{\alpha u} - e^{\alpha v})}\right] = \frac{\partial}{\partial u}\left[\frac{e^{\alpha(u+v)} - e^{\alpha v}}{(e^{\alpha} + e^{\alpha(u+v)} - e^{\alpha u} - e^{\alpha v})}\right]$$

$$c(u,v) = \frac{\alpha e^{\alpha(u+v)}}{(e^{\alpha} + e^{\alpha(u+v)} - e^{\alpha u} - e^{\alpha v})} - \frac{(e^{\alpha(u+v)} - e^{\alpha v})(\alpha e^{\alpha(u+v)} - \alpha e^{\alpha u})}{(e^{\alpha} + e^{\alpha(u+v)} - e^{\alpha u} - e^{\alpha v})^2} \tag{5.12}$$

$$c(u,v) = \frac{\alpha e^{\alpha(u+v)}(e^{\alpha}-1)}{(e^{\alpha} + e^{\alpha(u+v)} - e^{\alpha u} - e^{\alpha v})^2}$$

As in the previous sample problem, we use two standard uniform variables, $X$ and $Y$, where the CDFs between 0 and 1 are $x$ and $y$, respectively. Substituting $x$ and $y$ for $u$ and $v$, and setting $\alpha = 1$, we have:

$$c(x,y) = \frac{e^{(x+y)}(e-1)}{(e + e^{(x+y)} - e^x - e^y)^2}$$

Finally, to get the joint PDF, using Equation 5.11, we multiply the density function by the PDFs for $X$ and $Y$, $f(x)$ and $f(y)$, respectively. Because both variables are standard uniform random variables, their PDFs are equal to 1.

$$f(x,y) = c(u,v)f(x)f(y) = c(u,v) = \frac{e^{(x+y)}(e-1)}{(e+e^{(x+y)} - e^x - e^y)^2}$$

To check the result, we note that the final equation matches the result from the previous sample problem.

### Graphing Copulas

Exhibit 5.12 shows the joint PDF for a standard normal Frank's copula. As you can see from the exhibit, Frank's copula displays symmetric tail dependence. How do we actually go about creating one of these graphs? One of the easiest ways is to use Equation 5.11. For any point on the graph, $(x,y)$, we first calculate values for both the PDF and the CDF of $X$ and $Y$. We use the CDFs to calculate the copula density function, and then multiply this value by the value of the PDFs to determine the value of the joint distribution at that point.

For example, suppose that we want to graph the joint PDF of a Frank's copula for two standard normal variables with $\alpha = 2$. To determine the height of the graph at $(x,y) = (0,0)$, we start by calculating the cumulative distribution for both variables. At 0, the cumulative distribution for a standard normal variable is equal to 0.50. We can calculate this in Excel by using the NORMSDIST function. Plugging 0.50 into the copula's density function, Equation 5.12, for both $x$ and $y$ gives us a value of 1.08. Next, we multiply this by the value of the standard normal PDF, which for 0 is 0.40. You can get this in Excel by using the NORMDIST function, setting the cumulative option to false. Our final answer for the height of the distribution is then 0.17:

$$f(x,y) = c(u,v)f(x)f(y) = \frac{\alpha e^{\alpha(u+v)}(e^\alpha - 1)}{(e^\alpha + e^{\alpha(u+v)} - e^{\alpha u} - e^{\alpha v})^2}f(x)f(y)$$

$$f(x,y) = \frac{2e^{2(0.5+0.5)}(e^{0.5} - 1)}{(e^2 + e^{2(0.5+0.5)} - e^{2\cdot 0.5} - e^{2\cdot 0.5})^2} \cdot 0.40 \cdot 0.40 = 1.08 \cdot 0.40 \cdot 0.40 = 0.17$$

To complete the graph, we would continue to calculate values of the PDF for various combinations of $X$ and $Y$. Exhibit 5.12 was drawn using 441 evenly spaced $(x,y)$ pairs.

Because Equation 5.11 allows us to separate the copula density function and the marginal distributions, going from a normal-normal Frank's distribution to, say, a uniform-uniform Frank's distribution is relatively easy; we simply change the PDF and CDF functions from normal to uniform.

An Excel spreadsheet with several examples is available online.

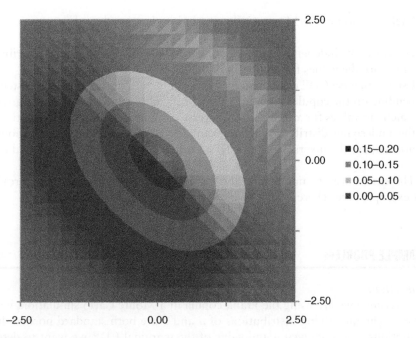

**EXHIBIT 5.12**  Bivariate Standard Normal PDF with Frank's Copula, $\alpha = 2$

## Using Copulas in Simulations

In this section, we demonstrate how copulas can be used in Monte Carlo simulations. Our example uses two random variables, but the same basic methodology can be extended to any number of variables.

In order to use copulas in a Monte Carlo simulation, we need to calculate the inverse marginal CDFs for the copula. To determine the marginal CDFs of a copula, we take the first derivative of the copula function with respect to one of the underlying distributions. For two cumulative distributions $u$ and $v$, the marginal CDFs would be:

$$C_1 = \frac{\partial C}{\partial u} = \int c(u,v)dv$$
$$C_2 = \frac{\partial C}{\partial v} = \int c(u,v)dv$$

(5.13)

For example, for Frank's copula the marginal CDF for $u$ would be:

$$C_1 = \frac{\partial C}{\partial u} = \frac{(e^{-\alpha u} - 1)(e^{-\alpha v} - 1) + (e^{-\alpha v} - 1)}{(e^{-\alpha u} - 1)(e^{-\alpha v} - 1) + (e^{-\alpha} - 1)}$$

(5.14)

$C_1$ is a proper CDF, and varies between 0% and 100%. To determine the inverse of $C_1$, we solve for $v$:

$$v = -\frac{1}{\alpha}\ln\left[1 + \frac{C_1(e^{-\alpha} - 1)}{1 + (e^{-\alpha u} - 1)(1 - C_1)}\right]$$

(5.15)

Each iteration in the Monte Carlo simulation then involves three steps:

1. Generate two independent random draws from a standard uniform distribution. These are the values for $u$ and $C_1$.
2. Use the inverse CDF of the copula to determine $v$. This is the essential step. Depending on the copula, different values of $v$ will be more or less likely, given $u$.
3. Calculate values for $x$ and $y$, using inverse cumulative distribution functions for the underlying distributions. For example, if the underlying distributions are normal, use the inverse normal CDF to calculate $x$ and $y$ based on $u$ and $v$.

The easiest way to understand this process is to see it in action. We provide a brief example here. There is also an Excel example available online.

---

**SAMPLE PROBLEM**

*Question:*
Assume we are using the Frank copula in a Monte Carlo simulation, with $\alpha = 3$. The underlying distributions of $u$ and $v$ are both standard normal distributions. For any given $u$ and value of the marginal CDF, we want to determine the corresponding value of $v$. If our random number generator produces $u = 0.20$ and $C_1 = 0.50$, what are the values of our underlying random variables $X$ and $Y$?

*Answer:*
First we determine $v$ using Equation 5.15:

$$v = -\frac{1}{3}\ln\left[1 + \frac{0.50(e^{-3} - 1)}{1 + (e^{-3\cdot0.20} - 1)(1 - 0.50)}\right] = 0.32$$

Notice that $u$, $v$, and $C_1$ are all between 0% and 100%. We then use an inverse standard normal function, NORMSINV() in Excel, to calculate $x$ and $y$ from $u$ and $v$. We get: $x = -0.84$ and $y = -0.48$. Notice that even though $C_1$ was 0.50, right in the center of its distribution, $y$ is negative. This is because $x$ is negative, and negative-negative pairs are more likely with the Frank copula.

---

### Parameterization of Copulas

Given a copula, we know how to calculate values for that copula, but how do we know which copula to use in the first place? The answer is a mixture of art and science.

In picking which type of copula to use, there are quantitative methods we could use, but in practice this choice is often based on the general characteristics of the data. If the data seem to exhibit increased correlation in crashes, then you should choose a copula that displays a higher probability in the negative-negative region such as the Clayton copula. Choosing a copula is often where the art comes into play.

Once we know which type of copula we are going to use, we need to determine the parameters of the copula. Take for example the Farlie-Gumbel-Morgenstern (FGM) copula, given by:

$$C = uv[1 + \alpha(1 - u)(1 - v)] \tag{5.16}$$

As with most copulas, there is a single parameter, $\alpha$, which needs to be determined, and this parameter is related to how closely the two underlying random variables are related to each other.

In statistics, the most popular method for measuring how closely two variables are related to each other is correlation. For two random variables, $X$ and $Y$, with standard deviation $\sigma_X$ and $\sigma_Y$, respectively, correlation is defined as follows:

$$\text{Correlation} = \frac{E[(X - E[X])(Y - E[Y])]}{\sigma_X \sigma_Y} \tag{5.17}$$

To avoid any ambiguity, this standard correlation is often referred to as Pearson's correlation or linear correlation. While this measure is extremely popular, there are other ways to quantify the relationship between two variables, and when working with copulas, two of these measures, Kendall's tau and Spearman's rho, are often preferred. Rather than being based directly on the values of the variables, both Kendall's tau and Spearman's rho are based on the order or rank of the variables. We start by exploring Kendall's tau.

Two data sets are presented in Exhibit 5.13. Both sets contain three points, A, B, and C. In Data Set #1, the variables $X$ and $Y$ are both perfectly correlated, $Y$ increases in exact proportion to $X$, always equal to 5 times $X$. It turns out that Kendall's tau is also equal to 100% for Data Set #1. Now look at Data Set #2. The $Y$ value of point C has changed. In Data Set #2 the correlation is less than 100%, but Kendall's tau is still 100%. This is because, even though the value of $Y$ for point C has changed, the rank of $Y$ for point C has not changed. The value of $Y$ for point C is the highest for all the points in both data sets, and only the ranks of the variables are relevant for Kendall's tau.

Interestingly, within both data sets if the $X$ value of one point is greater than the $X$ value of another point, then the $Y$ value is also greater. Likewise, if the $X$ value of one point is less than the $X$ value of another point, then the $Y$ value is also less. When the $X$ and $Y$ values of one point are both greater than or both less than the $X$ and $Y$ values of another point, we say that the two points are concordant. If two points are

**EXHIBIT 5.13**  Comparing Two Data Sets

| | Data Set #1 | | | | | Data Set #2 | | | |
|---|---|---|---|---|---|---|---|---|---|
| | X | Y | Rank[X] | Rank[Y] | | X | Y | Rank[X] | Rank[Y] |
| A | 1 | 5 | 3 | 3 | A | 1 | 5 | 3 | 3 |
| B | 2 | 10 | 2 | 2 | B | 2 | 10 | 2 | 2 |
| C | 3 | 15 | 1 | 1 | C | 3 | 18 | 1 | 1 |

not concordant, we say they are discordant. More formally, for two distinct points $i$ and $j$ we have:

$$\text{Concordance: } X_i > X_j \text{ and } Y_i > Y_j \text{ or } X_i < X_j \text{ and } Y_i < Y_j$$
$$\text{Disconcordance: } X_i < X_j \text{ and } Y_i > Y_j \text{ or } X_i > X_j \text{ and } Y_i < Y_j \quad (5.18)$$

Kendall's tau is defined as the probability of concordance minus the probability of discordance.

$$\tau = P[\text{concordance}] - P[\text{discordance}]$$

If $P[\text{concordance}]$ is 100%, then $P[\text{discordance}]$ must be 0%. Similarly, if $P[\text{discordance}]$ is 100%, $P[\text{concordance}]$ must be 0%. Because of this, like our standard correlation measure, Kendall's tau must vary between –100% and +100%.

To measure Kendall's tau in a given data set, we simply need to compare every possible pair of points and count how many are concordant and how many are discordant. In a data set with $n$ points, the number of unique combinations of two points is as follows (see Chapter 1):

$$\binom{n}{2} = \frac{n!}{(n-2)!2!} = \frac{1}{2}n(n-1)$$

For example, in Exhibit 5.13 each data set has three points, $A$, $B$, and $C$, and there are three possible combinations of two points: $A$ and $B$, $A$ and $C$, and $B$ and $C$. For a given data set, then, Kendall's tau is:

$$\tau = \frac{\#\text{ of concordant points} - \#\text{ of discordant points}}{\binom{n}{2}} \quad (5.19)$$

A potentially interesting feature of Kendall's tau is that it is less sensitive to outliers than Pearson's correlation. In Exhibit 5.13, as long as the $Y$ value of point $C$ is greater than 10, all of the points will be concordant and Kendall's tau will be unchanged. It could be 11 or 11,000. In this way, measures of dependence based on rank are analogous to the median when measuring averages.

---

**SAMPLE PROBLEM**

*Question:*
Given the following data set, calculate Kendall's tau:

|   | X | Y |
|---|---|---|
| A | 76 | 6 |
| B | 89 | 51 |
| C | 63 | 56 |
| D | 50 | 1 |

*Answer:*

Kendall's tau is 33%.

In this data set there are four data points, giving us six possible pairings: $0.5 \times 4 \times 3 = 6$. The first pair, $A$ and $B$, is concordant; 89 is greater than 76, and 51 is greater than 6. We determine each pair in turn:

| Pair | Concordant = +1, Discordant = −1 |
|------|:---:|
| A, B | +1 |
| A, C | −1 |
| A, D | +1 |
| B, C | −1 |
| B, D | +1 |
| C, D | +1 |

In all, there are four concordant pairs and two discordant pairs, giving us our final answer:

$$\tau = \frac{4-2}{6} = \frac{1}{3} = 33\%$$

As the number of points grows, the number of unique pairings increases rapidly. For 100 points there are 4,950 unique pairings. For large data sets, you will need to use a computer to calculate Kendall's tau.

We have not said anything yet about how to approach ties—that is, if $x_i = x_j$ or $y_i = y_j$. There is no universally agreed upon approach. The simplest solution is to ignore ties, but there are more complex methods. These different methods are often referred to as tau-a, tau-b, et cetera.

Besides being robust to outliers, measures of dependence based on rank are invariant under strictly increasing transformations. This is a fancy way of saying that we can stretch and twist our data set in certain ways, and, as long as we don't change the relative order of the points, Kendall's tau will not change. As an example, take a look at Exhibit 5.14, in which we have graphed two data sets. In both cases the relationship between the $Y$ values and the $X$ values is deterministic. In the first series, represented by circles, $y' = 4x$. In the second series, represented by ×'s, $y^* = \sin(2\pi x)$. The second series can be viewed as a transformation of the first, $y^* = \sin(0.5\pi y')$ for all values of $X$. Importantly, while we have moved the points, we have not changed the concordance; in both series a higher value of $X$ implies a higher value of $Y$. Because of this, Kendall's tau for both series is 100%.

Even though both relationships are deterministic, the correlation is 100% only for the first series, not for the second. In general, if the relationship between two variables can be described by a deterministic linear equation, then the correlation will be ±100%. If the correlation is deterministic but nonlinear, this will not be the case. This is why we describe our standard measure of correlation as being a linear measure of association.

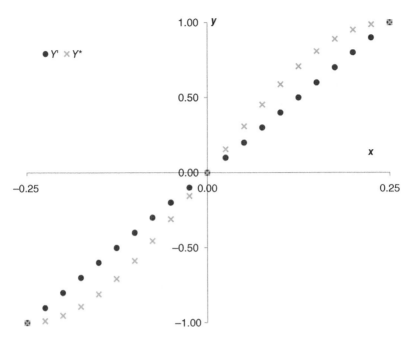

**EXHIBIT 5.14**   Example of Transformed Data

As it turns out, for many copulas, changing the value of the shape parameter, $\alpha$, will transform the data in a way that is similar to the way the data was transformed in Exhibit 5.14. Changing $\alpha$ will change the shape of the data, but it will not change the order. For a given type of copula, then, Kendall's tau is often a function of the copula's parameter, $\alpha$, and does not depend on what type of marginal distributions are being used. For example, for the FGM copula, Equation 5.16, Kendall's tau is equal to $2\alpha/9$. This leads to a simple method for setting the parameter of the copula. First, calculate Kendall's tau, and then set the shape parameter based on the appropriate formula for that copula relating Kendall's tau and the shape parameter.

Given an equation for a copula, $C(u,v)$ and its density function $c(u,v)$, Kendall's tau can be determined as follows:

$$\tau = 4E[C(u,v)] - 1 = 4\int_0^1\int_0^1 C(u,v)c(u,v)dudv - 1 \tag{5.20}$$

Formulas for copulas and their density functions are not always compact. Using Equation 5.20 to calculate Kendall's tau can be tedious, but once you've gone through the calculation you can use the result again and again. Appendix F includes formulas defining the relationship between Kendall's tau for several named copulas.

## SAMPLE PROBLEM

*Question:*
Using Equation 5.20, prove that Kendall's tau for the FGM distribution is equal to $2\alpha/9$. What would alpha be for a data set where Kendall's tau was equal to 10%?

*Answer:*
The FGM copula is defined by:

$$C = uv[1 + \alpha\ (1 - u)(1 - v)] = uv + \alpha(v - v^2)(u - u^2)$$

We first determine the density function, $c$, as follows:

$$\frac{\partial C}{\partial u} = v + \alpha(v - v^2)(1 - 2u)$$

$$c = \frac{\partial^2 C}{\partial u \partial v} = 1 + \alpha(1 - 2v)(1 - 2u)$$

To determine Kendall's tau, we need to integrate the product of the copula and the density function. There are a number of ways we could do this. It looks complicated, but simply by multiplying and rearranging terms we get:

$$Cc = uv[1 + \alpha(1 - u)(1 - v)][1 + \alpha(1 - 2u)(1 - 2v)]$$
$$Cc = [v + \alpha v(2 - 3v)]u + \alpha v(5v - 3)u^2 + \alpha^2 v(1 - 3v + 2v^2)(u - 3u^2 - 2u^3)$$

To get Kendall's tau, we need to integrate with respect to $u$ and $v$. Starting with $u$, we get:

$$\int_0^1 Cc\,du = \left[\frac{1}{2}(v + \alpha v(2 - 3v))u^2 + \frac{1}{3}\alpha v(5v - 3)u^3 \right.$$
$$\left. + \alpha^2 v(1 - 3v + 2v^2)\left(\frac{1}{2}u^2 - u^3 - \frac{1}{2}u^4\right)\right]_0^1$$

$$\int_0^1 Cc\,du = \left[\frac{1}{2}(v + \alpha v(2 - 3v)) + \frac{1}{3}\alpha v(5v - 3) + \alpha^2 v(1 - 3v + 2v^2)\left(\frac{1}{2} - 1 - \frac{1}{2}\right)\right]$$
$$- [0 + 0 + 0]$$

$$\int_0^1 Cc\,du = \left(\frac{1}{2} - \alpha^2\right)v + \left(\frac{1}{6}\alpha + 3\alpha^2\right)v^2 - 2\alpha^2 v^3$$

Using this result, we can calculate the following double integral:

$$\int_0^1 \int_0^1 Ccdudv = \int_0^1 \left( \left( \frac{1}{2} - \alpha^2 \right) v + \left( \frac{1}{6}\alpha + 3\alpha^2 \right) v^2 - 2\alpha^2 v^3 \right) dv$$

$$\int_0^1 \int_0^1 Ccdudv = \left[ \frac{1}{2} \left( \frac{1}{2} - \alpha^2 \right) v^2 + \frac{1}{3} \left( \frac{1}{6}\alpha + 3\alpha^2 \right) v^3 - \frac{1}{2}\alpha^2 v^4 \right]_0^1$$

$$\int_0^1 \int_0^1 Ccdudv = \frac{1}{4} + \frac{1}{18}\alpha$$

We then use this to calculate Kendall's tau:

$$\tau = 4 \int_0^1 \int_0^1 Ccdudv - 1 = 4 \left( \frac{1}{4} + \frac{1}{18}\alpha \right) - 1 = \frac{2}{9}\alpha$$

As expected, Kendall's tau for the FGM copula is equal to $2\alpha/9$.

We can rearrange this result to express alpha in terms of Kendall's tau:

$$\alpha = \frac{9}{2}\tau$$

If $\tau$ is equal to 10%, then $\alpha = 0.45$.

$$\alpha = \frac{9}{2}\frac{1}{10} = \frac{9}{20} = 0.45$$

The preceding process of choosing a copula and then determining the parameter of the copula based on Kendall's tau is extremely flexible. As we mentioned at the beginning of the section, there is another measure of dependence based on rank, Spearman's rho. Both Kendall's tau and Spearman's rho range between –1 and +1, and their values are often very similar. To calculate Spearman's rho from sample data, we simply calculate our standard correlation measure using the ranks of the data. We can also calculate Spearman's rho from a copula function:

$$\rho_s = 12 \int_0^1 \int_0^1 C(u,v)dudv - 3 \tag{5.21}$$

In many situations, we can use either Kendall's tau or Spearman's rho. Both are valid. The choice often comes down to familiarity and to which is easier to calculate. For some copulas there is no discrete solution for Spearman's rho. That said, when such a solution does exist, it is often easier to calculate Spearman's rho.

## PROBLEMS

1. Given the following joint probability density function, determine if $X$ and $Y$ are independent:

$$f(x,y) = \begin{cases} 0 & -2 > X > 2, -2 > Y > 2 \\ c(8 - x^2 - y^2) & -2 \leq X \leq 2, -2 \leq Y \leq 2 \end{cases}$$

where $c$ is equal to 3/256.

2. Calculate Kendall's tau and Spearman's rho for the following data set:

|   | X | Y |
|---|---|---|
| A | 70% | 5% |
| B | 40% | 35% |
| C | 20% | 10% |

3. Calculate Kendall's tau for the independent copula, $C(u,v)$, given by the following formula:

$$C(u, v) = uv$$

4. Calculate Spearman's rho for the FGM copula, Equation 5.16, in terms of $\alpha$.

## CHAPTER 6

# Bayesian Analysis

**B**ayesian analysis is an extremely broad topic. In this chapter we introduce Bayes' theorem and other concepts related to Bayesian analysis. We will begin to see how Bayesian analysis can help us tackle some very difficult problems in risk management.

## OVERVIEW

The foundation of Bayesian analysis is Bayes' theorem. Bayes' theorem is named after the eighteenth-century English mathematician Thomas Bayes, who first described the theorem. During his life, Bayes never actually publicized his eponymous theorem. Bayes' theorem might have been confined to the dustheap of history had not a friend submitted it to the Royal Society two years after his death.

Bayes' theorem itself is incredibly simple. For two random variables, $A$ and $B$, Bayes' theorem states that:

$$P[A \mid B] = \frac{P[B \mid A] \cdot P[A]}{P[B]} \tag{6.1}$$

In the next section we'll derive Bayes' theorem and explain how to interpret Equation 6.1. As we will see, the simplicity of Bayes' theorem is deceptive. Bayes' theorem can be applied to a wide range of problems, and its application can often be quite complex.

Bayesian analysis is used in a number of fields. It is most often associated with computer science and artificial intelligence, where it is used in everything from spam filters to machine translation and to the software that controls self-driving cars. The use of Bayesian analysis in finance and risk management has grown in recent years, and will likely continue to grow.

What follows makes heavy use of joint and conditional probabilities. If you have not already done so and you are not familiar with these topics, you can review them in Chapter 2.

## BAYES' THEOREM

Assume we have two bonds, Bond A and Bond B, each with a 10% probability of defaulting over the next year. Further assume that the probability that both bonds

**EXHIBIT 6.1**   Probability Matrix

|         |            | Bond A      |         |      |
|---------|------------|-------------|---------|------|
|         |            | No Default  | Default |      |
| Bond B  | No Default | 86%         | 4%      | 90%  |
|         | Default    | 4%          | 6%      | 10%  |
|         |            | 90%         | 10%     | 100% |

default is 6%, and that the probability that neither bond defaults is 86%. It follows that the probability that only Bond A *or* Bond B defaults is 4%. We can summarize all of this information in a probability matrix as shown in Exhibit 6.1.

As required, the rows and columns of the matrix add up, and the sum of all the probabilities is equal to 100%.

In the probability matrix, notice that the probability of both bonds defaulting is 6%. This is higher than the 1% probability we would expect if the default events were independent ($10\% \times 10\% = 1\%$). The probability that neither bond defaults, 86%, is also higher than what we would expect if the defaults were independent ($90\% \times 90\% = 81\%$). Because bond issuers are often sensitive to broad economic trends, bond defaults are often highly correlated.

We can also express features of the probability matrix in terms of conditional probabilities. What is the probability that Bond A defaults, given that Bond B has defaulted? Bond B defaults in 10% of the scenarios, but the probability that both Bond A and Bond B default is only 6%. In other words, Bond A defaults in 60% of the scenarios in which Bond B defaults. We write this as follows:

$$P[A \mid B] = \frac{P[A \cap B]}{P[B]} = \frac{6\%}{10\%} = 60\% \tag{6.2}$$

Notice that the conditional probability is different from the unconditional probability. The unconditional probability of default is 10%.

$$P[A] = 10\% \neq 60\% = P[A \mid B] \tag{6.3}$$

It turns out that Equation 6.2 is true in general. More often the equation is written as follows:

$$P[A \cap B] = P[A \mid B] \cdot P[B] \tag{6.4}$$

In other words, the probability of both $A$ and $B$ occurring is just the probability that $A$ occurs, given $B$, multiplied by the probability of $B$ occurring. What's more, the ordering of $A$ and $B$ doesn't matter. We could just as easily write:

$$P[A \cap B] = P[B \mid A] \cdot P[A] \tag{6.5}$$

Combining the right-hand side of both of these equations and rearranging terms leads us to Bayes' theorem:

$$P[A \mid B] = \frac{P[B \mid A] \cdot P[A]}{P[B]} \qquad (6.6)$$

The following sample problem shows how Bayes' theorem can be applied to a very interesting statistical question.

---

### SAMPLE PROBLEM

*Question:*

Imagine there is a disease that afflicts just 1 in every 100 people in the population. A new test has been developed to detect the disease that is 99% accurate. That is, for people with the disease, the test correctly indicates that they have the disease in 99% of cases. Similarly, for those who do not have the disease, the test correctly indicates that they do not have the disease in 99% of cases.

If a person takes the test and the result of the test is positive, what is the probability that he or she actually has the disease?

*Answer:*

While not exactly financial risk, this is a classic example of how conditional probability can be far from intuitive. This type of problem is also far from being an academic curiosity. A number of studies have asked doctors similar questions; see, for example, Gigerenzer and Edwards (2003). The results are often discouraging. The physicians' answers vary widely and are often far from correct.

If the test is 99% accurate, it is tempting to guess that there is a 99% chance that the person who tests positive actually has the disease. 99% is in fact a very bad guess. The correct answer is that there is only a 50% chance that the person who tests positive actually has the disease.

To calculate the correct answer, we first need to calculate the unconditional probability of a positive test. Remember from Chapter 2 that this is simply the probability of a positive test being produced by somebody with the disease plus the probability of a positive test being produced by somebody without the disease. Using a "+" to represent a positive test result, this can be calculated as:

$P[+] = P[+ \cap \text{have disease}] + P[+ \cap \overline{\text{have disease}}]$

$P[+] = P[+ \mid \text{have disease}] \cdot P[\text{have disease}] + P[+ \mid \overline{\text{have disease}}] \cdot P[\overline{\text{have disease}}]$

$P[+] = 99\% \cdot 1\% + 1\% \cdot 99\%$

$P[+] = 2\% \cdot 99\%$

Here we use the line above "have disease" to represent logical negation. In other words, $P[\overline{\text{have disease}}]$ is the probability of not having the disease.

We can then calculate the probability of having the disease given a positive test using Bayes' theorem:

$$P[\text{have disease} \mid +] = \frac{P[+ \mid \text{have disease}] \cdot P[\text{have disease}]}{P[+]}$$

$$P[\text{have disease} \mid +] = \frac{99\% \cdot 1\%}{2\% \cdot 99\%} = 50\%$$

The reason the answer is 50% and not 99% is because the disease is so rare. Most people don't have the disease, so even a small number of false positives overwhelms the number of actual positives. It is easy to see this in a matrix. Assume 10,000 trials:

|       |   | Actual | | |
|-------|---|-----|-------|--------|
|       |   | +   | −     |        |
| Test  | + | 99  | 99    | 198    |
|       | − | 1   | 9,801 | 9,802  |
|       |   | 100 | 9,900 | 10,000 |

If you check the numbers, you'll see that they work out exactly as described: 1% of the population with the disease, and 99% accuracy in each column. In the end, though, the number of positive test results is identical for the two populations, 99 in each. This is why the probability of actually having the disease given a positive test is 50%.

In order for a test for a rare disease to be meaningful, it has to be extremely accurate. In the case just described, 99% accuracy was not nearly accurate enough.

Bayes' theorem is often described as a procedure for updating beliefs about the world when presented with new information. For example, pretend you had a coin that you believed was fair, with a 50% chance of landing heads or tails when flipped. If you flip the coin 10 times and it lands heads each time, you might start to suspect that the coin is not fair. Ten heads in a row could happen, but the odds of seeing 10 heads in a row is only 1:1,024 for a fair coin, $(1/2)^{10} = 1/1,024$. How do you update your beliefs after seeing 10 heads? If you believed there was a 90% probability that the coin was fair before you started flipping, then after seeing 10 heads your belief that the coin is fair should probably be somewhere between 0% and 90%. You believe it is less likely that the coin is fair after seeing 10 heads (so less than 90%), but there is still some probability that the coin is fair (so greater than 0%). As the following sample problem will make clear, Bayes' theorem provides a framework for deciding exactly what our new beliefs should be.

## SAMPLE PROBLEM

*Question:*

You are an analyst at Astra Fund of Funds. Based on an examination of historical data, you determine that all fund managers fall into one of two groups. Stars are the best managers. The probability that a star will beat the market in any given year is 75%. Ordinary, nonstar managers, by contrast, are just as likely to beat the market as they are to underperform it. For both types of managers, the probability of beating the market is independent from one year to the next.

Stars are rare. Of a given pool of managers, only 16% turn out to be stars. A new manager was added to your portfolio three years ago. Since then, the new manager has beaten the market every year. What was the probability that the manager was a star when the manager was first added to the portfolio? What is the probability that this manager is a star now? After observing the manager beat the market over the past three years, what is the probability that the manager will beat the market next year?

*Answer:*

We start by summarizing the information from the problem and introducing some notation. The probability that a manager beats the market given that the manager is a star is 75%:

$$P[B \mid S] = 75\% = \frac{3}{4}$$

The probability that a nonstar manager will beat the market is 50%:

$$P[B \mid \bar{S}] = 50\% = \frac{1}{2}$$

At the time the new manager was added to the portfolio, the probability that the manager was a star was just the probability of any manager being a star, 16%, the unconditional probability:

$$P[S] = 16\% = \frac{4}{25}$$

To answer the second part of the question, we need to find $P[S \mid 3B]$, the probability that the manager is a star, given that the manager has beaten the market three years in a row. We can find this probability using Bayes' theorem:

$$P[S \mid 3B] = \frac{P[3B \mid S] P[S]}{P[3B]}$$

We already know $P[S]$. Because outperformance is independent from one year to the next, the other part of the numerator, $P[3B \mid S]$, is just the probability that a star beats the market in any given year to the third power:

$$P[3B \mid S] = \left(\frac{3}{4}\right)^3 = \frac{27}{64}$$

The denominator is the unconditional probability of beating the market for three years. This is just the weighted average probability of three market-beating years over both types of managers:

$$P[3B] = P[3B \mid S]P[S] + P[3B \mid \overline{S}]P[\overline{S}]$$

$$P[3B] = \left(\frac{3}{4}\right)^3 \frac{4}{25} + \left(\frac{1}{2}\right)^3 \frac{21}{25} = \frac{27}{64}\frac{4}{25} + \frac{1}{8}\frac{21}{25} = \frac{69}{400}$$

Putting it all together, we get our final result:

$$P[S \mid 3B] = \frac{\dfrac{27}{64}\dfrac{4}{25}}{\dfrac{69}{400}} = \frac{9}{23} = 39\%$$

Our updated belief about the manager being a star, having seen the manager beat the market three times, is 39%, a significant increase from our prior belief of 16%. A star is much more likely to beat the market three years in a row—more than three times as likely—so it makes sense that we believe our manager is more likely to be a star now.

Even though it is much more likely that a star will beat the market three years in a row, we are still far from certain that this manager is a star. In fact, at 39% the odds are more likely that the manager is *not* a star. As was the case in the medical test example, the reason has to do with the overwhelming number of false positives. There are so many nonstar managers that some of them are bound to beat the market three years in a row. The real stars are simply outnumbered by these lucky nonstar managers.

Next, we answer the final part of the question. The probability that the manager beats the market next year is just the probability that a star would beat the market plus the probability that a nonstar would beat the market, weighted by our new beliefs. Our updated belief about the manager being a star is 39% = 9/23, so the probability that the manager is not a star must be 61% = 14/23:

$$P[B] = P[B \mid S] \cdot P[S] + P[B \mid \overline{S}] \cdot P[\overline{S}]$$

$$P[B] = \frac{3}{4} \cdot \frac{9}{23} + \frac{1}{2} \cdot \frac{14}{23}$$

$$P[B] = 60\%$$

The probability that the manager will beat the market next year falls somewhere between the probability for a nonstar, 50%, and for a star, 75%, but is closer to the probability for a nonstar. This is consistent with our updated belief that there is only a 39% probability that the manager is a star.

When using Bayes' theorem to update beliefs, we often refer to prior and posterior beliefs and probabilities. In the preceding sample problem, the prior probability was 16%. That is, *before* seeing the manager beat the market three times, our belief that the manager was a star was 16%. The posterior probability for the sample problem was 39%. That is, *after* seeing the manager beat the market three times, our belief that the manager was a star was 39%.

We often use the terms *evidence* and *likelihood* when referring to the conditional probability on the right-hand side of Bayes' theorem. In the sample problem, the probability of beating the market, assuming that the manager was a star, $P[3B|S] = 27/64$, was the likelihood. In other words, the likelihood of the manager beating the market three times, assuming that the manager was a star, was 27/64.

$$\text{posterior} \longrightarrow P[S|3B] = \frac{\overset{\text{likelihood}}{P[3B|S]} \, \overset{\text{prior}}{P[S]}}{P[3B]} \tag{6.7}$$

## BAYES VERSUS FREQUENTISTS

Pretend that as an analyst you are given daily profit data for a fund, and that the fund has had positive returns for 560 of the past 1,000 trading days. What is the probability that the fund will generate a positive return tomorrow? Without any further instructions, it is tempting to say that the probability is 56%, (560/1,000 = 56%). In the previous sample problem, though, we were presented with a portfolio manager who beat the market three years in a row. Shouldn't we have concluded that the probability that the portfolio manager would beat the market the following year was 100% (3/3 = 100%), and not 60%? How can both answers be correct?

The last approach, taking three out of three positive results and concluding that the probability of a positive result next year is 100%, is known as the frequentist approach. The conclusion is based only on the observed frequency of positive results. Prior to this chapter we had been using the frequentist approach to calculate probabilities and other parameters.

The Bayesian approach, which we have been exploring in this chapter, also counts the number of positive results. The conclusion is different because the Bayesian approach starts with a prior belief about the probability.

Which approach is better? It's hard to say. Within the statistics community there are those who believe that the frequentist approach is always correct. On the other end of the spectrum, there are those who believe the Bayesian approach is always superior.

Proponents of Bayesian analysis often point to the absurdity of the frequentist approach when applied to small data sets. Observing three out of three positive results and concluding that the probability of a positive result next year is 100% suggests that we are absolutely certain and that there is absolutely no possibility of a negative result. Clearly this certainty is unjustified.

Proponents of the frequentist approach often point to the arbitrariness of Bayesian priors. In the portfolio manager example, we started our analysis with the assumption that 16% of managers were stars. In a previous example we assumed that there was a 90% probability that a coin was fair. How did we arrive at these priors? In most cases the prior is either subjective or based on frequentist analysis.

Perhaps unsurprisingly, most practitioners tend to take a more balanced view, realizing that there are situations that lend themselves to frequentist analysis and others that lend themselves to Bayesian analysis. Situations in which there is very little data, or in which the signal-to-noise ratio is extremely low, often lend themselves to Bayesian analysis. When we have lots of data, the conclusions of frequentist analysis and Bayesian analysis are often very similar, and the frequentist results are often easier to calculate.

In the example with the portfolio manager, we had only three data points. Using the Bayesian approach for this problem made sense. In the example where we had 1,000 data points, most practitioners would probably utilize frequentist analysis. In risk management, performance analysis and stress testing are examples of areas where we often have very little data, and the data we do have is very noisy. These areas are likely to lend themselves to Bayesian analysis.

## MANY-STATE PROBLEMS

In the two previous sample problems, each variable could exist in only one of two states: a person either had the disease or did not have the disease; a manager was either a star or a nonstar. We can easily extend Bayesian analysis to any number of possible outcomes. For example, suppose rather than stars and nonstars, we believe there are three types of managers: underperformers, in-line performers, and outperformers. The underperformers beat the market only 25% of the time, the in-line performers beat the market 50% of the time, and the outperformers beat the market 75% of the time. Initially we believe that a given manager is most likely to be an in-line performer, and is less likely to be an underperformer or an outperformer. More specifically, our prior belief is that a manager has a 60% probability of being an in-line performer, a 20% chance of being an underperformer, and a 20% chance of being an outperformer. We can summarize this as:

$$P[p = 0.25] = 20\%$$
$$P[p = 0.50] = 60\% \qquad (6.8)$$
$$P[p = 0.75] = 20\%$$

Now suppose the manager beats the market two years in a row. What should our updated beliefs be? We start by calculating the likelihoods, the probability of beating the market two years in a row, for each type of manager:

$$P[2B \mid p = 0.25] = \left(\frac{1}{4}\right)^2 = \frac{1}{16}$$

$$P[2B \mid p = 0.50] = \left(\frac{1}{2}\right)^2 = \frac{1}{4} = \frac{4}{16} \qquad (6.9)$$

$$P[2B \mid p = 0.75] = \left(\frac{3}{4}\right)^2 = \frac{9}{16}$$

The unconditional probability of observing the manager beat the market two years in a row, given our prior beliefs about $p$, is:

$$P[2B] = 20\%\frac{1}{16} + 60\%\frac{4}{16} + 20\%\frac{9}{16}$$

$$P[2B] = \frac{2}{10}\frac{1}{16} + \frac{6}{10}\frac{4}{16} + \frac{2}{10}\frac{9}{16} = \frac{44}{160} = 27.5\%$$

(6.10)

Putting this all together and using Bayes' theorem, we can calculate our posterior belief that the manager is an underperformer:

$$P[p = 0.25 \mid 2B] = \frac{P[2B \mid p = 0.25]P[p = 0.25]}{P[2B]} = \frac{\frac{1}{16}\frac{2}{10}}{\frac{44}{160}} = \frac{2}{44} = \frac{1}{22} = 4.55\%$$

(6.11)

Similarly, we can show that the posterior probability that the manager is an in-line performer is 54.55%:

$$P[p = 0.50 \mid 2B] = \frac{P[2B \mid p = 0.50]P[p = 0.50]}{P[2B]} = \frac{\frac{4}{16}\frac{6}{10}}{\frac{44}{160}} = \frac{24}{44} = \frac{12}{22} = 54.55\%$$

(6.12)

and that the posterior probability that the manager is an outperformer is 40.91%:

$$P[p = 0.75 \mid 2B] = \frac{P[2B \mid p = 0.75]P[p = 0.75]}{P[2B]} = \frac{\frac{9}{16}\frac{2}{10}}{\frac{44}{160}} = \frac{18}{44} = \frac{9}{22} = 40.91\%$$

(6.13)

As we would expect, given that the manager beat the market two years in a row, the posterior probability that the manager is an outperformer has increased, from 20% to 40.91%, and the posterior probability that the manager is an underperformer has decreased, from 20% to 4.55%. Even though the probabilities have changed, the sum of the probabilities is still equal to 100% (the percentages seem to add to 100.01%, but that is only a rounding error):

$$\frac{1}{22} + \frac{12}{22} + \frac{9}{22} = \frac{22}{22} = 1$$

(6.14)

At this point it is worth noting a useful shortcut. Notice that for each type of manager, the posterior probability was calculated as:

$$P[p = x \mid 2B] = \frac{P[2B \mid p = x]P[p = x]}{P[2B]}$$

(6.15)

In each case, the denominator on the right-hand side is the same, $P[2B]$, or 44/160. We can then rewrite this equation in terms of a constant, $c$:

$$P[p = x \mid 2B] = c \cdot P[2B \mid p = x]P[p = x]$$

(6.16)

We also know that the sum of all the posterior probabilities must equal one:

$$\sum_{i=1}^{3} c \cdot P[2B \mid p = x_i]P[p = x_i] = c\sum_{i=1}^{3} P[2B \mid p = x_i]P[p = x_i] = 1 \qquad (6.17)$$

In our current example we have:

$$c\left(\frac{1}{16}\frac{2}{10} + \frac{4}{16}\frac{6}{10} + \frac{9}{16}\frac{2}{10}\right) = c\frac{2 + 24 + 18}{160} = c\frac{44}{160} = 1$$
$$c = \frac{160}{44} \qquad (6.18)$$

We then use this to calculate each of the posterior probabilities. For example, the posterior probability that the manager is an underperformer is:

$$P[p = 0.25 \mid 2B] = c \cdot P[2B \mid p = 0.25]P[p = 0.25] = \frac{160}{44}\frac{1}{16}\frac{2}{10} = \frac{2}{44} = \frac{1}{22} \quad (6.19)$$

In the current example this might not seem like much of a shortcut, but, as we will see, with continuous distributions this approach can make seemingly intractable problems very easy to solve.

---

**SAMPLE PROBLEM**

*Question:*
    Using the same prior distributions as in the preceding example, what would the posterior probabilities be for an underperformer, an in-line performer, or an outperformer if instead of beating the market two years in a row, the manager beat the market in 6 of the next 10 years?

*Answer:*
    For each possible type of manager, the likelihood of beating the market 6 times out of 10 can be determined using a binomial distribution (see Chapter 4):

$$P[6B \mid p] = \binom{10}{6}p^6(1-p)^4$$

Using our shortcut, we first calculate the posterior probabilities in terms of an arbitrary constant, $c$. If the manager is an underperformer:

$$P[p = 0.25 \mid 6B] = c \cdot P[6B \mid p = 0.25] \cdot P[p = 0.25]$$

$$P[p = 0.25 \mid 6B] = c \cdot \binom{10}{6}\left(\frac{1}{4}\right)^6\left(\frac{3}{4}\right)^4 \cdot \frac{2}{10}$$

$$P[p = 0.25 \mid 6B] = c\binom{10}{6}\frac{2 \cdot 3^4}{10 \cdot 4^{10}}$$

Similarly, if the manager is an in-line performer or outperformer, we have:

$$P[p = 0.50 \mid 6B] = c\binom{10}{6}\frac{6 \cdot 2^{10}}{10 \cdot 4^{10}}$$

$$P[p = 0.75 \mid 6B] = c\binom{10}{6}\frac{2 \cdot 3^{6}}{10 \cdot 4^{10}}$$

Because all of the posterior probabilities sum to one, we have:

$$P[p = 0.25 \mid 6B] + P[p = 0.50 \mid 6B] + P[p = 0.75 \mid 6B] = 1$$

$$c\binom{10}{6}\frac{2 \cdot 3}{10 \cdot 4^{10}}(3^3 + 2^{10} + 3^5) = 1$$

$$c\binom{10}{6}\frac{2 \cdot 3}{10 \cdot 4^{10}}1{,}294 = 1$$

$$c = \frac{1}{\binom{10}{6}}\frac{10 \cdot 4^{10}}{2 \cdot 3}\frac{1}{1{,}294}$$

This may look unwieldy, but, as we will see, many of the terms will cancel out before we arrive at the final answers. Substituting back into the equations for the posterior probabilities, we have:

$$P[p = 0.25 \mid 6B] = c\binom{10}{6}\frac{2 \cdot 3^4}{10 \cdot 4^{10}} = \frac{3^3}{1{,}294} = \frac{27}{1{,}294} = 2.09\%$$

$$P[p = 0.50 \mid 6B] = c\binom{10}{6}\frac{6 \cdot 2^{10}}{10 \cdot 4^{10}} = \frac{2^{10}}{1{,}294} = \frac{1{,}024}{1{,}294} = 79.13\%$$

$$P[p = 0.75 \mid 6B] = c\binom{10}{6}\frac{2 \cdot 3^6}{10 \cdot 4^{10}} = \frac{3^5}{1{,}294} = \frac{243}{1{,}294} = 18.78\%$$

In this case, the probability that the manager is an in-line performer has increased from 60% to 79.13%. The probability that the manager is an outperformer decreased slightly from 20% to 18.78%. It now seems very unlikely that the manager is an underperformer (2.09% probability compared to our prior belief of 20%).

While the calculations looked rather complicated, using our shortcut saved us from actually having to calculate many of the more complicated terms. For more complex problems, and especially for problems involving continuous distributions, this shortcut can be extremely useful.

This sample problem involved three possible states. The basic approach for solving a problem with four, five, or any finite number of states is exactly the same, only the number of calculations increases. The end-of-chapter problems include one question with four possible states. Because the calculations are highly repetitive, it is often much easier to solve these problems using a spreadsheet or computer program. The online content includes an example involving 11 possible states.

## CONTINUOUS DISTRIBUTIONS

In the limit, as we increase the number of possible states, our prior and posterior distributions converge to continuous distributions. Our fundamental equation, Bayes' theorem, remains the same, only now the prior and posterior probabilities are replaced with prior and posterior probability density functions (PDFs):

$$P[A \mid B] = \frac{P[B \mid A]P[A]}{P[B]} \rightarrow f(A \mid B) = \frac{g(B \mid A)f(A)}{\int_{-\infty}^{+\infty} g(B \mid A)f(A)dA} \qquad (6.20)$$

Here $f(A)$ is the prior probability density function, and $f(A \mid B)$ is the posterior PDF. $g(B \mid A)$ is the likelihood. We can also mix discrete and continuous distributions. If the prior distribution is continuous, then the posterior distribution will almost always be continuous, but the likelihood can easily be discrete or continuous. Finally, the integral in the denominator represents the unconditional probability of $B$, $P[B]$. Calculating $P[B]$ through integration is analogous to how we calculated $P[B]$ for a discrete distribution by summing across all of the possible states.

Just as we did for the discrete case, we can rewrite Equation 6.20 using our shortcut from the previous section. For a constant, $c$, it must be true that:

$$f(A \mid B) = c \cdot g(B \mid A)f(A) \qquad (6.21)$$

For a discrete posterior distribution, it is necessary that all of the possible posterior distributions sum to one. In the continuous case, the analogous requirement is that the integral of the posterior PDF over the relevant range be equal to one:

$$\int_{-\infty}^{+\infty} f(A \mid B)dA = 1 \qquad (6.22)$$

In other words, we require that the posterior distribution be a proper distribution. Substituting Equation 6.21 into Equation 6.22, we have:

$$c\int_{-\infty}^{+\infty} g(B \mid A)f(A)dA = 1 \qquad (6.23)$$

We will put this result to use in the following sample problem.

## SAMPLE PROBLEM

*Question:*

As in the preceding sample problem, assume that we observe a portfolio manager beat the market in 6 out of 10 years. Instead of assuming that there are two or three types of managers, though, we assume that the manager can beat the market anywhere between 0% and 100% of the time. Prior to observing the manager, we believed that the manager was equally likely to be anywhere between 0% and 100%. That is, our prior distribution was a uniform distribution between 0% and 100%. Our PDF, $f(p)$, is:

$$f(p) = 1 \quad 0 \leq p \leq 1$$

What is the posterior distribution after observing the manager beat the market in 6 out of 10 years?

*Answer:*

As in the preceding sample problem, the likelihood is described by a binomial distribution:

$$g(6B \mid p) = \binom{10}{6} p^6 (1-p)^4$$

In the preceding equation and what follows, we assume $0 \leq p \leq 1$. For a constant, $c$, the posterior probability density function is then:

$$f(p \mid 6B) = c \cdot g(6B \mid p) f(p)$$

$$f(p \mid 6B) = c \cdot \binom{10}{6} p^6 (1-p)^4 \cdot 1$$

$$f(p \mid 6B) = c \cdot \binom{10}{6} p^6 (1-p)^4$$

Next, we note that the number of combinations is independent of $p$. Because of this, we can rewrite the posterior distribution in terms of a new constant, $k$:

$$f(p \mid 6B) = k \cdot p^6 (1-p)^4 \quad \text{where} \quad k = c \cdot \binom{10}{6}$$

The next step is the tricky part. Remember from Chapter 4 that the PDF for the beta distribution can be written as:

$$\beta(p; a, b) = \frac{1}{B(a,b)} p^{a-1} (1-p)^{b-1} \quad 0 \leq p \leq 1$$

Both our posterior distribution and the beta distribution are nonzero from zero to one, and, because they are distributions, the integral of their PDFs over this range must be equal to one:

$$\int_0^1 k \cdot p^6 (1-p)^4 \, dp = 1 = \int_0^1 \frac{1}{B(a,b)} p^{a-1}(1-p)^{b-1} \, dp$$

Taking the constants out of the integrals and rewriting the exponents, we have:

$$k \int_0^1 p^{7-1}(1-p)^{5-1} \, dp = \frac{1}{B(a,b)} \int_0^1 p^{a-1}(1-p)^{b-1} \, dp$$

If we set $a$ equal to 7 and $b$ equal to 5, it is clear that $k$ must equal $1/B(7,5)$ in order for the two sides of the equation to be equal. Replacing $k$ in our previous equation for the posterior distribution, we arrive at our final answer. The posterior distribution of our beliefs after seeing the manager beat the market in 6 out of 10 years is a beta distribution, $\beta(p; 7,5)$:

$$f(p \mid 6B) = \frac{1}{B(7,5)} p^6 (1-p)^4$$

The prior and posterior distributions are shown in Exhibit 6.2.

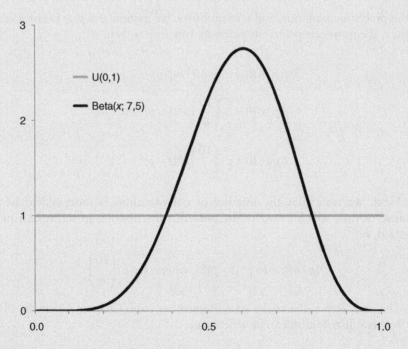

**EXHIBIT 6.2**   Prior and Posterior Distributions

The posterior distribution has a mode of 0.60 and a mean of 0.58. Extreme values (below 0.2 and above 0.9) are very unlikely for the posterior distribution.

Remember from Chapter 4 that the uniform distribution is a special case of the beta distribution, where both parameters, *a* and *b*, are equal to one. In the sample problem, then, both the prior and posterior distributions are beta distributions. This is not a coincidence. In general, if the prior distribution is a beta distribution and the likelihood function follows a binomial distribution, then the posterior distribution will be a beta distribution. More precisely, if we start with a beta distribution $\beta(x; a,b)$ and then observe *n* trials, of which *k* are successful and $(n - k)$ are unsuccessful, the posterior distribution will be $\beta(x; a + k, b + n - k)$. We simply add the number of successful trials to the first parameter of the beta distribution and add the number of unsuccessful trials to the second.

## SAMPLE PROBLEM

*Question:*
　　As in the previous sample problem, assume we are observing a portfolio manager whose probability of beating the market can range from 0% to 100%. Instead of believing that all probabilities are equally likely, though, our prior distribution puts more weight on probabilities closer to 50%. More specifically, our prior distribution is a beta distribution, $\beta(x; 2,2)$, as depicted in Exhibit 6.3. After 20 years, the portfolio manager has beaten the market only 9 times. What is the posterior distribution for the portfolio manager?

*Answer:*
　　Even though the problem seems complex, almost no calculation is required in this case. Adding the number of successes, 9, to the first parameter, and the number of failures, 11, to the second parameter, we arrive at our final answer, a posterior distribution of $\beta(x; 11,13)$.

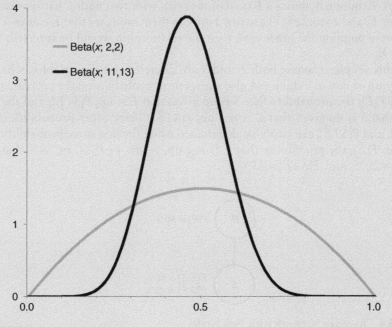

**EXHIBIT 6.3** Beta Distribution

As expected, the posterior distribution has a mean and median below 50%, and the most extreme probabilities are even less likely than they were prior to the observations.

It is not always the case that the prior and posterior distributions are of the same type. When both the prior and posterior distributions *are* of the same type, we say that they are conjugate distributions. As we just saw, the beta distribution is the conjugate distribution for the binomial likelihood distribution. Here is another useful set of conjugates: The normal distribution is the conjugate distribution for the normal likelihood when we are trying to estimate the distribution of the mean, and the variance is known.

Conjugate distributions are extremely easy to work with and make calculating posterior distributions very simple. This latter fact was extremely appealing before the widespread use of computers. Unfortunately, real-world problems need not involve conjugate distributions. The real world is not obligated to make our statistical calculations easy. In practice, prior and posterior distributions may be nonparametric and require numerical methods to solve. While all of this makes Bayesian analysis involving continuous distributions more complex, these are problems that are easily solved by computers. One reason for the increasing popularity of Bayesian analysis has to do with the rapidly increasing power of computers in recent decades.

## BAYESIAN NETWORKS

A Bayesian network illustrates the causal relationship between different random variables. Exhibit 6.4 shows a Bayesian network with two nodes that represent the economy, $E$, and a stock, $S$. The arrow between them indicates that $E$ causes $S$. If the arrow were pointing the other way, then the relationship would be reversed, with $S$ causing $E$.

In this simple example, both $E$ and $S$ are discrete random variables, which can be either up or down. Exhibit 6.4 also shows three probabilities: the probability that $E$ is up, $P[E]$; the probability that $S$ is up given that $E$ is up, $P[S\,|\,E]$; and the probability that $S$ is up given that $E$ is not up, $P[S\,|\,\bar{E}]$. Three other probabilities, $P[\bar{E}]$, $P[\bar{S}\,|\,E]$, and $P[\bar{S}\,|\,\bar{E}]$, can easily be determined using the first three probabilities. For example, $P[\bar{E}]$, the probability that $E$ is not up, is just $1 - P[E]$, or 50%. Similarly, $P[\bar{S}\,|\,E] = 20\%$, and $P[\bar{S}\,|\,\bar{E}] = 75\%$.

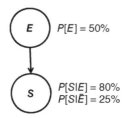

**EXHIBIT 6.4**  Bayesian Network with Two Nodes

Using Bayes' theorem, we can also calculate $P[E \mid S]$. This is the probability that $E$ is up given that we have observed $S$ being up:

$$P[E \mid S] = \frac{P[S \mid E]P[E]}{P[S]} = \frac{P[S \mid E]P[E]}{P[S \mid E]P[E] + P[S \mid \bar{E}]P[\bar{E}]} \tag{6.24}$$

$P[E \mid S]$ is the reverse probability of $P[S \mid E]$. Even though we can easily calculate both $P[S \mid E]$ and $P[E \mid S]$, most people find the concept of $P[E \mid S]$, the reverse probability, to be less intuitive. This is because human brains are wired to move from causes to effects, and not the other way around. If we believe that the state of the economy determines the performance of stocks, then it seems much more logical to ask, "What is the probability that the stock will be up, given that the economy is up?" It seems strange to ask the reverse, "What is the probability that the economy was up, given that the stock is up?" Our hunter-gatherer ancestors were more likely to ask, "What is the probability that the woolly mammoth will die if I hit it with a spear?" than to ask, "What is the probability that I hit the woolly mammoth with a spear, given that it is dead?" In Bayesian statistics we refer to these two alternative modes of evaluating a network as causal reasoning and diagnostic reasoning. Causal reasoning, $P[S \mid E]$, follows the cause-and-effect arrow of our Bayesian network. Diagnostic reasoning, $P[E \mid S]$, works in reverse.

For most people, causal reasoning is much more intuitive than diagnostic reasoning. Diagnostic reasoning is one reason why people often find Bayesian logic to be confusing. Bayesian networks do not eliminate this problem, but they do implicitly model cause and effect, allowing us to differentiate easily between causal and diagnostic relationships.

Bayesian networks are extremely flexible. Exhibit 6.5 shows a network with seven nodes. Nodes can have multiple inputs and multiple outputs. For example, node $B$ influences both nodes $D$ and $E$, and node $F$ is influenced by both nodes $C$ and $D$.

In a network with $n$ nodes, where each node can be in one of two states (for example, up or down), there are a total of $2^n$ possible states for the network. As we will see, an advantage of Bayesian networks is that we will rarely have to specify $2^n$ probabilities in order to define the network. For example, in Exhibit 6.4 with two nodes, there are four possible states for the network, but we only had to define three probabilities.

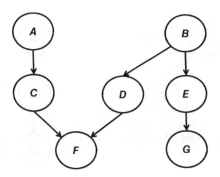

**EXHIBIT 6.5**   Bayesian Network with Seven Nodes

## BAYESIAN NETWORKS VERSUS CORRELATION MATRICES

Exhibit 6.6 shows two networks, each with three nodes. In each network $E$ is the economy and $S1$ and $S2$ are two stocks. In the first network, on the left, $S1$ and $S2$ are directly influenced by the economy. In the second network, on the right, $S1$ is still directly influenced by the economy, but $S2$ is only indirectly influenced by the economy, being directly influenced only by $S1$. In the first example, we might imagine that $S1$ and $S2$ represent the stocks of large, diverse corporations whose performance is largely determined by the state of the economy. In the second example, we might imagine that $S1$ is still the stock of a large, diverse company, but that $S2$ is now the stock of a supplier whose largest customer is $S1$. In the second network, $S2$ is still influenced by $E$, but the influence is indirect.

For each network in Exhibit 6.6 there are eight possible states: $2^3 = 8$. Given the probabilities supplied, we can figure out the entire joint distribution for each network; that is, we can figure out the probability of each state. For example, in the first network, the probability of $E$, $S1$, and $S2$ all occurring is 25.20%:

$$P[E, S1, S2] = P[E]P[S1 \mid E]P[S2 \mid E] = 60\% \cdot 70\% \cdot 60\% = 25.20\% \qquad (6.25)$$

Exhibit 6.7 shows all eight probabilities for both networks. In the table, the occurrence of an event is signified by a 1, and an event not occurring by a 0. For example, the probability of $E$, $S1$, and $S2$ occurring, $P[E,S1,S2]$, can be found in the last row of the table where $E$, $S1$, and $S2$ are all equal to 1. You should check all of the remaining values in the table to ensure that you understand how they are calculated.

As with any random variable, we can calculate the mean, standard deviation, and variance of $E$, $S1$, and $S2$. Also, because we know the joint distribution of all three variables, we can calculate their covariances and correlations as well. For example, the mean of $S1$ in both networks is 50%:

$$\begin{aligned} E[S1] &= E[S1 \mid E]P[E] + E[S1 \mid \bar{E}]P[\bar{E}] \\ E[S1] &= 70\% \cdot 60\% + 20\% \cdot (1 - 60\%) \\ E[S1] &= 50\% \end{aligned} \qquad (6.26)$$

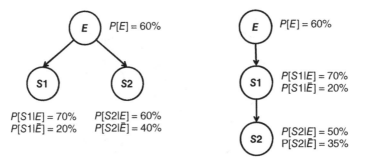

**EXHIBIT 6.6**   Two Bayesian Networks with Three Nodes Each

**EXHIBIT 6.7**  Probabilities of Networks

| E | S1 | S2 | Network 1 | Network 2 |
|---|----|----|-----------|-----------|
| 0 | 0 | 0 | 19.20% | 20.80% |
| 0 | 0 | 1 | 12.80% | 11.20% |
| 0 | 1 | 0 | 4.80% | 4.00% |
| 0 | 1 | 1 | 3.20% | 4.00% |
| 1 | 0 | 0 | 7.20% | 11.70% |
| 1 | 0 | 1 | 10.80% | 6.30% |
| 1 | 1 | 0 | 16.80% | 21.00% |
| 1 | 1 | 1 | 25.20% | 21.00% |
|   |   |   | 100.00% | 100.00% |

## SAMPLE PROBLEM

*Question:*

Using the probabilities for the first network in Exhibit 6.6, calculate the covariance between $E$ and $S1$.

*Answer:*

Using our equation for covariance from Chapter 3, the covariance of $E$ and $S1$ is:

$$\sigma_{E,S1} = E[(E - E[E])(S1 - E[S1])] = E[E \cdot S1] - E[E]E[S1]$$

We already know $E[S1]$ from Equation 6.26. We could calculate $E[E]$ in a similar fashion. Alternatively, we could read the values and probabilities straight from the joint probability distribution in Exhibit 6.7. The equation is longer, but the process is more mechanical and much easier to automate:

$$E[E] = 19.20\% \cdot 0 + 12.80\% \cdot 0 + 4.80\% \cdot 0 + 3.20\% \cdot 0 + 7.20\% \cdot 1 + 10.80\% \cdot 1$$
$$+ 16.80\% \cdot 1 + 25.20\% \cdot 1$$
$$E[E] = 7.20\% + 10.80\% + 16.80\% + 25.20\%$$
$$E[E] = 60\%$$

In the second line of the preceding equation, we see that calculating $E[E]$ is equivalent to adding up all the probabilities in Exhibit 6.7 where $E$ is equal to 1. We can calculate $E[E \cdot S1]$ in a similar fashion. $E \cdot S1$ is equal to 1 only if both $E$ and $S$ are equal to 1, which is true for only the last two lines of Exhibit 6.7. Therefore:

$$E[E \cdot S1] = 16.80\% + 25.20\% = 42.00\%$$

Putting this all together, we have our final answer:

$$\sigma_{E,S1} = E[E \cdot S1] - E[E]E[S1] = 42.00\% - 60.00\% \cdot 50.00\% = 12.00\%$$

**EXHIBIT 6.8**   Covariance Matrices

| Network 1 | | | | Network 2 | | |
|---|---|---|---|---|---|---|
| | E | S1 | S2 | | E | S1 | S2 |
| **E** | 24% | 12% | 5% | **E** | 24% | 12% | 2% |
| **S1** | 12% | 25% | 2% | **S1** | 12% | 25% | 4% |
| **S2** | 5% | 2% | 25% | **S2** | 2% | 4% | 24% |

The complete covariance matrices are provided in Exhibit 6.8. Calculating these covariance matrices and the corresponding correlation matrices is left as an exercise at the end of the chapter.

Not surprisingly, given the similarity of the Bayesian networks from which they were derived, the covariance matrices are very similar to each other. $E$, $S1$, and $S2$ are all positively correlated with each other in both cases.

One advantage of Bayesian networks is that they can be specified with very few parameters, relative to other approaches. In the preceding example, we were able to specify each network using only five probabilities, but each covariance matrix contains six nontrivial entries, and the joint probability table, Exhibit 6.7, contains eight entries for each network. As networks grow in size, this advantage tends to become even more dramatic.

Another advantage of Bayesian networks is that they are more intuitive. It is hard to have much intuition for entries in a covariance matrix or a joint probability table. Given the scenarios described in this example, it makes sense that the entries in the covariance matrices are positive, but beyond that it is difficult to say much. What if we were worried that we had accidentally reversed the data for the two networks? An equity analyst covering the two companies represented by $S1$ and $S2$ might be able to look at the Bayesian networks and say that the linkages and probabilities seem reasonable, but the analyst is unlikely to be able to say the same about the two covariance matrices.

Because Bayesian networks are more intuitive, they might be easier to update in the face of a structural change or regime change. In the second network, where we have described $S2$ as being a supplier to $S1$, suppose that $S2$ announces that it has signed a contract to supply another large firm, thereby making it less reliant on $S1$? With the help of our equity analyst, we might be able to update the Bayesian network immediately (for example, by decreasing the probabilities $P[S2 \mid S1]$ and $P[\overline{S2} \mid \overline{S1}]$), but it is not as obvious how we would directly update the covariance matrices.

## PROBLEMS

1. The probability that gross domestic product (GDP) decreases is 20%. The probability that unemployment increases is 10%. The probability that unemployment increases given that GDP has decreased is 40%. What is the probability that GDP decreases given that unemployment has increased?

2. An analyst develops a model for forecasting bond defaults. The model is 90% accurate. In other words, of the bonds that actually default, the model identifies

90% of them; likewise, of the bonds that do not default, the model correctly predicts that 90% will not default. You have a portfolio of bonds, each with a 5% probability of defaulting. Given that the model predicts that a bond will default, what is the probability that it actually defaults?

3. As a risk analyst, you are asked to look at EB Corporation, which has issued both equity and bonds. The bonds can either be downgraded, be upgraded, or have no change in rating. The stock can either outperform the market or underperform the market. You are given the following probability matrix from an analyst who had worked on the company previously, but some of the values are missing. Fill in the missing values. What is the conditional probability that the bonds are downgraded given that the equity has underperformed?

|  |  | Equity | | |
|---|---|---|---|---|
|  |  | Outperform | Underperform | |
| Bonds | Upgrade | W | 5% | 15% |
|  | No Change | 45% | X | 65% |
|  | Downgrade | Y | 15% | Z |
|  |  | 60% | 40% | |

4. Your firm is testing a new quantitative strategy. The analyst who developed the strategy claims that there is a 55% probability that the strategy will generate positive returns on any given day. After 20 days the strategy has generated a profit only 10 times. What is the probability that the analyst is right and the actual probability of positive returns for the strategy is 55%? Assume that there are only two possible states of the world: Either the analyst is correct, or there the strategy is equally likely to gain or lose money on any given day. Your prior assumption was that these two states of the world were equally likely.

5. Your firm has created two equity baskets. One is procyclical, and the other is countercyclical. The procyclical basket has a 75% probability of being up in years when the economy is up, and a 25% probability of being up when the economy is down or flat. The probability of the economy being down or flat in any given year is only 20%. Given that the procyclical index is up, what is the probability that the economy is also up?

6. You are an analyst at Astra Fund of Funds, but instead of believing that there are two or three types of portfolio managers, your latest model classifies managers into four categories. Managers can be underperformers, in-line performers, stars, or superstars. In any given year, these managers have a 40%, 50%, 60%, and 80% chance of beating the market, respectively. In general, you believe that managers are equally likely to be any one of the four types of managers. After observing a manager beat the market in three out of five years, what do you believe the probability is that the manager belongs in each of the four categories?

7. You have a model that classifies Federal Reserve statements as either bullish or bearish. When the Fed makes a bullish announcement, you expect the market to be up 75% of the time. The market is just as likely to be up as it is to be down

or flat, but the Fed makes bullish announcements 60% of the time. What is the probability that the Fed made a *bearish* announcement, given that the market was up?

8. You are monitoring a new strategy. Initially, you believed that the strategy was just as likely to be up as it was to be down or flat on any given day, and that the probability of being up was fairly close to 50%. More specifically, your initial assumption was that the probability of being up, $p$, could be described by a beta distribution, $\beta(4,4)$. Over the past 100 days, the strategy has been up 60 times. What is your new estimate for the distribution of the parameter $p$? What is the probability that the strategy will be up the next day?

9. For the Bayesian network in Exhibit 6.9, each node can be in one of three states: up, down, or no change. How many possible states are there for the entire network? What is the minimum number of probabilities needed to completely define the network?

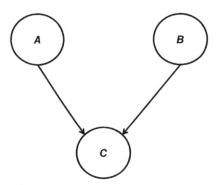

**EXHIBIT 6.9**   Three-State Network

10. Calculate the correlation matrix for Network 1, the network on the left, in Exhibit 6.6. Start by calculating the covariance matrix for the network.

11. Calculate the correlation matrix for Network 2, the network on the right, in Exhibit 6.6. Start by calculating the covariance matrix for the network.

## CHAPTER 7

# Hypothesis Testing and Confidence Intervals

**I**n this chapter we explore two closely related topics, confidence intervals and hypothesis testing. At the end of the chapter, we explore applications, including value at risk (VaR).

## SAMPLE MEAN REVISITED

Imagine taking the output from a standard random number generator on a computer, and multiply it by 100. The resulting data-generating process (DGP) is a uniform random variable, which ranges between 0 and 100, with a mean of 50. If we generate 20 draws from this DGP and calculate the sample mean of those 20 draws, it is unlikely that the sample mean will be exactly 50. The sample mean might round to 50, say 50.03906724, but exactly 50 is next to impossible. In fact, given that we have only 20 data points, the sample mean might not even be close to the true mean.

The sample mean is actually a random variable itself. If we continue to repeat the experiment—generating 20 data points and calculating the sample mean each time—the calculated sample mean will be different every time. As we proved in Chapter 3, even though we never get exactly 50, the expected value of each sample mean is in fact 50. It might sound strange to say it, but the mean of our sample mean is the true mean of the distribution. Using our standard notation:

$$E[\hat{\mu}] = \mu \tag{7.1}$$

If instead of 20 data points, what if we generate 1,000 data points? With 1,000 data points, the expected value of our sample mean is still 50, just as it was with 20 data points. While we still don't expect our sample mean to be exactly 50, our sample mean will tend to be closer when we are using 1,000 data points. The reason is simple: A single outlier won't have nearly the impact in a pool of 1,000 data points that it will in a pool of 20. If we continue to generate sets of 1,000 data points, it stands to reason that the standard deviation of our sample mean will be lower with 1,000 data points than it would be if our sets contained only 20 data points.

It turns out that the variance of our sample mean doesn't just decrease with the sample size; it decreases in a predictable way, in proportion to the sample size. If our sample size is $n$ and the true variance of our DGP is $\sigma^2$, then the variance of the sample mean is:

$$\sigma_{\hat{\mu}}^2 = \frac{\sigma^2}{n} \tag{7.2}$$

It follows that the standard deviation of the sample mean decreases with the square root of $n$. This square root is important. In order to reduce the standard deviation of the mean by a factor of 2, we need 4 times as many data points. To reduce it by a factor of 10, we need 100 times as much data. This is yet another example of the famous square root rule for independent and identically distributed (i.i.d.) variables.

In our current example, because the DGP follows a uniform distribution, we can easily calculate the variance of each data point using Equation 4.4. The variance of each data point is 833.33, $(100 - 0)^2/12 = 833.33$. This is equivalent to a standard deviation of 28.87. For 20 data points, the standard deviation of the mean will then be $28.87/\sqrt{20} = 6.45$, and for 1,000 data points, the standard deviation will be $28.87/\sqrt{1,000} = 0.91$.

We have the mean and the standard deviation of our sample mean, but what about the shape of the distribution? You might think that the shape of the distribution would depend on the shape of the underlying distribution of the DGP. If we recast our formula for the sample mean slightly, though:

$$\hat{\mu} = \frac{1}{n} \sum_{i=1}^{n} x_i = \sum_{i=1}^{n} \frac{1}{n} x_i \tag{7.3}$$

and regard each of the $(1/n)x_i$'s as a random variable in its own right, we see that our sample mean is equivalent to the sum of $n$ i.i.d. random variables, each with a mean of $\mu/n$ and a standard deviation of $\sigma/n$. Using the central limit theorem, we claim that the distribution of the sample mean converges to a normal distribution. For large values of $n$, the distribution of the sample mean will be extremely close to a normal distribution. Practitioners will often assume that the sample mean *is* normally distributed.

## SAMPLE PROBLEM

*Question:*
You are given 10 years of monthly returns for a portfolio manager. The mean monthly return is 2.3%, and the standard deviation of the return series is 3.6%. What is the standard deviation of the mean?

The portfolio manager is being compared against a benchmark with a mean monthly return of 1.5%. What is the probability that the portfolio manager's mean return exceeds the benchmark? Assume the sample mean is normally distributed.

*Answer:*

There is a total of 120 data points in the sample (10 years × 12 months per year). The standard deviation of the mean is then 0.33%:

$$\sigma_{\hat{\mu}} = \frac{\sigma}{\sqrt{n}} = \frac{3.6\%}{\sqrt{120}} = 0.33\%$$

The distance between the portfolio manager's mean return and the benchmark is –2.43 standard deviations: (1.50% – 2.30%)/0.33% = –2.43. For a normal distribution, 99.25% of the distribution lies above –2.43 standard deviations, and only 0.75% lies below. The difference between the portfolio manager and the benchmark is highly significant.

## SAMPLE VARIANCE REVISITED

Just as with the sample mean, we can treat the sample variance as a random variable. For a given DGP if we repeatedly calculate the sample variance, the expected value of the sample variance will equal the true variance, and the variance of the sample variance will equal:

$$E[(\hat{\sigma}^2 - \sigma^2)^2] = \sigma^4 \left( \frac{2}{n-1} + \frac{\kappa_{ex}}{n} \right) \tag{7.4}$$

where $n$ is the sample size, and $\kappa_{ex}$ is the excess kurtosis.

If the DGP has a normal distribution, then we can also say something about the shape of the distribution of the sample variance. If we have $n$ sample points and $\hat{\sigma}^2$ is the sample variance, then our estimator will follow a chi-squared distribution with $(n - 1)$ degrees of freedom:

$$(n-1)\frac{\hat{\sigma}^2}{\sigma^2} \sim \chi_{n-1}^2 \tag{7.5}$$

where $\sigma^2$ is the population variance. Note that this is true only when the DGP has a normal distribution. Unfortunately, unlike the case of the sample mean, we cannot apply the central limit theorem here. Even when the sample size is large, if the underlying distribution is nonnormal, the statistic in Equation 7.5 can vary significantly from a chi-squared distribution.

## CONFIDENCE INTERVALS

In our discussion of the sample mean, we assumed that the standard deviation of the underlying distribution was known. In practice, the true standard deviation is likely to be unknown. At the same time we are measuring the sample mean, we will typically be measuring the sample variance as well.

It turns out that if we first standardize our estimate of the sample mean using the sample standard deviation, the new random variable follows a Student's $t$ distribution with $(n - 1)$ degrees of freedom:

$$t = \frac{\hat{\mu} - \mu}{\hat{\sigma} / \sqrt{n}} \tag{7.6}$$

Here the numerator is simply the difference between the sample mean and the population mean, while the denominator is the sample standard deviation divided by the square root of the sample size. To see why this new variable follows a $t$ distribution, we simply need to divide both the numerator and the denominator by the population standard deviation. This creates a standard normal variable in the numerator, and the square root of a chi-square variable in the denominator with the appropriate constant. We know from the previous chapter on distributions that this combination of random variables follows a $t$ distribution. This standardized version of the population mean is so frequently used that it is referred to as a $t$-statistic, or simply a $t$-stat.

Technically, this result requires that the underlying distribution be normally distributed. As was the case with the sample variance, the denominator may not follow a chi-squared distribution if the underlying distribution is nonnormal. Oddly enough, for large sample sizes the overall $t$-statistic still converges to a $t$ distribution. However, if the sample size is small and the data distribution is nonnormal, the $t$-statistic, as defined here, may not be well approximated by a $t$ distribution.

By looking up the appropriate values for the $t$ distribution, we can establish the probability that our $t$-statistic is contained within a certain range:

$$P\left[ x_L \leq \frac{\hat{\mu} - \mu}{\hat{\sigma} / \sqrt{n}} \leq x_U \right] = \gamma \tag{7.7}$$

where $x_L$ and $x_U$ are constants, which, respectively, define the lower and upper bounds of the range within the $t$ distribution, and $\gamma$ is the probability that our $t$-statistic will be found within that range. Typically $\gamma$ is referred to as the confidence level. Rather than working directly with the confidence level, we often work with the quantity $1 - \gamma$, which is known as the significance level and is often denoted by $\alpha$. The smaller the confidence level is, the higher the significance level.

In practice, the population mean, $\mu$, is often unknown. By rearranging the previous equation we come to an equation with a more interesting form:

$$P\left[ \hat{\mu} - \frac{x_L \hat{\sigma}}{\sqrt{n}} \leq \mu \leq \hat{\mu} + \frac{x_U \hat{\sigma}}{\sqrt{n}} \right] = \gamma \tag{7.8}$$

Looked at this way, we are now giving the probability that the population mean will be contained within the defined range. When it is formulated this way, we call this range the confidence interval for the population mean. Confidence intervals are not limited to the population mean. Though it may not be as simple, in theory we can define a confidence level for any distribution parameter.

## HYPOTHESIS TESTING

One problem with confidence intervals is that they require us to settle on an arbitrary confidence level. While 95% and 99% are common choices for the confidence level in risk management, there is nothing sacred about these numbers. It would be perfectly legitimate to construct a 74.92% confidence interval. At the same time, we are often concerned with the probability that a certain variable exceeds a threshold. For example, given the observed returns of a mutual fund, what is the probability that the standard deviation of those returns is less than 20%?

In a sense, we want to turn the confidence interval around. Rather than saying there is an $x$% probability that the population mean is contained within a given interval, we want to know what the probability is that the population mean is greater than $y$. When we pose the question this way, we are in the realm of hypothesis testing.

Traditionally the question is put in the form of a null hypothesis. If we are interested in knowing whether the expected return of a portfolio manager is greater than 10%, we would write:

$$H_0 : \mu_r > 10\% \tag{7.9}$$

where $H_0$ is known as the null hypothesis. Even though the true population mean is unknown, for the hypothesis test we assume that the population mean *is* 10%. In effect, we are asking, *if* the true population mean *is* 10%, what is the probability that we would see a given sample mean? With our null hypothesis in hand, we gather our data, calculate the sample mean, and form the appropriate $t$-statistic. In this case, the appropriate $t$-statistic is:

$$t = \frac{\mu - 10\%}{\sigma / \sqrt{n}} \tag{7.10}$$

We can then look up the corresponding probability from the $t$ distribution.

In addition to the null hypothesis, we can offer an alternative hypothesis. In the previous example, where our null hypothesis is that the expected return is greater than 10%, the logical alternative would be that the expected return is less than or equal to 10%:

$$H_1 : \mu_r \leq 10\% \tag{7.11}$$

In principle, we could test any number of hypotheses. In practice, as long as the alternative is trivial, we tend to limit ourselves to stating the null hypothesis.

### Which Way to Test?

If we want to know if the expected return of a portfolio manager is greater than 10%, the obvious statement of the null hypothesis might seem to be $\mu_r > 10\%$. But we could just have easily have started with the alternative hypothesis, that $\mu_r \leq 10\%$. Finding that the first is true and finding that the second is false are logically equivalent.

Many practitioners construct the null hypothesis so that the desired result is false. If we are an investor trying to find good portfolio managers, then we would make the null hypothesis $\mu_r \leq 10\%$. That we want the expected return to be greater than 10% but we are testing for the opposite makes us seem objective. Unfortunately, in the case where there is a high probability that the manager's expected return is greater than 10% (a good result), we have to say, "We reject the null hypothesis that the manager's expected return is less than or equal to 10% at the $x\%$ level." This is very close to a double negative. Like a medical test where the good outcome is negative and the bad outcome is positive, we often find that the desired outcome for a null hypothesis is rejection.

To make matters more complicated, what happens if the portfolio manager doesn't seem to be that good? If we *rejected* the null hypothesis when there was a high probability that the portfolio manager's expected return was greater than 10%, should we *accept* the null hypothesis when there is a high probability that the expected return is less than 10%? In the realm of statistics, outright acceptance seems too certain. In practice, we can do two things. First, we can state that the probability of rejecting the null hypothesis is low (e.g., "The probability of rejecting the null hypothesis is only 4.2%"). More often, we say that we *fail to reject* the null hypothesis (e.g., "We fail to reject the null hypothesis at the 95.8% level").

---

## SAMPLE PROBLEM

*Question:*
    At the start of the year, you believed that the annualized volatility of XYZ Corporation's equity was 45%. At the end of the year, you have collected a year of daily returns, 256 business days' worth. You calculate the standard deviation, annualize it, and come up with a value of 48%. Can you reject the null hypothesis, $H_0: \sigma = 45\%$, at the 95% confidence level?

*Answer:*
    The appropriate test statistic is:

$$(n-1)\frac{\hat{\sigma}^2}{\sigma^2} = (256-1)\frac{0.48^2}{0.45^2} = 290.13 \sim \chi^2_{255}$$

    Notice that annualizing the standard deviation has no impact on the test statistic. The same factor would appear in the numerator and the denominator, leaving the ratio unchanged. For a chi-squared distribution with 255 degrees of freedom, 290.13 corresponds to a probability of 6.44%. We fail to reject the null hypothesis at the 95% confidence level.

---

### One Tail or Two?

Novice statisticians often get confused about the choice between one-tailed and two-tailed critical values. In many scientific fields where positive and negative deviations are equally important, two-tailed confidence levels are more prevalent. In risk management, more often than not we are more concerned with the probability of extreme negative outcomes, and this concern naturally leads to one-tailed tests.

A two-tailed null hypothesis could take the form:

$$H_0 : \mu = 0$$
$$H_1 : \mu \neq 0$$

(7.12)

In this case, $H_1$ implies that extreme positive or negative values would cause us to reject the null hypothesis. If we are concerned with both sides of the distribution (both tails), we should choose a two-tailed test.

A one-tailed test could be of the form:

$$H_0 : \mu > c$$
$$H_1 : \mu \leq c \tag{7.13}$$

In this case, we will reject $H_0$ only if the estimate of $\mu$ is significantly less than $c$. If we are only concerned with deviations in one direction, we should use a one-tailed test. As long as the null hypothesis is clearly stated, the choice of a one-tailed or two-tailed confidence level should be obvious.

The 95% confidence level is a very popular choice for confidence levels, both in risk management and in the sciences. Many non–risk managers remember from their science classes that a 95% confidence level is equivalent to approximately 1.96 standard deviations. For a two-tailed test this is correct; for a normal distribution 95% of the mass is within +/–1.96 standard deviations. For a one-tailed test, though, 95% of the mass is within either +1.64 or –1.64 standard deviations. Using 1.96 instead of 1.64 is a common mistake for people new to risk management.

Exhibit 7.1 shows common critical values for $t$-tests of varying degrees of freedom and for a normal distribution. Notice that all distributions are symmetrical. For small sample sizes, extreme values are more likely, but as the sample size increases, the $t$ distribution converges to the normal distribution. For 5% significance with 100 degrees of freedom, the difference between our rule of thumb based on the normal distribution, 1.64 standard deviations, is very close to the actual value of 1.66.

## The Confidence Level Returns

As we stated at the beginning of this section, one of the great things about a hypothesis test is that we are not required to choose an arbitrary confidence level. In practice, though, 95% and 99% confidence levels are such gold standards that we often end up referring back to them. If we can reject a null hypothesis at the 96.3% confidence level, some practitioners will simply say that the hypothesis was rejected at the 95% confidence level. The implication is that, even though we may be more confident, 95% is enough. This convention can be convenient when testing

**EXHIBIT 7.1**   Common Critical Values for Student's $t$ Distribution

|  | $t_{10}$ | $t_{100}$ | $t_{1,000}$ | $N$ |
|---|---|---|---|---|
| 1.0% | −2.76 | −2.36 | −2.33 | −2.33 |
| 2.5% | −2.23 | −1.98 | −1.96 | −1.96 |
| 5.0% | −1.81 | −1.66 | −1.65 | −1.64 |
| 10.0% | −1.37 | −1.29 | −1.28 | −1.28 |
| 90.0% | 1.37 | 1.29 | 1.28 | 1.28 |
| 95.0% | 1.81 | 1.66 | 1.65 | 1.64 |
| 97.5% | 2.23 | 1.98 | 1.96 | 1.96 |
| 99.0% | 2.76 | 2.36 | 2.33 | 2.33 |

a hypothesis repeatedly. As an example, we might want to test the validity of a risk model against new market data every day and be alerted only when the hypothesis cannot be rejected at the 95% confidence level. In the end, our inability to decide on a universal confidence level should serve as a reminder that, in statistics, there is no such thing as a sure bet; there is no such thing as absolute certainty.

## CHEBYSHEV'S INEQUALITY

In the preceding sections, we were working with sample statistics where the shape of the distribution was known. Amazingly, even if we do not know the entire distribution of a random variable, we can form a confidence interval, as long as we know the variance of the variable. For a random variable, $X$, with a standard deviation of $\sigma$, the probability that $X$ is within $n$ standard deviations of $\mu$ is less than or equal to $1/n^2$:

$$P[|X - \mu| \geq n\sigma] \leq \frac{1}{n^2} \qquad (7.14)$$

This is a result of what is known as Chebyshev's inequality.

For a given level of variance, Chebyshev's inequality places an upper limit on the probability of a variable being more than a certain distance from its mean. For a given distribution, the actual probability may be considerably less. Take, for example, a standard normal variable. Chebyshev's inequality tells us that the probability of being greater than two standard deviations from the mean is less than or equal to 25%. The exact probability for a standard normal variable is closer to 5%, which is indeed less than 25%.

Chebyshev's inequality makes clear how assuming normality can be very anti-conservative. If a variable is normally distributed, the probability of a three standard deviation event is very small, 0.27%. If we assume normality, we will assume that three standard deviation events are very rare. For other distributions, though, Chebyshev's inequality tells us that the probability could be as high as ⅑, or approximately 11%. Eleven percent is hardly a rare occurrence. Assuming normality when a random variable is in fact not normal can lead to a severe underestimation of risk. Risk managers take note!

## APPLICATION: VaR

Value at risk (VaR) is one of the most widely used risk measures in finance. VaR was popularized by J.P. Morgan in the 1990s. The executives at J.P. Morgan wanted their risk managers to generate one statistic at the end of each day, which summarized the risk of the firm's entire portfolio. What they came up with was VaR.

If the 95% VaR of a portfolio is $400, then we expect the portfolio will lose $400 or less in 95% of the scenarios, and lose more than $400 in 5% of the scenarios. We can define VaR for any confidence level, but 95% has become an extremely popular choice in finance. The time horizon also needs to be specified for VaR. On trading desks, with liquid portfolios, it is common to measure the one-day 95% VaR. In other settings, in which less liquid assets may be involved, time frames of up to one year are not uncommon. VaR is decidedly a one-tailed confidence interval.

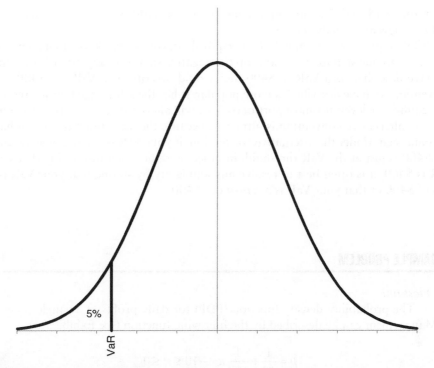

**EXHIBIT 7.2**　Example of 95% Value at Risk

If an actual loss equals or exceeds the predicted VaR threshold, that event is known as an exceedance. Another way to explain VaR is to say that for a one-day 95% VaR, the probability of an exceedance event on any given day is 5%.

Exhibit 7.2 provides a graphical representation of VaR at the 95% confidence level. The exhibit shows the probability density function for the returns of a portfolio. Because VaR is being measured at the 95% confidence level, 5% of the distribution is to the left of the VaR level, and 95% is to the right.

In order to formally define VaR, we begin by defining a random variable $L$, which represents the loss to our portfolio. $L$ is simply the negative of the return to our portfolio. If the return of our portfolio is –$600, then the loss, $L$, is +$600. For a given confidence level, $\gamma$, then, we can define value at risk as:

$$P\left[L \geq \text{VaR}_\gamma\right] = 1 - \gamma \qquad (7.15)$$

If a risk manager says that the one-day 95% VaR of a portfolio is $400, this means that there is a 5% probability that the portfolio will *lose* $400 or more on any given day (that $L$ will be more than $400).

We can also define VaR directly in terms of returns. If we multiply both sides of the inequality in Equation 7.15 by –1, and replace –$L$ with $R$, we come up with Equation 7.16:

$$P\left[R \leq -\text{VaR}_\gamma\right] = 1 - \gamma \qquad (7.16)$$

Equations 7.15 and 7.16 are equivalent. A loss of $400 or more and a return of –$400 or less are exactly the same.

While Equations 7.15 and 7.16 are equivalent, you should know that some risk managers go one step further and drop the negative sign from Equation 7.16. What we have described as a VaR of $400 they would describe as a VaR of –$400. The convention we have described is more popular. It has the advantage that for reasonable confidence levels for most portfolios, VaR will almost always be a positive number. The alternative convention is attractive because the VaR and returns will have the same sign. Under the alternative convention, if your VaR is –$400, then a return of –$400 is just at the VaR threshold. In practice, rather than just saying that your VaR is $400, it is often best to resolve any ambiguity by stating that your VaR is a *loss* of $400 or that your VaR is a *return* of –$400.

## SAMPLE PROBLEM

*Question:*

The probability density function (PDF) for daily profits at Triangle Asset Management can be described by the following function (see Exhibit 7.3):

$$p = \frac{1}{10} + \frac{1}{100}\pi \quad -10 \leq \pi \leq 0$$

$$p = \frac{1}{10} - \frac{1}{100}\pi \quad 0 < \pi \leq 10$$

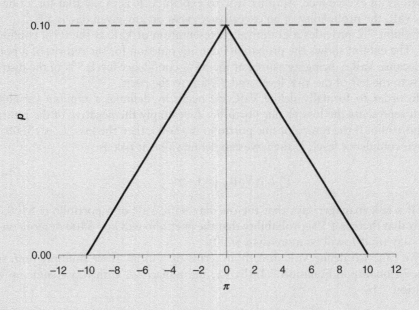

**EXHIBIT 7.3** Triangular Probability Density Function

What is the one-day 95% VaR for Triangle Asset Management?

*Answer:*
To find the 95% VaR, we need to find $a$, such that:

$$\int_{-10}^{a} pd\pi = 0.05$$

By inspection, half the distribution is below zero, so we need only bother with the first half of the function:

$$\int_{-10}^{a} \left( \frac{1}{10} + \frac{1}{100}\pi \right) d\pi = \left[ \frac{1}{10}\pi + \frac{1}{200}\pi^2 \right]_{-10}^{a}$$

$$\int_{-10}^{a} \left( \frac{1}{10} + \frac{1}{100}\pi \right) d\pi = \frac{1}{10}a + \frac{1}{200}a^2 + 0.50 = 0.05$$

$$a^2 + 20a + 90 = 0$$

Using the quadratic formula, we can solve for $a$:

$$a = \frac{-20 \pm \sqrt{400 - 4 \cdot 90}}{2} = -10 \pm \sqrt{10}$$

Because the distribution is not defined for $\pi < -10$, we can ignore the negative, giving us the final answer:

$$a = -10 + \sqrt{10} = -6.84$$

The one-day 95% VaR for Triangle Asset Management is a loss of 6.84.

## Backtesting

An obvious concern when using VaR is choosing the appropriate confidence interval. As mentioned, 95% has become a very popular choice in risk management. In some settings there may be a natural choice for the confidence level, but most of the time the exact choice is arbitrary.

A common mistake for newcomers is to choose a confidence level that is too high. Naturally, a higher confidence level sounds more conservative. A risk manager who measures one-day VaR at the 95% confidence level will, on average, experience an exceedance event every 20 days. A risk manager who measures VaR at the 99.9% confidence level expects to see an exceedance only once every 1,000 days. Is an event that happens once every 20 days really something that we need to worry about? It is tempting to believe that the risk manager using the 99.9% confidence level is concerned with more serious, riskier outcomes, and is therefore doing a better job.

The problem is that, as we go further and further out into the tail of the distribution, we become less and less certain of the shape of the distribution. In most cases, the assumed distribution of returns for our portfolio will be based on historical data. If we have 1,000 data points, then there are 50 data points to back up our 95% confidence level, but only one to back up our 99.9% confidence level. As with any distribution parameter, the variance of our estimate of the parameter decreases with the sample size. One data point is hardly a good sample size on which to base a parameter estimate.

A related problem has to do with backtesting. Good risk managers should regularly backtest their models. Backtesting entails checking the predicted outcome of a model against actual data. Any model parameter can be backtested.

In the case of VaR, backtesting is easy. As we saw in a problem at the end of Chapter 4, when assessing a VaR model, each period can be viewed as a Bernoulli trial. In the case of one-day 95% VaR, there is a 5% chance of an exceedance event each day, and a 95% chance that there is no exceedance. Because exceedance events are independent, over the course of $n$ days the distribution of exceedances follows a binomial distribution:

$$P[K = k] = \binom{n}{k} p^k (1 - p)^{n-k} \tag{7.17}$$

Here, $n$ is the number of periods that we are using in our backtest, $k$ is the number of exceedances, and $(1 - p)$ is our confidence level.

---

**SAMPLE PROBLEM**

*Question:*
    As a risk manager, you are tasked with calculating a daily 95% VaR statistic for a large fixed income portfolio. Over the past 100 days, there have been four exceedances. How many exceedances should you have expected? What was the probability of exactly four exceedances during this time? The probability of four or less? Four or more?

*Answer:*
    Over 100 days we would expect to see five exceedances: $(1 - 95\%) \times 100 = 5$. The probability of exactly four exceedances is 17.81%:

$$P[K = 4] = \binom{100}{4} 0.05^4 (1 - 0.05)^{100-4} = 0.1781$$

    Remember, by convention, for a 95% VaR the probability of an exceedance is 5%, not 95%.

    The probability of four or fewer exceedances is 43.60%. Here we simply do the same calculation as in the first part of the problem, but for zero, one, two, three, and four exceedances. It's important not to forget zero:

$$P[K \leq 4] = \sum_{k=0}^{4} \binom{100}{k} 0.05^k (1 - 0.05)^{100-k}$$

$$P[K \leq 4] = 0.0059 + 0.0312 + 0.0812 + 0.1396 + 0.1781$$

$$P[K \leq 4] = 0.4360$$

For the final result, we could use the brute force approach and calculate the probability for $k = 4, 5, 6, \ldots, 99, 100$, a total of 97 calculations. Instead we realize that the sum of all probabilities from 0 to 100 must be 100%; therefore, if the probability of $K \leq 4$ is 43.60%, then the probability of $K > 4$ must be $100\% - 43.60\% = 56.40\%$. Be careful, though, as what we want is the probability for $K \geq 4$. To get this, we simply add the probability that $K = 4$, from the first part of our question, to get the final answer, 74.21%:

$$P[K \geq 4] = P[K > 4] + P[K = 4]$$

$$P[K \geq 4] = 0.5640 + 0.1781 = 0.7412$$

The probability of a VaR exceedance should be conditionally independent of all available information at the time the forecast is made. In other words, if we are calculating the 95% VaR for a portfolio, then the probability of an exceedance should always be 5%. The probability shouldn't be different because today is Tuesday, because it was sunny yesterday, or because your firm has been having a good month. Importantly, the probability should not vary because there was an exceedance the previous day, or because risk levels are elevated.

A common problem with VaR models in practice is that exceedances often end up being serially correlated. When exceedances are serially correlated, you are more likely to see another exceedance in the period immediately after an exceedance than expected. To test for serial correlation in exceedances, we can look at the periods immediately following any exceedance events. The number of exceedances in these periods should also follow a binomial distribution. For example, pretend we are calculating the one-day 95% VaR for a portfolio, and we observed 40 exceedances over the past 800 days. To test for serial correlation in the exceedances, we look at the 40 days immediately following the exceedance events, and count how many of those were also exceedances. In other words, we count the number of back-to-back exceedances. Because we are calculating VaR at the 95% confidence level, of the 40 day-after days, we would expect that 2 of them, $5\% \times 40 = 2$, would also be exceedances. The actual number of these day-after exceedances should follow a binomial distribution with $n = 40$ and $p = 5\%$.

Another common problem with VaR models in practice is that exceedances tend to be correlated with the level of risk. It may seem counterintuitive, but we should be no more or less likely to see VaR exceedances in years when market volatility is high compared to when it is low. Positive correlation between exceedances and risk levels can happen when a model does not react quickly enough to changes in risk levels. Negative correlation can happen when model windows are too short. To test for correlation between exceedances and the level of risk, we can divide our exceedances into two or more buckets, based on the level of risk. As an example, pretend we have been calculating the one-day 95% VaR for a portfolio over the past 800 days. We divide the sample period in two, placing the 400 days with the highest forecasted VaR in one bucket and the 400 days with the lowest forecasted VaR in the other. After sorting the days, we would expect each 400-day bucket to contain 20 exceedances: $5\% \times 400 = 20$. The actual number of exceedances in each bucket should follow a binomial distribution with $n = 400$, and $p = 5\%$.

## Subadditivity

There is a reason VaR has become so popular in risk management. The appeal of VaR is its simplicity. Because VaR can be calculated for any portfolio, it allows us to easily compare the risk of different portfolios. Because it boils risk down to a single number, VaR provides us with a convenient way to track the risk of a portfolio over time. Finally, the concept of VaR is intuitive, even to those not versed in statistics.

Because it is so popular, VaR has come under a lot of criticism. The criticism generally falls into one of three categories.

At a very high level, financial institutions have been criticized for being overly reliant on VaR. This is not so much a criticism of VaR as it is a criticism of financial institutions for trying to make risk too simple.

At the other end of the spectrum, many experts have criticized how VaR is measured in practice. This is not so much a criticism of VaR as it is a criticism of specific implementations of VaR. For example, in the early days of finance it was popular to make what is known as a delta-normal assumption. That is, when measuring VaR, you would assume that all asset returns were normally distributed, and that all options could be approximated by their delta exposures. Further, the relationship between assets was based entirely on a covariance matrix (no coskewness or cokurtosis). These assumptions made calculating VaR very easy, even for large portfolios, but the results were often disappointing. As computing power became cheaper and more widespread, this approach quickly fell out of favor. Today VaR models can be extremely complex, but many people outside of risk management still remember when delta-normal was the standard approach, and mistakenly believe that this is a fundamental shortcoming of VaR.

In between, there are more sophisticated criticisms. One such criticism is that VaR is not a subadditive risk measure. It is generally accepted that a logical risk measure should have certain properties; see, for example, Artzner, Delbaen, Eber, and Heath (1999). One such property is known as subadditivity. Subadditivity is basically a fancy way of saying that diversification is good, and a good risk measure should reflect that.

Assume that our risk measure is a function $f$ that takes as its input a random variable representing an asset or portfolio of assets. Higher values of the risk measure are associated with greater risk. If we have two risky portfolios, $X$ and $Y$, then $f$ is said to be subadditive if:

$$f(X + Y) \leq f(X) + f(Y) \tag{7.18}$$

In other words, the risk of the combined portfolio, $X + Y$, is less than or equal to the sum of the risks of the separate portfolios. Variance and standard deviation are subadditive risk measures.

While there is a lot to recommend VaR, unfortunately it does not always satisfy the requirement of subadditivity. The following example demonstrates a violation of subadditivity.

## SAMPLE PROBLEM

*Question:*
Imagine a portfolio with two bonds, each with a 4% probability of defaulting. Assume that default events are uncorrelated and that the recovery rate of both bonds is 0%. If a bond defaults, it is worth $0; if it does not, it is worth $100. What is the 95% VaR of each bond separately? What is the 95% VaR of the bond portfolio?

*Answer:*
For each bond separately, the 95% VaR is $0. For an individual bond, in (over) 95% of scenarios, there is no loss.

In the combined portfolio, however, there are three possibilities, with the following probabilities:

| $P[x]$ | $x$ |
|--------|--------|
| 0.16% | -$200 |
| 7.68% | -$100 |
| 92.16% | $0 |

As we can easily see, there are no defaults in only 92.16% of the scenarios, $(1 - 4\%)^2 = 92.16\%$. In the other 7.84% of scenarios, the loss is greater than or equal to $100. The 95% VaR of the portfolio is therefore $100.

For this portfolio, VaR is not subadditive. Because the VaR of the combined portfolio is greater than the sum of the VaRs of the separate portfolios, VaR seems to suggest that there is no diversification benefit, even though the bonds are uncorrelated. It seems to suggest that holding $200 of either bond would be less risky than holding a portfolio with $100 of each. Clearly this is not correct.

This example makes clear that when assets have payout functions that are discontinuous near the VaR critical level, we are likely to have problems with subadditivity. By the same token, if the payout functions of the assets in a portfolio are continuous, then VaR will be subadditive. In many settings this is not an onerous assumption. In between, we have large, diverse portfolios, which contain some assets with discontinuous payout functions. For these portfolios subadditivity will likely be only a minor issue.

### Expected Shortfall

Another criticism of VaR is that it does not tell us anything about the tail of the distribution. Two portfolios could have the exact same 95% VaR but very different distributions beyond the 95% confidence level.

More than VaR, then, what we really want to know is how big the loss will be when we have an exceedance event. Using the concept of conditional probability, we can define the expected value of a loss, given an exceedance, as follows:

$$E[L \mid L \geq \text{VaR}_\gamma] = S \tag{7.19}$$

We refer to this conditional expected loss, $S$, as the expected shortfall.

If the profit function has a probability density function given by $f(x)$, and VaR is the VaR at the $\gamma$ confidence level, we can find the expected shortfall as:

$$S = -\frac{1}{1-\gamma} \int_{-\infty}^{\text{VaR}} x f(x) dx \tag{7.20}$$

As with VaR, we have defined expected shortfall in terms of losses. Just as VaR tends to be positive for reasonable confidence levels for most portfolios, expected shortfall, as we have defined it in Equation 7.20, will also tend to positive. As with VaR, this convention is not universal, and risk managers should be careful to avoid ambiguity when quoting expected shortfall numbers.

Expected shortfall does answer an important question. What's more, expected shortfall turns out to be subadditive, thereby avoiding one of the major criticisms of VaR. As our discussion on backtesting suggests, though, because it is concerned with the tail of the distribution, the reliability of our expected shortfall measure may be difficult to gauge.

---

### SAMPLE PROBLEM

*Question:*

In a previous example, the probability density function of Triangle Asset Management's daily profits could be described by the following function:

$$p = \frac{1}{10} + \frac{1}{100}\pi \quad -10 \leq \pi \leq 0$$

$$p = \frac{1}{10} - \frac{1}{100}\pi \quad 0 < \pi \leq 10$$

The PDF is also shown in Exhibit 7.4. We calculated Triangle's one-day 95% VaR as a loss of $(10 - \sqrt{10}) = 6.84$. For the same confidence level and time horizon, what is the expected shortfall?

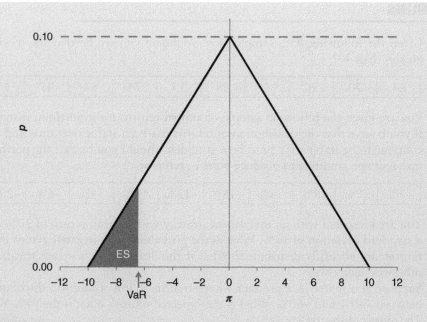

**EXHIBIT 7.4** Triangular PDF, VaR, and Expected Shortfall

*Answer:*

Because the VaR occurs in the region where $\pi < 0$, we need to utilize only the first half of the function. Using Equation 7.20, we have:

$$S = \frac{1}{0.05} \int_{-10}^{\mathrm{VaR}} \pi p \, d\pi = 20 \int_{-10}^{\mathrm{VaR}} \pi \left( \frac{1}{10} + \frac{1}{100} \pi \right) d\pi$$

$$S = \int_{-10}^{\mathrm{VaR}} \left( 2\pi + \frac{\pi^2}{5} \right) d\pi = \left[ \pi^2 + \frac{1}{15} \pi^3 \right]_{-10}^{\mathrm{VaR}}$$

$$S = \left( \left( -10 + \sqrt{10} \right)^2 + \frac{1}{15} \left( -10 + \sqrt{10} \right)^3 \right) - \left( (-10)^2 + \frac{1}{15} (-10)^3 \right)$$

$$S = -10 + \frac{2}{3} \sqrt{10} = -7.89$$

Thus, the expected shortfall is a loss of 7.89. Intuitively this should make sense. The expected shortfall must be greater than the VaR, 6.84, but less than the maximum loss of 10. Because extreme events are less likely (the height of the PDF decreases away from the center), it also makes sense that the expected shortfall is closer to the VaR than it is to the maximum loss.

## PROBLEMS

1. Given the following data sample, how confident can we be that the mean is greater than 40?

| 64 | 70 | 20 | 3 | 58 | 13 | 74 | 84 | 47 | 17 |

2. You are given the following sample of annual returns for a portfolio manager. If you believe that the distribution of returns has been stable over time and will continue to be stable over time, how confident should you be that the portfolio manager will continue to produce positive returns?

| –7% | 7% | 19% | 23% | –18% | –12% | 49% | 34% | –6% | –20% |

3. You are presented with an investment strategy with a mean return of 20% and a standard deviation of 10%. What is the probability of a negative return if the returns are normally distributed? What if the distribution is symmetrical, but otherwise unknown?

4. Suppose you invest in a product whose returns follow a uniform distribution between –40% and +60%. What is the expected return? What is the 95% VaR? The expected shortfall?

5. You are the risk manager for a portfolio with a mean daily return of 0.40% and a daily standard deviation of 2.3%. Assume the returns are normally distributed (not a good assumption to make, in general). What is the 95% VaR?

6. You are told that the log annual returns of a commodities index are normally distributed with a standard deviation of 40%. You have 33 years of data, from which you calculate the sample variance. What is the standard deviation of this estimate of the sample variance?

7. In the previous question, you were told that the *actual* standard deviation was 40%. If, instead of 40%, the measured standard deviation turns out to be 50%, how confident can you be in the initial assumption? State a null hypothesis and calculate the corresponding probability.

8. A hedge fund targets a mean annual return of 15% with a 10% standard deviation. Last year, the fund returned –5%. What is the probability of a result this bad or worse happening, given the target mean and standard deviation? Assume the distribution is symmetrical.

9. A fund of funds has investments in 36 hedge funds. At the end of the year, the mean return of the constituent hedge funds was 18%. The standard deviation of the funds' returns was 12%. The benchmark return for the fund of funds was 14%. Is the difference between the average return and the benchmark return statistically significant at the 95% confidence level?

10. The probability density function for daily profits at Box Asset Management can be described by the following function (see Exhibit 7.5):

$$p = \frac{1}{200} \quad -100 \le \pi \le 100$$
$$p = 0 \quad -100 > \pi > 100$$

What is the one-day 95% VaR of Box Asset Management?

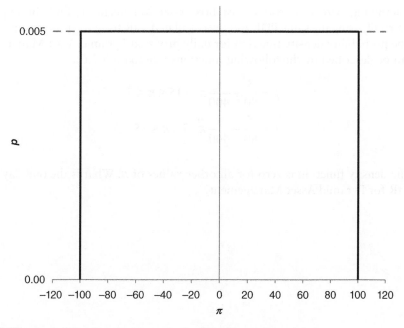

**EXHIBIT 7.5**   Probability Density Function for Box Asset Management

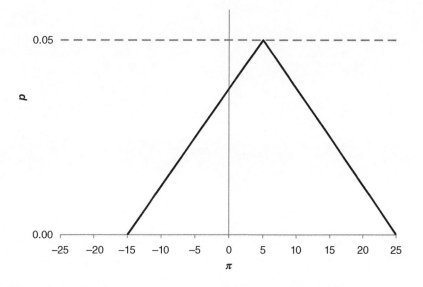

**EXHIBIT 7.6**   Probability Density Function for Pyramid Asset Management

11. Continuing with our example of Box Asset Management, find the expected shortfall, using the same PDF and the calculated VaR from the previous question.

12. The probability density function for daily profits at Pyramid Asset Management can be described by the following functions (see Exhibit 7.6):

$$p = \frac{3}{80} + \frac{1}{400}\pi \quad -15 \leq \pi \leq 5$$

$$p = \frac{5}{80} - \frac{1}{400}\pi \quad 5 < \pi \leq 25$$

The density function is zero for all other values of $\pi$. What is the one-day 95% VaR for Pyramid Asset Management?

## CHAPTER 8

# Matrix Algebra

**T**his chapter starts with a brief review of matrix notation and operations. We then explore the application of matrix algebra to risk management.

## MATRIX NOTATION

A matrix is a two-dimensional array of numbers, or variables. By convention, the size of a matrix is denoted by the number of rows, and then by the number of columns. For example, the following is a $3 \times 2$ matrix (pronounced "three by two"):

$$\mathbf{A} = \begin{bmatrix} 3 & 5 \\ -9 & 3 \\ 10 & 8 \end{bmatrix} \tag{8.1}$$

Matrices with only one column are also known as vectors. The following is a $4 \times 1$ vector:

$$\mathbf{b} = \begin{bmatrix} 43 \\ 17 \\ -56 \\ 64 \end{bmatrix} \tag{8.2}$$

In matrix algebra, we typically refer to ordinary real numbers or variables as scalars. The elements of matrices $\mathbf{A}$ and $\mathbf{b}$ shown here are all scalars. Traditionally, as here, matrices are denoted by bold letters. Matrices with more than one column are designated by bold capital letters, whereas vectors (i.e., one-column matrices) are designated by bold lowercase letters. Scalars, including the elements of a matrix, are denoted by nonbold lowercase letters.

The various elements of a matrix are differentiated by subscripts, which indicate first the row and then the column of the element. For example:

$$\mathbf{C} = \begin{bmatrix} c_{1,1} & c_{1,2} \\ c_{2,1} & c_{2,2} \end{bmatrix} \tag{8.3}$$

In the case of a vector like **b**, if it does not cause any ambiguity, we often just use a single subscript for each of the elements:

$$\mathbf{b} = \begin{bmatrix} b_1 \\ b_2 \\ b_3 \\ b_4 \end{bmatrix} \tag{8.4}$$

Matrices like **C** with the same number of rows and columns are known as square matrices. The main diagonal of a square matrix consists of the entries running down the diagonal from the top-left corner to the bottom-right corner. In other words, all the entries $x_{i,j}$, where $i = j$. If all of the entries above the main diagonal are zero, then a matrix is said to be a lower triangular matrix. The following is a $3 \times 3$ lower triangular matrix:

$$\mathbf{L} = \begin{bmatrix} l_{1,1} & 0 & 0 \\ l_{2,1} & l_{2,2} & 0 \\ l_{3,1} & l_{3,2} & l_{3,3} \end{bmatrix} \tag{8.5}$$

Similarly, a matrix in which all of the entries below the main diagonal are zero is said to be an upper triangular matrix. The following is a $3 \times 3$ upper diagonal matrix:

$$\mathbf{U} = \begin{bmatrix} u_{1,1} & u_{1,2} & u_{1,3} \\ 0 & u_{2,2} & u_{2,3} \\ 0 & 0 & u_{3,3} \end{bmatrix} \tag{8.6}$$

If all of the entries both above and below the main diagonal are zero, then the matrix is said to be diagonal. The following are all diagonal matrices:

$$\begin{bmatrix} 15 & 0 & 0 \\ 0 & -9 & 0 \\ 0 & 0 & 2 \end{bmatrix} \quad \begin{bmatrix} 5.6 & 0 \\ 0 & 23.9 \end{bmatrix} \quad \begin{bmatrix} 47 & 0 & 0 \\ 0 & 0 & 0 \\ 0 & 0 & 3 \end{bmatrix} \tag{8.7}$$

## MATRIX OPERATIONS

The following sections introduce some basic matrix operations. Just as we can add, subtract, and multiply scalars, we can also add, subtract, and multiply matrices. We rarely talk about matrix division, but there is inversion, which is analogous. Finally, there are operations, such as transposition, that are unique to matrices.

### Addition and Subtraction

To add two matrices together, we simply add the corresponding elements in each matrix together. Matrix addition can occur only between matrices with the same number of rows and columns. As an example, suppose we have two matrices, **D** and **E**:

$$D = \begin{bmatrix} 32 & 51 \\ -10 & 0 \end{bmatrix} \quad E = \begin{bmatrix} 25 & -21 \\ 3 & 14 \end{bmatrix} \tag{8.8}$$

We could add them together as follows:

$$D + E = \begin{bmatrix} (d_{1,1} + e_{1,1}) & (d_{1,2} + e_{1,2}) \\ (d_{2,1} + e_{2,1}) & (d_{2,2} + e_{2,2}) \end{bmatrix} = \begin{bmatrix} 57 & 30 \\ -7 & 14 \end{bmatrix} \tag{8.9}$$

Matrix addition is commutative; that is, the order of the matrices does not matter when we are adding:

$$D + E = E + D \tag{8.10}$$

Matrix addition is also associative. If we want to add together more than two matrices, the order in which we carry out the addition is not important. Given three matrices, **D**, **E**, and **F**, all the same size:

$$D + (E + F) = (D + E) + F \tag{8.11}$$

In other words, we can add **E** and **F** together first, and then add the result to **D**, or we can add **D** and **E** first and add that to **F**. The result is the same.

We can also multiply a matrix by a scalar. The result is a new matrix, the same size as the original, but with all the elements multiplied by the scalar value. Using the matrix **A**, from before, and a scalar, s = 10:

$$sA = 10 \begin{bmatrix} 3 & 5 \\ -9 & 3 \\ 10 & 8 \end{bmatrix} = \begin{bmatrix} 30 & 50 \\ -90 & 30 \\ 100 & 80 \end{bmatrix} \tag{8.12}$$

To subtract one matrix from another matrix, we simply subtract the corresponding elements in each matrix. Again the matrices must be of the same size. Using our matrices **D** and **E**:

$$D - E = \begin{bmatrix} 32 & 51 \\ -10 & 0 \end{bmatrix} - \begin{bmatrix} 25 & -21 \\ 3 & 14 \end{bmatrix}$$

$$D - E = \begin{bmatrix} 32 - 25 & 51 + 21 \\ -10 - 3 & 0 - 14 \end{bmatrix} \tag{8.13}$$

$$D - E = \begin{bmatrix} 7 & 72 \\ -13 & -14 \end{bmatrix}$$

Subtraction is equivalent to adding a matrix to a second matrix multiplied by $-1$. It's slightly more complicated, but we get the same result:

$$\mathbf{D} - \mathbf{E} = \begin{bmatrix} 32 & 51 \\ -10 & 0 \end{bmatrix} + (-1) \begin{bmatrix} 25 & -21 \\ 3 & 14 \end{bmatrix}$$

$$\mathbf{D} - \mathbf{E} = \begin{bmatrix} 32 & 51 \\ -10 & 0 \end{bmatrix} + \begin{bmatrix} -25 & 21 \\ -3 & -14 \end{bmatrix} \tag{8.14}$$

$$\mathbf{D} - \mathbf{E} = \begin{bmatrix} 7 & 72 \\ -13 & -14 \end{bmatrix}$$

Because matrix subtraction can also be turned into matrix addition, matrix subtraction is also commutative and associative.

## Multiplication

We can also multiply two matrices together. In order to multiply two matrices together, the number of columns in the first matrix must be equal to the number of rows in the second matrix. The resulting matrix has the same number of rows as the first matrix and the same number of columns as the second. For example, the product of a $3 \times 2$ matrix and a $2 \times 5$ matrix is a $3 \times 5$ matrix. To determine each entry in the new matrix, we multiply the corresponding elements from the same row in the first matrix by the corresponding elements in the same column in the second matrix. For example, for the following matrices, $\mathbf{G}$ and $\mathbf{H}$, to get the first element of the product matrix, $\mathbf{J} = \mathbf{GH}$, we go across the first row of $\mathbf{G}$ and down the first column of $\mathbf{H}$:

$$\mathbf{G} = \begin{bmatrix} 6 & 1 \\ 9 & 5 \end{bmatrix} \quad \mathbf{H} = \begin{bmatrix} 2 & 3 \\ 8 & 4 \end{bmatrix}$$

$$\mathbf{J} = \mathbf{GH} = \begin{bmatrix} 6 & 1 \\ 9 & 5 \end{bmatrix}\begin{bmatrix} 2 & 3 \\ 8 & 4 \end{bmatrix} = \begin{bmatrix} 6 \cdot 2 + 1 \cdot 8 & ? \\ ? & ? \end{bmatrix} = \begin{bmatrix} 20 & ? \\ ? & ? \end{bmatrix} \tag{8.15}$$

Similarly, to get the first entry in the second row, we go across the second row of $\mathbf{G}$ and down the first column of $\mathbf{H}$:

$$\mathbf{GJ} = \mathbf{GH} = \begin{bmatrix} 6 & 1 \\ 9 & 5 \end{bmatrix}\begin{bmatrix} 2 & 3 \\ 8 & 4 \end{bmatrix} = \begin{bmatrix} 6 \cdot 2 + 1 \cdot 8 & ? \\ 9 \cdot 2 + 5 \cdot 8 & ? \end{bmatrix} = \begin{bmatrix} 20 & ? \\ 58 & ? \end{bmatrix} \tag{8.16}$$

To get the second entry in the first row, we go across the first row of $\mathbf{G}$ and down the second column of $\mathbf{H}$:

$$\mathbf{J} = \mathbf{GH} = \begin{bmatrix} 6 & 1 \\ 9 & 5 \end{bmatrix}\begin{bmatrix} 2 & 3 \\ 8 & 4 \end{bmatrix} = \begin{bmatrix} 6 \cdot 2 + 1 \cdot 8 & 6 \cdot 3 + 1 \cdot 4 \\ 9 \cdot 2 + 5 \cdot 8 & ? \end{bmatrix} = \begin{bmatrix} 20 & 22 \\ 58 & ? \end{bmatrix} \tag{8.17}$$

Finally, to get the last entry in **J**, we go across the second row of **G**, and down the second column of **H**:

$$\mathbf{J} = \begin{bmatrix} 6 & 1 \\ 9 & 5 \end{bmatrix}\begin{bmatrix} 2 & 3 \\ 8 & 4 \end{bmatrix} = \begin{bmatrix} 6\cdot2+1\cdot8 & 6\cdot3+1\cdot4 \\ 9\cdot2+5\cdot8 & 9\cdot3+5\cdot4 \end{bmatrix} = \begin{bmatrix} 20 & 22 \\ 58 & 47 \end{bmatrix} \tag{8.18}$$

More formally, for the entry in **J** in the $i$th row and $j$th column, $j_{i,j}$, we have:

$$j_{i,j} = \sum_{k=1}^{2} g_{i,k} h_{k,j} \tag{8.19}$$

We can generalize this to larger matrices. Assuming **G** is $m \times n$ and **H** is $n \times p$, we would obtain an $m \times p$ matrix **J** = **GH**, as follows:

$$\mathbf{GH} = \begin{bmatrix} g_{1,1} & g_{1,2} & \cdots & g_{1,n} \\ g_{2,1} & g_{2,2} & \cdots & g_{2,n} \\ \vdots & \vdots & \ddots & \vdots \\ g_{m,1} & g_{m,2} & \cdots & g_{m,n} \end{bmatrix}\begin{bmatrix} h_{1,1} & h_{1,2} & \cdots & h_{1,p} \\ h_{2,1} & h_{2,2} & \cdots & h_{2,p} \\ \vdots & \vdots & \ddots & \vdots \\ h_{n,1} & h_{n,2} & \cdots & h_{n,p} \end{bmatrix}$$

$$\mathbf{GH} = \begin{bmatrix} \sum_{i=1}^{n} g_{1,i}h_{i,1} & \sum_{i=1}^{n} g_{1,i}h_{i,2} & \cdots & \sum_{i=1}^{n} g_{1,i}h_{i,p} \\ \sum_{i=1}^{n} g_{2,i}h_{i,1} & \sum_{i=1}^{n} g_{2,i}h_{i,2} & \cdots & \sum_{i=1}^{n} g_{2,i}h_{i,p} \\ \vdots & \vdots & \ddots & \vdots \\ \sum_{i=1}^{n} g_{m,i}h_{i,1} & \sum_{i=1}^{n} g_{m,i}h_{i,2} & \cdots & \sum_{i=1}^{n} g_{m,i}h_{i,p} \end{bmatrix} \tag{8.20}$$

As with matrix addition, matrix multiplication is associative. If we have three matrices of the appropriate size, **G**, **H**, and **J**, it does not matter if we multiply **H** and **J** together first or multiply **G** and **H** together first. That is:

$$\mathbf{G(HJ)} = \mathbf{(GH)J} \tag{8.21}$$

Be careful, though; unlike matrix addition or scalar multiplication, the *order* of matrix multiplication does matter. Matrix multiplication is not commutative.

$$\mathbf{GH} \neq \mathbf{HG} \tag{8.22}$$

Clearly, this is true for matrices that are of different size. We can multiply a $10 \times 5$ matrix by a $5 \times 6$ matrix, but if we try to reverse the order and multiply a $5 \times 6$ matrix by a $10 \times 5$ matrix, the number of columns and rows will not match. Even if the matrices are square and we can reverse the order of multiplication, the result will not necessarily be the same.

## SAMPLE PROBLEM

*Question:*
   Given the following matrices **M** and **N**, find the products **MN** and **NM**:

$$\mathbf{M} = \begin{bmatrix} 3 & 5 \\ 9 & 8 \end{bmatrix} \quad \mathbf{N} = \begin{bmatrix} 2 & 6 \\ 1 & 5 \end{bmatrix}$$

*Answer:*

$$\mathbf{MN} = \begin{bmatrix} 3 \cdot 2 + 5 \cdot 1 & 3 \cdot 6 + 5 \cdot 5 \\ 9 \cdot 2 + 8 \cdot 1 & 9 \cdot 6 + 8 \cdot 5 \end{bmatrix} = \begin{bmatrix} 11 & 43 \\ 26 & 94 \end{bmatrix}$$

$$\mathbf{NM} = \begin{bmatrix} 2 \cdot 3 + 6 \cdot 9 & 2 \cdot 5 + 6 \cdot 8 \\ 1 \cdot 3 + 5 \cdot 9 & 1 \cdot 5 + 5 \cdot 8 \end{bmatrix} = \begin{bmatrix} 60 & 58 \\ 48 & 45 \end{bmatrix}$$

As you might have guessed, in this case, **MN** does not equal **NM**.

Because a square matrix has the same number of rows and columns, a square matrix can always be multiplied by itself. Because the resulting matrix has the same dimensions, we can multiply the resulting product matrix by the original square matrix. We can continue doing this as many times as we want. Just as with scalars, we denote this repeated multiplication, or exponentiation, with an exponent:

$$\mathbf{MM} = \mathbf{M}^2$$
$$\mathbf{MMM} = \mathbf{M}^3 \tag{8.23}$$
$$\vdots$$

There is a distributive law for matrix multiplication, too. Assuming the matrices are of the correct size, we have:

$$\mathbf{F(D + E)} = \mathbf{FD + FE}$$
$$(\mathbf{M + N})\mathbf{P} = \mathbf{MP + NP} \tag{8.24}$$

Because multiplication is involved, it is important that we have preserved the order of the matrices. In the first line, **F** is always before **D** and **E**, and in the second line, **P** remains after **M** and **N**.

One matrix that comes up again and again in matrix algebra is the identity matrix. The identity matrix is a diagonal matrix with 1's along its main diagonal. An identity matrix with $n$ rows and columns is typically denoted $\mathbf{I}_n$, or simply by **I** if the number or rows and columns can be inferred.

$$\mathbf{I}_2 = \begin{bmatrix} 1 & 0 \\ 0 & 1 \end{bmatrix} \quad \mathbf{I}_3 = \begin{bmatrix} 1 & 0 & 0 \\ 0 & 1 & 0 \\ 0 & 0 & 1 \end{bmatrix} \tag{8.25}$$

When we multiply a matrix by the appropriately sized identity matrix, the result is the original matrix. If we have an $r \times c$ matrix **A**, then:

$$\mathbf{AI}_c = \mathbf{I}_r\mathbf{A} = \mathbf{A} \qquad (8.26)$$

The identity matrix leads us to define the inverse of a matrix. The inverse of a matrix **A** is denoted $\mathbf{A}^{-1}$. If we multiply a matrix by its inverse, we get an identity matrix:

$$\mathbf{AA}^{-1} = \mathbf{A}^{-1}\mathbf{A} = \mathbf{I} \qquad (8.27)$$

### SAMPLE PROBLEM

*Question:*
    The following matrices, **A** and $\mathbf{A}^{-1}$, are inverses of each other. Prove this by showing that the products $\mathbf{AA}^{-1}$ and $\mathbf{A}^{-1}\mathbf{A}$ are both equal to the identity matrix.

$$\mathbf{A} = \begin{bmatrix} 1 & 4 \\ 2 & 9 \end{bmatrix} \quad \mathbf{A}^{-1} = \begin{bmatrix} 9 & -4 \\ -2 & 1 \end{bmatrix}$$

*Answer:*

$$\mathbf{AA}^{-1} = \begin{bmatrix} 1\cdot9 + 4\cdot(-2) & 1\cdot(-4) + 4\cdot1 \\ 2\cdot9 + 9\cdot(-2) & 2\cdot(-4) + 9\cdot1 \end{bmatrix} = \begin{bmatrix} 1 & 0 \\ 0 & 1 \end{bmatrix}$$

$$\mathbf{A}^{-1}\mathbf{A} = \begin{bmatrix} 9\cdot1 + (-4)\cdot2 & 9\cdot4 + (-4)\cdot9 \\ (-2)\cdot1 + 1\cdot2 & -2\cdot4 + 1\cdot9 \end{bmatrix} = \begin{bmatrix} 1 & 0 \\ 0 & 1 \end{bmatrix}$$

In the preceding example, if the inverse matrix hadn't been given to us, how would we calculate it? There are well-established methods for finding the inverse of a matrix. For relatively small matrices, these methods are straightforward, and can often be carried out by hand. For even moderately sized matrices, these methods grow quickly in complexity. Finding the inverse of a $4 \times 4$ matrix by hand might be possible, but it will certainly be tedious. For large matrices, calculating the inverse can be very complex. Because of the potentially large number of steps involved, a simple algorithm is likely to be very slow and susceptible to rounding errors. A good statistics software package will use algorithms that are both accurate and efficient, but often very complex. While both the simple and the complex methods are interesting, in practice most risk management applications will involve large matrices, which will necessitate using a statistics program to calculate inverses. In practice, understanding the properties of a matrix is much more important. Because there is a possibility of rounding error, it never hurts to check the output of a statistical package by making sure that the product of a matrix and the calculated inverse is, in fact, equal to an identity matrix.

It is important to note that not every matrix has an inverse. Take, for example, the following matrix:

$$U = \begin{bmatrix} 1 & 1 \\ 1 & 1 \end{bmatrix} \tag{8.28}$$

There is no matrix with which we can multiply U to get an identity matrix. U has no inverse. While this is easy to see with U, it is not always obvious when matrices are noninvertible.

### Zero Matrix

In addition to the identity matrix, we will often find it convenient to define a zero matrix, where all the entries are zero. We will denote the zero matrix with a bold zero, 0.

The zero matrix has similar properties to its scalar equivalent. First, if we multiply anything by an appropriately sized zero matrix, we get the zero matrix:

$$0A = A0 = 0 \tag{8.29}$$

Second, if we add the zero matrix to anything, we get back the original matrix. Again, assuming the matrices are of the appropriate size:

$$0 + A = A + 0 = A \tag{8.30}$$

Because of this last relationship, some texts refer to 0 as the additive identity matrix, and to I as the multiplicative identity matrix. From here on out, we will refer to 0 as a zero matrix, and continue to refer to I as an identity matrix. The zero matrix is another example of a noninvertible matrix.

### Transpose

The transpose of a matrix can be formed by swapping the columns and rows of the original matrix. For a matrix A, we denote its transpose by A' (pronounced "A prime" or "A transpose").[1] We can easily determine each element of the transpose matrix by reversing the row index and column index of each element of the original matrix:

$$a'_{ij} = a_{ji} \tag{8.31}$$

The following are examples of matrices and their transposes:

$$A = \begin{bmatrix} 3 & 5 \\ -9 & 3 \\ 10 & 8 \end{bmatrix} \quad A' = \begin{bmatrix} 3 & -9 & 10 \\ 5 & 3 & 8 \end{bmatrix}$$

$$M = \begin{bmatrix} 3 & 5 \\ 9 & 8 \end{bmatrix} \quad M' = \begin{bmatrix} 3 & 9 \\ 5 & 8 \end{bmatrix} \tag{8.32}$$

---

[1] Another common way to denote the transpose of a matrix is with a superscript T, as in $A^T$. In finance and economics, the prime notation seems to be more popular, and we will use that convention throughout the rest of the book.

Note that for a square matrix, taking the transpose can be thought of as reflecting the matrix across the main diagonal.

If we reverse the row and column indexes of an element and then reverse them again, we get back our original indexes. This means that if we take the transpose of a transpose, we get back the original matrix:

$$(\mathbf{A}')' = \mathbf{A} \tag{8.33}$$

A square matrix that is equal to its own transpose is said to be symmetrical. The following matrices are both symmetrical:

$$\mathbf{S_1} = \begin{bmatrix} 6 & -7 \\ -7 & 6 \end{bmatrix}$$

$$\mathbf{S_2} = \begin{bmatrix} 9 & 5 & 8 \\ 5 & 3 & -2 \\ 8 & -2 & 14 \end{bmatrix} \tag{8.34}$$

In the second application section, we will work with covariance matrices. Covariance and correlation matrices are examples of symmetrical matrices.

## APPLICATION: TRANSITION MATRICES

A ratings transition matrix provides the probability that a bond's rating will change or stay the same over a given time period, given its rating at the start of the period. At the end of Chapter 2, we looked at the following problem: Given the following one-year ratings transition matrix, what is the probability that a bond that starts with a B rating defaults over two years?

| 1-Year | | To a rating of: | | | |
|---|---|---|---|---|---|
| | | A | B | C | D |
| | A | 90% | 8% | 2% | 0% |
| From a | B | 10% | 80% | 8% | 2% |
| rating of: | C | 0% | 25% | 60% | 15% |
| | D | 0% | 0% | 0% | 100% |

For a bond with a B rating, over the first year the probability of migrating to A is 10%, the probability of staying at B is 80%, the probability of migrating to C is 8%, and the probability of defaulting is 2%. Over two years, there are four ways in which the bond could default: It could migrate to A in the first year and then default; it could remain at B during the first year and then default; it could migrate to C and then default; or it could default the first year and stay defaulted. We can easily calculate each of these probabilities. For example, the probability of migrating from B to C to D is just the probability of migrating from B to C, multiplied by the probability of migrating from C to D, or $8\% \times 15\% = 1.2\%$. The probability of the bond migrating from B to D over two years is just the sum of the probabilities of the four possible paths. The following set of equations shows this calculation, with the final result, 4.80%.

$$P[\text{B}\to\text{D}] = P[\text{B}\to\text{A}\to\text{D}] + P[\text{B}\to\text{B}\to\text{D}] + P[\text{B}\to\text{C}\to\text{D}] + P[\text{B}\to\text{D}\to\text{D}]$$

$$= x_{21}x_{14} \qquad + x_{22}x_{24} \qquad + x_{23}x_{34} \qquad + x_{24}x_{44}$$

$$= 10\% \cdot 0\% \quad + 80\% \cdot 2\% \quad + 8\% \cdot 15\% \quad + 2\% \cdot 100\% = 4.80\%$$

In the second row, we have expressed the problem in terms of our standard matrix notation. Notice that for the first element in each product, we are just going across the second row of the transition matrix, and for the second element in each product we are going down the fourth column. This is exactly what we would do to get the element in the second row and fourth column if we were multiplying the transition matrix by itself. This is no coincidence. It turns out rather conveniently that we can calculate the complete two-year transition matrix by multiplying the one-year transition matrix by itself. If $\mathbf{T}_1$ is our one-year transition matrix, and $\mathbf{T}_2$ is our two-year transition matrix, then:

$$\mathbf{T}_2 = \mathbf{T}_1\mathbf{T}_1 = \mathbf{T}_1^2$$

Interested readers should check this for themselves by calculating additional values for the two-year matrix.

What is even more convenient is that we can generalize this formula. To calculate the $n$-year transition matrix, we simply raise $\mathbf{T}_1$ to the $n$th power:

$$\mathbf{T}_n = \mathbf{T}_1^n$$

The following would be the five-year transition matrix based on the one-year transition matrix:

| 5-Year | | To a rating of: | | | |
|---|---|---|---|---|---|
| | | A | B | C | D |
| | A | 64.7% | 24.8% | 6.7% | 3.7% |
| From a | B | 28.1% | 46.0% | 12.1% | 13.8% |
| rating of: | C | 11.8% | 35.0% | 14.3% | 39.0% |
| | D | 0.0% | 0.0% | 0.0% | 100.0% |

In this example, A-rated bonds have a high probability of maintaining their rating and zero probability of defaulting over one year. Over five years, though, they have a much lower probability of staying at the same rating and a much higher probability of defaulting.

## APPLICATION: MONTE CARLO SIMULATIONS PART II: CHOLESKY DECOMPOSITION

In risk management, it is often useful to generate simulations in which we can specify the covariance between different variables. Imagine that we wanted to create a Monte Carlo simulation of a portfolio containing $N$ stocks. The variance of the portfolio will be a function of the variance of each of the stocks, the position sizes, and the covariances between the stocks. In Chapter 4, we saw how we could create uncorrelated normally distributed random variables. We also saw how we could create two correlated normal variables using linear combinations of uncorrelated normal variables. We can use matrix algebra to extend this approach to a large number of variables.

Imagine that we have $N$ random variables, $X_1, X_2, \ldots, X_N$, representing the returns of different stocks. In order to describe the relationships between each of the variables, we could form an $N \times N$ covariance matrix, where each element, $\sigma_{i,j}$, corresponds to the covariance between the $i$th and $j$th random variables:

$$\Sigma = \begin{bmatrix} \sigma_{1,1} & \sigma_{1,2} & \cdots & \sigma_{1,n} \\ \sigma_{2,1} & \sigma_{2,2} & \cdots & \sigma_{2,n} \\ \vdots & \vdots & \ddots & \vdots \\ \sigma_{n,1} & \sigma_{n,2} & \cdots & \sigma_{n,n} \end{bmatrix} \text{ s.t. } \sigma_{i,j} = E[(X_i - E[X_i])(X_j - E[X_j])] \quad (8.35)$$

Each of the elements along the main diagonal represents the covariance of a random variable with itself, which is simply that variable's variance. For the off-diagonal elements, because $\sigma_{i,j} = \sigma_{j,i}$, the covariance matrix is necessarily symmetrical.

If the covariance matrix satisfies certain minimum requirements, we can decompose the covariance matrix, rewriting it in terms of a lower triangular matrix, $\mathbf{L}$, and its transpose, $\mathbf{L}'$, which is an upper triangular matrix:

$$\Sigma = \mathbf{L}\mathbf{L}' \quad (8.36)$$

This is what is known as a Cholesky decomposition.

It turns out that if we take the matrix $\mathbf{L}$ from our Cholesky decomposition and multiply it by a vector of i.i.d. standard normal variables, we will obtain a new vector of normal variables that satisfy the original covariance matrix, $\Sigma$. To see why this is the case, designate an $N \times 1$ vector of i.i.d. standard normal variables as $\Phi$, and the resulting product as $\mathbf{C}$:

$$\mathbf{L}\Phi = \mathbf{C} \quad (8.37)$$

As with any matrix product, we can write any element of $\mathbf{C}$ as follows:

$$c_i = \sum_{j=1}^{N} l_{i,j}\phi_i \quad (8.38)$$

We can see that the $c_i$'s are normally distributed random variables, because each is a linear combination of independent normal variables; furthermore, it is easy to see that the expected value of each $c_i$ is zero:

$$E[c_i] = E\left[\sum_{m=1}^{N} l_{i,m}\phi_m\right] = \sum_{m=1}^{N} l_{i,m}E[\phi_m] = \sum_{j=1}^{N} l_{i,m} \cdot 0 = 0 \qquad (8.39)$$

For the last step, we were able to set $E[\phi_m]$ equal to zero, since the mean of any standard normal variable is zero by definition.

Now that we have the means of each of the $c_i$'s, we can easily calculate the covariance between any two elements:

$$\text{Cov}[c_i c_j] = E[c_i c_j] - E[c_i]E[c_j] = E[c_i c_j]$$

$$\text{Cov}[c_i c_j] = E\left[\sum_{m=1}^{N} l_{i,m}\phi_m \sum_{n=1}^{N} l_{j,n}\phi_n\right]$$

$$\text{Cov}[c_i c_j] = E\left[\sum_{m=1}^{N} l_{i,m}l_{j,m}\phi_m^2 + \sum_{m=1}^{N}\sum_{n\neq m} l_{i,m}l_{j,n}\phi_m\phi_n\right]$$

$$\text{Cov}[c_i c_k] = \sum_{m=1}^{N} l_{i,m}l_{j,m}E[\phi_m^2] + \sum_{m=1}^{N}\sum_{n\neq m} l_{i,m}l_{j,n}E[\phi_m\phi_n] \qquad (8.40)$$

$$\text{Cov}[c_i c_j] = \sum_{m=1}^{N} l_{i,m}l_{j,m} \cdot 1 + \sum_{m=1}^{N}\sum_{n\neq m} l_{i,m}l_{j,n} \cdot 0$$

$$\text{Cov}[c_i c_k] = \sum_{m=1}^{N} l_{i,m}l_{j,m} = \sigma_{i,k}$$

For the second to last row we relied on the fact that the variance of a standard normal variable is 1, and the covariance between any two i.i.d. variables is, by definition, 0. The last line follows from our initial decomposition of $\Sigma$ into $LL'$.

Given $\Sigma$, how do we go about getting $L$ and $L'$ in the first place, though? Many statistical packages will perform a Cholesky decomposition, and, in practice, that might be the best solution. That said, there is a simple algorithm that can be used to perform the decomposition. Given our covariance matrix $\Sigma$, with entries $\sigma_{i,j}$, we can calculate entries in $L$, $l_{i,j}$, proceeding row by row, from left to right:

$$l_{i,i} = \sqrt{\sigma_{i,i} - \sum_{m=1}^{i-1} l_{i,m}^2}$$

$$l_{i,j} = \frac{1}{l_{j,j}}\left(\sigma_{i,j} - \sum_{m=1}^{j-1} l_{i,m}l_{j,m}\right) \forall i > j \qquad (8.41)$$

$$l_{i,j} = 0 \quad \forall i < j$$

## SAMPLE PROBLEM

*Question:*

Given the following covariance matrix, $\Sigma$, develop a set of equations that converts three uncorrelated normal variables into three correlated normal variables:

$$\Sigma = \begin{bmatrix} 16 & 8 & 12 \\ 8 & 29 & 26 \\ 12 & 26 & 61 \end{bmatrix}$$

*Answer:*

We can use our Cholesky algorithm to calculate the entries of a lower triangular matrix, **L**:

$$l_{1,1} = \sqrt{16} = 4$$

$$l_{2,1} = \frac{1}{4}(8) = 2$$

$$l_{2,2} = \sqrt{29 - 2^2} = 5$$

$$l_{3,1} = \frac{1}{4}(12) = 3$$

$$l_{3,2} = \frac{1}{5}(26 - 3 \cdot 2) = 4$$

$$l_{3,3} = \sqrt{61 - 3^2 - 4^2} = 6$$

Next, place the entries in a matrix:

$$\mathbf{L} = \begin{bmatrix} 4 & 0 & 0 \\ 2 & 5 & 0 \\ 3 & 4 & 6 \end{bmatrix}$$

Given a vector of three uncorrelated standard normal variables, $\Phi$, and using Equation 8.37,

$$\mathbf{L}\Phi = \mathbf{C}$$

we can create a vector of correlated random variables, **C**. The elements of **C** are:

$$c_1 = 4\phi_1$$
$$c_2 = 2\phi_1 + 5\phi_2$$
$$c_3 = 3\phi_1 + 4\phi_2 + 6\phi_3$$

## PROBLEMS

1. Given the following matrices, what is $\mathbf{A} + \mathbf{B}$? $\mathbf{BC}$? $\mathbf{CB}$?

$$\mathbf{A} = \begin{bmatrix} -10 & 9 \\ 8 & 7 \end{bmatrix} \mathbf{B} = \begin{bmatrix} 2 & 9 \\ 1 & 1 \end{bmatrix} \mathbf{C} = \begin{bmatrix} -5 & 7 \\ -10 & 7 \end{bmatrix}$$

2. Using the same matrices from problem 1, what is $\mathbf{B} + (\mathbf{A} + \mathbf{C})$? What is $\mathbf{B}(\mathbf{A} - \mathbf{C})$?
3. Using the same matrices from problem 1, what is the transpose of $\mathbf{A}$? Of $\mathbf{C}$?
4. Given the following matrices, what is $\mathbf{F} + \mathbf{G}$? $\mathbf{FG}'$? $\mathbf{F}'\mathbf{G}$?

$$\mathbf{F} = \begin{bmatrix} -6 & 1 \\ -8 & 2 \\ -6 & -3 \end{bmatrix} \mathbf{G} = \begin{bmatrix} 5 & 0 \\ 0 & -1 \\ -8 & -7 \end{bmatrix}$$

5. Given the following matrices, what is $\mathbf{UI}$? $\mathbf{I}^2$? $\mathbf{U}^2$? $\mathbf{AU}$?

$$\mathbf{A} = \begin{bmatrix} -10 & 9 \\ 8 & 7 \end{bmatrix} \mathbf{U} = \begin{bmatrix} 1 & 1 \\ 1 & 1 \end{bmatrix} \mathbf{I} = \begin{bmatrix} 1 & 0 \\ 0 & 1 \end{bmatrix}$$

6. Given the following matrices, prove that $\mathbf{J}$ is the inverse of $\mathbf{K}$.

$$\mathbf{J} = \begin{bmatrix} 4 & 1 \\ 9 & 2 \end{bmatrix} \mathbf{K} = \begin{bmatrix} -2 & 1 \\ 9 & -4 \end{bmatrix}$$

7. Given the matrix $\mathbf{M}$, what is $\mathbf{M}^5$?

$$\mathbf{M} = \begin{bmatrix} 2 & 0 \\ 0 & 2 \end{bmatrix}$$

8. You are the risk manager for a large corporate bond portfolio. At the start of the year, 60% of the bonds in the portfolio are rated A, and 40% are rated B. Given the following one-year rating transition matrix, what is the expected distribution of ratings after one year?

| 1-Year | | To | | | |
|---|---|---|---|---|---|
| | | A | B | C | D |
| | A | 95% | 4% | 1% | 0% |
| From | B | 10% | 85% | 4% | 1% |
| | C | 0% | 20% | 65% | 15% |
| | D | 0% | 0% | 0% | 100% |

9. Using the one-year rating transition matrix from the previous question, calculate the corresponding two-year transition matrix.
10. Calculate the Cholesky decomposition for the following covariance matrix:

$$\Sigma = \begin{bmatrix} 4 & 14 & 16 \\ 14 & 50 & 58 \\ 16 & 58 & 132 \end{bmatrix}$$

## CHAPTER 9

# Vector Spaces

In this chapter we introduce the concept of vector spaces. At the end of the chapter we introduce principal component analysis and explore its application to risk management.

## VECTORS REVISITED

In the previous chapter we stated that matrices with a single column could be referred to as vectors. While not necessary, it is often convenient to represent vectors graphically. For example, the elements of a $2 \times 1$ matrix can be thought of as representing a point or a vector in two dimensions,[1] as shown in Exhibit 9.1.

$$\mathbf{v}_1 = \begin{bmatrix} 10 \\ 2 \end{bmatrix} \tag{9.1}$$

Similarly, a $3 \times 1$ matrix can be thought of as representing a point or vector in three dimensions, as shown in Exhibit 9.2.

$$\mathbf{v}_2 = \begin{bmatrix} 5 \\ 10 \\ 4 \end{bmatrix} \tag{9.2}$$

While it is difficult to visualize a point in higher dimensions, we can still speak of an $n \times 1$ vector as representing a point or vector in $n$ dimensions, for any positive value of $n$.

In addition to the operations of addition and scalar multiplication that we explored in the previous chapter, with vectors we can also compute the Euclidean inner product, often simply referred to as the inner product. For two vectors, the Euclidean

---

[1] In physics, a vector has both magnitude and direction. In a graph, a vector is represented by an arrow connecting two points, the direction indicated by the head of the arrow. In risk management, we are unlikely to encounter problems where this concept of direction has any real physical meaning. Still, the concept of a vector can be useful when working through the problems. For our purposes, whether we imagine a collection of data to represent a point or a vector, the math will be the same.

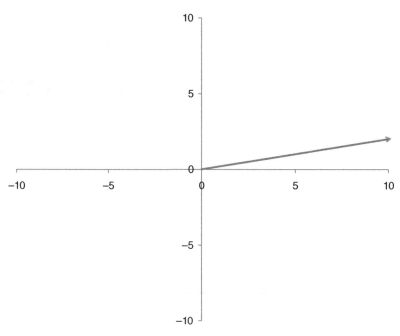

**EXHIBIT 9.1** Two-Dimensional Vector

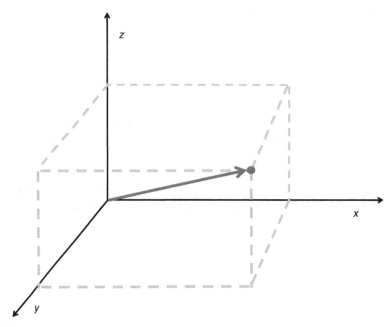

**EXHIBIT 9.2** Three-Dimensional Vector

inner product is defined as the sum of the product of the corresponding elements in the vector. For two vectors, **a** and **b**, we denote the inner product as **a** · **b**:

$$\mathbf{a} \cdot \mathbf{b} = a_1 b_1 + a_2 b_2 + \cdots + a_n b_n \tag{9.3}$$

We can also refer to the inner product as a *dot product*, so referred to because of the dot between the two vectors.[2] The inner product is equal to the matrix multiplication of the transpose of the first vector and the second vector:

$$\mathbf{a} \cdot \mathbf{b} = \mathbf{a}' \mathbf{b} \tag{9.4}$$

We can use the inner product to calculate the length of a vector. To calculate the length of a vector, we simply take the square root of the inner product of the vector with itself:

$$\| \mathbf{a} \| = \sqrt{\mathbf{a} \cdot \mathbf{a}} \tag{9.5}$$

The length of a vector is alternatively referred to as the norm, the Euclidean length, or the magnitude of the vector.

Every vector exists within a vector space. A vector space is a mathematical construct consisting of a set of related vectors that obey certain axioms. For the interested reader, a more formal definition of a vector space is provided in Appendix C. In risk management we are almost always working in a space $\mathbf{R}^n$, which consists of all of the vectors of length $n$, whose elements are real numbers.

---

### SAMPLE PROBLEM

*Question:*
Given the following vectors in $\mathbf{R}^3$,

$$\mathbf{a} = \begin{bmatrix} 5 \\ -2 \\ 4 \end{bmatrix} \quad \mathbf{b} = \begin{bmatrix} 10 \\ 6 \\ 1 \end{bmatrix} \quad \mathbf{c} = \begin{bmatrix} 4 \\ 0 \\ 4 \end{bmatrix}$$

find the following:

1. **a** · **b**
2. **b** · **c**
3. The magnitude of **c**

---

[2] In physics and other fields, the inner product of two vectors is often denoted not with a dot, but with pointy brackets. Under this convention, the inner product of **a** and **b** would be denoted <a,b>. The term *dot product* can be applied to any ordered collection of numbers, not just vectors, while an *inner product* is defined relative to a vector space. For our purposes, when talking about vectors, the terms can be used interchangeably.

*Answer:*

1. $\mathbf{a} \cdot \mathbf{b} = 5 \cdot 10 + (-2) \cdot 6 + 4 \cdot 1 = 42$
2. $\mathbf{b} \cdot \mathbf{c} = 10 \cdot 4 + 6 \cdot 0 + 1 \cdot 4 = 44$
3. $\| \mathbf{c} \| = \sqrt{\mathbf{c} \cdot \mathbf{c}} = \sqrt{4 \cdot 4 + 0 \cdot 0 + 4 \cdot 4} = \sqrt{32} = 4\sqrt{2}$

## ORTHOGONALITY

We can use matrix addition and scalar multiplication to combine vectors in a linear combination. The result is a new vector in the same space. For example, in $\mathbf{R}^4$, combining three vectors, $\mathbf{v}$, $\mathbf{w}$, and $\mathbf{x}$, and three scalars, $s_1$, $s_2$, and $s_3$, we get $\mathbf{y}$:

$$s_1\mathbf{v} + s_2\mathbf{w} + s_3\mathbf{x} = s_1 \begin{bmatrix} v_1 \\ v_2 \\ v_3 \\ v_4 \end{bmatrix} + s_2 \begin{bmatrix} w_1 \\ w_2 \\ w_3 \\ w_4 \end{bmatrix} + s_3 \begin{bmatrix} x_1 \\ x_2 \\ x_3 \\ x_4 \end{bmatrix} = \begin{bmatrix} y_1 \\ y_2 \\ y_3 \\ y_4 \end{bmatrix} = \mathbf{y} \tag{9.6}$$

Rather than viewing this equation as creating $\mathbf{y}$, we can read the equation in reverse, and imagine decomposing $\mathbf{y}$ into a linear combination of other vectors.

A set of $n$ vectors, $\mathbf{v}_1, \mathbf{v}_2, \ldots, \mathbf{v}_n$, is said to be linearly independent if, and only if, given the scalars $c_1, c_2, \ldots, c_n$, the solution to the equation:

$$c_1\mathbf{v}_1 + c_2\mathbf{v}_2 + \cdots + c_n\mathbf{v}_n = 0 \tag{9.7}$$

has only the trivial solution, $c_1 = c_2 = \cdots = c_n = 0$. A corollary to this definition is that if a set of vectors is linearly independent, then it is impossible to express any vector in the set as a linear combination of the other vectors in the set.

## SAMPLE PROBLEM

*Question:*

Given a set of linear independent vectors, $S = \{\mathbf{v}_1, \mathbf{v}_2, \ldots, \mathbf{v}_n\}$, and a set of constants, $c_1, c_2, \ldots, c_n$, prove that the equation:

$$c_1\mathbf{v}_1 + c_2\mathbf{v}_2 + \cdots + c_n\mathbf{v}_n = 0$$

has a nontrivial solution if any of the vectors in $S$ can be expressed as a linear combination of the other vectors in the set.

*Answer:*

Let us start by assuming that the first vector, $\mathbf{v}_1$, can be expressed as a linear combination of the vectors $\mathbf{v}_2, \mathbf{v}_3, \ldots, \mathbf{v}_m$, where $m < n$; that is:

$$\mathbf{v}_1 = k_2\mathbf{v}_2 + \cdots + k_n\mathbf{v}_m$$

where $k_2, \ldots, k_n$, are constants. We can rearrange this equation as:

$$\mathbf{v}_1 - k_2\mathbf{v}_2 - \cdots - k_n\mathbf{v}_m = 0$$

Now if we set all the constants, $c_{m+1}, c_{m+2}, \ldots, c_n$, to zero, for the other vectors we have:

$$c_{m+1}\mathbf{v}_{m+1} + c_{m+2}\mathbf{v}_{m+2} + \cdots + c_n\mathbf{v}_n = 0$$

Combining the two equations, we have:

$$\mathbf{v}_1 - k_2\mathbf{v}_2 - \cdots - k_m\mathbf{v}_m + c_{m+1}\mathbf{v}_{m+1} + \cdots + c_n\mathbf{v}_n = 0 + 0 = 0$$

This then is a nontrivial solution for the original equation. In terms of the original constants, the solution is:

$$c_1 = 1$$
$$c_2 = -k_2, c_3 = -k_3, \ldots, c_m = -k_m$$
$$c_{m+1} = 0, c_{m+2} = 0, \ldots, c_n = 0$$

Moreover, this is a general proof, and not limited to the case where $\mathbf{v}_1$ can be expressed as a linear combination of $\mathbf{v}_2, \mathbf{v}_3, \ldots, \mathbf{v}_m$. Because matrix addition is commutative, the order of the addition is not important. The result would have been the same if any one vector had been expressible as a linear combination of any subset of the other vectors.

We can use the concept of linear independence to define a basis for a vector space, **V**. A basis is a set of linearly independent vectors, $S = \{\mathbf{v}_1, \mathbf{v}_2, \ldots, \mathbf{v}_n\}$, such that every vector within **V** can be expressed as a unique linear combination of the vectors in $S$. As an example, we provide the following set of two vectors, which form a basis, $B_1 = \{\mathbf{v}_1, \mathbf{v}_2\}$, for $\mathbf{R}^2$:

$$\mathbf{v}_1 = \begin{bmatrix} 1 \\ 0 \end{bmatrix} \quad \mathbf{v}_2 = \begin{bmatrix} 0 \\ 1 \end{bmatrix} \tag{9.8}$$

First, note that the vectors are linearly independent. We cannot multiply either vector by a constant to get the other vector. Next, note that any vector in $\mathbf{R}^2$, $[x\ y]'$, can be expressed as a linear combination of the two vectors:

$$\begin{bmatrix} x \\ y \end{bmatrix} = x\mathbf{v}_1 + y\mathbf{v}_2 \tag{9.9}$$

The scalars on the right-hand side of this equation, $x$ and $y$, are known as the coordinates of the vector. We can arrange these coordinates in a vector to form a coordinate vector.

$$\mathbf{c} = \begin{bmatrix} c_1 \\ c_2 \end{bmatrix} = \begin{bmatrix} x \\ y \end{bmatrix} \tag{9.10}$$

In this case, the vector and the coordinate vector are the same, but this need not be the case.

As another example, take the following basis, $B_2 = \{\mathbf{w}_1, \mathbf{w}_2\}$, for $\mathbf{R}^2$:

$$\mathbf{w}_1 = \begin{bmatrix} 7 \\ 0 \end{bmatrix} \quad \mathbf{w}_2 = \begin{bmatrix} 0 \\ 10 \end{bmatrix} \tag{9.11}$$

These vectors are still linearly independent, and we can create any vector, $[x\ y]'$, from a linear combination of $\mathbf{w}_1$ and $\mathbf{w}_2$. In this case, however, the coordinate vector is not the same as the original vector. To find the coordinate vector, we solve the following equation for $c_1$ and $c_2$ in terms of $x$ and $y$:

$$\begin{bmatrix} x \\ y \end{bmatrix} = c_1\mathbf{w}_1 + c_2\mathbf{w}_2 = c_1\begin{bmatrix} 7 \\ 0 \end{bmatrix} + c_2\begin{bmatrix} 0 \\ 10 \end{bmatrix} = \begin{bmatrix} 7c_1 \\ 10c_2 \end{bmatrix} \tag{9.12}$$

Therefore, $x = 7c_1$ and $y = 10c_2$. Solving for $c_1$ and $c_2$, we get our coordinate vector relative to the new basis:

$$\mathbf{c} = \begin{bmatrix} c_1 \\ c_2 \end{bmatrix} = \begin{bmatrix} \dfrac{x}{7} \\ \dfrac{y}{10} \end{bmatrix} \tag{9.13}$$

Finally, the following set of vectors, $B_3 = \{\mathbf{x}_1, \mathbf{x}_2\}$, would also be a legitimate basis for $\mathbf{R}^2$:

$$\mathbf{x}_1 = \begin{bmatrix} \dfrac{1}{\sqrt{2}} \\ \dfrac{1}{\sqrt{2}} \end{bmatrix} \quad \mathbf{x}_2 = \begin{bmatrix} 0 \\ 1 \end{bmatrix} \tag{9.14}$$

These vectors are also linearly independent. For this third basis, the coordinate vector for a vector, $[x\ y]'$, would be:

$$\mathbf{c} = \begin{bmatrix} \sqrt{2}x \\ y - x \end{bmatrix} \tag{9.15}$$

Of the three bases, is one preferable to the others? We can't really say that one basis is the best—this would be subjective—but we can describe certain features of a basis, which may make them more or less interesting in certain applications.

The first way to characterize a basis is to measure the length of its vectors. Note that the vectors in $B_2$ are really just scalar multiples of the vector in $B_1$.

$$\mathbf{w}_1 = 7\mathbf{v}_1 \quad \mathbf{w}_2 = 10\mathbf{v}_2 \tag{9.16}$$

This is not a coincidence. For any vector space, we can create a new basis simply by multiplying some or all the vectors in one basis by nonzero scalars. Multiplying a vector by a scalar doesn't change the vector's orientation in space; it just changes the vector's length. We can see this if we plot both sets of vectors as in Exhibit 9.3.

If the lengths of the vectors in a basis don't matter, then one logical choice is to set all the vectors to unit length, $\|\mathbf{v}\| = 1$. A vector of unit length is said to be normal or normalized.

The second way to characterize a basis has to do with how the vectors in the basis are oriented with respect to each other. The vectors in $B_3$ are also of unit length, but, as we can see in Exhibit 9.4, if we plot the vectors, the vectors in $B_1$ are at right angles to each other, whereas the vectors in $B_3$ form a 45-degree angle.

When vectors are at right angles to each other, we say that they are orthogonal to each other. One way to test for orthogonality is to calculate the inner product between two vectors. If two vectors are orthogonal, then their inner product will be equal to zero. For $B_1$ and $B_3$, then:

$$\mathbf{v}_1 \cdot \mathbf{v}_2 = 1 \cdot 0 + 0 \cdot 1 = 0$$
$$\mathbf{x}_1 \cdot \mathbf{x}_2 = \frac{1}{\sqrt{2}} \cdot 0 + \frac{1}{\sqrt{2}} \cdot 1 = \frac{1}{\sqrt{2}} \tag{9.17}$$

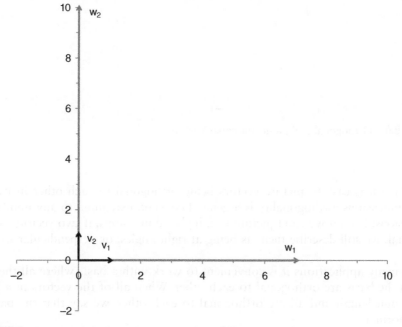

**EXHIBIT 9.3** Vectors with Same Orientation but Different Lengths

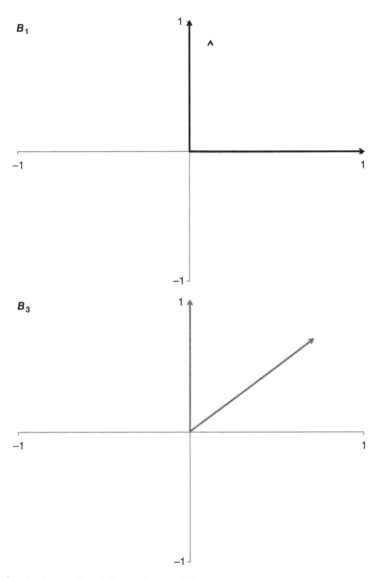

**EXHIBIT 9.4**  Orthogonal and Nonorthogonal Vectors

While it is easy to picture vectors being orthogonal to each other in two or three dimensions, orthogonality is a general concept, extending to any number of dimensions. Even if we can't picture it in higher dimensions, if two vectors are orthogonal, we still describe them as being at right angles, or perpendicular to each other.

In many applications it is convenient to work with a basis where all the vectors in the basis are orthogonal to each other. When all of the vectors in a basis are of unit length and all are orthogonal to each other, we say that the basis is orthonormal.

## ROTATION

In the preceding section, we saw that the following set of vectors formed an orthonormal basis for $\mathbf{R}^2$:

$$\mathbf{v}_1 = \begin{bmatrix} 1 \\ 0 \end{bmatrix} \quad \mathbf{v}_2 = \begin{bmatrix} 0 \\ 1 \end{bmatrix} \tag{9.18}$$

This basis is known as the standard basis for $\mathbf{R}^2$. In general, for the space $\mathbf{R}^n$, the standard basis is defined as the set of vectors:

$$\mathbf{v}_1 = \begin{bmatrix} 1 \\ 0 \\ \vdots \\ 0 \end{bmatrix} \quad \mathbf{v}_2 = \begin{bmatrix} 0 \\ 1 \\ \vdots \\ 0 \end{bmatrix} \quad \cdots \quad \mathbf{v}_n = \begin{bmatrix} 0 \\ 0 \\ \vdots \\ 1 \end{bmatrix} \tag{9.19}$$

where the $i$th element of the $i$th vector is equal to one, and all other elements are zero. The standard basis for each space is an orthonormal basis. The standard bases are not the only orthonormal bases for these spaces, though. For $\mathbf{R}^2$, the following is also an orthonormal basis:

$$\mathbf{z}_1 = \begin{bmatrix} \dfrac{1}{\sqrt{2}} \\ \dfrac{1}{\sqrt{2}} \end{bmatrix} \quad \mathbf{z}_2 = \begin{bmatrix} -\dfrac{1}{\sqrt{2}} \\ \dfrac{1}{\sqrt{2}} \end{bmatrix} \tag{9.20}$$

## SAMPLE PROBLEM

*Question:*
    Prove that the following basis is orthonormal:

$$\mathbf{z}_1 = \begin{bmatrix} \dfrac{1}{\sqrt{2}} \\ \dfrac{1}{\sqrt{2}} \end{bmatrix} \quad \mathbf{z}_2 = \begin{bmatrix} -\dfrac{1}{\sqrt{2}} \\ \dfrac{1}{\sqrt{2}} \end{bmatrix} \tag{9.21}$$

*Answer:*
    First, we show that the length of each vector is equal to one:

$$\| \mathbf{z}_1 \| = \sqrt{\mathbf{z}_1 \cdot \mathbf{z}_1} = \sqrt{\frac{1}{\sqrt{2}}\frac{1}{\sqrt{2}} + \frac{1}{\sqrt{2}}\frac{1}{\sqrt{2}}} = \sqrt{\frac{1}{2} + \frac{1}{2}} = \sqrt{1} = 1$$

$$\| \mathbf{z}_2 \| = \sqrt{\mathbf{z}_2 \cdot \mathbf{z}_2} = \sqrt{\left(-\frac{1}{\sqrt{2}}\right)\left(-\frac{1}{\sqrt{2}}\right) + \frac{1}{\sqrt{2}}\frac{1}{\sqrt{2}}} = \sqrt{\frac{1}{2} + \frac{1}{2}} = \sqrt{1} = 1 \tag{9.22}$$

Next, we show that the two vectors are orthogonal to each other, by showing that their inner product is equal to zero:

$$\mathbf{z}_1 \cdot \mathbf{z}_2 = \frac{1}{\sqrt{2}}\left(-\frac{1}{\sqrt{2}}\right) + \frac{1}{\sqrt{2}}\frac{1}{\sqrt{2}} = -\frac{1}{2} + \frac{1}{2} = 0 \tag{9.23}$$

All of the vectors are of unitary length and are orthogonal to each other; therefore, the basis is orthonormal.

The difference between the standard basis for $\mathbf{R}^2$ and our new basis can be viewed as a rotation about the origin, as shown in Exhibit 9.5.

It is common to describe a change from one orthonormal basis to another as a rotation in higher dimensions as well.

It is often convenient to form a matrix from the vectors of a basis, where each column of the matrix corresponds to a vector of the basis. If the vectors $\mathbf{v}_1, \mathbf{v}_2, \ldots, \mathbf{v}_n$ form an orthonormal basis, and we denote the $j$th element of the $i$th vector, $\mathbf{v}_i$, as $v_{i,j}$, we have:

$$\mathbf{V} = \begin{bmatrix} \mathbf{v}_1 & \mathbf{v}_2 & \cdots & \mathbf{v}_n \end{bmatrix} = \begin{bmatrix} v_{11} & v_{21} & \cdots & v_{n1} \\ v_{21} & v_{22} & \cdots & v_{v2} \\ \vdots & \vdots & \ddots & \vdots \\ v_{n1} & v_{n2} & \cdots & v_{nn} \end{bmatrix} \tag{9.24}$$

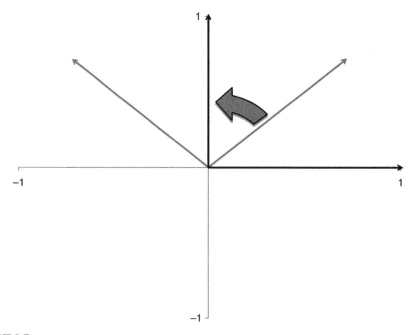

**EXHIBIT 9.5** Basis Rotation

For an orthonormal basis, this matrix has the interesting property that its transpose and its inverse are the same.

$$VV' = VV^{-1} = I \qquad (9.25)$$

The proof is not difficult. If we multiply $V$ by its transpose, every element along the diagonal is the inner product of a basis vector with itself. This is just the length of the vector, which by definition is equal to one. The off-diagonal elements are the inner product of different vectors in the basis with each other. Because they are orthogonal, these inner products will be zero. In other words, the matrix that results from multiplying $V$ by $V'$ is the identity matrix, so $V'$ must be the inverse of $V$.

This property makes calculating the coordinate vector for an orthonormal basis relatively simple. Given a vector $x$ of length $n$, and the matrix $V$, whose columns form an orthonormal basis in $R^n$, the corresponding coordinate vector can be found as follows:

$$c = V^{-1}x = V'x \qquad (9.26)$$

The first part of the equation, $c = V^{-1}x$, would be true even for a nonorthonormal basis.

Rather than picture the basis as rotating and the vector as remaining still, it would be equally valid to picture a change of basis as a rotation of a vector, as in Exhibit 9.6.

If we premultiply both sides of this Equation 9.26 by $V$, we have $Vc = V\ V'x = Ix = x$. In other words, if $V'$ rotates $x$ into the new vector space, then multiplying by $V$ performs the reverse transformation, rotating $c$ back into the original vector space. It stands to reason that $V'$ is also an orthonormal basis. If the vectors of a matrix form an orthonormal basis in $R^n$, then the rows of that matrix also form an orthonormal basis in $R^n$. It is also true that if the columns of a square matrix are orthogonal, then the rows are orthogonal, too. Because of this, rather than saying the columns and rows of a matrix are orthogonal or orthonormal, it is enough to say that the matrix is orthogonal or orthonormal.

## SAMPLE PROBLEM

*Question:*

Given the following basis for $R^2$,

$$z_1 = \begin{bmatrix} \dfrac{1}{\sqrt{2}} \\ \dfrac{1}{\sqrt{2}} \end{bmatrix} \quad z_2 = \begin{bmatrix} -\dfrac{1}{\sqrt{2}} \\ \dfrac{1}{\sqrt{2}} \end{bmatrix}$$

find the coordinate vector for the vector $x$, where $x' = [9\ 4]$.

*Answer:*

$$\mathbf{c} = \mathbf{Z}'\mathbf{x} = \begin{bmatrix} \dfrac{1}{\sqrt{2}} & \dfrac{1}{\sqrt{2}} \\ -\dfrac{1}{\sqrt{2}} & \dfrac{1}{\sqrt{2}} \end{bmatrix} \begin{bmatrix} 9 \\ 4 \end{bmatrix} = \begin{bmatrix} \dfrac{13}{\sqrt{2}} \\ -\dfrac{5}{\sqrt{2}} \end{bmatrix}$$

We can verify this result as follows:

$$c_1\mathbf{z}_1 + c_2\mathbf{z}_2 = \frac{13}{\sqrt{2}} \begin{bmatrix} \dfrac{1}{\sqrt{2}} \\ \dfrac{1}{\sqrt{2}} \end{bmatrix} - \frac{5}{\sqrt{2}} \begin{bmatrix} -\dfrac{1}{\sqrt{2}} \\ \dfrac{1}{\sqrt{2}} \end{bmatrix}$$

$$c_1\mathbf{z}_1 + c_2\mathbf{z}_2 = \begin{bmatrix} \dfrac{13}{2} + \dfrac{5}{2} \\ \dfrac{13}{2} - \dfrac{5}{2} \end{bmatrix} = \begin{bmatrix} 9 \\ 4 \end{bmatrix} = \mathbf{x}$$

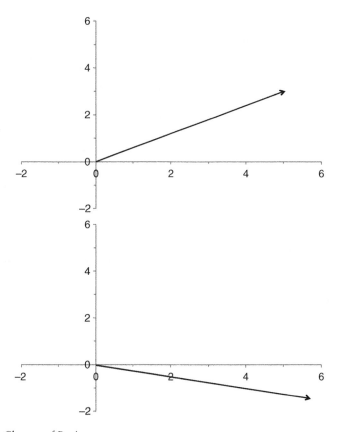

**EXHIBIT 9.6**    Change of Basis

## PRINCIPAL COMPONENT ANALYSIS

For any given vector space, there is potentially an infinite number of orthonormal bases. Can we say that one orthonormal basis is better than another? As before, the decision is ultimately subjective, but there are factors we could take into consideration when trying to decide on a suitable basis. Due to its simplicity, the standard basis would seem to be an obvious choice in many cases. Another approach is to choose a basis based on the data being considered. This is the basic idea behind principal component analysis (PCA). In risk management, PCA can be used to examine the underlying structure of financial markets. Common applications, which we explore at the end of the chapter, include the development of equity indexes for factor analysis, and describing the dynamics of yield curves.

In PCA, a basis is chosen so that the first vector in the basis, now called the first principal component, explains as much of the variance in the data being considered as possible. For example, we have plotted annual returns over 10 years for two hedge funds, Fund X and Fund Y, in Exhibit 9.7 using the standard basis and in Exhibit 9.8 using an alternative basis. The returns are also presented in Exhibit 9.9. As can be seen in the chart, the returns in Exhibit 9.7 are highly correlated. On the right-hand side of Exhibit 9.9 and in Exhibit 9.8, we have transformed the data using the basis from the previous example (readers should verify this). In effect, we've rotated the data 45 degrees. Now almost all of the variance in the data is along the X'-axis.

By transforming the data, we are calling attention to the underlying structure of the data. In this case, the X and Y data are highly correlated, and almost all of the variance in the data can be described by variance in X', our first principal component. It might be that the linear transformation we used to construct X' corresponds to an underlying process, which is generating the data. In this case, maybe both funds are invested in some of the same securities, or maybe both funds have similar investment styles.

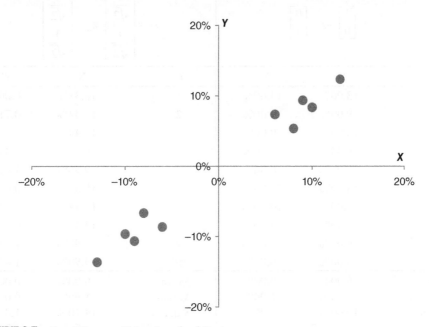

**EXHIBIT 9.7**   Fund Returns Using Standard Basis

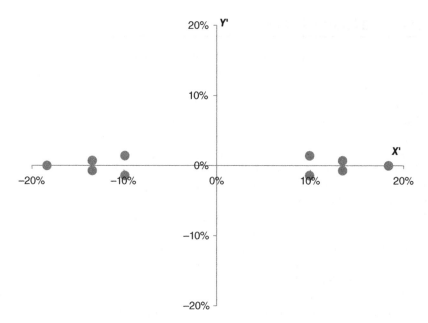

**EXHIBIT 9.8**   Fund Returns Using Alternative Basis

**EXHIBIT 9.9**   Change of Basis

| | Standard Basis | | | Alternative Basis | |
|---|---|---|---|---|---|
| | $s_1 = \begin{bmatrix} 1 \\ 0 \end{bmatrix}$  $s_2 = \begin{bmatrix} 0 \\ 1 \end{bmatrix}$ | | | $z_1 = \begin{bmatrix} \dfrac{1}{\sqrt{2}} \\ \dfrac{1}{\sqrt{2}} \end{bmatrix}$  $z_2 = \begin{bmatrix} \dfrac{1}{\sqrt{2}} \\ \dfrac{1}{\sqrt{2}} \end{bmatrix}$ | | |
| $t$ | X | Y | $t$ | X′ | Y′ |
| 1 | 13.00% | 13.00% | 1 | 18.38% | 0.00% |
| 2 | 9.00% | 10.00% | 2 | 13.44% | 0.71% |
| 3 | 10.00% | 9.00% | 3 | 13.44% | −0.71% |
| 4 | 6.00% | 8.00% | 4 | 9.90% | 1.41% |
| 5 | 8.00% | 6.00% | 5 | 9.90% | −1.41% |
| 6 | −13.00% | −13.00% | 6 | −18.38% | 0.00% |
| 7 | −9.00% | −10.00% | 7 | −13.44% | −0.71% |
| 8 | −10.00% | −9.00% | 8 | −13.44% | 0.71% |
| 9 | −6.00% | −8.00% | 9 | −9.90% | −1.41% |
| 10 | −8.00% | −6.00% | 10 | −9.90% | 1.41% |
| Mean | 0.00% | 0.00% | Mean | 0.00% | 0.00% |
| Variance | 1.00% | 1.00% | Variance | 1.99% | 0.01% |
| Std. dev. | 10.00% | 10.00% | Std. dev. | 14.10% | 1.05% |

The transformed data can also be used to create an index to analyze the original data. In this case, we could use the transformed data along the first principal component as our index (possibly scaled). This index could then be used to benchmark the performances of both funds.

Tracking the index over time might also be interesting, in and of itself. For a summary report, we might not need to know how each fund is performing. With the index, rather than tracking two data points every period, we only have to track one. This reduction in the number of data points is an example of dimensionality reduction. In effect we have taken what was a two-dimensional problem (tracking two funds) and reduced it to a one-dimensional problem (tracking one index). Many problems in risk management can be viewed as exercises in dimensionality reduction—taking complex problems and simplifying them.

## SAMPLE PROBLEM

*Question:*
Using the first principal component from the previous example, construct an index with the same standard deviation as the original series. Calculate the tracking error of each fund in each period.

*Answer:*
In order to construct the index, we simply multiply each value of the first component of the transformed data, X′, by the ratio of the standard deviation of the original series to X′: 10.00%/14.10%. The tracking error for the original series is then found by subtracting the index values from the original series.

|  | Index | Error[X] | Error[Y] |
|---|---|---|---|
|  | 13.04% | −0.04% | −0.04% |
|  | 9.53% | −0.53% | 0.47% |
|  | 9.53% | 0.47% | −0.53% |
|  | 7.02% | −1.02% | 0.98% |
|  | 7.02% | 0.98% | −1.02% |
|  | −13.04% | 0.04% | 0.04% |
|  | −9.53% | 0.53% | −0.47% |
|  | −9.53% | −0.47% | 0.53% |
|  | −7.02% | 1.02% | −0.98% |
|  | −7.02% | −0.98% | 1.02% |
| Mean | 0.00% | 0.00% | 0.00% |
| Variance | 1.00% | 0.01% | 0.01% |
| Std. dev. | 10.00% | 0.75% | 0.75% |

We can easily extend the concept of PCA to higher dimensions using the techniques we have covered in this chapter. In higher dimensions, each successive principal component explains the maximum amount of variance in the residual data, after taking into account all of the preceding components. Just as the first principal component explained as much of the variance in the data as possible, the second principal component explains as much of the variance in the residuals, after taking out the variance explained by the first component. Similarly, the third principal component explains the maximum amount of variance in the residuals, after taking out the variance explained by the first and second components.

Now that we understand the properties of principal components, how do we actually go about calculating them? A general approach to PCA involves three steps:

1. Transform the raw data.
2. Calculate a covariance matrix of the transformed data.
3. Decompose the covariance matrix.

Assume we have a $T \times N$ matrix of data, where each column represents a different random variable, and each row represents a set of observations of those variables. For example, we might have the daily returns of $N$ different equity indexes over $T$ days. The first step is to transform the data so that the mean of each series is zero. This is often referred to as centering the data. To do this, we simply calculate the mean of each series and subtract that value from each point in that series. In certain situations we may also want to standardize the variance of each of the series. To do this, we calculate the standard deviation of each series, and divide each point in the series by that value. Imagine that one of our series is much more volatile than all of the other series. Because PCA is trying to account for the maximum amount of variance in the data, the first principal component might be dominated by this highly volatile series. If we want to call attention to the relative volatility of different series, this may be fine and we do not need to standardize the variance. However, if we are more interested in the correlation between the series, the high variance of this one series would be a distraction, and we should fully standardize the data.

Next, we need to calculate the covariance matrix of our transformed data. Denote the $T \times N$ matrix of transformed data as **X**. Because the data is centered, the covariance matrix, $\Sigma$, can be found as follows:

$$\Sigma = \frac{1}{N}\mathbf{X}'\mathbf{X} \tag{9.27}$$

Here we assume that we are calculating the population covariance, and divide by $N$. If instead we wish to calculate the sample covariance, we can divide by $(N-1)$. If we had standardized the variance of each series, then this matrix would be equivalent to the correlation matrix of the original series.

For the third and final step, we need to rely on the fact that $\Sigma$ is a symmetrical matrix. It turns out that any symmetrical matrix, where all of the entries are real numbers, can be diagonalized; that is, it can be expressed as the product of three matrices:

$$\Sigma = \mathbf{PDP}' \tag{9.28}$$

where the $N \times N$ matrix $\mathbf{P}$ is orthonormal, and the $N \times N$ matrix $\mathbf{D}$ is diagonal.[3] Combining the two equations and rearranging, we have:

$$\mathbf{X}' = N\mathbf{P}\mathbf{D}\mathbf{P}'\mathbf{X}^{-1} = \mathbf{P}\mathbf{D}\mathbf{M} \tag{9.29}$$

where $\mathbf{M} = N\mathbf{P}'\mathbf{X}^{-1}$. If we order the column vectors of $\mathbf{P}$ so that the first column explains most of the variance in $\mathbf{X}$, the second column vector explains most of the residual variance, and so on, then this is the PCA decomposition of $\mathbf{X}$. The column vectors of $\mathbf{P}$ are now viewed as the principal components, and serve as the basis for our new vector space.

To transform the original matrix $\mathbf{X}$, we simply multiply by the matrix $\mathbf{P}$:

$$\mathbf{Y} = \mathbf{X}\mathbf{P} \tag{9.30}$$

As we will see in the following application sections, the values of the elements of the matrix, $\mathbf{P}$, often hint at the underlying structure of the original data.

## APPLICATION: THE DYNAMIC TERM STRUCTURE OF INTEREST RATES

A yield curve plots the relationship between yield to maturity and time to maturity for a given issuer or group of issuers. A typical yield curve is concave and upward-sloping. An example is shown in Exhibit 9.10.

Over time, as interest rates change, the shape of the yield curve will change, too. At times, the yield curve can be close to flat, or even inverted (downward-sloping). Examples of flat and inverted yield curves are shown in Exhibits 9.11 and 9.12.

Because the points along a yield curve are driven by the same or similar fundamental factors, they tend to be highly correlated. Points that are closer together on the yield curve and have similar maturities tend to be even more highly correlated.

Because the points along the yield curve tend to be highly correlated, the ways in which the yield curve can move are limited. Practitioners tend to classify movements in yield curves as a combination of shifts, tilts, or twists. A shift in the yield curve occurs when all of the points along the curve increase or decrease by an equal amount. A tilt occurs when the yield curve either steepens (points further out on the curve increase relative to those closer in) or flattens (points further out decrease relative to those closer in). The yield curve is said to twist when the points in the middle of the curve move up or down relative to the points on either end of the curve. Exhibits 9.13, 9.14, and 9.15 show examples of these dynamics.

These three prototypical patterns—shifting, tilting, and twisting—can often be seen in PCA. The following is a principal component matrix obtained from daily U.S. government rates from March 2000 through August 2000. For each day, there were

---

[3] We have not formally introduced the concept of eigenvalues and eigenvectors. For the reader familiar with these concepts, the columns of $\mathbf{P}$ are the eigenvectors of $\Sigma$, and the entries along the diagonal of $\mathbf{D}$ are the corresponding eigenvalues. For small matrices, it is possible to calculate the eigenvectors and eigenvalues by hand. In practice, as with matrix inversion, for large matrices this step almost always involves the use of commercial software packages.

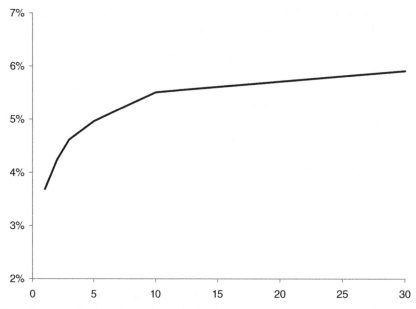

**EXHIBIT 9.10**    Upward-Sloping Yield Curve

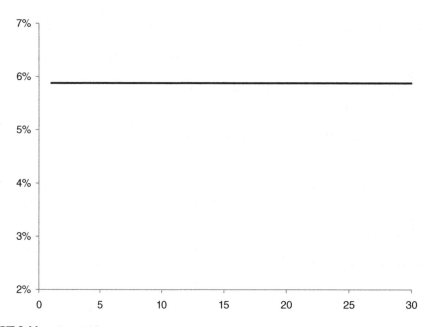

**EXHIBIT 9.11**    Flat Yield Curve

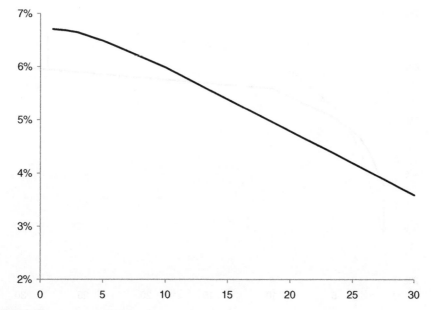

**EXHIBIT 9.12**  Inverted Yield Curve

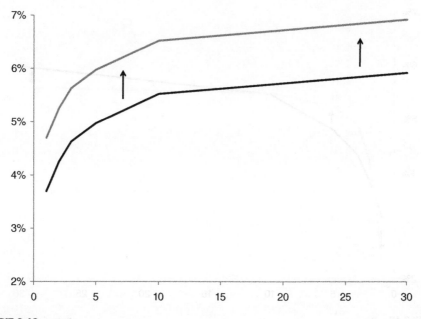

**EXHIBIT 9.13**  Shift

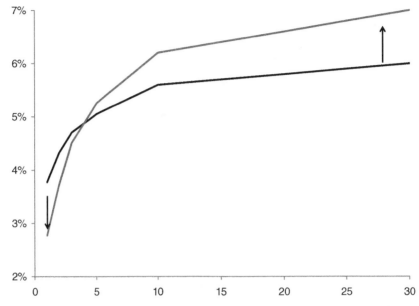

**EXHIBIT 9.14**  Tilt

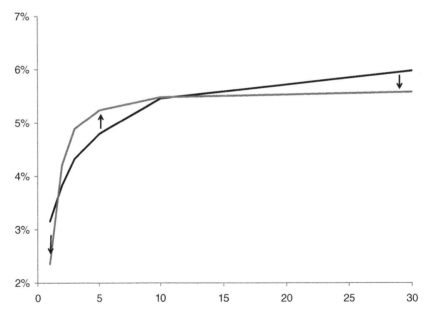

**EXHIBIT 9.15**  Twist

six points on the curve representing maturities of 1, 2, 3, 5, 10, and 30 years. Before calculating the covariance matrix, all of the data were centered and standardized.

$$
P = \begin{bmatrix}
0.39104 & -0.53351 & -0.61017 & 0.33671 & 0.22609 & 0.16020 \\
0.42206 & -0.26300 & 0.03012 & -0.30876 & -0.26758 & -0.76476 \\
0.42685 & -0.16318 & 0.19812 & -0.35626 & -0.49491 & 0.61649 \\
0.42853 & 0.01135 & 0.46043 & -0.17988 & 0.75388 & 0.05958 \\
0.41861 & 0.29495 & 0.31521 & 0.75553 & -0.24862 & -0.07604 \\
0.35761 & 0.72969 & -0.52554 & -0.24737 & 0.04696 & 0.00916
\end{bmatrix} \tag{9.31}
$$

The first column of the matrix is the first principal component. Notice that all of the elements are positive and of similar size. We can see this if we plot the elements in a chart, as in Exhibit 9.16. This flat, equal weighting represents the shift of the yield curve. A movement in this component increases or decreases all of the points on the yield curve by the same amount (actually, because we standardized all of the data, it shifts them in proportion to their standard deviation). Similarly, the second principal component shows an upward trend. A movement in this component tends to tilt the yield curve. Finally, if we plot the third principal component, it is bowed, high in the center and low on the ends. A shift in this component tends to twist the yield curve.

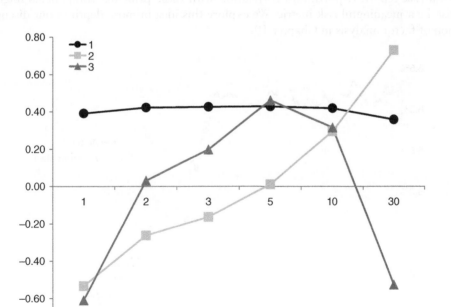

**EXHIBIT 9.16** First Three Principal Components of the Yield Curve

It's worth pointing out that, if we wanted to, we could change the sign of any principal component. That is, we could multiply all of the elements in one column of the principal component matrix, **P**, by −1. As we saw previously, we can always multiply a vector in a basis by a nonzero scalar to form a new basis. Multiplying by −1 won't change the length of a vector, just the direction; therefore, if our original matrix is orthonormal, the matrix that results from changing the sign of one or more columns will still be an orthonormal matrix. Normally, the justification for doing this is purely aesthetic. For example, our first principal component could be composed of all positive elements or all negative elements. The analysis is perfectly valid either way, but many practitioners would have a preference for all positive elements.

Not only can we see the shift, tilt, and twist in the principal components, but we can also see their relative importance in explaining the variability of interest rates. In this example, the first principal component explains 90% of the variance in interest rates. As is often the case, these interest rates are highly correlated with each other, and parallel shifts explain most of the evolution of the yield curve over time. If we incorporate the second and third principal components, fully 99.9% of the variance is explained. The two charts in Exhibits 9.17 and 9.18 show approximations to the 1-year and 30-year rates, using just the first three principal components. The differences between the actual rates and the approximations are extremely small. The actual and approximate series are almost indistinguishable.

Because the first three principal components explain so much of the dynamics of the yield curve, they could serve as a basis for an interest rate model or as the basis for a risk report. A portfolio's correlation with these principal components might also be a meaningful risk metric. We explore this idea in more depth in our discussion of factor analysis in Chapter 10.

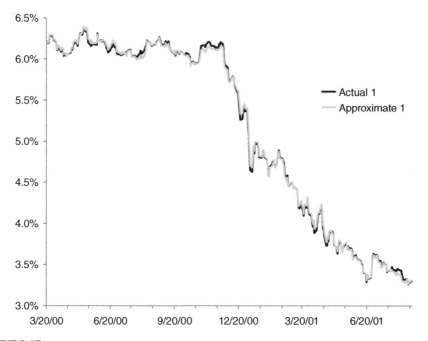

**EXHIBIT 9.17**   Actual and Approximate 1-Year Rates

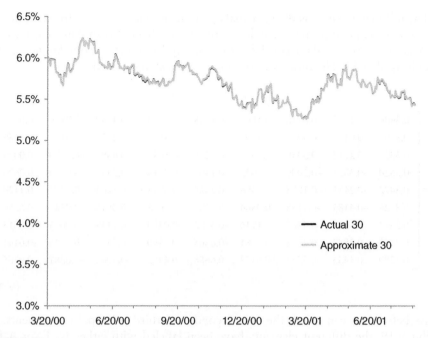

**EXHIBIT 9.18** Actual and Approximate 30-Year Rates

## APPLICATION: THE STRUCTURE OF GLOBAL EQUITY MARKETS

Principal component analysis can be used in many different ways when analyzing equity markets. At the highest level, we can analyze the relationship between different market indexes in different countries. Global equity markets are increasingly linked. Due to similarities in their economies or because of trade relationships, equity markets in different countries will be more or less correlated. PCA can highlight these relationships.

Within countries, PCA can be used to describe the relationships between groups of companies in industries or sectors. In a novel application of PCA, Kritzman, Li, Page, and Rigobon (2010) suggest that the amount of variance explained by the first principal components can be used to gauge systemic risk within an economy. The basic idea is that as more and more of the variance is explained by fewer and fewer principal components, the economy is becoming less robust and more susceptible to systemic shocks. In a similar vein, Meucci (2009) proposes a general measure of portfolio diversification based in part on principal component analysis. In this case, a portfolio can range from undiversified (all the variance is explained by the first principal component) to fully diversified (each of the principal components explains an equal amount of variance).

In many cases, PCA analysis of equity markets is similar to the analysis of yield curves: The results are simply confirming and quantifying structures that we already believed existed. PCA can be most interesting, however, when it points to relationships that we were previously unaware of. For example, as the economy changes over time, new industries form and business relationships change. We can perform PCA on individual stocks to try to tease out these relationships.

The following matrix is the principal component matrix formed from the analysis of nine broad equity market indexes, three each from North America, Europe, and Asia. The original data consisted of monthly log returns from January 2000 through April 2011. The returns were centered and standardized.

$$
P = \begin{bmatrix}
0.3604 & -0.1257 & 0.0716 & -0.1862 & 0.1158 & -0.1244 & 0.4159 & 0.7806 & 0.0579 \\
0.3302 & -0.0197 & 0.4953 & -0.4909 & -2.1320 & 0.4577 & 0.2073 & -0.3189 & -0.0689 \\
0.3323 & 0.2712 & 0.3359 & -0.2548 & 0.2298 & -0.5841 & -0.4897 & -0.0670 & -0.0095 \\
0.3520 & -0.3821 & -0.2090 & 0.1022 & -0.1805 & 0.0014 & -0.2457 & 0.0339 & -0.7628 \\
0.3472 & -0.2431 & -0.1883 & 0.1496 & 0.2024 & -0.3918 & 0.5264 & -0.5277 & 0.1120 \\
0.3426 & -0.4185 & -0.1158 & 0.0804 & -0.3707 & 0.0675 & -0.3916 & 0.0322 & 0.6256 \\
0.2844 & 0.6528 & -0.4863 & -0.1116 & -0.4782 & -0.0489 & 0.1138 & -0.0055 & -0.0013 \\
0.3157 & 0.2887 & 0.4238 & 0.7781 & -0.0365 & 0.1590 & 0.0459 & 0.0548 & -0.0141 \\
0.3290 & 0.1433 & -0.3581 & -0.0472 & 0.6688 & 0.4982 & -0.1964 & -0.0281 & 0.0765
\end{bmatrix}
$$

$$(9.32)$$

As before, we can graph the first, second, and third principal components. In Exhibit 9.19, the different elements have been labeled with either N, E, or A for North America, Europe, and Asia, respectively.

As before, the first principal component appears to be composed of an approximately equal weighting of all the component time series. This suggests that these equity markets are highly integrated, and most of their movement is being driven by

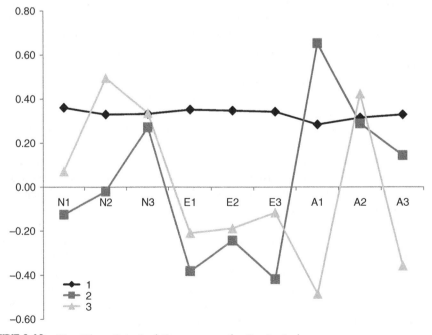

**EXHIBIT 9.19**   First Three Principal Components for Equity Indexes

a common factor. The first component explains just over 75% of the total variance in the data. Diversifying a portfolio across different countries might not prove as risk-reducing as one might hope.

The second factor could be described as long North America and Asia and short Europe. Going long or short this spread might be an interesting strategy for somebody with a portfolio that is highly correlated with the first principal component. Because the two components are uncorrelated by definition, investing in both may provide good diversification. That said, the pattern for the second principal component certainly is not as distinct as the patterns we saw in the yield curve example. For the equity indexes, the second component explains only an additional 7% of the variance.

By the time we get to the third principal component, it is difficult to posit any fundamental rationale for the component weights. Unlike our yield curve example, in which the first three components explained 99.9% of the variance in the series, in this example the first three components explain only 87% of the total variance. This is still a lot, but it suggests that these equity returns are much more distinct.

Trying to ascribe a fundamental explanation to the third and possibly even the second principal component highlights one potential pitfall of PCA analysis: identification. When the principal components account for a large part of the variance and conform to our prior expectations, they likely correspond to real fundamental risk factors. When the principal components account for less variance and we cannot associate them with any known risk factors, they are more likely to be spurious. Unfortunately, it is these components, which do not correspond to any previously known risk factors, which we are often hoping that PCA will identify.

Another closely related problem is stability. If we are going to use PCA for risk analysis, we will likely want to update our principal component matrix on a regular basis. The changing weights of the components over time might be interesting, illuminating how the structure of a market is changing. Unfortunately, nearby components will often change place, the second becoming the third and the third becoming the second, for example. If the weights are too unstable, tracking components over time can be difficult or impossible.

## PROBLEMS

1. Given the following vectors, **a**, **b**, and **c**, are **a** and **b** orthogonal? Are **b** and **c** orthogonal?

$$\mathbf{a} = \begin{bmatrix} 10 \\ -5 \\ 4 \end{bmatrix} \quad \mathbf{b} = \begin{bmatrix} 6 \\ 2 \\ -4 \end{bmatrix} \quad \mathbf{c} = \begin{bmatrix} 5 \\ 5 \\ 10 \end{bmatrix}$$

2. Find $x$ such that **A** is an orthonormal basis:

$$\mathbf{A} = \begin{bmatrix} x & \dfrac{1}{3} \\ \dfrac{1}{3} & \dfrac{2\sqrt{2}}{3} \end{bmatrix}$$

**3.** Find $x$ and $y$ such that **B** is an orthonormal basis:

$$\mathbf{B} = \begin{bmatrix} x & \dfrac{1}{5} \\ y & \dfrac{2\sqrt{6}}{5} \end{bmatrix}$$

**4.** Given the following matrix **B**, whose columns are orthonormal and form a vector space in $\mathbf{R}^2$, find the coordinate vector for the vector **x**:

$$\mathbf{B} = \begin{bmatrix} \dfrac{1}{\sqrt{2}} & -\dfrac{1}{\sqrt{2}} \\ \dfrac{1}{\sqrt{2}} & \dfrac{1}{\sqrt{2}} \end{bmatrix} \quad \mathbf{x} = \begin{bmatrix} 6 \\ 4 \end{bmatrix}$$

**5.** Given the following matrix **B**, whose columns form a vector space in $\mathbf{R}^3$, find the coordinate vector for the vector **x**:

$$\mathbf{B} = \begin{bmatrix} 4 & 2 & -46 \\ 1 & -18 & -1 \\ 5 & 2 & 37 \end{bmatrix} \quad \mathbf{x} = \begin{bmatrix} -170 \\ -19 \\ 165 \end{bmatrix}$$

# Linear Regression Analysis

This chapter provides a basic introduction to linear regression models. At the end of the chapter, we will explore two risk management applications, factor analysis and stress testing.

## LINEAR REGRESSION (ONE REGRESSOR)

One of the most popular models in statistics is the linear regression model. Given two constants, $\alpha$ and $\beta$, and a random error term, $\varepsilon$, in its simplest form the model posits a relationship between two variables, $X$ and $Y$:

$$Y = \alpha + \beta X + \varepsilon \tag{10.1}$$

As specified, $X$ is known as the regressor or independent variable. Similarly, $Y$ is known as the regressand or dependent variable. As *dependent* implies, traditionally we think of $X$ as *causing* $Y$. This relationship is not necessary, and in practice, especially in finance, this cause-and-effect relationship is either ambiguous or entirely absent. In finance, it is often the case that both $X$ and $Y$ are being driven by a common underlying factor.

The linear regression relationship is often represented graphically as a plot of $Y$ against $X$, as shown in Exhibit 10.1. The solid line in the chart represents the deterministic portion of the linear regression equation, $Y = \alpha + \beta X$. For any particular point, the distance above or below the line is the error, $\varepsilon$, for that point.

Because there is only one regressor, this model is often referred to as a univariate regression. Mainly, this is to differentiate it from the multivariate model, with more than one regressor, which we will explore later in this chapter. While everybody agrees that a model with two or more regressors is multivariate, not everybody agrees that a model with one regressor is univariate. Even though the univariate model has one regressor, $X$, it has two variables, $X$ and $Y$, which has led some people to refer to Equation 10.1 as a bivariate model. The former convention seems to be more common within financial risk management. From here on out, we will refer to Equation 10.1 as a univariate model.

In Equation 10.1, $\alpha$ and $\beta$ are constants. In the univariate model, $\alpha$ is typically referred to as the intercept, and $\beta$ is often referred to as the slope. $\beta$ is referred to as

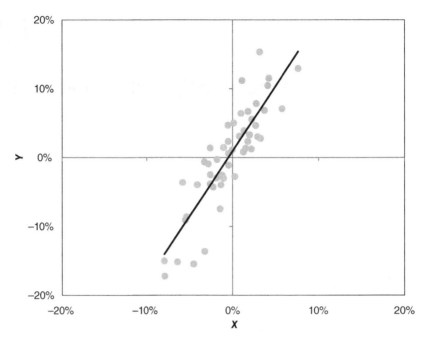

**EXHIBIT 10.1**   Linear Regression Example

the slope because it measures the slope of the solid line when $Y$ is plotted against $X$. We can see this by taking the derivative of $Y$ with respect to $X$:

$$\frac{dY}{dX} = \beta \tag{10.2}$$

The final term in Equation 10.1, $\varepsilon$, represents a random error, or residual. The error term allows us to specify a relationship between $X$ and $Y$ even when that relationship is not exact. In effect, the model is incomplete; it is an approximation. Changes in $X$ may drive changes in $Y$, but there are other variables, which we are not modeling, that also impact $Y$. These unmodeled variables cause $X$ and $Y$ to deviate from a purely deterministic relationship. That deviation is captured by $\varepsilon$, our residual.

In risk management, this division of the world into two parts, a part that can be explained by the model and a part that cannot, is a common dichotomy. We refer to risk that can be explained by our model as systematic risk, and to the part that cannot be explained by the model as idiosyncratic risk. In our regression model, $Y$ is divided into a systematic component, $\alpha + \beta X$, and an idiosyncratic component, $\varepsilon$.

$$Y = \underbrace{\alpha + \beta X}_{\text{systematic}} + \underbrace{\varepsilon}_{\text{idiosyncratic}} \tag{10.3}$$

Which component of the overall risk is more important? It depends on what our objective is. As we will see, portfolio managers who wish to hedge certain risks in their portfolios are basically trying to reduce or eliminate systematic risk. Portfolio managers who try to mimic the returns of an index, on the other hand, can be viewed as trying to minimize idiosyncratic risk.

## Ordinary Least Squares

The univariate regression model is conceptually simple. In order to uniquely determine the parameters in the model, though, we need to make some assumption about our variables. While relatively simple, these assumptions allow us to derive some very powerful statistical results.

By far the most popular linear regression model is ordinary least squares (OLS). The objective of OLS is to explain as much of the variation in $Y$ as possible, based on the constants $\alpha$ and $\beta$. This is equivalent to minimizing the role of $\varepsilon$, the error term. More specifically, OLS attempts to minimize the sum of the squared error terms (hence "least squares").

OLS makes several assumptions about the form of the regression model, which can be summarized as follows:

A1: The relationship between the regressor and the regressand is linear.

A2: $E[\varepsilon | X] = 0$

A3: $\text{Var}[\varepsilon | X] = \sigma^2$

A4: $\text{Cov}[\varepsilon_i, \varepsilon_j] = 0 \ \forall i \neq j$

A5: $\varepsilon_i \sim N(0, \sigma^2) \ \forall \varepsilon_i$

A6: The regressor is nonstochastic.

We examine each assumption in turn.

The first assumption A1 really just reiterates what Equation 10.1 implies, that we are assuming a linear relationship between $X$ and $Y$. This assumption is not nearly as restrictive as it sounds. Suppose we suspect that default rates are related to interest rates in the following way:

$$D = \alpha + \beta R^{3/4} + \varepsilon \tag{10.4}$$

Because of the exponent on $R$, the relationship between $D$ and $R$ is clearly nonlinear. Still, the relationship between $D$ and $R^{3/4}$ *is* linear. Though not necessary, it is perfectly legitimate to substitute $X$, where $X = R^{3/4}$, into the equation to make this explicit.

As specified, the model implies that the linear relationship should be true for *all* values of $D$ and $R$. In practice, we often only require that the relationship is linear within a given range. In this example, we don't have to assume that the model is true for negative interest rates or rates over 500%. As long as we can restrict ourselves to a range within which the relationship is linear, this is not a problem. What could be a problem is if the relationship takes one form over most of the range, but changes for extreme but plausible values. In our example, maybe interest rates tend to vary between 0% and 15%; there is a linear relationship between $D$ and $R^{3/4}$ in this range, but beyond 15% the relationship becomes highly nonlinear. As risk managers, these extreme but plausible outcomes are what we are most interested in. We will return to this topic at the end of the chapter when we discuss stress testing.

Assumption A2 states that for any realization of $X$, the expected value of $\varepsilon$ is zero. From a very practical standpoint, this assumption resolves any ambiguity between $\alpha$ and $\varepsilon$. Imagine $\varepsilon$ could be modeled as:

$$\varepsilon = \alpha' + \varepsilon' \tag{10.5}$$

where $\alpha'$ is a nonzero constant and $\varepsilon'$ is mean zero. By substituting this equation into Equation 10.1, we have:

$$Y = (\alpha + \alpha') + \beta X + \varepsilon' \tag{10.6}$$

In practice, there is no way to differentiate between $\alpha$ and $\alpha'$, and it is the combined term $(\alpha + \alpha')$, that is our constant.

Using assumption A2 and taking the expectation of both sides of Equation 10.1, we arrive at our first result for the OLS model, namely:

$$E[Y|X] = \alpha + \beta X \tag{10.7}$$

Given $X$, the expected value of $Y$ is fully determined by $\alpha$ and $\beta$. In other words, the model provides a very simple linear and unbiased estimator of $Y$.

Assumption A2 also implies that the error term is independent of $X$. We can express this as:

$$\text{Cov}[X, \varepsilon] = 0 \tag{10.8}$$

This result will prove useful in deriving other properties of the OLS model.

Assumption A3 states that the variance of the error term is constant. This property of constant variance is known as homoscedasticity, in contrast to heteroscedasticity, where the variance is nonconstant. This assumption means that the variance of the error term does not vary over time or depending on the level of the regressor. In finance, many models that appear to be linear often violate this assumption. As we will see in the next chapter, interest rate models often specify an error term that varies in relation to the level of interest rates.

Assumption A4 states that the error terms for various data points should be uncorrelated with each other. As we will also see in the next chapter, this assumption is often violated in time series models, where today's error is correlated with the previous day's error. Assumptions A3 and A4 are often combined. A random variable that has constant variance and is uncorrelated with itself is termed spherical. OLS assumes spherical errors.

Combining assumptions A2 and A3 allows us to derive a very useful relationship, which is widely used in finance. Given $X$ and $Y$ in Equation 10.1:

$$\beta = \frac{\text{Cov}[X, Y]}{\sigma_X^2} = \rho_{XY} \frac{\sigma_Y}{\sigma_X} \tag{10.9}$$

where $\sigma_X$ and $\sigma_Y$ are the standard deviation of $X$ and $Y$, respectively, and $\rho_{XY}$ is the correlation between the two. The proof is left as an exercise at the end of the chapter.

One of the most popular uses of regression analysis in finance is to regress stock returns against market index returns. As specified in Equation 10.1, index returns are represented by $X$, and stock returns by $Y$. This regression is so popular that we frequently speak of a stock's beta, which is simply $\beta$ from the regression equation. While there are other ways to calculate a stock's beta, the functional form given in Equation 10.9 is extremely popular, as it relates two values, $\sigma_X$ and $\sigma_Y$, with which traders and risk managers are often familiar, to two other terms, $\rho_{XY}$ and $\beta$, which should be rather intuitive.

## OPTIMAL HEDGING REVISITED

In Chapter 3, we determined that the optimal hedge ratio for two assets, $A$ and $B$, was given by:

$$h^* = -\rho_{AB}\frac{\sigma_A}{\sigma_B}$$

where $\sigma_A$ is the standard deviation of the returns of asset $A$, $\sigma_B$ is the standard deviation of the returns of asset $B$, and $\rho_{AB}$ is the correlation between the returns of $A$ and $B$.

Although we didn't know it at the time, our optimal hedge ratio is just the negative of our slope from the following regression:

$$r_A = \alpha + \beta r_B + \varepsilon$$
$$h^* = -\beta \qquad\qquad (10.10)$$

In other words, in order to minimize the variance of the portfolio, we need to short $\beta$ units of asset $B$. This completely negates the $\beta r_B$ term in the portfolio, leaving us with a constant, $\alpha$, and the idiosyncratic residual, $\varepsilon$, which cannot be hedged:

$$r_A - \beta r_B = \alpha + \varepsilon$$

This is the minimum variance portfolio.

As an example, pretend we are monitoring a portfolio with \$100 million worth of assets, and the portfolio manager wishes to hedge the portfolio's exposure to fluctuations in the price of oil. We perform an OLS analysis and obtain the following regression equation, where $r_{\text{portfolio}}$ is the portfolio's percentage return, and $r_{\text{oil}}$ is the return associated with the price of oil:

$$r_{\text{portfolio}} = 0.01 + 0.43 r_{\text{oil}} + \varepsilon$$

This tells us that for every unit of the portfolio, the optimal hedge would be to short 0.43 units of oil. For the entire \$100 million portfolio, the hedge would be –\$43 million of oil.

Assumption A5 states that the error terms in the model should be normally distributed. Many of the results of the OLS model are true, regardless of this assumption. This assumption is most useful when it comes to defining confidence levels for the model parameters.

Finally, assumption A6 assumes that the regressor is nonstochastic, or nonrandom. In science, the regressor is often carefully controlled by an experimenter. A researcher might vary the amount of a drug given to mice, to determine the impact of the drug on their weight. One mouse gets one unit of the drug each day, the next gets two, the next three, and so on. Afterward, the regressand, the weight of each mouse, is measured. Ignoring measurement errors, the amount of the drug given to the mice is nonrandom. The experiment could be repeated, with another researcher providing the exact same dosages as in the initial experiment. Unfortunately, the ability to carefully control the independent variable and repeat experiments is rare in finance. More often than not, all of the variables of interest are random. Take, for example, the regression of stock returns on index returns. As the model is specified, we are basically stating that the index's return *causes* the stock's return. In reality, both the index's return and the stock's return are random variables, determined by a number of factors, some of which they might have in common. At some point, the discussion around assumption A6 tends to become deeply philosophical. From a practical standpoint, most of the results of OLS hold true, regardless of assumption A6. In many cases the conclusion needs to be modified only slightly.

### Estimating the Parameters

Now that we have the model, how do we go about determining the constants, $\alpha$ and $\beta$? In the case of OLS, we need only find the combination of constants that minimizes the squared errors. In other words, given a sample of regressands, $y_1, y_2, \ldots, y_n,$ and a set of corresponding regressors, $x_1, x_2, \ldots, x_n,$ we want to minimize the following sum:

$$\text{RSS} = \sum_{i=1}^{n}\varepsilon_i^2 = \sum_{i=1}^{n}(y_i - \alpha - \beta x_i)^2 \tag{10.11}$$

where RSS is the commonly used acronym for the residual sum of squares (sum of squared residuals would probably be a more accurate description, but RSS is the convention). In order to minimize this equation, we first take its derivative with respect to $\alpha$ and $\beta$ separately. We set the derivatives to zero and solve the resulting simultaneous equations. The result is the equations for OLS parameters:

$$\alpha = \bar{Y} - \beta \bar{X}$$

$$\beta = \frac{\sum_{i=1}^{n}x_i y_i - n\bar{Y}\bar{X}}{\sum_{i=1}^{n}x_i^2 - n\bar{X}^2} \tag{10.12}$$

where $\bar{X}$ and $\bar{Y}$ are the sample mean of $X$ and $Y$, respectively. The proof is left for an exercise at the end of the chapter.

## Evaluating the Regression

Unlike a controlled laboratory experiment, the real world is a very noisy and complicated place. In finance it is rare that a simple univariate regression model is going to completely explain a large data set. In many cases, the data are so noisy that we must ask ourselves if the model is explaining anything at all. Even when a relationship appears to exist, we are likely to want some quantitative measure of just how strong that relationship is.

Probably the most popular statistic for describing linear regressions is the coefficient of determination, commonly known as $R$-squared, or just $R^2$. $R^2$ is often described as the goodness of fit of the linear regression. When $R^2$ is one, the regression model completely explains the data. If $R^2$ is one, all the residuals are zero, and the residual sum of squares (RSS) is zero. At the other end of the spectrum, if $R^2$ is zero, the model does not explain any variation in the observed data. In other words, $Y$ does not vary with $X$, and $\beta$ is zero.

To calculate the coefficient of determination, we need to define two additional terms: the total sum of squares (TSS) and the explained sum of squares (ESS). They are defined as:

$$\text{TSS} = \sum_{i=1}^{n}\left(y_i - \bar{Y}\right)^2$$
$$\text{ESS} = \sum_{i=1}^{n}\left(\hat{y}_i - \bar{Y}\right)^2 = \sum_{i=1}^{n}\left(\alpha + \beta x_i - \bar{Y}\right)^2 \tag{10.13}$$

Here, as before, $\bar{Y}$ is the sample mean of $Y$.

These two sums are related to the previously encountered residual sum of squares, as follows:

$$\text{TSS} = \text{ESS} + \text{RSS} \tag{10.14}$$

In other words, the total variation in our regressand, TSS, can be broken down into two components, the part the model can explain, ESS, and the part the model cannot, RSS. These sums can be used to compute $R^2$:

$$R^2 = \frac{\text{ESS}}{\text{TSS}} = 1 - \frac{\text{RSS}}{\text{TSS}} \tag{10.15}$$

As promised, when there are no residual errors, when RSS is zero, $R^2$ is one. Also, when ESS is zero, or when the variation in the errors is equal to TSS, $R^2$ is zero. It turns out that for the univariate linear regression model, $R^2$ is also equal to the correlation between $X$ and $Y$, squared. If $X$ and $Y$ are perfectly correlated ($\rho_{xy} = 1$) or perfectly negatively correlated ($\rho_{xy} = -1$), then $R^2$ will equal one.

Estimates of the regression parameters are just like the parameter estimates we examined in the preceding chapter, and subject to hypothesis testing. In regression analysis, the most common null hypothesis is that the slope parameter, $\beta$, is zero. If $\beta$ is zero, then the regression model does not explain any variation in the regressand.

In finance, we often want to know if $\alpha$ is significantly different from zero, but for different reasons. In modern finance, *alpha* has become synonymous with the ability of a portfolio manager to generate excess returns. This is because, in a regression equation modeling the returns of a portfolio manager, after we remove all the randomness, $\varepsilon$, and the influence of the explanatory variable, $X$, if $\alpha$ is still positive, then it is suggested that the portfolio manager is producing positive excess returns, something that should be very difficult in efficient markets. Of course, it's not just enough that $\alpha$ is positive; we require that the $\alpha$ be positive *and* statistically significant.

In order to test the significance of the regression parameters, we first need to calculate the variance of $\alpha$ and $\beta$, which we can obtain from the following formulas:

$$\hat{\sigma}_\alpha^2 = \frac{\sum_{i=1}^{n} x_i^2}{n \sum_{i=1}^{n} (x_i - \bar{x})^2} \hat{\sigma}_\varepsilon^2$$

$$\hat{\sigma}_\beta^2 = \frac{\hat{\sigma}_\varepsilon^2}{\sum_{i=1}^{n} (x_i - \bar{x})^2} \tag{10.16}$$

$$\hat{\sigma}_\varepsilon^2 = \frac{\sum_{i=1}^{n} \varepsilon_i^2}{n - 2}$$

where the last formula gives the variance of the error term, $\varepsilon$, which is simply the RSS divided by the degrees of freedom for the regression. Using the equations for the variance of our estimators, we can then form an appropriate $t$-statistic. For example, for $\beta$ we would have:

$$\frac{\hat{\beta} - \beta}{\hat{\sigma}_\beta} \sim t_{n-2} \tag{10.17}$$

The most common null hypothesis when testing regression parameters is that the parameters are equal to zero. More often than not, we do not care if the parameters are significantly greater than or less than zero; we just care that they are significantly different. Because of this, rather than using the standard $t$-statistics as in Equation 10.17, some practitioners prefer to use the absolute value of the $t$-statistic. Some software packages also follow this convention.

## SAMPLE PROBLEM

*Question:*
  As a risk manager and expert on statistics, you are asked to evaluate the performance of a long/short equity portfolio manager. You are given 10 years of monthly return data. You regress the log returns of the portfolio manager against the log returns of a market index.

$$r_{\text{portfolio\_manager}} = \alpha + \beta r_{\text{market}} + \varepsilon$$

Assume both series are normally distributed and homoscedastic. From this analysis, you obtain the following regression results:

|  | Constant | Beta |
| --- | --- | --- |
| Value | 1.13% | 20.39% |
| Standard deviation | 0.48% | 9.71% |
| $R^2$ | 8.11% | |

What can we say about the performance of the portfolio manager?

*Answer:*

The $R^2$ for the regression is low. Only 8.11% of the variation in the portfolio manager's returns can be explained by the constant, beta, and variation in the market. The rest is idiosyncratic risk, and is unexplained by the model.

That said, both the constant and the beta seem to be statistically significant (i.e., they are statistically different from zero). We can get the *t*-statistic by dividing the value of the coefficient by its standard deviation. For the constant, we have:

$$\frac{\hat{\alpha} - \alpha}{\hat{\sigma}_\alpha} = \frac{1.13\% - 0\%}{0.48\%} = 2.36$$

Similarly, for beta we have a *t*-statistic of 2.10. Using a statistical package, we calculate the corresponding probability associated with each *t*-statistic. This should be a two-tailed test with 118 degrees of freedom (10 years × 12 months per year – 2 parameters). We can reject the hypothesis that the constant and slope are zero at the 2% level and the 4% level, respectively. In other words, there seems to be a significant market component to the fund manager's return, but the manager is also generating statistically significant excess returns.

In the preceding example, both regression parameters were statistically significant, even though the $R^2$ was fairly modest. Which is more important, $R^2$ or the significance of the regression parameters? Of course this is a subjective question and both measures are useful, but in finance one is tempted to say that the *t*-statistics, and not $R^2$, are more useful. For many who are new to finance, this is surprising. Many of us first encounter regression analysis in the sciences. In a scientific experiment where conditions can be precisely controlled, it is not unusual to see $R^2$ above 90%. In finance, where so much is not being measured, the error term tends to dominate, and $R^2$ is typically much lower. That $\beta$ can be statistically significant even with a low $R^2$ may seem surprising, but in finance this is often the case.

## LINEAR REGRESSION (MULTIVARIATE)

Univariate regression models are extremely common in finance and risk management, but sometimes we require a slightly more complicated model. In these cases, we might use a multivariate regression model. The basic idea is the same, but instead of one regressand and one regressor, we have one regressand and multiple regressors. Our basic equation will look something like the following:

$$Y = \beta_1 + \beta_2 X_2 + \beta_3 X_3 + \cdots + \beta_n X_n \tag{10.18}$$

Notice that rather than denoting the first constant with $\alpha$, we chose to go with $\beta_1$. This is the more common convention in multivariate regression. To make the equation even more regular, we can assume that there is an $X_1$, which, unlike the other $X$'s, is constant and always equal to one. This convention allows us to easily express a set of observations in matrix form. For $t$ observations and $n$ regressands, we can write:

$$\begin{bmatrix} y_1 \\ y_2 \\ \vdots \\ y_t \end{bmatrix} = \begin{bmatrix} x_{11} & x_{12} & \cdots & x_{1n} \\ x_{21} & x_{22} & \cdots & x_{2n} \\ \vdots & \vdots & \ddots & \\ x_{t1} & x_{t2} & & x_{tn} \end{bmatrix} \begin{bmatrix} \beta_1 \\ \beta_2 \\ \vdots \\ \beta_n \end{bmatrix} + \begin{bmatrix} \varepsilon_1 \\ \varepsilon_2 \\ \vdots \\ \varepsilon_t \end{bmatrix} \tag{10.19}$$

where the first column of the **X** matrix—$x_{11}, x_{21}, \ldots, x_{t1}$—is understood to consist entirely of ones. The entire equation can be written more succinctly as:

$$\mathbf{Y} = \mathbf{X}\boldsymbol{\beta} + \boldsymbol{\varepsilon} \tag{10.20}$$

where, as before, we have used bold letters to denote matrices.

## Multicollinearity

In order to determine the parameters of the multivariate regression, we again turn to our OLS assumptions. In the multivariate case, the assumptions are the same as before, but with one addition. In the multivariate case, we require that all of the independent variables be linearly independent of each other. We say that the independent variables must lack multicollinearity:

A7: The independent variables have no multicollinearity.

To say that the independent variables lack multicollinearity means that it is impossible to express one of the independent variables as a linear combination of the others.

This additional assumption is required to remove ambiguity. To see why this is the case, imagine that we attempt a regression with two independent variables where the second independent variable, $X_3$, can be expressed as a linear function of the first independent variable, $X_2$:

$$Y = \beta_1 + \beta_2 X_2 + \beta_3 X_3 + \varepsilon_1$$
$$X_3 = \lambda_1 + \lambda_2 X_2 + \varepsilon_2 \tag{10.21}$$

If we substitute the second line of Equation 10.21 into the first, we get:

$$Y = (\beta_1 + \beta_3 \lambda_1) + (\beta_2 + \beta \lambda_2) X_2 + (\beta_3 \varepsilon_2 + \varepsilon_1)$$
$$Y = \beta_4 + \beta_5 X_2 + \varepsilon_3 \tag{10.22}$$

In the second line, we have simplified by introducing new constants and a new error term. We have replaced $(\beta_1 + \beta_3\lambda_1)$ with $\beta_4$, replaced $(\beta_2 + \beta_3\lambda_2)$ with $\beta_5$, and replaced $(\beta_3\varepsilon_2 + \varepsilon_1)$ with $\varepsilon_3$. $\beta_5$ can be uniquely determined in a univariate regression, but there is an infinite number of combinations of $\beta_2$, $\beta_3$, and $\lambda_2$ that we could choose to equal $\beta_5$. If $\beta_5 = 10$, any of the following combinations would work:

$$\begin{aligned}
\beta_2 &= 10, & \beta_3 &= 0, & \lambda_2 &= 100 \\
\beta_2 &= 0, & \beta_3 &= 10, & \lambda_2 &= 1 \\
\beta_2 &= 500, & \beta_3 &= -49, & \lambda_2 &= 10
\end{aligned} \tag{10.23}$$

In other words, $\beta_2$ and $\beta_3$ are ambiguous in the initial equation. This ambiguity is why we want to avoid multicollinearity.

Even in the presence of multicollinearity, the regression model still works in a sense. In the preceding example, even though $\beta_2$ and $\beta_3$ are ambiguous, any combination where $(\beta_2 + \beta_3\lambda_2)$ equals $\beta_5$ will produce the same value of $Y$ for a given set of $X$'s. If our only objective is to predict $Y$, then the regression model still works. The problem is that the value of the parameters will be unstable. A slightly different data set can cause wild swings in the value of the parameter estimates, and may even flip the signs of the parameters. A variable that we expect to be positively correlated with the regressand may end up with a large negative beta. This makes interpreting the model difficult. Parameter instability is often a sign of multicollinearity.

There is no well-accepted procedure for dealing with multicollinearity. The easiest course of action is often simply to eliminate a variable from the regression. While easy, this is hardly satisfactory.

Another possibility is to transform the variables, to create uncorrelated variables out of linear combinations of the existing variables. In the previous example, even though $X_3$ is correlated with $X_2$, $X_3 - \lambda_2 X_2$ *is* uncorrelated with $X_2$.

$$\begin{aligned}
X_3 - \lambda_2 X_2 &= \lambda_1 + \varepsilon_3 \\
\text{Cov}[X_2, X_3 - \lambda_2 X_2] &= \text{Cov}[X_2, \lambda_1 + \varepsilon_3] = \text{Cov}[X_2, \varepsilon_3] = 0
\end{aligned} \tag{10.24}$$

One potential problem with this approach is similar to what we saw with principal component analysis (which is really just another method for creating uncorrelated variables from linear combinations of correlated variables). If we are lucky, a linear combination of variables will have a simple economic interpretation. For example, if $X_2$ and $X_3$ are two equity indexes, then their difference might correspond to a familiar spread. Similarly, if the two variables are interest rates, their difference might bear some relation to the shape of the yield curve. Other linear combinations might be difficult to interpret, and if the relationship is not readily identifiable, then the relationship is more likely to be unstable or spurious.

Global financial markets are becoming increasingly integrated. More now than ever before, multicollinearity is a problem that risk managers need to be aware of.

### Estimating the Parameters

Assuming our variables meet all of the OLS assumptions, how do we go about estimating the parameters of our multivariate model? The math is a bit more complicated, but the process is the same as in the univariate case. Using our regression equation, we calculate the residual sum of squares and seek to minimize its value through the choice of our parameters. The result is our OLS estimator for $\beta$, $\hat{\beta}$:

$$\hat{\beta} = (\mathbf{X}'\mathbf{X})^{-1}\mathbf{X}'\mathbf{Y} \qquad (10.25)$$

Where we had two parameters in the univariate case, now we have a vector of $n$ parameters, which define our regression equation.

Given the OLS assumptions—actually, we don't even need assumption A6, that the regressors are nonstochastic—$\hat{\beta}$ is the best linear unbiased estimator of $\beta$. This result is known as the Gauss-Markov theorem.

### Evaluating the Regression

Just as with the univariate model, once we have calculated the parameters of our multivariate model, we need to be able to evaluate how well the model explains the data.

We can use the same process that we used in the univariate case to calculate $R^2$ for the multivariate regression. All of the necessary sums, RSS, ESS, and TSS, can be calculated without further complication. As in the univariate case, in the multivariate model, $R^2$ varies between zero and one, and indicates how much of the dependent variable is being explained by the model. One problem in the multivariate setting is that $R^2$ tends to increase as we add independent variables to our regression. In fact, adding variables to a regression can never decrease the $R^2$. At worst, $R^2$ stays the same. This might seem to suggest that adding variables to a regression is always a good thing, even if they have little or no explanatory power. Clearly there should be some penalty for adding variables to a regression. An attempt to rectify this situation is the adjusted $R^2$, which is typically denoted by $\bar{R}^2$, and defined as:

$$\bar{R}^2 = 1 - (1 - R^2)\frac{t-1}{t-n} \qquad (10.26)$$

where $t$ is the number of sample points and $n$ is the number of regressors, including the constant term. While there is clearly a penalty for adding independent variables and increasing $n$, one odd thing about $\bar{R}^2$ is that the value can turn negative in certain situations.

Just as with the univariate model, we can calculate the variance of the error term. Given $t$ data points and $n$ regressors, the variance of the error term is:

$$\hat{\sigma}_\varepsilon^2 = \frac{\sum_{i=1}^{t}\varepsilon_i^2}{t-n} \qquad (10.27)$$

The variance of the $i$th estimator is then:

$$\hat{\sigma}_i^2 = \hat{\sigma}_\varepsilon^2[(\mathbf{X}'\mathbf{X})^{-1}]_{i,i} \qquad (10.28)$$

where the final term on the right-hand side is the $i$th diagonal element of the matrix $(\mathbf{X'X})^{-1}$. We can then use this to form an appropriate $t$-statistic, with $t - n$ degrees of freedom:

$$\frac{\hat{\beta}_i - \beta_i}{\hat{\sigma}_i} \sim t_{t-n} \tag{10.29}$$

Instead of just testing one parameter, we can actually test the significance of all of the parameters, excluding the constant, using what is known as an $F$-test. The $F$-statistic can be calculated using $R^2$:

$$\frac{R^2 / (n-1)}{(1 - R^2) / (t - n)} \sim F_{n-1, t-n} \tag{10.30}$$

As the name implies, the $F$-statistic follows an $F$-distribution with $n - 1$ and $t - n$ degrees of freedom. Not surprisingly, if the $R^2$ is zero, the $F$-statistic will be zero as well.

Exhibit 10.2 shows 5% and 10% critical values for the $F$-distribution for various values of $n$ and $t$, where the appropriate degrees of freedom are $n - 1$ and $t - n$. For a univariate regression, $n = 2$, with a large number of data points, a good rule of thumb is that values over 4.00 will be significant at the 5% level.

In general, we want to keep our models as simple as possible. We don't want to add variables just for the sake of adding variables. This principle is known as parsimony. $\bar{R}^2$, $t$-tests, and $F$-tests are often used in deciding whether to include an additional variable in a regression. In the case of $\bar{R}^2$, a variable will be added only if it improves $\bar{R}^2$. In finance, even when the statistical significance of the betas is high, $R^2$ and $\bar{R}^2$ are often very low. For this reason, it is common to evaluate the addition of a variable on the basis of its $t$-statistic. If the $t$-statistic of the additional variable is statistically significant, then it is kept in the model. It is less common, but it is possible to have a collection of variables, none of which are statistically significant by themselves, but which are jointly significant. This is why it is important to monitor the $F$-statistic as well. When applied systematically, this process of adding or removing variables from a regression model is referred to as stepwise regression.

**EXHIBIT 10.2**   *F*-Distribution Critical Values

| $n$ | $t$ | 5% | 10% |
|-----|------|------|------|
| 2 | 20 | 4.41 | 3.01 |
| 2 | 50 | 4.04 | 2.81 |
| 2 | 100 | 3.94 | 2.76 |
| 2 | 1,000 | 3.85 | 2.71 |
| 4 | 20 | 3.24 | 2.46 |
| 4 | 50 | 2.81 | 2.21 |
| 4 | 100 | 2.70 | 2.14 |
| 4 | 1,000 | 2.61 | 2.09 |

## APPLICATION: FACTOR ANALYSIS

In risk management, factor analysis is a form of risk attribution, which attempts to identify and measure common sources of risk within large, complex portfolios.[1] These underlying sources of risk are known as factors. Factors can include equity market risk, sector risk, region risk, country risk, interest rate risk, inflation risk, or style risk (large-cap versus small-cap, value versus growth, momentum, etc.). Factor analysis is most popular for equity portfolios, but can be applied to any asset class or strategy.

In a large, complex portfolio, it is sometimes far from obvious how much exposure a portfolio has to a given factor. Depending on a portfolio manager's objectives, it may be desirable to minimize certain factor exposures or to keep the amount of risk from certain factors within a given range. It typically falls to risk management to ensure that the factor exposures are maintained at acceptable levels.

The classic approach to factor analysis can best be described as risk taxonomy. For each type of factor, each security would be associated with one and only one factor. If we were trying to measure country exposures, each security would be assigned to a specific country—France, South Korea, the United States, and so on. If we were trying to measure sector exposures, each security would similarly be assigned to an industry, such as technology, manufacturing, or retail. After we had categorized all of the securities, we would simply add up the exposures of the various securities to get our portfolio-level exposures. Exhibit 10.3 shows how a portfolio's exposure to different regions and countries could be broken down.

**EXHIBIT 10.3**  Geographic Exposures

|  | Market Value |
|---|---|
| Asia | |
| China | $359 |
| Japan | $3,349 |
| Europe | |
| Germany | –$823 |
| Ireland | $500 |
| North America | |
| United States | $4,865 |
| Mexico | $2,393 |
| Total | $10,643 |

---

[1] In statistics, factor analysis can also refer to a specific method of data analysis, similar to principal component analysis (PCA). What we are exploring in this section might be more formally referred to as risk factor analysis. Risk factor analysis is a much more general concept, which might utilize statistical factor analysis, regression analysis, PCA, or any number of statistical methods.

In this portfolio, which has a total value of $10,643, there is $359 of exposure to China and a net –$323 of exposure to Europe. Importantly, the classic approach is binary. A security is an investment in either China or Germany; it is either in utilities or in agriculture. It can't be one-third in Russia and two-thirds in Poland, or just 42% in value stocks. This creates a problem in the real world. What do you do with a company that is headquartered in France, has all of its manufacturing capacity in China, sells its products in North America, and has listed shares on both NASDAQ and the London Stock Exchange? Is a company that sells electronics a technology company or a retailer?

These kinds of obvious questions led to the development of various statistical approaches to factor analysis. One very popular approach is to associate each factor with an index, and then to use that index in a regression analysis to measure a portfolio's exposure to that factor. For example, if we want to measure a portfolio's exposure to Japan, we would run a regression of our portfolio's returns against the returns of a Japanese index:

$$r_{\text{portfolio}} = \alpha + \beta r_{\text{index}} + \varepsilon \tag{10.31}$$

The Japanese index could be a publicly available index, such as the Nikkei, or it could be an index of our own construction based on a basket of Japanese securities. The return series for our portfolio should reflect what the returns of the current portfolio would have been, given the current holdings of the portfolio. This type of return series is often referred to as a what-if or backcast return series. This is as opposed to the actual return series, which would be impacted by the changing composition of the portfolio over time. Of course this analysis assumes that both return series obey all the OLS assumptions.

In Equation 10.31, $\beta$ now represents our factor exposure. The exposure will be in the same units as the portfolio returns. If the portfolio returns are in U.S. dollars, the exposure will be in U.S. dollars, too. From this equation, we would already be able to predict that if the index return was –10%, then the impact on the portfolio's return would be $-0.10\beta$. Being able to summarize the risk of a large, complex portfolio in such simple terms is what makes regression analysis so powerful.

Another nice thing about factor analysis is that the factor exposures can be added across portfolios. If Portfolio A has $100 of exposure to technology, and Portfolio B has $200 of exposure to the same factor, then a combined portfolio, Portfolio A + B, would have $300 of exposure to technology. This result can be obtained by simply adding together the regression equations of Portfolio A and Portfolio B:

$$\begin{aligned}
r_A &= \alpha_A + \beta_A r_{\text{index}} + \varepsilon_A \\
r_B &= \alpha_B + \beta_B r_{\text{index}} + \varepsilon_B \\
r_{A+B} &= (\alpha_A + \alpha_B) + (\beta_A + \beta_B) r_{\text{index}} + (\varepsilon_A + \varepsilon_B)
\end{aligned} \tag{10.32}$$

Because factor exposures are additive, this makes hedging a factor exposure relatively simple. If we have $300 of exposure to technology, and assuming the technology index is tradable, we can hedge this factor by shorting $300 of the technology index; $300 less $300 leaves us with $0 of factor exposure.

Exhibit 10.4 shows a sample exposure breakdown for an unspecified factor. Notice how the factor exposures are not necessarily proportional to the market values or even of the same sign. Even though there is not a fixed relationship between

**EXHIBIT 10.4**    Adding Factor Exposures across Portfolios

|             | Market Value | Factor Exposure |
|-------------|-------------|-----------------|
| Portfolio A | $9,378      | –$30,592        |
| Portfolio B | $39,348     | $45,829         |
| Portfolio C | –$2,938     | –$2,674         |
| Total       | $45,788     | $12,563         |

market value and factor exposure across portfolios, the market values and the factor exposures can each be added up separately to arrive at their respective totals.

In addition to giving us the factor exposure, the factor analysis allows us to divide the risk of a portfolio into systematic and idiosyncratic components. In this case, systematic risk refers to the risk in a portfolio that can be attributed to a factor. The risk that is not systematic (i.e., that cannot be attributed to a factor) is referred to as idiosyncratic risk. In an equity portfolio, this is often referred to as stock-specific risk. From our OLS assumptions, we know that $r_{index}$ and $\varepsilon$ are not correlated. Calculating the variance of $r_{portfolio}$ in Equation 10.31, we arrive at the following:

$$\sigma^2_{portfolio} = \beta^2 \sigma^2_{index} + \sigma^2_\varepsilon \tag{10.33}$$

In other words, the variance of the portfolio can be broken into two components, $\beta^2 \sigma^2_{index}$, the systematic component, and $\sigma^2_\varepsilon$, the idiosyncratic component. As mentioned previously, depending on the objective of the portfolio, we might consider more or less idiosyncratic variance desirable. If our objective is to replicate an index, we might want to minimize idiosyncratic risk. If our goal is to produce portfolio returns that are uncorrelated with the market, we would want to minimize the systematic risk in the portfolio.

In theory, there is no reason why we cannot extend our factor analysis using multivariate regression analysis. In practice, many of the factors we are interested in will be highly correlated (most equity indexes are highly correlated with each other). This leads naturally to the use of spreads between indexes for secondary factors in order to avoid multicollinearity. For example, if we are using a broad market index as a primary factor, then the spread between that index and a country factor might be an interesting secondary factor. As outlined in the section on multicollinearity, we can use the residuals from the regression of our secondary index on the primary index to construct a return series that is uncorrelated with the primary series.

In theory, factors can be based on almost any kind of return series. The advantage of indexes based on publicly traded securities is that it makes hedging very straightforward. At the same time, there might be some risks that are not captured by any publicly traded index. Some risk managers have attempted to resolve this problem by using statistical techniques, such as principal component analysis (PCA) or cluster analysis, to develop more robust factors. Besides the fact that these factors might be difficult to hedge, they might also be unstable, and it might be difficult to associate these factors with any identifiable macroeconomic variable. Even using these statistical techniques, there is always the possibility that we have failed to identify a factor that is an important source of risk for our portfolio. Factor analysis is a very powerful tool, but it is not without its shortcomings.

## APPLICATION: STRESS TESTING

In risk management, stress testing assesses the likely impact of an extreme, but plausible, scenario on a portfolio. There is no universally accepted method for performing stress tests. One popular approach, which we consider here, is closely related to factor analysis.

The first step in stress testing is defining a scenario. Scenarios can be either ad hoc or based on a historical episode. An ad hoc scenario might assume that equity markets decline 20% or that interest rates jump 5%, for example. A historical scenario might examine the Russian debt crisis of 1998 or the Asian currency crisis of 1997. Black Monday, the equity market crash of 1987, is probably one of the most popular scenarios for historical stress tests. For both the ad hoc and the historical approaches, we want to quantify our scenario by specifying the returns of a few key instruments, or factors. For the 5% jump in interest rates, we might specify that 10-year U.S. Treasury rates increase by 5%, BBB credit spreads increase 2%, and the Standard & Poor's 500 index decreases 10%. In the Black Monday scenario, we might choose to focus on the change in the Dow Jones Industrial Average, the price of gold, and the London Interbank Offered Rate (LIBOR). Just as with our factor analysis, we need to be careful that the instruments defining our scenario are not highly correlated.

In the second step, we need to define how all other underlying financial instruments react, given our scenario. In order to do this, we construct multivariate regressions. We regress the returns of each underlying financial instrument against the returns of the instruments that define our scenario. What might seem strange is that, even in the case of the historical scenarios, we use recent returns in our regression. In the case of the historical scenarios, why don't we just use the actual returns from that period? The reason we use current returns and not returns from the historical episode is partly practical. Consider Black Monday, 1987. Credit default swaps didn't exist in 1987. The euro, the world's second largest currency, didn't exist. Many of today's largest companies didn't exist, including Google (IPO in 2004) and Exxon Mobil (Exxon and Mobil did not merge until 1999). If our current portfolio holds any of these securities and we tried to use actual returns from the stress period, we would have no data to use for those securities. Even if we did have historical returns for all of the securities in our portfolio, would we want to use them? The world has changed significantly over the past 30 years. Companies and relationships between companies are likely to be very different now than they were 30 years ago. To put it another way, we choose a specific historical episode not because we expect that event to repeat exactly, in every detail, but because we expect something *like* that event could happen again. As Mark Twain was supposed to have said, "History does not repeat itself, but it often rhymes."

In the final step, after we have generated the returns for all of the underlying financial instruments, we price any options or other derivatives. This last step is important. While using delta approximations might have been acceptable for calculating value at risk statistics at one point in time, it should never have been acceptable for stress testing. By definition, stress testing is the examination of extreme events, and the accurate pricing of nonlinear instruments is critical.

As an example of how a stress test might work in practice, let's imagine a scenario that we'll call Simple Oil Crisis. In this scenario, crude oil prices increase 20% and the Standard & Poor's 500 index decreases by 10%. Imagine that our portfolio consists solely of $100 worth of shares in Exxon Mobil. To see how Exxon Mobil reacts, we would construct the following regression:

$$r_{\text{Exxon\_Mobil}} = \beta_1 + \beta_2 r_{\text{oil}} + \beta_3 r_{\text{equity\_index}} + \varepsilon \qquad (10.34)$$

where the returns would be based on recent historical data, say the past year of daily returns. In order to avoid issues with multicollinearity, we'll assume that $r_{\text{oil}}$ and $r_{\text{equity\_index}}$ are uncorrelated. Assume that the OLS regression produces the following equation describing Exxon Mobil's returns:

$$r_{\text{Exxon\_Mobil}} = 0.0000 + 0.0899 r_{\text{oil}} + 0.7727 r_{\text{equity\_index}} + \varepsilon \qquad (10.35)$$

Based on this equation, we expect Exxon Mobil to return −5.93% in our stress scenario:

$$\begin{aligned} E\left[r_{\text{Exxon\_Mobil}} \middle| \text{stress}\right] &= 0.0000 + 0.0899 \cdot 0.20 + 0.7727 \cdot (-0.10) \\ E\left[r_{\text{Exxon\_Mobil}} \middle| \text{stress}\right] &= -0.0593 \end{aligned} \qquad (10.36)$$

Given our starting value of $100, we would expect to lose $5.93 in this scenario. To evaluate the expected return of a portfolio with multiple securities, we could proceed stepwise, evaluating each security in turn and adding up the gains or losses. Alternatively, we could calculate the backcast dollar return series for the entire portfolio, and use this series in our regression analysis to calculate the expected portfolio return directly.

Earlier in the chapter, when we were reviewing the assumptions of the OLS model, we noted that the model assumes that the linear relationship between the regressand and regressors is true over the entire range being considered. We cautioned that this assumption could be problematic if the relationship takes one form over most of the range, but changes for extreme but plausible values. Stress testing is, by definition, about extreme but plausible values. In Chapter 12, we discuss some alternative approaches to regression that may be better suited to the analysis of extreme returns. Regardless of which form of regression analysis we settle on, the other steps in constructing the stress test remain the same.

## PROBLEMS

1. The following regression equation describes the daily returns of stock XYZ, $r_{\text{XYZ}}$, in terms of an index return, $r_{\text{index}}$, and a mean zero disturbance term, $\varepsilon$:

$$r_{\text{XYZ}} = \alpha + \beta r_{\text{index}} + \varepsilon$$

where $\alpha$ and $\beta$ are constants, $\varepsilon$ is mean zero with a standard deviation of 1.0%, $\alpha$ is 0.01%, and $\beta$ is 1.20. If the index return on a given day is 5%, what is the expected return of XYZ?

2. In addition to the assumptions in the previous question, assume $r_{\text{index}}$ has a mean of 0.05% and a standard deviation of 1.5%. What is the expected value of $r_{\text{XYZ}}$? What is the standard deviation of $r_{\text{XYZ}}$?

3. Using all the information from the previous two questions, determine the correlation between the index returns and the returns of XYZ.

4. You perform a regression analysis of a hedge fund's returns against an industry benchmark. You have 50 data points. The total sum of squares (TSS) is 13.50%. The residual sum of squares (RSS) is 10.80%. What is the $R^2$?

5. In the previous question, what is the critical value for the $F$-test? Is the $F$-statistic significant at the 95% confidence level?

6. An initial univariate regression produces an $R^2$ of 60%. There are 20 data points. In an effort to improve the model, two additional regressors are added, which boost the $R^2$ to 64%. Determine which model is better based on adjusted $R^2$.

7. Based on your analysis of Company ABC's stock returns, $r_{ABC}$, you develop the following OLS regression model:

$$r_{ABC} = 0.01 + 1.25r_A + 0.34r_B + \varepsilon$$

where $r_A$ and $r_B$ are two uncorrelated indexes, and $\varepsilon$ is a mean zero disturbance term. If $r_A = 10\%$ and $r_B = 50\%$, what is the expected value of $r_{ABC}$?

8. You perform the following multivariate regression:

$$r = \beta_1 + \beta_2 X_2 + \beta_3 X_3 + \varepsilon_1$$

Upon closer inspection you notice that $X_2$ and $X_3$ are, in fact, correlated. Their relationship can be described in the following regression:

$$X_3 = \beta_4 + \beta_5 X_2 + \varepsilon_2$$

Suggest a new model that avoids the problem of multicollinearity.

9. Prove Equation 10.9. That is, given the standard univariate regression,

$$Y = \alpha + \beta X + \varepsilon$$

prove that:

$$\beta = \frac{\text{Cov}[X, Y]}{\sigma_X^2} = \rho_{XY} \frac{\sigma_Y}{\sigma_X}$$

where $\sigma_X$ and $\sigma_Y$ are the standard deviations of $X$ and $Y$, respectively, and $\rho_{XY}$ is the correlation between the two. Hint: Start by calculating the covariance between $X$ and $Y$.

10. The equation for the residual sum of squares (RSS) of the univariate regression model is:

$$\text{RSS} = \sum_{i=1}^{n} \varepsilon_i^2 = \sum_{i=1}^{n} (y_i - \alpha - \beta x_i)^2$$

Take the derivatives of this equation, first with respect to $\alpha$, then with respect to $\beta$. Set the two resulting equations to zero, and solve to get the standard equations for the OLS regression parameters, Equation 10.12. Technically, we should also prove that this solution is a minimum and not a maximum, but that is beyond the scope of this book.

## CHAPTER 11

# Time Series Models

In this chapter, we provide an introduction to time series analysis. Time series describe how random variables evolve over time and form the basis of many financial models.

## RANDOM WALKS

A time series is an equation or set of equations describing how a random variable or variables evolve over time. Probably the most basic time series is the random walk. For a random variable $X$, with a realization $x_t$ at time $t$, the following conditions describe a random walk:

$$
\begin{aligned}
x_t &= x_{t-1} + \varepsilon_t \\
E[\varepsilon_t] &= 0 \\
E[\varepsilon_t^2] &= \sigma^2 \\
E[\varepsilon_s \varepsilon_t] &= 0 \;\; \forall s \neq t
\end{aligned}
\tag{11.1}
$$

In other words, $X$ is equal to its value from the previous period, plus a random disturbance, $\varepsilon_t$; $\varepsilon_t$ is mean zero, with a constant variance. The last condition in Equation 11.1, combined with the fact that $\varepsilon_t$ is mean zero, tells us that the $\varepsilon$'s from different periods will be uncorrelated with each other. In time series analysis, we typically refer to $x_{t-1}$ as the first lagged value of $x_t$, or just the first lag of $x_t$. By this convention, $x_{t-2}$ would be the second lag, $x_{t-3}$ the third, and so on.

We can also think in terms of changes in $X$. Subtracting $x_{t-1}$ from both sides of our initial equation:

$$
\Delta x_t = x_t - x_{t-1} = \varepsilon_t
\tag{11.2}
$$

In this basic random walk, $\Delta x_t$ has all of the properties of our stochastic term, $\varepsilon_t$. Both are mean zero. Both have a constant variance, $\sigma^2$. Most important, the error terms are uncorrelated with each other. This system is not affected by its past. This is the defining feature of a random walk.

How does the system evolve over time? Note that Equation 11.1 is true for all time periods. All of the following equations are valid:

$$x_t = x_{t-1} + \varepsilon_t$$
$$x_{t-1} = x_{t-2} + \varepsilon_{t-1}$$
$$\vdots$$
$$x_{t-i} = x_{t-i-1} + \varepsilon_{t-i}$$

(11.3)

By substituting the equation into itself, we can see how the equation evolves over multiple periods:

$$x_t = x_{t-1} + \varepsilon_t = x_{t-2} + \varepsilon_{t-1} + \varepsilon_t = x_0 + \sum_{i=1}^{t} \varepsilon_i$$

(11.4)

At time $t$, $X$ is simply the sum of its initial value, $x_0$, plus a series of random steps. Using this formula, it is easy to calculate the conditional mean and variance of $x_t$:

$$E[x_t | x_0] = x_0$$
$$\mathrm{Var}[x_t | x_0] = t\sigma^2$$

(11.5)

If the variance increases proportionally with $t$, then the standard deviation increases with the square root of $t$. This is our familiar square root rule for independent and identically distributed (i.i.d.) variables. For a random walk, our best guess for the future value of the variable is simply the current value, but the probability of finding it near the current value becomes increasingly small.

Though the proof is omitted here, it is not difficult to show that, for a random walk, skewness is proportional to $t^{-0.5}$ and kurtosis is proportional to $t^{-1}$. In other words, while variance, and standard deviation increase over longer time spans, skewness and kurtosis become smaller.

The simple random walk is not a great model for equities, where we expect prices to increase over time, or for interest rates, which cannot be negative. With some rather trivial modification, though, we can accommodate both of these requirements.

## DRIFT-DIFFUSION MODEL

One simple modification we can make to the random walk is to add a constant term, in the following way:

$$p_t = \alpha + p_{t-1} + \varepsilon_t$$

(11.6)

Now the current realization of our random variable $p_t$ is a function of a constant, $\alpha$, its previous value, $p_{t-1}$, and our random disturbance, $\varepsilon_t$. Just as before, the variance of $\varepsilon_t$ is constant over time, and the various $\varepsilon_t$'s are uncorrelated with each other.

The choice of $p_t$ for our random variable is intentional. If $p_t$ is the log price, then rearranging terms, we obtain an equation for the log return:

$$r_t = \Delta p_t = \alpha + \varepsilon_t \tag{11.7}$$

The constant term, $\alpha$, is often referred to as the drift term, for reasons that will become apparent. In these cases, $\varepsilon_t$ is typically referred to as the diffusion term. Outside of finance, these types of models are most famously used in physics to describe the motion of particles. We can imagine a bunch of particles starting out close together, randomly drifting about, and filling a space, or diffusing. Putting these two terms together, the entire equation is known as a drift-diffusion model.

When equity returns follow a drift-diffusion process, we say that equity markets are perfectly efficient. We say they are efficient because the return is impossible to forecast based on past prices or returns. Put another way, the conditional and unconditional returns are equal. Mathematically:

$$E[r_t \mid r_{t-1}] = E[r_t] = \alpha \tag{11.8}$$

If this was not the case—if there was some information in the past that suggested that tomorrow's return should be higher than average—then buyers should enter the market to buy the security, in the process pushing up the price. In a perfectly efficient market, this process would continue until there was no opportunity for excess profit, until tomorrow's expected return was no higher or lower than the unconditional mean return.

As with the random walk equation, we can iteratively substitute the drift-diffusion model into itself:

$$p_t = 2\alpha + p_{t-2} + \varepsilon_t + \varepsilon_{t-1} = t\alpha + p_0 + \sum_{i=1}^{t} \varepsilon_i \tag{11.9}$$

And just as before, we can calculate the conditional mean and variance of our drift-diffusion model:

$$\begin{aligned} E[p_t \mid p_0] &= p_0 + t\alpha \\ \mathrm{Var}[p_t \mid p_0] &= t\sigma^2 \end{aligned} \tag{11.10}$$

As with the random walk, the variance of the drift-diffusion process is proportional to $t$. This time, however, the mean is not constant. The expected value of $p_t$ continues to increase or decrease steadily, to drift, as time goes by, at a rate of $\alpha$. This is why $\alpha$ is known as the drift term.

## AUTOREGRESSION

The next modification we'll make to our time series model is to multiply the lagged term by a constant:

$$r_t = \alpha + \lambda r_{t-1} + \varepsilon_t \tag{11.11}$$

Here, both $\alpha$ and $\lambda$ are constants. Depending on the value of $\lambda$, the behavior of this model can vary greatly. As we'll see, when $|\lambda|$ is less than one, this model can produce a stable time series. Exhibit 11.1 shows the results of a Monte Carlo simulation based on Equation 11.11, with $\alpha = 0.50$ and $\lambda = 0.90$. As we will see later in the chapter, models similar to this can be used to model interest rates.

Equation 11.11 is known as an autoregressive (AR) model. More specifically, Equation 11.11 is known as an AR(1) model, since $r_t$ depends only on its first lag. The random walk is then just a special case of the AR(1) model, where $\alpha$ is zero and $\lambda$ is equal to one. Although our main focus will be on AR(1) models, we can easily construct an AR($n$) model as follows:

$$r_t = \alpha + \lambda_1 r_{t-1} + \lambda_2 r_{t-2} + \cdots + \lambda_n r_{t-n} + \varepsilon_t \tag{11.12}$$

where $\alpha$ and the $\lambda$'s are all constants.

How does the addition of $\lambda$ to our equation change the behavior of $r_t$? To find out, just as we did before, we can iteratively substitute our AR(1) model into itself to obtain the following equation:

$$r_t = \alpha \sum_{i=0}^{n-1} \lambda^i + \lambda^n r_{t-n} + \sum_{i=0}^{n-1} \lambda^i \varepsilon_{t-i} \tag{11.13}$$

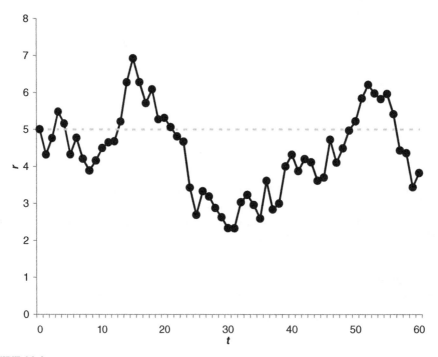

**EXHIBIT 11.1**   Mean Reversion ($\alpha = 0.50$; $\lambda = 0.90$)

To proceed further, we can use methods developed in Chapter 1 for summing geometric series. The conditional mean and variance are now:

$$E[r_t \,|\, r_{t-n}] = \frac{1 - \lambda^n}{1 - \lambda} \alpha + \lambda^n r_{t-n}$$

$$\text{Var}[r_t \,|\, r_{t-n}] = \frac{1 - \lambda^{2n}}{1 - \lambda^2} \sigma^2$$

(11.14)

As you might expect, for values of $|\lambda|$ greater than one, the variance of $r_t$ increases exponentially as $n$ increases. We say that the series diverges or that it is unstable. For values of $|\lambda|$ greater than one, $r$ will tend to move further and further away from its starting value as $n$ increases. Exhibit 11.2 shows the results of a Monte Carlo simulation based on Equation 11.11, with $\alpha = -0.10$ and $\lambda = 1.02$. The standard deviation of the error term is 0.50.

For values of $|\lambda|$ less than one, notice that the impact of $r_{t-n}$ on the expected value of $r_t$ decreases as $n$ increases, but never goes to zero. This may seem a bit strange. It's as if the system has infinite memory. If we use this as an interest rate model, then a spike in rates from 100 years ago would still be impacting current rates. In practical terms, the impact would be so small as to be negligible, but it is a potential criticism of autoregressive models.

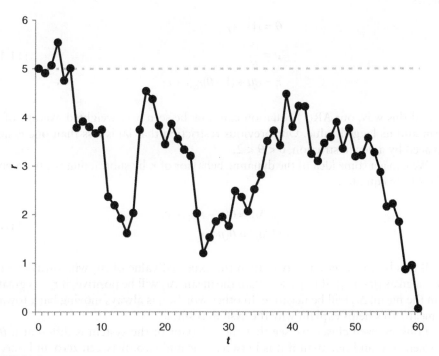

**EXHIBIT 11.2**  Divergent Series ($\alpha = -0.10$; $\lambda = 1.02$; $\sigma = 0.50$)

For values of $|\lambda|$ less than one, the AR(1) process is stable. If we continue to extend the series back in time, as $n$ approaches infinity, $\lambda^n$ becomes increasingly small, causing $\lambda^n r_{t-n}$ to approach zero. In this case:

$$r_t = \frac{1}{1-\lambda}\alpha + \sum_{i=0}^{\infty}\lambda^i \varepsilon_{t-i} \tag{11.15}$$

Continuing to use our geometric series techniques, we then arrive at the following results for the mean and variance:

$$E[r_t] = \frac{1}{1-\lambda}\alpha$$
$$\text{Var}[r_t] = \frac{1}{1-\lambda^2}\sigma^2 \tag{11.16}$$

So, for values of $|\lambda|$ less than one, as $n$ approaches infinity, the initial state of the system ceases to matter. The mean and variance are only a function of the constants.

For a random walk, the conditional and unconditional means are equal. This is not the case for an AR(1) process. For an AR(1) process, because this period's value is a function of the previous period's value, knowing the value from the previous period will impact our expectation of the value in this period.

Using these results suggests an interesting way to reformulate our original AR(1) equation. We define two new constants, $\mu$ and $\theta$, and rewrite Equation 11.11 as follows:

$$\theta = (1 - \lambda)$$
$$\mu = \frac{\alpha}{\theta} \tag{11.17}$$
$$r_t = \theta\mu + (1 - \theta)r_{t-1} + \varepsilon_t$$

Viewed this way, our AR(1) equation can now be seen as a weighted average of its mean and its lagged value. Our previous restriction that $|\lambda|$ is less than one is now replaced by a new restriction, $0 < \theta < 2$.

We can get some idea of the dynamic behavior of $r_t$ by subtracting $r_{t-1}$ from both sides of the equation:

$$\Delta r_t = \theta(\mu - r_{t-1}) + \varepsilon_t$$
$$E[\Delta r_t] = \theta(\mu - r_{t-1}) \tag{11.18}$$

If $\theta$ is between zero and two, then the expected value of $\Delta r_t$ will always be the same sign as $(\mu - r_{t-1})$. If $r_{t-1}$ is less than the mean, $\Delta r_t$ will be positive; if $r_{t-1}$ is greater than the mean, $\Delta r_t$ will be negative. In other words, $r_t$ is always moving back toward its mean. This helps explain why the system is stable.

Looking even closer, we see that the behavior of the system is different if $\theta$ is between zero and one than if it is between one and two. Between zero and one, at each step, the expected value of $\Delta r_t$ is a fraction of the distance between $r_{t-1}$ and $\mu$.

For $0 < \theta < 1$, $r$ tends to move closer to the mean with each step. This property is known as mean reversion and is thought to be a common feature of many financial time series. For $1 < \theta < 2$, the series tends to overshoot the mean. If $\theta = 1.5$, we expect that $\Delta r_t$ will be 1.5 times $(\mu - r_{t-1})$, so $r$ will tend to overshoot $\mu$ by 0.5 times $(\mu - r_{t-1})$. Exhibit 11.3 shows the results of a Monte Carlo simulation based on Equation 11.17, which exhibits mean reversion with overshooting. This system is stable, but this constant overshooting is unusual in practice. In finance, more often than not, for AR(1) systems, we expect $\theta$ to be between zero and one, and for the system to exhibit mean reversion.

We can quantify the level of mean reversion by calculating the correlation of $r_t$ with its first lag. This is known as autocorrelation or serial correlation. For our AR(1) series, we have:

$$\rho_{t,t-1} = 1 - \theta = \lambda \qquad (11.19)$$

The proof is left as an exercise. Clearly this makes sense only when $|\lambda|$ is less than one. Remember that covariance and correlation look at expected deviations from the mean. In light of our discussion of the dynamics of AR(1) systems, this result should make sense. For $0 < \theta < 1$, if $r_{t-1}$ is below the mean, we expect $r_t$ to also be below the mean, and the autocorrelation is positive. Similarly, for $1 < \theta < 2$, if $r_{t-1}$ is below the mean, we expect the process to overshoot, causing $r_t$ to be above the mean, and the autocorrelation is negative.

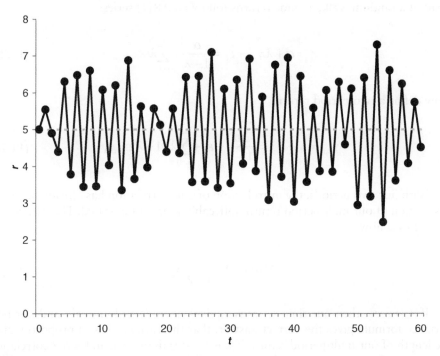

**EXHIBIT 11.3** Mean Reversion with Overshooting ($\mu = 5.0$; $\lambda = -0.90$; $\theta = 1.90$)

## VARIANCE AND AUTOCORRELATION

Autocorrelation has a very important impact on variance as we look at longer and longer time periods. For our random walk, as we look at longer and longer periods, the variance grows in proportion to the length of time.

Assume returns follow a random walk:

$$r_t = \varepsilon_t \tag{11.20}$$

where $\varepsilon_t$ is an i.i.d. disturbance term. Now define $y_{n,t}$ as an $n$ period return; that is:

$$y_{n,t} = \sum_{i=0}^{n-1} r_{t-i} = \sum_{i=0}^{n-1} \varepsilon_{t-i} \tag{11.21}$$

As stated before, the variance of $y_{n,t}$ is proportional to $n$:

$$\text{Var}[y_{n,t}] = n\sigma_\varepsilon^2 \tag{11.22}$$

and the standard deviation of $y_{n,t}$ is proportional to the square root of $n$. In other words, if the daily standard deviation of an equity index is 1% and the returns of the index follow a random walk, then the standard deviation of 25-day returns will be 5%, and the standard deviation of 100-day returns will be 10%.

When we introduce autocorrelation, this square root rule no longer holds. Instead of a random walk, assume returns follow an AR(1) series:

$$r_t = \alpha + \lambda r_{t-1} + \varepsilon_t = \frac{\alpha}{1-\lambda} + \sum_{i=0}^{\infty} \lambda^i \varepsilon_{t-i} \tag{11.23}$$

Now define a two-period return:

$$y_{2,t} = r_t + r_{t-1} = \frac{2\alpha}{1-\lambda} + \varepsilon_t + \sum_{i=0}^{\infty} \lambda^i (1+\lambda)\varepsilon_{t-i-1} \tag{11.24}$$

With just two periods, the introduction of autocorrelation has already made the description of our multiperiod return noticeably more complicated. The variance of this series is now:

$$\text{Var}[y_{2,t}] = \frac{2}{1-\lambda}\sigma_\varepsilon^2 \tag{11.25}$$

If $\lambda$ is zero, then our time series is equivalent to a random walk and our new variance formula gives the correct answer: that the variance is still proportional to the length of our multiperiod return. If $\lambda$ is greater than zero, and serial correlation is positive, then the two-period variance will be more than twice as great as the single-period variance. If $\lambda$ is less than zero, and the serial correlation is negative, then the two-period variance will be less than twice the single-period variance. This makes sense. For series with negative serial correlation, a large positive excess return will tend to be followed by a negative excess return, pulling the series back toward its mean, thereby reducing the multiperiod variance. The opposite is true for series with positive serial correlation.

Time series with slightly positive or negative serial correlation abound in finance. It is a common mistake to assume that variance is linear in time, when in fact it is not. Assuming no serial correlation when it does exist can lead to a serious overestimation or underestimation of risk.

## STATIONARITY

In the preceding section we discussed unstable series whose means and variances tend to grow without bound. There are many series in the real world that tend to grow exponentially—stock market indexes and gross domestic product (GDP), for example—while other series such as interest rates, inflation, and exchange rates typically fluctuate in narrow bands. This dichotomy, between series that tend to grow without limit and those series that tend to fluctuate around a constant level, is extremely important in statistics. We call series that tend to fluctuate around a constant level stationary time series. In contrast, series that are divergent are known as nonstationary. Determining whether a series is stationary is often the first step in time series analysis.

To be more precise, we say that a random variable $X$ is stationary if for all $t$ and $n$:

1. $E[x_t] = \mu$ and $|\mu| < \infty$
2. $\text{Var}[x_t] = \sigma^2$ and $|\sigma^2| < \infty$ $\qquad\qquad\qquad\qquad$ (11.26)
3. $\text{Cov}[x_t, x_{t-n}] = \sigma_{t,\,t-n}$

where $\mu$, $\sigma^2$, and $\sigma_{t,t-n}$ are constants. These three conditions state that the mean, variance, and serial correlation should be constant over time. We also require that the mean and variance be finite. In addition, some statisticians include the condition that the distribution of $X$ is stable over time. This is often called strong stationarity, as opposed to weak stationarity when only the first three conditions are met.

While we can calculate a sample mean or variance for a nonstationary series, these statistics are not very useful. Because the mean and variance are changing, by definition, these sample statistics will not tell us anything about the mean and variance of the distribution in general.

Regression analysis on nonstationary series is likely to be even more meaningless. If a series is nonstationary because its volatility varies over time, then it violates the ordinary least squares (OLS) requirement of homoscedasticity. Even if the variance is constant, but the mean is drifting, any conclusions we might draw about the relationship between two nonstationary series will almost certainly be spurious.

## SAMPLE PROBLEM

As an example of this type of spurious correlation, imagine two AR(1) series with nonzero drifts. To make the calculations easier, we also assume that both series start at zero:

$$p_t = \alpha_p + p_{t-1} + \varepsilon_{p,t} \quad \text{where} \quad \alpha_p \neq 0, \; p_0 = 0$$
$$q_t = \alpha_q + q_{t-1} + \varepsilon_{q,t} \quad \text{where} \quad \alpha_q \neq 0, \; q_0 = 0$$

We assume that both disturbance terms are mean zero and uncorrelated, which can be summarized as:

$$E[\varepsilon_{p,t}] = E[\varepsilon_{q,t}] = 0$$
$$E[\varepsilon_{p,t}\varepsilon_{q,t}] = 0$$

The two series are independent by design; $p_t$ is not a function of $q_t$, nor is $q_t$ a function of $p_t$; $p_t$ might be a model of milk prices in Germany, and $q_t$ a model of life expectancy in Singapore. The two series have no causal relationship.

At any given point in time, the expected value of $p$ is just $t\alpha_p$:

$$p_t = \alpha_p + p_{t-1} + \varepsilon_{p,t} = n\alpha_p + p_{t-n} + \sum_{i=0}^{n-1} \varepsilon_{p,t-i} = t\alpha_p + \sum_{i=0}^{t-1} \varepsilon_{p,t-i}$$

$$E[p_t] = E\left[ t\alpha_p + \sum_{i=0}^{t-1} \varepsilon_{p,t-i} \right] = t\alpha_p$$

Imagine that we tried to calculate the mean of $p$ between 0 and $t$:

$$\tilde{p} = \frac{1}{t+1} \sum_{i=0}^{t} p_i$$

It is quite simple to calculate the expected value of this sample mean:

$$E[\tilde{p}] = \frac{1}{t+1} \sum_{i=0}^{t} E[p_i] = \frac{1}{t+1} \sum_{i=0}^{t} i\alpha_p$$

$$E[\tilde{p}] = \frac{\alpha_p}{t+1} \sum_{i=0}^{t} i = \frac{\alpha_p}{t+1} \frac{t(t+1)}{2} = E[\tilde{p}] = \alpha_p \frac{t}{2}$$

As expected, the sample mean is not independent of $t$. The result for our second series, $q$, is similar, only replacing $\alpha_p$ with $\alpha_q$. If we take these sample means as given, we could try to construct a sample covariance:

$$\tilde{\sigma}_{p,q} = \frac{1}{t+1} \sum_{i=0}^{t} p_i q_i - E[\tilde{p}]E[\tilde{q}] = \frac{1}{t+1} \sum_{i=0}^{t} p_i q_i - \alpha_p \alpha_q \frac{t^2}{4}$$

To calculate the expected value of this series, we need to know that the sum of series, $0, 1, 4, 9, \ldots (t-1)^2, t^2$ is equal to $t(t+1)(2t+1)/6$:

$$E[\tilde{\sigma}_{p,q}] = \alpha_p \alpha_q \frac{t^2 + 2t}{12}$$

Clearly, if both $\alpha_p$ and $\alpha_q$ are nonzero, then this sample covariance estimator will also be nonzero, despite the fact that the series are uncorrelated by design. We could imagine trying to calculate a similar variance estimator (variance is just the covariance of a variable with itself) and using the result to create an estimate of the slope in a regression of $p$ on $q$:

$$\beta = \frac{\tilde{\sigma}_{p,q}}{\tilde{\sigma}_p^2} = \frac{\alpha_p \alpha_q \dfrac{t^2 + 2t}{12}}{\alpha_p^2 \dfrac{t^2 + 2t}{12}} = \frac{\alpha_q}{\alpha_p}$$

Though it was a long time in coming, this result is rather intuitive. If $\alpha_p$ is twice the value of $\alpha_q$, then at any point in time we will expect $p$ to be twice the value of $q$.

Exhibit 11.4 shows one iteration from a Monte Carlo simulation with $\alpha_p = 2$, $\alpha_q = 1$. If we plotted these two series against each other, the points would tend to line up along a line with a slope equal to 2.

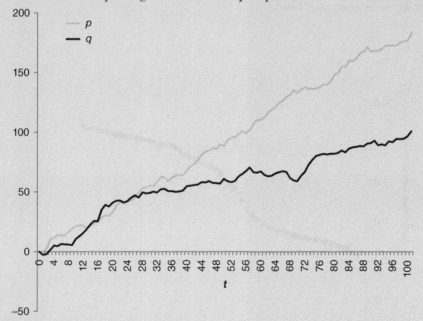

**EXHIBIT 11.4**   Two Nonstationary Time Series

This should all seem very wrong. If two variables are independent, we expect them to have zero covariance, but because these series both have nonzero drift terms, the sample covariance and beta will also tend to be nonzero. The results are clearly spurious.

In a situation such as our sample problem, you could argue that even though the two AR(1) series are independent, the positive sample covariance is telling us something meaningful: that both series have nonzero drift terms. How meaningful is this? Not very, as it turns out. Any random variable with a nonzero mean can be turned into a nonstationary series. Log returns of equities tend to be stationary, but the addition of those returns over time, log prices, are nonstationary.

To show just how silly all of this can get, in a classic example, Hendry (1980) showed how, if statistical analysis is done incorrectly, you might conclude that cumulative rainfall in the United Kingdom and the UK price index where causally related. In most stable economies, inflation tends to be slightly positive on average, and stationary. The accumulation of this inflation over time results in ever-increasing prices. Rainfall, which in any given year will be equal to or greater than zero—almost certainly greater than zero in the United Kingdom—can also safely be assumed to be a stationary series. But if we plot the *cumulative* rainfall in the United Kingdom since 1900, say, this series will be constantly growing, and nonstationary. Rainfall doesn't cause inflation, or the opposite way around, but if done improperly, statistical analysis might make you think it did.

Exhibit 11.5 shows a regression of cumulative rainfall and the log price index in the United Kingdom between 1949 and 2010. We use the log price level to ensure that the relationship is linear (remember from Chapter 1: plotted on a logarithmic scale, a series whose growth rate is constant over time will have a constant slope and appear as a straight line). The two series are highly correlated, but only because both series are increasing over time.

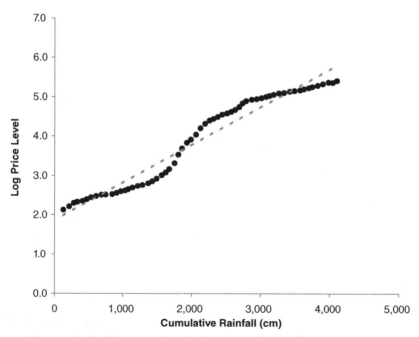

**EXHIBIT 11.5** United Kingdom: Log Price Level and Cumulative Rainfall, 1949–2010
*Sources:* Met Office and Office for National Statistics, United Kingdom.

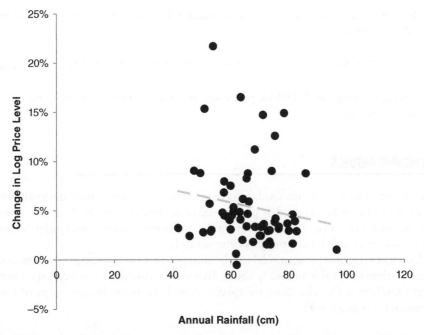

**EXHIBIT 11.6**  United Kingdom: Change in Log Price Level and Annual Rainfall, 1949–2010
*Sources:* Met Office and Office for National Statistics, United Kingdom.

The remedy for stationarity in statistical analysis is clear. Just as we can construct a nonstationary series from a stationary one by summing over time, we can usually create a stationary series from a nonstationary series by taking its difference. Transforming a price series into returns is by now a familiar example. Occasionally additional steps will need to be taken (e.g., differencing twice), but for most financial and economic series, this will suffice.

Exhibit 11.6 shows a regression based on the same data set we used in Exhibit 11.5, only now instead of cumulative rainfall we are using annual rainfall, and instead of the log price level we are using changes in the log price index. This new chart looks very different. The regression line is very close to being flat, and the slope parameter is in fact not significant. In other words, rainfall has no meaningful impact on inflation, just as we would expect.

Ascribing a causal relationship when none exists is a serious mistake. Unfortunately, in this day and age, it is easy to gather massive amounts of data and perform  a quick regression analysis. When performing statistical analysis of time series data, it is important to check for stationarity.

## MOVING AVERAGE

Besides autoregressive (AR) series, the other major class of time series is moving averages (MAs). An MA($n$) series takes the form:

$$x_t = \varepsilon_t + \theta_1 \varepsilon_{t-1} + \cdots + \theta_n \varepsilon_{t-n} \tag{11.27}$$

Moving average series can be combined with autoregressive series to form ARMA($p,q$) processes:

$$x_t = \lambda_1 x_{t-1} + \lambda_2 x_{t-2} + \cdots + \lambda_p x_{t-p} + \varepsilon_t + \theta_1 \varepsilon_{t-1} + \cdots + \theta_q \varepsilon_{t-q} \qquad (11.28)$$

Moving averages and ARMA processes are important in statistics, but are less common in finance.

## CONTINUOUS MODELS

Up until now, our time series models have all assumed discrete time intervals. From time $t - 1$ to $t$ to $t + 1$, our models progressed in uniform intervals. Time just jumped from one instance to the next. By contrast, continuous time series models define a system as a function of a continuous time variable.

A continuous time series model can be thought of as a discrete time series model, where the time interval is infinitely short. To see how this works, we can start with a discrete random walk. This time we specify that there are $n$ discrete steps of length $h$ between $t = 0$ and $t = T$:

$$p_t = p_{t-1} + \varepsilon_t \quad t = 0, h, 2h, 3h \cdots nh \quad nh = T \qquad (11.29)$$

Unlike in previous examples where the disturbance term was continuous, we imagine that the disturbance term is also discrete. At the start of each time interval, the time series jumps by positive or negative $\Delta$, with equal probability:

$$P[\varepsilon_t = \Delta] = 0.5$$
$$P[\varepsilon_t = -\Delta] = 0.5 \qquad (11.30)$$

In a discrete model, what happens between $t$ and $(t + 1)$ is unknown. To make our model continuous, we only need to specify what happens in this interval. We start by assuming the model is constant between jumps. In other words, plotted over time, the series would look something like Exhibit 11.7.

This type of process is often described as a step function. We can write the relationship between the discrete and continuous series formally as:

$$p_n(t) = p_{[t/h]} \qquad (11.31)$$

Here, $p_n(t)$ is a continuous function defined for any real value of $t$ between 0 and $T$. The square brackets, $[\cdot]$, signify the greatest integer function. For example, if our time interval is two units, for $t = 8.648$ we get: $[8.648/2] = [4.324] = 5$. This series, $p_n(t)$, is continuous but not differentiable.

At the time $t = T$, the mean and variance of $p_n(t)$ are:

$$E[p_n(T)] = 0$$
$$\text{Var}[p_n(t)] = \frac{T}{h}\Delta^2 \qquad (11.32)$$

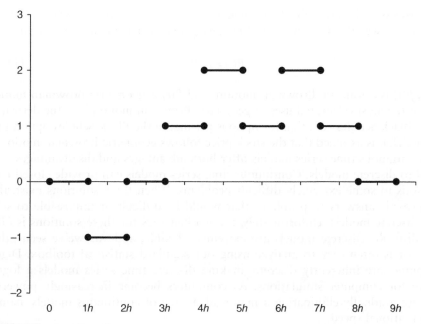

**EXHIBIT 11.7**   Step Function

To make this process both continuous and differentiable, we imagine shrinking $h$ down to zero, which is equivalent to letting $n$ go to infinity. The trick is to define $\Delta$ in such a way that the variance is well behaved (i.e., finite) as $n$ goes to infinity. It would also be nice if the variance was linear in time; therefore, we specify:

$$\text{Var}[p_n(t)] = \frac{T}{h}\Delta^2 = \sigma^2 T \qquad (11.33)$$

We can solve for $\Delta$ to get:

$$\Delta = \sigma\sqrt{h} \qquad (11.34)$$

In the limit, as $h$ goes to zero, $\Delta$ remains proportional to the square root of $h$. In the limit, this process is referred to as a Wiener process, or Brownian motion. When the mean is zero and the variance is one, we refer to the process as standard Brownian motion, which is often denoted as $B(t)$. The proof is beyond the scope of this book, but it might not be surprising to learn that Brownian motion is also normally distributed.[1] We can summarize this as:

$$B(t) \sim N(0,1) \qquad (11.35)$$

Standard Brownian motion forms the basis for a more general class of processes known as arithmetic Brownian motion, which can be formulated as:

$$p(t) = \mu t + \sigma B(t) \qquad (11.36)$$

---

[1] For a more formal version of this derivation and an excellent introduction to stochastic differential equations, see Campbell, Lo, and MacKinlay (1996).

This process is also normally distributed, but with a mean of $\mu$ and a standard deviation of $\sigma$. If we take the exponent of $p(t)$, we get geometric Brownian motion:

$$P(t) = e^{p(t)} \qquad (11.37)$$

Here, $p(t)$ is arithmetic Brownian motion, and $P(t)$ is geometric Brownian motion. One of the most celebrated uses of geometric Brownian motion is in the derivation of the Black-Scholes equation for options pricing. In the Black-Scholes option pricing model, it is assumed that the stock price follows geometric Brownian motion.

Continuous time series models offer both advantages and disadvantages compared to discrete models. Continuous time series models can provide closed-form solutions to some extremely difficult problems. When these solutions exist, they can provide answers to problems that would be difficult or impossible to solve with discrete models. Unfortunately, the mathematics for these solutions is often very difficult. Discrete models are extremely flexible, and—as we've seen—their behavior is often easy to analyze using our standard statistical toolbox. Digital computers are inherently discrete, making discrete time series models a logical choice for computer simulations. As computers become increasingly powerful, they are gradually eliminating a major advantage of continuous models, namely computational speed.

## APPLICATION: GARCH

Up until this point, all of our time series models have assumed that the variance of the disturbance term remains constant over time. In financial markets, variance appears to be far from constant. Both prolonged periods of high variance and prolonged periods of low variance are observed. While the transition from low to high variance can be sudden, more often we observe serial correlation in variance, with gradual mean reversion. When this is the case, periods of above-average variance are more likely to be followed by periods of above-average variance, and periods of below-average variance are likely to be followed by periods of below-average variance. For risk managers, this is one of the most important features of financial markets. It implies that risk varies over time, and that this variation in risk is, in part, predictable.

Exhibit 11.8 shows the rolling annualized 60-day standard deviation of the S&P 500 index between 1928 and 2008. Notice how the level of the standard deviation is far from random. There are periods of sustained high volatility (e.g., 1996–2003) and periods of sustained low volatility (e.g., 1964–1969).

One of the most popular models of time-varying volatility is the autoregressive conditional heteroscedasticity (ARCH) model. We start by defining a disturbance term at time $t$, $\varepsilon_t$, in terms of an independent and identically distributed (i.i.d.) standard normal variable, $u_t$, and a time varying standard deviation, $\sigma_t$:

$$\varepsilon_t = \sigma_t u_t \qquad (11.38)$$

 Because the standard deviation of $u_t$ is 1, the standard deviation of $\varepsilon_t$ must be $\sigma_t$. With the exception of the degenerate case, where $\sigma_t$ is constant, $\varepsilon_t$ will not be

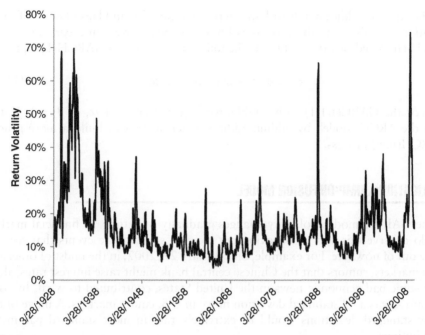

**EXHIBIT 11.8**    S&P 500, Annualized 60-Day Return Standard Deviation, 1928–2008

i.i.d. This is a departure from all of the models that we have seen up until now. In the simplest ARCH model, we can model the evolution of the variance as:

$$\sigma_t^2 = \alpha_0 \bar{\sigma}^2 + \alpha_1 \sigma_{t-1}^2 u_{t-1}^2 = \alpha_0 \bar{\sigma}^2 + \alpha_1 \varepsilon_{t-1}^2 \qquad (11.39)$$

where $\alpha_0$ and $\alpha_1$ are constants, and $\bar{\sigma}^2$ is the long-run variance. To ensure that $\sigma^2$ remains positive, we square $u_{t-1}$ and $\varepsilon_{t-1}$ and require $\alpha_0 > 0$, $\alpha_1 \geq 0$, and $\sigma_0^2 > 0$.

For $\sigma^2$ to be stable over time, we require that $\alpha_0 + \alpha_1 = 1$. Because $u_t$ is standard normal, the expected value of $u_{t-1}^2$ is equal to 1. Because $u_t$ is mean zero and independent of $\sigma_t$, we also know that $E\left[\sigma_{t-1}^2 u_{t-1}^2\right] = E\left[\sigma_{t-1}^2\right]E\left[u_{t-1}^2\right]$. Putting this altogether, we have:

$$E\left[\sigma_t^2\right] = \alpha_0 \bar{\sigma}^2 + \alpha_1 E\left[\sigma_{t-1}^2\right] \qquad (11.40)$$

The requirement that $\alpha_0 + \alpha_1 = 1$ is then equivalent to requiring that the expected value of the variance equal the long-run variance, $E\left[\sigma_t^2\right] = E\left[\sigma_{t-1}^2\right] = \bar{\sigma}^2$.

Notice how $\sigma_t$ is influenced by the lagged value of the disturbance term, $\varepsilon_{t-1}$. If there is a large disturbance (positive or negative) and $\alpha_1$ is greater than zero, then $\sigma_t$ will be greater than when the disturbance is small. This leads to serial correlation in our disturbance term. High volatility begets high volatility. Equation 11.39 is typically referred to as an ARCH(1) model. By adding more lagged terms containing $\sigma^2$ and $u^2$, we can generalize to an ARCH($n$) specification.

$$\sigma_t^2 = \alpha_0 \bar{\sigma}^2 + \sum_{i=1}^{n} \alpha_i \sigma_{t-i}^2 u_{t-i}^2 \qquad (11.41)$$

Besides the additional disturbance terms, we can also add lags of $\sigma^2$ itself to the equation. In this form, the process is known as generalized autoregressive conditional heteroscedasticity (GARCH). The following describes a GARCH(1,1) process:

$$\sigma_t^2 = \alpha_0 \bar{\sigma}^2 + \alpha_1 \sigma_{t-1}^2 u_{t-1}^2 + \beta \sigma_{t-1}^2 \qquad (11.42)$$

For the GARCH(1,1) to be stable, we require that $\alpha_0 + \alpha_1 + \beta = 1$. Just as with the ARCH model, by adding additional terms we can build a more general GARCH($n,m$) process.

## APPLICATION: JUMP-DIFFUSION MODEL

In the GARCH model, volatility changes gradually over time. In financial markets we do observe this sort of behavior, but we also see extreme events that seem to come out of nowhere. For example, on February 27, 2007, in the midst of otherwise calm markets, rumors that the Chinese central bank might raise interest rates, along with some bad economic news in the United States, contributed to what, by some measures, was a –8 standard deviation move in U.S. equity markets. A move of this many standard deviations would be extremely rare in most standard parametric distributions.

 One popular way to generate this type of extreme return is to add a so-called jump term to our standard time series model. This can be done by adding a second disturbance term:

$$r_t = \alpha + \varepsilon_t + [I_t]u_t \qquad (11.43)$$

Here, $r_t$ is the market return at time $t$, $\alpha$ is a constant drift term, and $\varepsilon_t$ is our standard mean zero diffusion term. As specified, our jump term has two components: $[I_t]$, an indicator variable that is either zero or one, and $u_t$, an additional disturbance term. Not surprisingly, as specified, this time series model is referred to as a jump-diffusion model.

The jump-diffusion model is really just a mixture model. To get the type of behavior we want—moderate volatility punctuated by rare extreme events—we can set the variance of $\varepsilon_t$ to relatively modest levels. We then specify the probability of $[I_t]$ equaling one at some relatively low level, and set the variance of $u_t$ at a relatively high level. If we believe that extreme negative returns are more likely than extreme positive returns, we can also make the distribution of $u_t$ asymmetrical.

GARCH and jump-diffusion are not mutually exclusive. By combining GARCH and jump-diffusion, we can model and understand a wide range of market environments and dynamics.

## APPLICATION: INTEREST RATE MODELS

In our discussion of autoregressive processes, we mentioned that these models, or models similar to them, might be used to model interest rates. In this section we give a very brief introduction to quantitative interest rate models. Most of these models were originally developed as continuous time models, but it is easy enough to describe discrete time counterparts for each. The availability of cheap computer power and the use of more complex derivatives has made these discrete models increasingly popular. For these reasons and for consistency with the rest of this chapter, we present the interest rate models in their discrete form, without further comment.

The simplest interest rate models are known as one-factor models. They describe the evolution of one interest rate, typically the short rate (the current, continuously compounded interest rate). The rest of the interest rate curve can then be derived from the short rate. Though less rigorous, most interest rate models can be used to model an interest rate of a specific term directly. If all you are interested in is the 10-year Treasury rate, then there is no need to model the whole interest rate curve.

One popular interest rate model, known as the Vasicek model, simply describes interest rates as an AR(1) process:

$$r_t = \lambda r_{t-1} + (1-\lambda)\theta + \sigma r_{t-1}^{1/2}\varepsilon_t \quad \varepsilon \sim N(0,1), 0 \leq \lambda \leq 1 \qquad (11.44)$$

Here, we've split our disturbance term into two parts. Now $\varepsilon$ is a standard normal variable, and we're multiplying it by a constant, $\sigma$, to alter the standard deviation of the disturbance term. This is entirely equivalent to having a disturbance term with a standard deviation of $\sigma$. Neither way of representing the disturbance term is necessarily better, but this functional form is popular in finance, and very popular for interest rate models.

As with any AR(1) process, the expected value of the process, the expected interest rate, is $\theta$. Also, $\lambda$ determines how quickly the process mean reverts. In this case a value of $\lambda$ closer to zero causes the interest rate to move more quickly back toward the mean level, $\theta$. A value closer to one implies that the interest rate is closer to a random walk, and reverts more slowly to the mean.

One problem with the Vasicek model is that it allows interest rates to take on negative values. In the real world, nominal interest rates are almost never negative. In practice, if $\theta$ is high enough and $\sigma$ is low, the probability of generating negative rates can be kept very low. If a negative interest rate is generated, we can discard it or override it with some very small nonnegative value. This solution is not very elegant, and it will alter the statistical properties of the model, but in certain settings this may be acceptable.

A slightly more complex model known as the Cox-Ingersoll-Ross (CIR) model aims to solve the negative interest rate problem by varying the disturbance term as the level of the interest rate changes. As the interest rate approaches zero, the magnitude of the disturbance term becomes smaller and smaller. This is accomplished by adding one additional term to the Vasicek model:

$$r_t = \lambda r_{t-1} + (1-\lambda)\theta + \sigma r_{t-1}^{1/2}\varepsilon_t \quad \varepsilon \sim N(0,1), 0 \leq \lambda \leq 1 \qquad (11.45)$$

As you can see, the disturbance term is now proportional to the square root of the interest rate. As interest rates approach zero, the volatility of interest rates declines. In the continuous case, this is enough to keep interest rates from ever becoming zero. In the discrete case, rates can still become negative, but it is much less likely to happen.

Modifying the disturbance term in this way solves one problem, but it is not without its drawbacks. Chief among the drawbacks is that our standard trick of iteratively substituting the model into itself will no longer work. In order to derive the statistical properties of this process—the mean and variance, for example—we would need to use other methods.

Besides preventing interest rates from becoming negative, the CIR model is appealing because the volatility of interest rates does appear to vary with the level of interest rates. When interest rates are high—say 15% to 20%—they are likely to be much more volatile than when they are low—say 0% to 5%. This pattern can be observed historically, between countries, and between different financial instruments within countries.

Interest rate volatility tends to increase as interest rates rise, but does it vary exactly with the square root of interest rates as implied by the CIR model? This square root rule has some theoretical advantages, but might seem arbitrary. The obvious solution is to make the exponent in the disturbance term variable as well:

$$r_t = \lambda r_{t-1} + (1-\lambda)\theta + \sigma r_{t-1}^\phi \varepsilon_t \quad \varepsilon \sim N(0,1), 0 \le \lambda \le 1 \qquad (11.46)$$

This is known as the constant elasticity of volatility (CEV) model. For a particular instrument, the new parameter, $\phi$, can be determined by examining interest rate data over time. As it turns out, many empirical studies have ended up with values for $\phi$ very close to 0.5. This has led some practitioners to stick with the simpler CIR model.

To avoid negative rates, the Black-Karasinski interest rate model utilizes log rates:

$$\ln(r_t) = \lambda \ln(r_{t-1}) + (1-\lambda)\theta + \sigma \varepsilon_t \quad \varepsilon \sim N(0,1), 0 \le \lambda \le 1 \qquad (11.47)$$

Note that this is not the log of $(1 + r)$, but simply the log of $r$. Unlike the use of log returns in equity models, where we want to ensure that returns are greater than −100%, here we want to ensure that rates are greater than zero. Unfortunately, while the log of $(1 + r)$ is very close in value to $r$, the log of $r$ is nothing like $r$. For example, the log of 4% is approximately −3.22.

One-factor interest rate models display a wide variety of adaptations aimed at solving real-world problems. They begin to hint at the flexibility and complexity of time series modeling in practice.

## PROBLEMS

1. Classify each of the following time series models in terms of the random variable $r_t$:
   a. $r_t = \alpha + \lambda_1 r_{t-1} + \lambda_2 r_{t-2} + \varepsilon_t$
   b. $r_t = \theta\mu + (1-\theta)r_{t-1} + \varepsilon_t$
   c. $r_t = \lambda_1 r_{t-1} + \lambda_2 r_{t-2} + \varepsilon_t + \theta_1 \varepsilon_{t-1}$
   d. $r_t = \alpha + \varepsilon_t$
2. You are given the following time series model. What is the long-term expected value of $r_t$?

$$r_t = 0.02 + 0.8 r_{t-1} + \varepsilon_t$$

3. Assume that a credit spread evolves according to the following time series equation:

$$r_t = 0.01 + 0.30r_{t-1} - 0.20r_{t-2} + \varepsilon_t$$

Further, assume $r_t$ was 2% during the most recent period, and 4% during the period before that. What is the expected value of $r_t$ in the next period? The period after that?

4. Assume that daily stock returns for RW Corporation can be described by the following equation:

$$r_t = \Delta p_t = \varepsilon_t$$

where $r_t$ is a log return, and the error term, $\varepsilon_t$, is i.i.d., with a mean of zero and a standard deviation of 1.5%. What is the expected log return over one year? What is the standard deviation of this annual log return? Ignore weekends, and assume 256 business days per year.

5. Assume that daily stock returns for Drift Corporation can be described by the following equation:

$$r_t = \Delta p_t = \alpha + \varepsilon_t$$

where $r_t$ is a log return; the error term, $\varepsilon_t$, is i.i.d., with a mean of zero and a standard deviation of 1.5%; and $\alpha$ is a constant equal to 0.10%. What is the expected log return over one year? What is the standard deviation of this annual log return? Ignore weekends, and assume 256 business days per year.

6. Assume that daily stock returns for Reversion Corporation can be described by the following time series equation:

$$r_t = \alpha + \lambda r_{t-1} + \varepsilon_t$$

where $r_t$ is a log return; the error term, $\varepsilon_t$, is i.i.d., with a mean of zero and a standard deviation of 1.5%; $\alpha$ is a constant equal to 0.10%; and $\lambda$ is a constant equal to 0.50. What is the expected log return over two days? What is the standard deviation of this two-day return? Ignore weekends, and assume that $r_t$ was equal to zero in the distant past. What would the mean and standard deviation of the two-day return be if $\lambda$ was equal to –0.50?

7. Assume that interest rates evolve according to the following Vasicek model:

$$r_t = \lambda r_{t-1} + (1 - \lambda)\theta + \sigma\varepsilon_t \qquad \varepsilon \sim N(0,1)$$
$$\lambda = 0.50$$
$$\theta = 0.04$$
$$\sigma = 0.02$$

What is the unconditional expected value of $r_t$? Assuming interest rates are currently 6%, what is the conditional expected value of $r_t$ over the next three periods?

8. Assume the spread between two equity indexes can be described by the following time series equation:

$$r_t = \rho r_{t-1} + \varepsilon_t \quad \varepsilon \sim N(0, \sigma^2), |\rho| \leq 1$$

$$\text{Cov}[\varepsilon_{t-i}, \varepsilon_{t-j}] = 0 \quad \forall i \neq j$$

Derive equations for the unconditional mean and variance of this process.

9. For the time series equation in the previous problem, what is the correlation between $r_t$ and a previous return, $r_{t-n}$?

10. Given our AR(1) process, Equation 11.11,

$$r_t = \alpha + \lambda r_{t-1} + \varepsilon_t$$

prove that the serial correlation is equal to $\lambda$.

11. You are provided with 10 years of monthly log returns for a mutual fund. The mean monthly log return is 2.0%, the standard deviation of the returns is 1.5%, the skewness is −1.0, and the kurtosis is 2.4. Assuming the log returns are i.i.d., what are the expected annualized mean, standard deviation, skewness, and kurtosis of the log returns?

## CHAPTER 12

# Decay Factors

In this chapter we explore a class of estimators that has become very popular in finance and risk management for analyzing historical data. These models hint at the limitations of the type of analysis that we have explored in previous chapters.

## MEAN

In previous chapters, we showed that the best linear unbiased estimator (BLUE) for the sample mean of a random variable was given by:

$$\hat{\mu} = \frac{1}{n} \sum_{i=0}^{n-1} x_{t-i} \qquad (12.1)$$

For a practitioner, this formula immediately raises the question of what value to use for $n$. Because this chapter is concerned with historical data, what value to choose for $n$ is equivalent to asking how far back in time we should look for data. Should we use 10 years of data? One year? Thirty days? A popular choice in many fields is simply to use all available data. If we have only 20 days of data, use 20 days; if we have 80 years, use 80 years. While this can be a sensible approach in some circumstances, it is much less common in modern finance. Using all available data has three potential drawbacks. First, the amount of available data for different variables may vary dramatically. If we are trying to calculate the mean return for two fixed-income portfolio managers, and we have 20 years of data for one and only two years of data for another, and the last two years have been particularly good years for fixed-income portfolio managers, a direct comparison of the means will naturally favor the manager with only two years of data. We could limit ourselves to the length of the shortest series, but there are potential drawbacks to this approach as well.

The second problem that arises when we use all available data is that our series length changes over time. If we have 500 days of data today, we will have 501 tomorrow, 502 the day after that, and so on. This is not necessarily a bad thing—more data may lead to a more accurate forecast—but, in practice, it is often convenient to maintain a constant window length. Among other advantages, a constant window length makes it easier to compare the accuracy of models over time.

Finally, there is the problem that the world is constantly changing. The Dow Jones Industrial Average has been available since 1896. There were initially just

12 companies in the index, including American Cotton Oil Company and Distilling & Cattle Feeding Company. That same year, Utah became the 45th U.S. state, and Queen Victoria became the longest-ruling monarch in British history. Forget computers; in 1896, the Model T had not yet been introduced (1908), and the Wright Brothers' famous flight at Kitty Hawk was still some years off (1903). Does it make any sense to use stock market data from 1896 to evaluate the risk of a securities portfolio today? It is easy to argue that the world was so different in the distant past—and in finance, the distant past is not necessarily that distant—that using extremely old data makes little sense.

If we are not going to use all available data, then a logical alternative is a constant window length. This is not without its own problems. If we use Equation 12.1 with a constant window length, then in each successive period, we add the most recent point to our data set and drop the oldest. The first objection to this method is philosophical. How can it be that the oldest point in our data set is considered just as legitimate as all the other points in our data set today (they have the same weight), yet in the very next period, the oldest point becomes completely illegitimate (zero weight)?

The second objection is more aesthetic. As extreme points enter and leave our data set, this can cause dramatic changes in our estimator. Exhibit 12.1 shows a sample time series. Notice the outlier in the series at time $t = 50$. Exhibit 12.2 shows the rolling 40-day mean for the series.

Notice how the spike in the original time series causes a sudden rise and drop in our estimate of the mean in Exhibit 12.2. Because of its appearance, this phenomenon

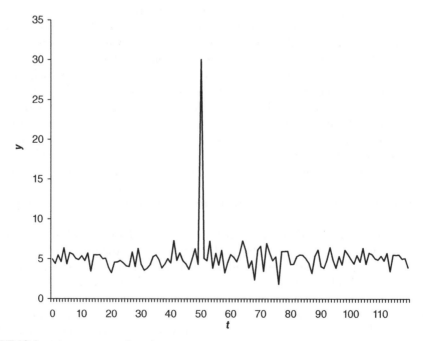

**EXHIBIT 12.1**    Time Series with Spike

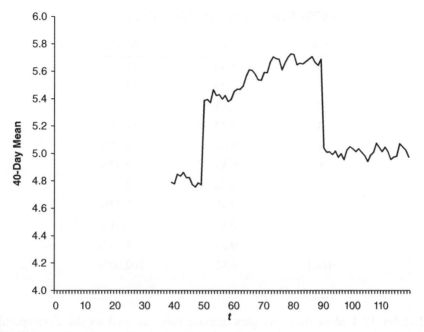

**EXHIBIT 12.2**   Rolling Mean of Time Series with Spike

is often referred to as plateauing. Technically, there is nothing wrong with plateauing, but many practitioners find this type of behavior unappealing.

In the end, the window length chosen is often arbitrary. Rarely in risk management are we presented with an obvious right choice for window length. Practitioners often choose windows that correspond to standard calendar units (one week, one month, one year) or round numbers (100 days, 500 days). While they are convenient and widely used, it is difficult to see why these common window lengths are better than, say, one year plus five days or 142 days.

One approach that addresses many of these objections is known as an exponentially weighted moving average (EWMA). An EWMA is a weighted mean in which the weights decrease exponentially as we go back in time. The EWMA estimator of the mean can be formulated as:

$$\hat{\mu}_t = \frac{1-\delta}{1-\delta^n} \sum_{i=0}^{n-1} \delta^i x_{t-i} \qquad (12.2)$$

Here, $\delta$ is a decay factor, where $0 < \delta < 1$. For the remainder of this chapter, unless noted otherwise, assume that any decay factor, $\delta$, is between zero and one. The term in front of the summation is the—by now familiar—inverse of the summation of $\delta$ from 0 to $n - 1$.

In the EWMA, more weight is placed on more recent events. For example, if we have 10 sample points and a decay factor of 0.90, then the first point gets approximately 15% of the total weight, and the last point gets less than 6%. Exhibit 12.3 shows the weights for all 10 points.

**EXHIBIT 12.3**   Example of EWMA Weights

| Age | $\delta^i$ | Weight |
| --- | --- | --- |
| 0 | 1.00 | 15.35% |
| 1 | 0.90 | 13.82% |
| 2 | 0.81 | 12.44% |
| 3 | 0.73 | 11.19% |
| 4 | 0.66 | 10.07% |
| 5 | 0.59 | 9.07% |
| 6 | 0.53 | 8.16% |
| 7 | 0.48 | 7.34% |
| 8 | 0.43 | 6.61% |
| 9 | 0.39 | 5.95% |
| Total | 6.51 | 100.00% |

Exhibit 12.4 plots these weights against time, as well as the corresponding weights for the standard equally weighted BLUE.

As you can see, the EWMA weights form a smooth exponential curve that fades at a constant rate as we go back in time. By contrast, because of the shape of the chart, we often refer to the equally weighted estimator as a rectangular window.

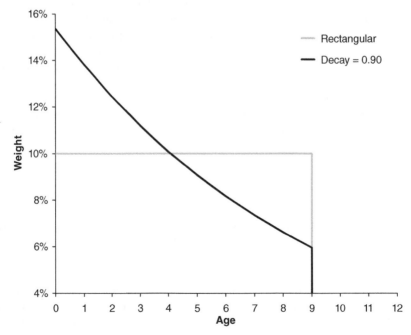

**EXHIBIT 12.4**   EWMA versus Rectangular Weights

One way we can characterize an EWMA is by its half-life. Half of the weight of the average comes before the half-life, and half after. We can find the half-life by solving for $h$ in the following equation:

$$\sum_{i=0}^{h-1}\delta^i = \frac{1}{2}\sum_{i=0}^{n-1}\delta^i \qquad (12.3)$$

The solution is:

$$h = \frac{\ln(0.5+0.5\delta^n)}{\ln(\delta)} \qquad (12.4)$$

For a sample of 250 data points and a decay factor of 0.98, the half-life is approximately 34. In other words, half of the weight of the estimator would be captured by the most recent 34 data points, and half in the remaining 216. A rectangular window of 250 data points, by comparison, would have a half-life of 125. Looked at another way, the EWMA with 250 data points and a decay factor of 0.98 has the same half-life as a rectangular window with 68 data points.

The EWMA can solve the problem of plateauing. The addition of an extreme data point to our data set can still cause a sudden change in our estimator, but the impact of that data point will slowly fade over time. Just before it exits the data set, the weight on the data point is likely to be so small that its removal will hardly be noticed. Exhibit 12.5 shows the same series as we saw in Exhibit 12.2. In addition to the estimator based on an equally weighted 40-day window, we have added an estimator based on a 40-day window with a decay factor of 0.95. As you can see, for the series with the decay factor, the second transition is much more gradual.

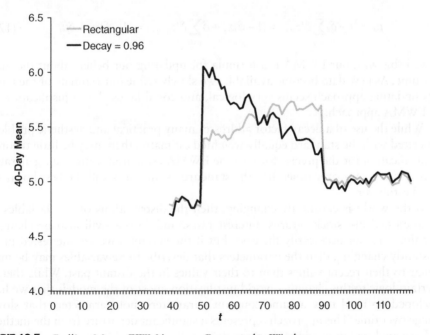

**EXHIBIT 12.5**   Rolling Mean, EWMA versus Rectangular Window

Besides addressing the aesthetic issue of plateauing, the EWMA estimator also addresses our philosophical objection to fixed windows. Rather than suddenly dropping out of the data set, the weight on any point is slowly reduced over time.

Finally, a fixed window length with a decay factor can be viewed as a compromise between a rectangular window of arbitrary length and using all available data. Because $|\delta|$ is less than one, as $n$ goes to infinity, Equation 12.2 can be rewritten as:

$$\hat{\mu}_t = (1-\delta)\sum_{i=0}^{\infty}\delta^i x_{t-i} \qquad (12.5)$$

Clearly an infinite series, if it did exist, would be using all available data. In practice, though, for reasonable decay factors, there will be very little weight on points from the distant past. Because of this, we can use a finite window length, but capture almost all of the weight of the infinite series. Using our geometric series math:

$$\frac{\text{Weight of finite series}}{\text{Weight of infinite series}} = \frac{\dfrac{1-\delta^n}{1-\delta}}{\dfrac{1}{1-\delta}} = 1-\delta^n \qquad (12.6)$$

For a decay factor of 0.98, if our window length is 250, we would capture 99.4% of the weight of the infinite series. Ultimately, the window length is still arbitrary, but the precise choice becomes less important. Whether we choose a window length that captures 99% of the weight or 99.9% will typically have little impact on our estimator.

By carefully rearranging Equation 12.5, we can express the EWMA estimator as a weighted average of its previous value and the most recent observation:

$$\hat{\mu}_t = (1-\delta)\sum_{i=0}^{\infty}\delta^i x_{t-i} = (1-\delta)x_t + \delta\sum_{i=0}^{\infty}\delta^i x_{t-i-1} = (1-\delta)x_t + \delta\hat{\mu}_{t-1} \qquad (12.7)$$

Viewed this way, our EWMA is a formula for updating our beliefs about the mean over time. As new data become available, we slowly refine our estimate of the mean. This updating approach seems very logical, and could be used as a justification for the EWMA approach.

While the use of a decay factor addresses many practical and aesthetic problems associated with the standard equally weighted estimator, there may be little theoretical justification for the precise form of the EWMA estimator. If our data-generating process is constant over time, then the standard estimator is still the best linear unbiased estimator.

If the world is constantly changing, then the distributions of the variables we are interested in—stock returns, interest rates, and so on—will also be changing over time. It's not necessarily the case, but if the variables we are interested in are constantly changing, then the parameters that describe these variables may be more similar to their recent values than to their values in the distant past. While there is a certain logic to this changing world justification, most of the models that we have developed up until now assume constant parameters, not parameters that slowly change over time. This approach represents a significant departure from the methods we have explored in previous chapters.

## VARIANCE

Just as we used a decay factor when calculating the mean, we can use a decay factor when calculating other estimators. For an estimator of the sample variance, when the mean is known, the following is an unbiased estimator:

$$\hat{\sigma}_t^2 = \frac{1-\delta}{1-\delta^n} \sum_{i=0}^{n-1} \delta^i (r_{t-i} - \mu)^2 \quad 0 < \delta < 1 \tag{12.8}$$

If we imagine an estimator of infinite length, then the term $\delta^n$ goes to zero, and we have:

$$\hat{\sigma}_t^2 = (1-\delta) \sum_{i=0}^{\infty} \delta^i (r_{t-i} - \mu)^2 \quad 0 < \delta < 1 \tag{12.9}$$

This formula, in turn, leads to a useful updating rule:

$$\hat{\sigma}_t^2 = (1-\delta)(r_t - \mu)^2 + \delta \hat{\sigma}_{t-1}^2 \tag{12.10}$$

As with our estimator of the mean, using a decay factor is equivalent to an updating rule. In this case, the new value of our estimator is a weighted average of the previous estimator and the most recent squared deviation.

As mentioned in connection with the standard estimator for variance, it is not uncommon in finance for the mean to be close to zero and much smaller than the standard deviation of returns. If we assume the mean is zero, then our updating rule simplifies even further to:

$$\hat{\sigma}_t^2 = (1-\delta)r_t^2 + \delta \hat{\sigma}_{t-1}^2 \tag{12.11}$$

Remember that the preceding formula is valid only if we assume the mean is known and equal to zero.

In the case where the mean is unknown and must also be estimated, our estimator takes on a slightly more complicated form:

$$\hat{\sigma}_t^2 = A \sum_{i=0}^{n-1} \delta^i r_{t-i}^2 - B \hat{\mu}_t^2 \tag{12.12}$$

where $\hat{\mu}_t$ is our estimator of the sample mean, based on the same decay factor, $\delta$, and $A$ and $B$ are constants defined as:

$$
\begin{aligned}
A &= \frac{S_1}{S_1^2 - S_2} \\
B &= S_1 A \\
S_1 &= \frac{1-\delta^n}{1-\delta} \\
S_2 &= \frac{1-\delta^{2n}}{1-\delta^2}
\end{aligned} \tag{12.13}
$$

Though these constants should look familiar by now, the addition of a decay factor has certainly made our variance estimator more complicated.

It is not too difficult to prove that in the limit, as $\delta$ approaches one—that is, as our estimator becomes a rectangular window—$A$ approaches $1/(n-1)$ and $B$ converges to $n/(n-1)$. Just as we would expect, in the limit our new estimator converges to the standard variance estimator.

If we wish to know the standard deviation of a time series using a decay factor, we can simply take the square root of the appropriate estimator of the variance. No additional steps are required.

## WEIGHTED LEAST SQUARES

To apply the same decay factor logic to linear regression analysis, we simply need to multiply all of the sample data, both the regressors and regressands, by the appropriate decay factors. Recall from Chapter 10 that, for a multivariate regression, the ordinary least squares (OLS) estimator is defined as:

$$\hat{\beta} = (\mathbf{X}'\mathbf{X})^{-1}\mathbf{X}'\mathbf{Y} \tag{12.14}$$

where $\mathbf{X}$ is a $t \times n$ matrix for our regressor, and $\mathbf{Y}$ is a $t \times 1$ matrix for our regressand. To integrate our decay factor into this analysis, we start by defining $\lambda$ as the square root of our decay factor, $\delta$. Next, we construct a diagonal weight matrix, $\mathbf{W}$, whose diagonal elements are a geometric progression of $\lambda$:

$$\mathbf{W} = \begin{bmatrix} \lambda^{n-1} & \cdots & 0 & 0 \\ \vdots & \ddots & 0 & 0 \\ 0 & 0 & \lambda & 0 \\ 0 & 0 & 0 & 1 \end{bmatrix} \tag{12.15}$$

We can then form a new estimator for our regression parameters:

$$\tilde{\beta} = (\mathbf{X}'\mathbf{W}'\mathbf{W}\mathbf{X})^{-1}\mathbf{X}'\mathbf{W}'\mathbf{W}\mathbf{Y} \tag{12.16}$$

This estimator is known as the weighted least squares estimator.

One way to view what we are doing is to redefine our regressors and regressands as follows:

$$\begin{aligned} \mathbf{X}^* &= \mathbf{W}\mathbf{X} \\ \mathbf{Y}^* &= \mathbf{W}\mathbf{Y} \end{aligned} \tag{12.17}$$

The new matrices take our original data, and multiply the data at time $t - i$ by $\lambda^i$. The effect is to make data points from the distant past smaller, which decreases their variance and decreases their impact on our parameter estimates. With these new matrices in hand, our weighted least squares estimator can now be written as:

$$\tilde{\beta} = (X^{*\prime} X^*)^{-1} X^{*\prime} Y^* \tag{12.18}$$

In this way, our weighted least squares estimator can be viewed as the OLS estimator of our transformed data.

One potential problem with the weighted least squares approach, as described here, involves heteroscedasticity. If the initial data set is homoscedastic, then clearly the transformed data will be heteroscedastic. As with our mean and variance estimators, when we use a decay factor, the resulting estimator will be unbiased, but it will not be the BLUE.

Why did we choose to define $W$ using the square root of $\delta$, and not $\delta$ itself? By defining $W$ this way, we are being consistent with the way we defined our variance estimator in the previous section.

## OTHER POSSIBILITIES

So far we have explored two weighting schemes for estimating population parameters. The traditional approach applies an equal weight to all data points, while our decay factor approach applies weights that decline at a constant rate as we go back in time. In theory, there is an infinite number of possible weighting schemes we could use, but one novel approach pioneered by Philip Hua and Paul Wilmott is worth mentioning (Hua and Wilmott 1997).

As risk managers, if we are ultimately concerned with extreme markets, then the suggestion is that we should be placing more weight on data from extreme markets, and little or no weight on data from normal markets. This approach seems particularly appropriate for stress testing, where, by definition, we are dealing with extreme events.

One way to implement this approach would be to define a cutoff return that separates extreme markets and normal markets, and use only the data from extreme markets to calculate statistics (weights are zero or one). Alternatively, we could define weights as a function of how extreme the returns are (e.g., the weights are equal to the square of the return of a given index). When applied to stress testing or value at risk (VaR), Hua and Wilmott refer to this as the CrashMetrics approach. Looked at more generally, it provides a novel third way of calculating sample parameters.

## APPLICATION: HYBRID VaR

One of the simplest approaches to estimating value at risk (VaR) is the historical method or historical simulation. In this approach, we calculate the backcast returns of a portfolio of assets, and take these as the portfolio's return distribution. To calculate the 95th percentile VaR, we would simply find the least worst of the worst

5% of returns. For example, suppose we have 100 returns, ranked from lowest to highest:

| | | |
|---|---|---|
| **Worst** | 1 | −1.40% |
| | 2 | −0.82% |
| | 3 | −0.75% |
| | 4 | −0.73% |
| | 5 | **−0.68%** |
| | 6 | −0.66% |
| | 7 | −0.65% |
| | ... | ... |
| | 97 | 0.93% |
| | 98 | 0.95% |
| | 99 | 1.17% |
| **Best** | 100 | 1.52% |

Here the 95th percentile VaR would correspond to the fifth return, −0.68%.

Instead of giving equal weight to all data, we can use a decay factor to weight more recent data more heavily. Rather than finding the fifth worst return, we would order the returns and find the point where we have 5% of the total weight. Using the same returns as in the preceding example:

| | Rank | Return | Weight | Percentage of Total Weight |
|---|---|---|---|---|
| **Worst** | 1 | −1.40% | 0.83 | 1.9% |
| | 2 | −0.82% | 0.27 | 2.5% |
| | 3 | **−0.75%** | **0.42** | **3.5%** |
| | 4 | −0.73% | 0.87 | 5.5% |
| | 5 | −0.68% | 0.52 | 6.7% |
| | 6 | −0.66% | 0.74 | 8.4% |
| | 7 | −0.65% | 0.31 | 9.1% |
| | ... | ... | ... | ... |
| | 97 | 0.93% | 0.16 | 96.4% |
| | 98 | 0.95% | 0.63 | 97.9% |
| | 99 | 1.17% | 0.25 | 98.5% |
| **Best** | 100 | 1.52% | 0.67 | 100.0% |

In this case, we get to 5% of the total weight between the third and fourth returns. At this point there are two approaches. The more conservative approach is to take the third return, −0.75%. The alternative is to interpolate between the third and fourth returns, to come up with −0.74%. Unless there is a strong justification for choosing the interpolation method, the conservative approach is recommended.

This general approach, using historical returns with decreasing weights, is often called the hybrid approach because it combines aspects of standard historical simulation and weighted parametric approaches; see, for example, Allen, Boudoukh, and Saunders (2004).

## PROBLEMS

1. For an estimator based on $n$ data points, with a decay factor of $\delta$, prove that the half-life, $h$, is given by:

$$h = \frac{\ln(0.5 + 0.5\delta^n)}{\ln(\delta)}$$

2. Using a decay factor of 0.95, calculate the mean, sample variance, and sample standard deviation of the following series. Assume $t = 7$ is the most recent data point, and use all eight points:

| $t$ | 0 | 1 | 2 | 3 | 4 | 5 | 6 | 7 |
|-----|----|----|----|----|----|----|----|----|
| $x$ | 11 | 84 | 30 | 73 | 56 | 58 | 52 | 35 |

3. Given the following set of data, calculate the mean using no decay factor (rectangular window), a decay factor of 0.99, and a decay factor of 0.90. Assume time $t = 10$ is the most recent data point, and use all 11 points:

| $t$ | 0 | 1 | 2 | 3 | 4 | 5 | 6 | 7 | 8 | 9 | 10 |
|-----|------|------|------|------|------|------|------|------|------|------|------|
| $x$ | 0.04 | 0.84 | 0.28 | 0.62 | 0.42 | 0.46 | 0.66 | 0.69 | 0.39 | 0.99 | 0.37 |

4. Calculate the sample standard deviation for the data set in problem 3, also using no decay factor, a decay factor of 0.99, and a decay factor of 0.90.

5. You are estimating the expected value of the annual return of a stock market index using an EWMA estimator with a decay factor of 0.98. The current estimate of the mean is 10%. Over the next three years, the index returns 15%, –4%, and finally 8%. Recalculate the estimate of the mean in each of these three years.

6. What is the half-life for an estimator with a decay factor of 0.95 and 200 data points? What is the half-life for the same decay factor with 1,000 data points?

7. What is the half-life of an EWMA estimator with a decay factor of 0.96 and 32 data points? What is the length of a rectangular window with the most similar half-life?

8. Assume we have an EWMA estimator with a decay factor of 0.96 and 50 data points. What percentage of the weight is captured with this estimator, compared to an estimator with the same decay factor and an infinite length?

9. Assume that the mean of a data-generating process is known and equal to 10%. The initial estimate of the standard deviation is 20%, when you observe a return of 15%. What is your updated estimate of the mean? Assume the data series is of infinite length, and use a decay factor of 0.97.

10. Assume that the mean of a data generating process is known and equal to zero. Your initial estimate of the standard deviation is 10%. You observe the following returns ($t = 6$ is the most recent period). Assume that the initial estimator was generated from an infinitely long series, and use a decay factor of 0.95. What is your updated estimate of the standard deviation?

| $t$ | 1 | 2 | 3 | 4 | 5 | 6 |
|---|---|---|---|---|---|---|
| $r$ | −5% | 18% | 16% | −2% | 5% | −10% |

# Binary Numbers

**B**inary numbers are important in risk management for two reasons. First, most of the mathematics and statistics in this book will end up being implemented on computers. Implementation can often be as difficult as, if not more difficult than, the theoretical aspects of a problem. Even if you're not doing the programming yourself, understanding programming can make the transition from theory to working systems easier. Understanding programming means understanding computers, and binary is the language that computers speak. The second reason that binary numbers are of interest is that—just by chance—they provide a very useful shortcut for doing some very common risk management calculations. Even if you're building highly complex systems, you'll often need to perform these back-of-the-envelope calculations.

Ordinarily, when we're doing arithmetic, we're using decimal numbers. If you see 157, this is usually shorthand for:

$$1 \cdot 10^2 + 5 \cdot 10^1 + 7 \cdot 10^0$$

We say that decimal is base 10. Binary, by contrast, is base 2. In binary, 1,001 is shorthand for:

$$1 \cdot 2^3 + 0 \cdot 2^2 + 0 \cdot 2^1 + 1 \cdot 2^0$$

If you work this out, you'll see that binary 1,001 is equivalent to decimal 9.

Computers work in binary. The standard unit for most computers is the byte, which consists of 8 bits. Coincidentally, $2^{10}$ is 1,024, which is very close to 1,000. This is why kilobytes are 1,024 bytes, not 1,000 bytes. Megabytes are $2^{20} = 1,048,576$ bytes, not 1 million bytes. Knowing that $2^{10}$ is close to 1,000 is very useful.

Just as $2^{10}$ turns out to be very close to 1,000, $2^8$ equals 256, which is very close to the number of business days in a year. It is often the case that we need to convert from daily standard deviations to annualized standard deviation, or vice versa. If returns are independent and identically distributed (i.i.d.), then translating daily standard deviations into annualized standard deviations requires multiplying by the square root of the number of business days in a year. If we use 256 business days per year as an approximation, then we would annualize daily standard deviations by multiplying by 16:

$$256 = 2^8 = 2^4 \cdot 2^4 = 16 \cdot 16$$

So if the daily standard deviation of a stock is 1%, then the annualized standard deviation is close to 16%. If the annualized standard deviation is close to 48%, then the daily standard deviation is close to 3%. This is a very useful approximation to be familiar with.

If returns are normally distributed—not an assumption you should make lightly—then the 95% value at risk (VaR) of a security will be approximately 1.6 standard deviations. Combining this with our approximate annualization factor, it is very easy to see why the one-day VaR should be close to one-tenth of the annualized standard deviation. A stock with a quoted annualized standard deviation of 43% will often have a one-day 95% VaR close to 4.3%. You should always be careful when using this kind of approximation, but being able to perform this calculation quickly can be very useful.

# Taylor Expansions

A Taylor series expansion can be used to provide approximations to a function. Given a function $f(x)$, assuming the necessary derivatives exist, we can define the Taylor series:

$$f(x) = f(a) + f'(a)(x-a) + \frac{1}{2!} f''(a)(x-a)^2 + \frac{1}{3!} f^{(3)}(a)(x-a)^3 + \cdots$$

$$+ \frac{1}{n!} f^{(n)}(a)(x-a)^n + \cdots$$

where $f'$, $f''$, and $f^{(3)}$ are, respectively, the first, second, and third derivatives of $f(x)$ with respect to $x$.

We can talk about an $n$th-order Taylor series expansion, which would extend to the $n$th term,

$$\frac{1}{n!} f^{(n)}(a)(x-a)^n$$

As an example, take the exponential function. The corresponding Taylor series expansion is:

$$e^x \approx e^a + e^a(x-a) + \frac{1}{2!} e^a(x-a)^2 + \frac{1}{3!} e^a(x-a)^3 + \cdots + \frac{1}{n!} e^a(x-a)^n$$

An obvious choice for $a$ is $a = 0$, which would give us $e^a = 1$. In this case, we say that we are expanding $e^x$ around zero. The expansion then simplifies to:

$$e^x \approx 1 + x + \frac{1}{2!} x^2 + \frac{1}{3!} x^3 + \cdots + \frac{1}{n!} x^n$$

Exhibit B.1 shows the first few approximations for $e^x$, expanded around zero, for various values of $x$.

The last row is the exact value of the function, which would be equal to the infinite expansion. Notice that as we add more terms, the approximation gets closer and closer to the real value. Also notice that the closer $x$ is to the expansion point, the better the approximation. Be careful: While many functions exhibit this type of

**EXHIBIT B.1** Taylor Approximations for $e^x$

| Order | $x$ −0.5 | 0.5 | 1 | 2 |
|-------|------|------|------|------|
| 1 | 0.50 | 1.50 | 2.00 | 3.00 |
| 2 | 0.63 | 1.63 | 2.50 | 5.00 |
| 3 | 0.60 | 1.65 | 2.67 | 6.33 |
| 4 | 0.61 | 1.65 | 2.71 | 7.00 |
| 5 | 0.61 | 1.65 | 2.72 | 7.27 |
| Exact | 0.61 | 1.65 | 2.72 | 7.39 |

convergence, this need not be the case. One important counterexample is the natural logarithm. The Taylor expansion for $\ln(x)$ around one is:

$$\ln(x) = (x-1) - \frac{1}{2}(x-1)^2 + \frac{1}{3}(x-1)^3 - \cdots - (-1^n)\frac{1}{n}(x-1)^n + \cdots$$

In this case, for values $x$ such that $0 < x \leq 2$, the Taylor series expansion converges as we increase the order of the approximation. As can be seen in Exhibit B.2, however, for values of $x$ greater than 2, increasing the order of the approximation can actually make matters worse.

**EXHIBIT B.2** Taylor Approximations for $\ln(x)$

| Order | $x$ −0.5 | 1.5 | 2 | 3 |
|-------|-------|------|------|------|
| 1 | −0.50 | 0.50 | 1.00 | 2.00 |
| 2 | −0.63 | 0.38 | 0.50 | 0.00 |
| 3 | −0.67 | 0.42 | 0.83 | 2.67 |
| 4 | −0.68 | 0.40 | 0.58 | −1.33 |
| 5 | −0.68 | 0.39 | 0.38 | −7.73 |
| Exact | −0.69 | 0.41 | 0.69 | 1.10 |

# Vector Spaces

**W**e can define a vector space more formally. Given three vectors, **v**, **w**, and **x**, and two scalars, $s$ and $t$, we begin by defining two operations:

1. Addition, **v** + **w**, which produces a sum.
2. Scalar multiplication, $s$**v**, which produces a scalar multiple.

In the most general definition of a vector space, these operations need not conform to the standard definitions we have explored in real vector spaces, $\mathbf{R}^n$. What we do require is that the following 10 axioms are satisfied:

1. If **v** and **w** exist in **V**, then **v** + **w** exists in **V** as well.
2. **v** + **w** = **w** + **v**.
3. **u** + (**v** + **w**) = (**u** + **v**) + **w**.
4. There is a zero vector in **V**, **0**, such that **0** + **v** = **v** + **0** = **v** for all **v**.
5. For every **v**, there is a negative of **v**, –**v**, such that **v** + (–**v**) = (–**v**) + **v** = **0**.
6. For any scalar, $s$, and any vector in **V**, **v**, $s$**v** is also in **V**.
7. $s$(**v** + **w**) = $s$**v** + $s$**w**.
8. $(s + t)$**v** = $s$**v** + $t$**v**.
9. $s(t$**v**$) = (st)$**v**.
10. 1**v** = **v**.

# 3

# Vector Spaces

# Greek Alphabet

| | | | | | | |
|---|---|---|---|---|---|---|
| A | $\alpha$ | Alpha | N | $\nu$ | Nu |
| B | $\beta$ | Beta | $\Xi$ | $\xi$ | Xi |
| $\Gamma$ | $\gamma$ | Gamma | O | $o$ | Omicron |
| $\Delta$ | $\delta$ | Delta | $\Pi$ | $\pi$ | Pi |
| E | $\varepsilon$ | Epsilon | P | $\rho$ | Rho |
| Z | $\zeta$ | Zeta | $\Sigma$ | $\sigma$ | Sigma |
| H | $\eta$ | Eta | T | $\tau$ | Tau |
| $\Theta$ | $\theta$ | Theta | Y | $\upsilon$ | Upsilon |
| I | $\iota$ | Iota | $\Phi$ | $\phi$ | Phi |
| K | $\kappa$ | Kappa | X | $\chi$ | Chi |
| $\Lambda$ | $\lambda$ | Lambda | $\Psi$ | $\psi$ | Psi |
| M | $\mu$ | Mu | $\Omega$ | $\omega$ | Omega |

# Common Abbreviations

**D**oes your DGP produce a PDF that leads to an MSE of *e*? What follows is a list of some common abbreviations from statistics and risk management:

| | |
|---|---|
| avg.: | average |
| BLUE: | best linear unbiased estimator |
| CDF: | cumulative density function or cumulative distribution function |
| DGP: | data-generating process |
| ESS: | explained sum of squares |
| EWMA: | exponentially weighted moving average |
| i.i.d.: | independent and identically distributed |
| MSE: | mean squared error |
| OLS: | ordinary least squares |
| PDF: | probability density function or probability distribution function |
| RNG: | random number generator |
| RSS: | residual sum of squares |
| s.d. or std. dev.: | standard deviation |
| s.t.: | such that |
| TSS: | total sum of squares |
| Var or var: | variance |
| VaR: | value at risk |

# Copulas

The following is a summary of the properties of various named copulas. Formulas are given in terms of two cumulative distribution functions (CDFs), but these definitions can be extended to any number of variables. The following notation is used for each copula:

- $g$: the generator function for the copula
- $g^{-1}$: inverse of the generator function
- $C$: the copula in terms of two CDFs, $u$ and $v$
- $C_1$: the marginal CDF of the copula, $\dfrac{\partial c}{\partial u}$
- $c$: the copula's density function
- $\tau$: Kendall's tau
- $\rho$: Spearman's rho

## Clayton

$$g^{-1} = (1 + t)^{-\frac{1}{\alpha}}$$

$$g = t^{-\alpha} - 1$$

$$C = (u^{-\alpha} + v^{-\alpha} - 1)^{-\frac{1}{\alpha}}$$

$$C_1 = \frac{\partial C}{\partial u} = u^{-(\alpha+1)}(u^{-\alpha} + v^{-\alpha} - 1)^{-\frac{1+\alpha}{\alpha}}$$

$$v = u\left(C_1^{-\frac{\alpha}{1+\alpha}} + u^{\alpha} - 1\right)^{-\frac{1}{\alpha}}$$

$$c = (1 + \alpha)(uv)^{-(\alpha+1)}(u^{-\alpha} + v^{-\alpha} - 1)^{-\frac{1+2\alpha}{\alpha}}$$

$$\alpha > 0$$

$$\tau = \frac{\alpha}{\alpha + 2}$$

## Farlie-Gumbel-Morgenstern (FGM)

$$C = uv[1 + \alpha(1 - u)(1 - v)]$$

$$C_1 = v(1 + \alpha - 2\alpha u) + v^2\alpha (2u - 1)$$

$$c = 1 + \alpha (1 - 2u)(1 - 2v)$$

$$-1 \leq \alpha \leq + 1$$

$$\tau = \frac{2}{9}\alpha$$

$$\rho = \frac{1}{3}\alpha$$

## Frank

$$g^{-1} = \frac{1}{\alpha}\ln[1 - (1 - e^\alpha)e^{-t}]$$

$$g = -\ln\left(\frac{1 - e^{\alpha t}}{1 - e^\alpha}\right)$$

$$C = \frac{1}{\alpha}\ln\left[1 + \frac{(e^{\alpha u} - 1)(e^{\alpha v} - 1)}{e^\alpha - 1}\right]$$

$$C_1 = \frac{\partial C}{\partial u} = \frac{(e^{\alpha u} - 1)(e^{\alpha v} - 1) + (e^{\alpha v} - 1)}{(e^{\alpha u} - 1)(e^{\alpha v} - 1) + (e^\alpha - 1)}$$

$$v = \frac{1}{\alpha}\ln\left[1 + \frac{C_1(e^\alpha - 1)}{1 + (e^{\alpha u} - 1)(1 - C_1)}\right]$$

$$c = \alpha(e^\alpha - 1)\frac{e^{\alpha(u+v)}}{[(e^{\alpha u} - 1)(e^{\alpha v} - 1) + (e^\alpha - 1)]^2}$$

$$\alpha \neq 0$$

$$\tau = 1 + \frac{4}{\alpha}\left[1 + \frac{1}{\alpha}\int_0^{-\alpha}\frac{t}{e^t - 1}dt\right]$$

$$\rho = 1 - \frac{12}{\alpha}\left[\frac{1}{\alpha}\int_0^{-\alpha}\frac{t}{e^t - 1}dt + \frac{1}{\alpha^2}\int_0^{-\alpha}\frac{t^2}{e^t - 1}dt\right]$$

## Gumbel

$$g^{-1} = e^{-t^{\frac{1}{\alpha}}}$$

$$g = (-\ln t)^\alpha$$

$$C = e^{-[(-\ln u)^\alpha + (-\ln v)^\alpha]^{\frac{1}{\alpha}}}$$

$$C_1 = \frac{\partial C}{\partial u} = \frac{1}{u}(-\ln u)^{\alpha - 1}C[(-\ln u)^\alpha + (-\ln v)^\alpha]^{\frac{1-\alpha}{\alpha}}$$

$$c = \frac{1}{uv}[(\ln u)(\ln v)]^{\alpha-1} C[(-\ln u)^{\alpha} + (-\ln v)^{\alpha}]^{\frac{1-2\alpha}{\alpha}} \left[ \alpha - 1 + ((-\ln u)^{\alpha} + (-\ln v)^{\alpha})^{\frac{1}{\alpha}} \right]$$

$$\alpha \geq 1$$

$$\tau = \frac{\alpha - 1}{\alpha}$$

## Independent

$$g^{-1} = e^{-t}$$

$$g = -\ln t$$

$$C = uv$$

$$C_1 = \frac{\partial C}{\partial u} = v$$

$$v = C_1$$

$$c = 1$$

$$\tau = 0$$

$$\rho = 0$$

## Joe

$$g^{-1} = 1 - (1 - e^{-t})^{\frac{1}{\alpha}}$$

$$g = -\ln[1 - (1 - t)^{\alpha}]$$

$$C = 1 - [(1-u)^{\alpha} + (1-v)^{\alpha} - (1-u)^{\alpha}(1-v)^{\alpha}]^{\frac{1}{\alpha}} = 1 - D^{\frac{1}{\alpha}}$$

$$c = (1-u)^{\alpha-1}(1-v)^{\alpha-1} D^{\frac{1-2\alpha}{\alpha}} (1-\alpha-D)$$

$$\alpha \geq 0$$

$$\tau = 1 - 4 \sum_{i=1}^{\infty} \frac{1}{i(\alpha i + 2)(\alpha(i-1) + 2)}$$

# Answers

## CHAPTER 1

**1. a.** $y = 5$
   **b.** $y = \ln(1) - \ln(e) = 0 - 1 = -1$
   **c.** $y = \ln(10) + \ln(e) = \ln(10) + 1 = 3.3026$

**2.** Annual rate = 5.12%; semiannual rate = 5.05%; continuous rate = 4.99%.

**3.** $100 \cdot e^{0.112} = 111.85$

**4.** $C(10,2) = \binom{10}{2} = \dfrac{10!}{2!(10-2)!} = \dfrac{10 \cdot 9 \cdot 8!}{2! \cdot 8!} = \dfrac{10 \cdot 9}{2} = 45$

**5.** $V = \displaystyle\sum_{i=1}^{\infty} \dfrac{100}{1.04^i} = 100 \sum_{i=1}^{\infty} \left(\dfrac{1}{1.04}\right)^i = 100 \dfrac{\frac{1}{1.04}}{1 - \frac{1}{1.04}} = 100 \dfrac{1}{1.04 - 1} = \$2,500$

**6.** $V = \dfrac{1.00}{1.06} + \dfrac{1.05}{1.06^2} + \dfrac{1.05^2}{1.06^3} + \cdots = \dfrac{1}{1.06}\left(1 + \dfrac{1.05}{1.06} + \dfrac{1.05^2}{1.06^2} + \cdots\right)$

$V = \dfrac{1}{1.06} \dfrac{1}{1 - \frac{1.05}{1.06}} = \dfrac{1}{1.06}\dfrac{1.06}{0.01} = \$100$

**7.** $V = \dfrac{6}{1.08} + \dfrac{6}{1.08^2} + \cdots \dfrac{6}{1.08^9} + \dfrac{106}{1.08^{10}} = 6 \cdot 6.71 + 46.32 = \$86.58$

**8.** $\ln(\ln(10)) = 0.8340$

**9.** $S = \displaystyle\sum_{i=0}^{9}(-0.5)^i = 1 + (-0.5) + (-0.5)^2 + \cdots + (-0.5)^8 + (-0.5)^9$

$-0.5S = (-0.5) + (-0.5)^2 + \cdots (-0.5)^9 + (-0.5)^{10}$

$= S - 1 + (-0.5)^{10}$

$S = \dfrac{1 - (-0.5)^{10}}{1.5} = \dfrac{1 - \frac{1}{1,024}}{1.5} = \dfrac{1,023}{1,536} = 0.67$

**10.** $\binom{10}{4} = \dfrac{10!}{4!6!} = 210$

11. The bond will pay 10 coupons of $2, starting in a year's time. In addition, the notional value of the bond will be returned with the final coupon payment in 10 years. The present value, $V$, is then:

$$V = \sum_{i=1}^{10} \frac{\$2}{(1.05)^i} + \frac{\$100}{(1.05)^{10}} = \$2\sum_{i=1}^{10} \frac{1}{(1.05)^i} + \frac{\$100}{(1.05)^{10}}$$

We start by evaluating the summation, using a discount factor of $\delta = 1/1.05 \approx 0.95$:

$$S = \sum_{i=1}^{10} \frac{1}{(1.05)^i} = \sum_{i=1}^{10}\left(\frac{1}{1.05}\right)^i = \sum_{i=1}^{10} \delta^i = \delta + \delta^2 + \cdots + \delta^9 + \delta^{10}$$

$$\delta S = \delta^2 + \delta^3 + \cdots + \delta^{10} + \delta^{11} = S - \delta + \delta^{11}$$

$$S(1-\delta) = \delta - \delta^{11}$$

$$S = \frac{\delta - \delta^{11}}{1-\delta} = 7.72$$

Inserting this result into the initial equation, we obtain our final result:

$$V = \$2 \times 7.72 + \frac{\$100}{(1.05)^{10}} = \$76.83$$

Note that the present value of the bond, $76.83, is less than the notional value of the bond, $100. This is what we would expect, given that there is no risk of default, and the coupon rate is less than the discount rate.

## CHAPTER 2

1. Probability that both generate positive returns = 60% × 70% = 42%.
   Probability that both funds lose money = (1 − 60%) × (1 − 70%) = 40% × 30% = 12%.
2. 88%. The sum of all three events—upgrade, downgrade, and no change—must sum to one. There is no other possible outcome. 88% + 8% + 4% = 100%.
3. 50%. The outcomes are mutually exclusive; therefore, 20% + 30% = 50%.
4. $P[\text{oil up} \cap \text{stock market down}] = P[\text{stock market down} | \text{oil up}] \cdot P[\text{oil up}]$

   $P[\text{oil up} \cap \text{stock market down}] = 60\% \cdot 30\% = 18\%$

5. Given the density function, we can find $c$ by noting that the sum of probabilities must be equal to one:

$$\int_{-\infty}^{\infty} f(x)dx = \int_{-10}^{10} c(100 - x^2)dx = c\left[100x - \frac{1}{3}x^3\right]_{-10}^{10}$$

$$c = \frac{3}{4,000}$$

6. First we check that this is a valid CDF, by calculating the value of the CDF for the minimum and maximum values of $x$:

$$F(0) = \frac{0}{100}(20 - 0) = 0$$

$$F(10) = \frac{10}{100}(20 - 10) = 1$$

Next we calculate the PDF by taking the first derivative of the CDF:

$$f(x) = \frac{d}{dx}F(x) = \frac{20}{100} - \frac{2x}{100} = \frac{1}{50}(10 - x)$$

7. We first calculate the CDF by integrating the PDF:

$$F(x) = \int_1^x f(t)dt = \int_1^x \frac{c}{t}dt = c[\ln t]_1^x = c\ln x$$

We first try to find $c$ using the fact that the CDF is zero at the minimum value of $x$, $x = 0$.

$$F(0) = c\ln(1) = c \cdot 0 = 0$$

As it turns out, any value of $c$ will satisfy this constraint, and we cannot use this to determine $c$.

If we use the fact that the CDF is 1 for the maximum value of $x$, $x = e$, we find that $c = 1$:

$$F(e) = c\ln(e) = c \cdot 1 = c$$

$$\therefore c = 1$$

The CDF can then be expressed simply as:

$$F(x) = \ln(x)$$

8. $P[\text{both bonds default}] = 30\% \times 30\% = 9\%$.

$P[\text{one defaults}] = 2 \times 30\% \times (1 - 30\%) = 42\%$.

$P[\text{neither defaults}] = (1 - 30\%) \times (1 - 30\%) = 49\%$.

For the second part of the question, remember that there are two scenarios in which only one bond defaults: Either the first defaults and the second does not, or the second defaults and the first does not.

9. The probability that a B-rated bond defaults over one year is 2%. This can be read directly from the last column of the second row of the ratings transition matrix.

The probability of default over two years is 4.8%. During the first year, a B-rated bond can either be upgraded to an A rating, stay at B, be downgraded to C, or default. From the transition matrix, we know that the probability of these events is 10%, 80%, 8%, and 2%, respectively. If the bond is upgraded to A, then there is zero probability of default in the second year (the last column of the first row of the matrix is 0%). If it remains at B, there is a 2% probability of default in the second year, the same as in the first year. If it is downgraded to C, there is a 15% probability of default in the second year. Finally, if a bond defaulted in the first year, it stays defaulted (the last column of the last row is 100%). Putting all this together, we have:

$$P[\text{default}] = 10\% \times 0\% + 80\% \times 2\% + 8\% \times 15\% + 2\% \times 100\%$$
$$= 4.8\%$$

10. Using $M$ to represent the market and $X$ to represent the portfolio manager, we are given the following information:

$$P[M_{\text{up}}] = 50\%$$
$$P[M_{\text{dn}}] = 20\%$$
$$P[M_{\text{flat}}] = 30\%$$
$$P[X_{\text{up}} \mid M_{\text{up}}] = 80\%$$
$$P[X_{\text{up}} \mid M_{\text{dn}}] = 10\%$$
$$P[X_{\text{up}} \mid M_{\text{flat}}] = 50\%$$

The unconditional probability that the manager is up next year, $P[X_{\text{up}}]$, is then 57%:

$$P[X_{\text{up}}] = P[X_{\text{up}} \mid M_{\text{up}}] \cdot P[M_{\text{up}}] + P[X_{\text{up}} \mid M_{\text{dn}}] \cdot P[M_{\text{dn}}] + P[X_{\text{up}} \mid M_{\text{flat}}] \cdot P[M_{\text{flat}}]$$
$$P[X_{\text{up}}] = 80\% \cdot 50\% + 10\% \cdot 20\% + 50\% \cdot 30\%$$
$$P[X_{\text{up}}] = 40\% + 2\% + 15\% = 57\%$$

## CHAPTER 3

1. Mean = 6.43%; median = 5%.
2. Mean = 3%; standard deviation = 6.84%.

3. $$\hat{\mu} = \frac{1}{n}\sum_{i=1}^{n} r_i = \frac{1}{n}(r_1 + r_2 + \cdots + r_{n-1} + r_n)$$

$$E[\hat{\mu}] = \frac{1}{n}\sum_{i=1}^{n} E[r_i] = \frac{1}{n}\sum_{i=1}^{n} \mu = \frac{1}{n} \cdot n \cdot \mu = \mu$$

4. Using the results of question 3, we first calculate the variance of the estimator of the mean:

$$E[(\hat{\mu} - \mu)^2] = E\left[\left(\frac{1}{n}\sum_{i=1}^{n} r_i - \mu\right)^2\right] = E\left[\left(\frac{1}{n}\sum_{i=1}^{n}(r_i - \mu)\right)^2\right]$$

$$E[(\hat{\mu} - \mu)^2] = \frac{1}{n^2} E\left[\sum_{i=1}^{n}(r_i - \mu)^2 + \sum_{i=1}^{n}\sum_{i \neq j}(r_i - \mu)(r_j - \mu)\right]$$

$$E[(\hat{\mu} - \mu)^2] = \frac{1}{n^2} E\left[\sum_{i=1}^{n}(r_i - \mu)^2\right] + \frac{1}{n^2} E\left[\sum_{i=1}^{n}\sum_{i \neq j}(r_i - \mu)(r_j - \mu)\right]$$

$$E[(\hat{\mu} - \mu)^2] = \frac{1}{n^2} \sum_{i=1}^{n} E[(r_i - \mu)^2] + \frac{1}{n^2} \sum_{i=1}^{n}\sum_{i \neq j} E[(r_i - \mu)(r_j - \mu)]$$

$$E[(\hat{\mu} - \mu)^2] = \frac{1}{n^2} \sum_{i=1}^{n} \sigma^2 + \frac{1}{n^2} \sum_{i=1}^{n}\sum_{i \neq j} 0$$

$$E[(\hat{\mu} - \mu)^2] = \frac{1}{n^2} n\sigma^2 = \frac{\sigma^2}{n}$$

where $\sigma$ is the standard deviation of $r$. In the second to last line, we rely on the fact that, because the data points are i.i.d., the covariance between different data points is zero. We obtain the final answer by taking the square root of the variance of the estimator:

$$\sigma_{\hat{\mu}} = \sqrt{\frac{\sigma^2}{n}} = \frac{\sigma}{\sqrt{n}}$$

5. Covariance = 0.0487; correlation = 82.40%.
6. Series #1: Mean = 0, standard deviation = 39, skewness = 0.
   Series #2: Mean = 0, standard deviation = 39, skewness = –0.63.
7. Series #1: Mean = 0, standard deviation = 17, kurtosis = 1.69.
   Series #2: Mean = 0, standard deviation = 17, kurtosis = 1.
8. The mean, $\mu$, is

$$\mu = \int_0^6 x \frac{x}{18} dx = \left[\frac{x^3}{3 \cdot 18}\right]_0^6 = \frac{6^3}{3 \cdot 18} - \frac{0^3}{3 \cdot 18} = \frac{6^2}{3^2} = 4$$

The variance, $\sigma^2$, is then:

$$\sigma^2 = \int_0^6 (x - 4)^2 \frac{x}{18} dx = \frac{1}{18} \int_0^6 (x^3 - 8x^2 + 16x) dx$$

$$\sigma^2 = \frac{1}{18}\left[\frac{1}{4}x^4 - \frac{8}{3}x^3 + 8x^2\right]_0^6 = \frac{6^2}{18}\left(\frac{1}{4}6^2 - \frac{8}{3}6 + 8\right)$$

$$\sigma^2 = 2(9 - 16 + 8) = 2$$

9. We start by expanding the mean:

$$\hat{\sigma}_x^2 = \frac{1}{n-1} \sum_{i=1}^{n}(x_i - \hat{\mu}_x)^2 = \frac{1}{n-1} \sum_{i=1}^{n}\left(\frac{n-1}{n}x_i - \frac{1}{n}\sum_{j \neq i} x_j\right)^2$$

By carefully rearranging terms, we are left with:

$$\hat{\sigma}_x^2 = \frac{1}{n}\sum_{i=1}^{n}x_i^2 - \frac{1}{n(n-1)}\sum_{i=1}^{n}\sum_{j\neq i}x_ix_j$$

Assuming that all the different values of $X$ are uncorrelated with each other, we can use the following two relationships:

$$E[x_i^2] = \sigma^2 + \mu^2$$

$$E[x_ix_j] = \mu_i\mu_j \ \textit{iff} \ \sigma_{ij} = 0 \ \forall \ i \neq j$$

Then:

$$E[\hat{\sigma}_x^2] = \frac{1}{n}n(\sigma^2 + \mu^2) - \frac{1}{n(n-1)}n(n-1)\mu^2 = \sigma^2$$

10. First we note that the expected value of $X_A$ plus $X_B$ is just the sum of the means:

$$E[X_A + X_B] = E[X_A] + E[X_B] = \mu_A + \mu_B$$

Substituting into our equation for variance, and rearranging, we get:

$$\text{Var}[X_A + X_B] = E[(X_A + X_B - E[X_A + X_B])^2]$$
$$= E[((X_A - \mu_A) + (X_B - \mu_B))^2]$$

Expanding the squared term and solving:

$$\text{Var}[X_A + X_B] = E[(X_A - \mu_A)^2 + (X_B - \mu_B)^2 + 2(X_A - \mu_A)(X_B - \mu_B)]$$

$$\text{Var}[X_A + X_B] = E[(X_A - \mu_A)^2] + E[(X_B - \mu_B)^2] + 2E[(X_A - \mu_A)(X_B - \mu_B)]$$

$$\text{Var}[X_A + X_B] = \sigma_A^2 + \sigma_B^2 + 2\text{Cov}[X_A, X_B]$$

Using our definition of covariance, we arrive at our final answer:

$$\text{Var}[X_A + X_B] = \sigma_A^2 + \sigma_B^2 + 2\rho_{AB}\sigma_A\sigma_B$$

11. If the bond does not default, you will receive \$100. If the bond does default, you will receive $40\% \times \$100 = \$40$. The future value, the expected value of the bond at the end of the year, is then \$94:

$$E[V] = 0.90 \cdot \$100 + 0.10 \cdot \$40 = \$94$$

The present value of the bond is approximately \$89.42:

$$PV = e^{-0.05}\$94 = \$89.42$$

## CHAPTER 4

1. The number of times XYZ Corporation exceeds consensus estimates follows a binomial distribution; therefore:

$$P[X = 3] = \binom{4}{3} 0.30^3 0.70^1 = 4 \cdot 0.30^3 \cdot 0.70 = 7.56\%$$

2. The number of exceedance events follows a binomial distribution; therefore:

$$P[X = 2] = \binom{20}{2} 0.05^2 0.95^{18} = 18.87\%$$

3. Because the annual returns of both funds are normally distributed and independent, the difference in their returns is also normally distributed:

$$R_{B-A} \sim N(\mu_B - \mu_A, \sigma_A^2 + \sigma_B^2)$$

The mean of this distribution is 10%, and the standard deviation is 50%. At the end of the year, the difference in the expected returns is 92%. This is 82% above the mean, or 1.64 standard deviations. Using Excel or consulting the table of confidence levels in the chapter, we see that this is a rare event. The probability of more than a 1.64 standard deviation event is only 5%.

4. The average number of defaults over five months is 10; therefore:

$$P[x = 5] = \frac{10^5}{5!} e^{-10} = 3.78\%$$

$$P[x = 10] = \frac{10^{10}}{10!} e^{-10} = 12.51\%$$

$$P[x = 15] = \frac{10^{15}}{15!} e^{-10} = 3.47\%$$

5. If the returns of the fund are normally distributed with a mean of 10% and a standard deviation of 15%, then the returns of $200 million invested in the fund are also normally distributed, but with an expected return of $20 million and a standard deviation of $30 million. A loss of $18.4 million represents a –1.28 standard deviation move:

$$z = \frac{-\$18.4 - \$20}{\$30} = -1.28$$

This is a one-tailed problem. By consulting the table of confidence intervals or using a spreadsheet, we determine that just 10% of the normal distribution lies below –1.28 standard deviations.

6. The return of –30% is approximately a –1.64 standard deviation event:

$$z = \frac{-30\% - 20.60\%}{30.85\%} = -1.64$$

According to the table of confidence intervals, 5% of the normal distribution lies below –1.64 standard deviations. The probability of a return less than –30% is then 5%.

7. For the mean:

$$\mu = \int_{x_1}^{x_2} cx\,dx = c\int_{x_1}^{x_2} x\,dx = c\left[\frac{1}{2}x^2\right]_{x_1}^{x_2} = c\frac{1}{2}(x_2^2 - x_1^2)$$

From a previous example, we know that $c = 1/(x_2 - x_1)$; therefore:

$$\mu = \frac{1}{2}\frac{(x_2^2 - x_1^2)}{(x_2 - x_1)} = \frac{1}{2}\frac{(x_2 - x_1)(x_2 + x_1)}{(x_2 - x_1)} = \frac{1}{2}(x_2 + x_1)$$

For the variance:

$$\sigma^2 = \int_{x_1}^{x_2} c(x - \mu)^2 dx = c\int_{x_1}^{x_2}(x^2 - 2\mu x + \mu^2)dx = c\left[\frac{1}{3}x^3 - \mu x^2 + \mu^2 x\right]_{x_1}^{x_2}$$

Substituting in for $c$ and $\mu$ from above:

$$\sigma^2 = \frac{1}{x_2 - x_1}\left[\frac{1}{3}(x_2^3 - x_1^3) - \frac{1}{2}(x_2 + x_1)(x_2^2 - x_1^2) + \frac{1}{4}(x_2 + x_1)^2(x_2 - x_1)\right]$$

For the final step, we need to know that:

$$x_2^3 - x_1^3 = (x_2 - x_1)(x_2^2 + x_1^2 + x_1 x_2)$$

Substituting in and solving, we have:

$$\sigma^2 = \frac{1}{12}(x_2 - x_1)^2$$

8. Using integration by substitution, define a new variable $y$ and solve:

$$y = \frac{x - \mu}{\sqrt{2}\sigma}$$

$$dx = \sqrt{2}\sigma\,dy$$

$$\int_{-\infty}^{\infty}\frac{1}{\sigma\sqrt{2\pi}}e^{-\frac{(\mu - x)^2}{2\sigma^2}}dx = \frac{1}{\sqrt{\pi}}\int_{-\infty}^{\infty}e^{-y^2}dy = \frac{1}{\sqrt{\pi}}\sqrt{\pi} = 1$$

9. Using the same substitution as in the previous question:

$$y = \frac{x - \mu}{\sqrt{2}\sigma}$$

$$dx = \sigma\sqrt{2}\,dy$$

$$\int_{-\infty}^{\infty} x\frac{1}{\sigma\sqrt{2\pi}}e^{-\frac{(\mu - x)^2}{2\sigma^2}}dx = \frac{1}{\sqrt{\pi}}\int_{-\infty}^{\infty}(\sigma\sqrt{2}y + \mu)e^{-y^2}dy$$

$$\int_{-\infty}^{\infty} x \frac{1}{\sigma\sqrt{2\pi}} e^{-\frac{(\mu-x)^2}{2\sigma^2}} dx = \frac{\sigma\sqrt{2}}{\sqrt{\pi}} \int_{-\infty}^{\infty} y e^{-y^2} dy + \frac{\mu}{\sqrt{\pi}} \int_{-\infty}^{\infty} e^{-y^2} dy$$

$$\int_{-\infty}^{\infty} x \frac{1}{\sigma\sqrt{2\pi}} e^{-\frac{(\mu-x)^2}{2\sigma^2}} dx = \frac{\sigma\sqrt{2}}{\sqrt{\pi}} [-2y e^{-y^2}]_{-\infty}^{\infty} + \mu$$

$$\int_{-\infty}^{\infty} x \frac{1}{\sigma\sqrt{2\pi}} e^{-\frac{(\mu-x)^2}{2\sigma^2}} dx = \mu$$

**10.** Using the same substitution as before:

$$y = \frac{x - \mu}{\sqrt{2}\sigma}$$

$$dx = \sigma\sqrt{2}dy$$

$$\mathrm{Var}[x] = \int_{-\infty}^{\infty} (x-\mu)^2 \frac{1}{\sigma\sqrt{2\pi}} e^{-\frac{(\mu-x)^2}{2\sigma^2}} dx = \frac{2\sigma^2}{\sqrt{\pi}} \int_{-\infty}^{\infty} y^2 e^{-y^2} dy$$

For the final step, we need to know that:

$$\int_{-\infty}^{\infty} x^2 e^{-x^2} dx = \frac{1}{2}\sqrt{\pi}$$

Using this result, we achieve the desired result:

$$\mathrm{Var}[x] = \frac{2\sigma^2}{\sqrt{\pi}} \frac{1}{2} \sqrt{\pi} = \sigma^2$$

**11.** First we note that the mean of $X_A$ is zero:

$$E[X_A] = E[\sqrt{\rho}X_1 + \sqrt{1-\rho}X_2] = \sqrt{\rho}E[X_1] + \sqrt{1-\rho}E[X_2]$$
$$= \sqrt{\rho} \cdot 0 + \sqrt{1-\rho} \cdot 0 = 0$$

Similarly, the mean of $X_B$ is zero.

Next, we want to calculate the variance. In order to do that, it will be useful to know two relationships. First we rearrange the equation for variance, Equation 3.20, to get:

$$E[X_i^2] = \mathrm{Var}[X_i] + E[X_i]^2 = 1 + 0^2 = 1 \text{ for } i = 1, 2, 3$$

Similarly, we can rearrange our equation for covariance, Equation 3.26, to get:

$$E[X_i X_j] = \mathrm{Cov}[X_i, X_j] + E[X_i]E[X_j] = 0 + 0 \cdot 0 = 0 \ \forall \ i \neq j$$

With these results in hand, we now show that the variance of $X_A$ is one:

$$\text{Var}[X_A] = E[X_A^2] - E[X_A]^2 = E[X_A^2]$$

$$\text{Var}[X_A] = E[\rho X_1^2 + 2\sqrt{\rho(1-\rho)}X_1 X_2 + (1-\rho)X_2^2]$$

$$\text{Var}[X_A] = \rho E[X_1^2] + 2\sqrt{\rho(1-\rho)}E[X_1 X_2] + (1-\rho)E[X_2^2]$$

$$\text{Var}[X_A] = \rho \cdot 1 + 2\sqrt{\rho(1-\rho)} \cdot 0 + (1-\rho) \cdot 1 = 1$$

The variance of $X_B$ is similarly 1. Next we calculate the covariance of $X_A$ and $X_B$:

$$\text{Cov}[X_A, X_B] = E[X_A X_B] - E[X_A]E[X_B] = E[X_A X_B]$$

$$\text{Cov}[X_A, X_B] = E[\rho X_1^2 + \sqrt{\rho}\sqrt{1-\rho}(X_1 X_2 + X_1 X_3) + (1-\rho)X_2 X_3]$$

$$\text{Cov}[X_A, X_B] = \rho E[X_1^2] + \sqrt{\rho}\sqrt{1-\rho}(E[X_1 X_2] + E[X_1 X_3])$$
$$+ (1-\rho)E[X_2 X_3]$$

$$\text{Cov}[X_A, X_B] = \rho \cdot 1 + \sqrt{\rho}\sqrt{1-\rho}(0+0) + (1-\rho) \cdot 0 = \rho$$

Putting the last two results together completes the proof:

$$\text{Corr}[X_A, X_B] = \frac{\text{Cov}[X_A, X_B]}{\sqrt{\text{Var}[X_A] \cdot \text{Var}[X_B]}} = \frac{\rho}{\sqrt{1 \cdot 1}} = \rho$$

12. For the portfolio consisting of 50% $A$ and 50% $B$, we can proceed two ways. The PDF of the portfolio is a triangle, from –0.5 to +0.5, with height of 2.0 at 0. We can argue that the mean is zero based on geometric arguments. Also, because both distributions are just standard uniform variables shifted by a constant, they must have variance of 1/12; 50% of each asset would have a variance of 1/4 this amount, and—only because the variables are independent—we can add the variance of the variables, giving us:

$$\sigma^2 = 2\frac{1}{4}\frac{1}{12} = \frac{1}{24}$$

$$\sigma = \sqrt{\frac{1}{24}} = \frac{1}{2}\sqrt{\frac{1}{6}}$$

Alternatively, we could calculate the mean and variance by integration:

$$\mu = \int_{-0.5}^{0} x(2+4x)dx + \int_{0}^{+0.5} x(2-4x)dx$$

$$\mu = \left[x^2 + \frac{4}{3}x^3\right]_{-0.5}^{0} + \left[x^2 - \frac{4}{3}x^3\right]_{0}^{+0.5} = 0$$

$$\sigma^2 = \int_{-0.5}^{0} x^2(2+4x)dx + \int_{0}^{+0.5} x^2(2-4x)dx$$

$$\sigma^2 = \left[\frac{2}{3}x^3 + x^4\right]_{-0.5}^{0} + \left[\frac{2}{3}x^3 - x^4\right]_{0}^{+0.5} = \frac{1}{24}$$

This confirms our earlier answer.

For the 50/50 mixture distribution, the PDF is bimodal and symmetrical around zero, giving a mean of zero:

$$\mu = 0.5\int_{-2}^{-1} x\,dx + 0.5\int_{+1}^{+2} x\,dx = 0.5\left(\left[\frac{1}{2}x^2\right]_{-2}^{-1} + \left[\frac{1}{2}x^2\right]_{1}^{2}\right)$$

$$\mu = 0.5\frac{1}{2}(1 - 4 + 4 - 1) = 0$$

For the variance we have:

$$\sigma^2 = 0.5\left(\int_{-2}^{-1} x^2\,dx + \int_{+1}^{+2} x^2\,dx\right) = 0.5\left(\left[\frac{1}{3}x^3\right]_{-2}^{-1} + \left[\frac{1}{3}x^3\right]_{+1}^{+2}\right)$$

$$\sigma^2 = \frac{1}{6}(-1 + 8 + 8 - 1) = \frac{7}{3}$$

$$\sigma = \sqrt{\frac{7}{3}}$$

Notice that, while the mean is the same, the variance for the mixture distribution is significantly higher.

# CHAPTER 5

**1.** The shape of the PDF resembles a truncated parabola.

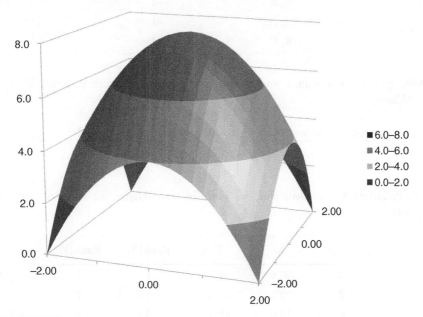

Legend:
- 6.0–8.0
- 4.0–6.0
- 2.0–4.0
- 0.0–2.0

**EXHIBIT 5.A1**   Joint Probability Density Function

To see if $X$ and $Y$ are independent, we start by calculating the marginal distribution of $X$:

$$f_x(x) = \int_y f(x,t)dt = \int_{-2}^{+2} c(8 - x^2 - t^2)dt = c\left[8t - tx^2 - \frac{1}{3}t^3\right]_{-2}^{+2} = 4c\left(\frac{20}{3} - x^2\right)$$

The marginal distribution of $Y$ is:

$$f_y(y) = \int_x f(t,y)dt = \int_{-2}^{+2} c(8 - t^2 - y^2)dt = c\left[8t - ty^2 - \frac{1}{3}t^3\right]_{-2}^{+2} = 4c\left(\frac{20}{3} - y^2\right)$$

Putting the two together, we can see that the product of the marginal distributions does not equal the joint distribution.

$$f_x(x)f_y(y) = 16c^2\left(\frac{20}{3} - x^2\right)\left(\frac{20}{3} - y^2\right) = \frac{1}{16^3}(400 - 60x^2 - 60y^2 + 9x^2y^2) \neq f(x,y)$$

We conclude that $X$ and $Y$ are not independent.

2. Kendall's tau is –33% and Spearman's rho is –50%.

   To calculate Kendall's tau, we start by examining the concordance of all possible pairs of points. With three points there are three distinct pairs:

| Pair | Concordant = +1, Discordant = –1 |
|------|----------------------------------|
| $A, B$ | –1 |
| $A, C$ | –1 |
| $B, C$ | +1 |

One pair is concordant and two are discordant; therefore, Kendall's tau is –33%:

$$\tau = \frac{\text{\# of concordant points} - \text{\# of discordant points}}{\binom{n}{2}} = \frac{1-2}{3} = -33\%$$

To calculate Spearman's rho, we start by calculating the rank of each data point:

|   | $X$ | $Y$ | Rank[$X$] | Rank[$Y$] |
|---|-----|-----|-----------|-----------|
| $A$ | 70% | 5%  | 1 | 3 |
| $B$ | 40% | 35% | 2 | 1 |
| $C$ | 20% | 10% | 3 | 2 |

The general formula for correlation is:

$$\mathrm{Corr}[X, Y] = \frac{\sum_{i=1}^{n}(x_i - \bar{x})(y_i - \bar{y})}{\sqrt{\sum_{i=1}^{n}(x_i - \bar{x})^2}\sqrt{\sum_{i=1}^{n}(y_i - \bar{y})^2}}$$

where $\bar{x}$ and $\bar{y}$ are the mean of $X$ and $Y$ respectively. To calculate Spearman's rho, we use not $X$ and $Y$ values, but their ranks. The mean of both Rank[$X$] and Rank[$Y$] is 2; therefore:

$$\rho_s = \frac{(1-2)(3-2) + (2-2)(1-2) + (3-2)(2-2)}{\sqrt{(1-2)^2 + (2-2)^2 + (3-2)^2}\sqrt{(3-2)^2 + (1-2)^2 + (2-2)^2}}$$

$$\rho_s = \frac{(-1) + 0 + 0}{\sqrt{1+0+1}\sqrt{1+1+0}} = \frac{-1}{\sqrt{2}\sqrt{2}} = \frac{-1}{2} = -50\%$$

In this example, Spearman's rho and Kendall's tau share the same sign, but they are not equal.

3. We start by calculating the copula's density function, $c(u,v)$:

$$c(u,v) = \frac{\partial^2 C(u,v)}{\partial u \partial v} = \frac{\partial^2}{\partial u \partial v}uv = \frac{\partial}{\partial u}u = 1$$

We next calculate the expected value of the copula:

$$\int_0^1 \int_0^1 C(u,v)c(u,v)dudv = \int_0^1 \int_0^1 uv \, dudv$$

$$\int_0^1 \int_0^1 C(u,v)c(u,v)dudv = \int_0^1 \left[\frac{1}{2}u^2 v\right]_0^1 dv$$

$$\int_0^1 \int_0^1 C(u,v)c(u,v)dudv = \frac{1}{2}\int_0^1 v \, dv = \frac{1}{2}\left[\frac{1}{2}v^2\right]_0^1 = \frac{1}{4}$$

Substituting into our equation for Kendall's tau:

$$\tau = 4\int_0^1 \int_0^1 C(u,v)c(u,v)dudv - 1 = 4\frac{1}{4} - 1 = 0$$

Not surprisingly for something called the independent copula, Kendall's tau is zero.

4. To calculate Spearman's rho, we first integrate the copula, $C(u,v)$, function with respect to $u$:

$$\int_0^1 C(u,v)du = \int_0^1 uv[1 + \alpha(1-u)(1-v)]du$$

$$\int_0^1 C(u,v)du = \int_0^1 [u(v + \alpha v(1-v)) - u^2\alpha v(1-v)]du$$

$$\int_0^1 C(u,v)du = \left[\frac{1}{2}u^2\left(v+\alpha v(1-v)\right)-\frac{1}{3}u^3\alpha v(1-v)\right]_0^1$$

$$\int_0^1 C(u,v)du = \left[\frac{1}{2}\left(v+\alpha v(1-v)\right)-\frac{1}{3}\alpha v(1-v)\right]-[0-0]$$

$$\int_0^1 C(u,v)du = \left(\frac{1}{2}+\frac{1}{6}\alpha\right)v-\frac{1}{6}\alpha v^2$$

Next we integrate this result with respect to $v$:

$$\int_0^1\int_0^1 C(u,v)dudv = \int_0^1\left[\left(\frac{1}{2}+\frac{1}{6}\alpha\right)v-\frac{1}{6}\alpha v^2\right]dv$$

$$\int_0^1\int_0^1 C(u,v)dudv = \left[\frac{1}{2}\left(\frac{1}{2}+\frac{1}{6}\alpha\right)v^2-\frac{1}{18}\alpha v^3\right]_0^1$$

$$\int_0^1\int_0^1 C(u,v)dudv = \left[\frac{1}{2}\left(\frac{1}{2}+\frac{1}{6}\alpha\right)-\frac{1}{18}\alpha\right]-[0-0]$$

$$\int_0^1\int_0^1 C(u,v)dudv = \frac{1}{4}+\frac{1}{36}\alpha$$

Finally, we use this result to calculate Spearman's rho:

$$\rho = 12\int_0^1\int_0^1 C(u,v)dudv-3$$

$$\rho = 12\left(\frac{1}{4}+\frac{1}{36}\alpha\right)-3 = \frac{1}{3}\alpha$$

## CHAPTER 6

1.     $P[\text{GDP down}|\text{unemployment up}] =$

$$\frac{P[\text{unemployment up}|\text{GDP down}]\cdot P[\text{GDP down}]}{P[\text{unemployment up}]}$$

$$P[\text{GDP down}|\text{unemployment up}] = \frac{40\%\cdot 20\%}{10\%} = 80\%$$

2. 32.14%. By applying Bayes' theorem, we can calculate the result:

$$P[\text{actual}=\text{D}|\text{model}=\text{D}] = \frac{P[\text{model}=\text{D}|\text{actual}=\text{D}]\cdot P[\text{actual}=\text{D}]}{P[\text{model}=\text{D}]}$$

$$P[\text{actual}=\text{D}|\text{model}=\text{D}] = \frac{90\%\cdot 5\%}{90\%\cdot 5\%+10\%\cdot 95\%} = 32.14\%$$

Even though the model is 90% accurate, 95% of the bonds don't default, and of those 95% the model predicts that 10% of them will default. Within the bond portfolio, the model identifies 9.5% of the bonds as likely to default, even though they won't. Of the 5% of bonds that actually default, the model correctly identifies 90%, or 4.5% of the portfolio. This 4.5% correctly identified is overwhelmed by the 9.5% incorrectly identified.

|  |  | Actual | | |
|---|---|---|---|---|
|  |  | D | No D | |
| Model | D | 4.5 | 9.5 | 14.0 |
|  | No D | 0.5 | 85.5 | 86.0 |
|  |  | 5.0 | 95.0 | 100.0 |

3. We can start by summing across the first row to get $W$:

$$W + 5\% = 15\%$$
$$W = 10\%$$

In a similar fashion, we can find $X$ by summing across the second row:

$$45\% + X = 65\%$$
$$X = 20\%$$

To calculate $Y$, we can sum down the first column, using our previously calculated value for $W$:

$$W + 45\% + Y = 10\% + 45\% + Y = 60\%$$
$$Y = 5\%$$

Using this result, we can sum across the third row to get $Z$:

$$Y + 15\% = 5\% + 15\% = Z$$
$$Z = 20\%$$

The completed probability matrix is:

|  |  | Equity | | |
|---|---|---|---|---|
|  |  | Outperform | Underperform | |
|  | Upgrade | 10% | 5% | 15% |
| Bonds | No Change | 45% | 20% | 65% |
|  | Downgrade | 5% | 15% | 20% |
|  |  | 60% | 40% | 100% |

The last part of the question asks us to find the conditional probability, which we can express as:

$$P[\text{Downgrade}|\text{Underperform}]$$

We can solve this by taking values from the completed probability matrix. The equity underperforms in 40% of scenarios. The equity underperforms and the bonds are downgraded in 15% of scenarios. Dividing, we get our final answer, 37.5%.

$$P[\text{Downgrade} \mid \text{Underperform}] = \frac{P[\text{Downgrade} \cap \text{Underperform}]}{P[\text{Underperform}]}$$

$$P[\text{Downgrade} \mid \text{Underperform}] = \frac{15\%}{40\%} = 37.5\%$$

**4.** The prior probabilities are:

$$P[p = 0.55] = 50\%$$
$$P[p = 0.50] = 50\%$$

The probability of the strategy generating 10 positive returns over 20 days if the analyst is correct is:

$$P[10+ \mid p = 0.55] = \binom{20}{10} 0.55^{10} 0.45^{10}$$

The unconditional probability of 10 positive returns is:

$$P[10+] = P[10+ \mid p = 0.55]P[p = 0.55] + P[10+ \mid p = 0.50]P[p = 0.50]$$

$$P[10+] = \binom{20}{10} 0.55^{10} 0.45^{10} \cdot 0.50 + \binom{20}{10} 0.50^{10} 0.50^{10} \cdot 0.50$$

$$P[10+] = 0.50 \binom{20}{10} (0.55^{10} 0.45^{10} + 0.50^{10} 0.50^{10})$$

To get our final answer, the probability that $p = 0.55$ given the 10 positive returns, we use Bayes' theorem:

$$P[p = 0.55 \mid 10+] = \frac{P[10+ \mid p = 0.55]P[p = 0.55]}{P[10+]}$$

$$P[p = 0.55 \mid 10+] = \frac{\binom{20}{10} 0.55^{10} 0.45^{10} \cdot 0.50}{0.50 \binom{20}{10} (0.55^{10} 0.45^{10} + 0.50^{10} 0.50^{10})}$$

$$P[p = 0.55 \mid 10+] = \frac{0.55^{10} 0.45^{10}}{(0.55^{10} 0.45^{10} + 0.50^{10} 0.50^{10})}$$

$$P[p = 0.55 \mid 10+] = \frac{1}{1 + \left(\dfrac{100}{99}\right)^{10}} = 47.49\%$$

The final answer is 47.49%. The strategy generated a profit in only 10 out of 20 days, so our belief in the analyst's claim has decreased. That said, with only 20 data points, it is hard to tell the difference between a strategy that generates profits 55% of the time and a strategy that generates profits 50% of the time. Our belief decreased, but not by much.

5. The final answer is 92.31%. Use + to signify the procyclical index being up, $G$ to signify that the economy is up (growing), and $\bar{G}$ to signify that the economy is down or flat (not growing). We are given the following information:

$$P[+ \mid G] = 75\%$$
$$P[+ \mid \bar{G}] = 25\%$$
$$P[\bar{G}] = 20\%$$

We are asked to find $P[G \mid +]$. Using Bayes' theorem, we have:

$$P[G \mid +] = \frac{P[+ \mid G]P[G]}{P[+]}$$

We were not given $P[G]$, but we know the economy must be either growing or not growing; therefore:

$$P[G] = 1 - P[\bar{G}] = 80\%$$

We can also calculate the unconditional probability that the index is up, $P[+]$:

$$P[+] = P[+ \mid G]P[G] + P[+ \mid \bar{G}]P[\bar{G}]$$
$$P[+] = 75\% \cdot 80\% + 25\% \cdot 20\%$$
$$P[+] = 60\% + 5\% = 65\%$$

Putting it all together, we arrive at our final answer:

$$P[G \mid +] = \frac{P[+ \mid G]P[G]}{P[+]} = \frac{75\% \cdot 80\%}{65\%}$$
$$P[G \mid +] = \frac{60\%}{65\%} = 92.31\%$$

6. The prior beliefs for beating the market in any given year are:

$$P[p = 0.40] = \frac{1}{4}$$
$$P[p = 0.50] = \frac{1}{4}$$
$$P[p = 0.60] = \frac{1}{4}$$
$$P[p = 0.80] = \frac{1}{4}$$

The probability of beating the market three out of five years is:

$$P[3B \mid p = p_i] = \binom{5}{3} p_i^3 (1 - p_i)^2$$

Given a constant, $c$, the posterior probability can be defined as:

$$P[p = p_i \mid 3B] = c \cdot P[3B \mid p = p_i] \cdot P[p = p_i]$$

$$P[p = p_i \mid 3B] = c \cdot \binom{5}{3} p_i^3 (1 - p_i)^2 \cdot \frac{1}{4}$$

We know that all of the posterior probabilities must add to one:

$$\sum_{i=1}^{4} P[p = p_i \mid 3B] = 1$$

$$c \cdot \binom{5}{3} \cdot \frac{1}{4} \sum_{i=1}^{4} p_i^3 (1 - p_i)^2 = 1$$

$$c = \frac{4}{\binom{5}{3} \sum_{i=1}^{4} p_i^3 (1 - p_i)^2}$$

The posterior probabilities are then:

$$P[p = p_i \mid 3B] = \frac{4}{\binom{5}{3} \sum_{i=1}^{4} p_i^3 (1 - p_i)^2} \cdot \binom{5}{3} p_i^3 (1 - p_i)^2 \cdot \frac{1}{4}$$

$$P[p = p_i \mid 3B] = \frac{p_i^3 (1 - p_i)^2}{\sum_{i=1}^{4} p_i^3 (1 - p_i)^2}$$

To get the final answer, we simply substitute in the four possible values for $p_i$. For example, the posterior probability that the manager is an underperformer is:

$$P[p = 0.40 \mid 3B] = \frac{0.40^3 (1 - 0.40)^2}{\sum_{i=1}^{4} p_i^3 (1 - p_i)^2}$$

$$P[p = 0.40 \mid 3B] = \frac{0.40^3 0.60^2}{0.40^3 0.60^2 + 0.50^3 0.50^2 + 0.60^3 0.40^2 + 0.80^3 0.20^2}$$

$$P[p = 0.40 \mid 3B] = \frac{4^3 6^2}{4^3 6^2 + 5^3 5^2 + 6^3 4^2 + 8^3 2^2}$$

$$P[p = 0.40 \mid 3B] = \frac{2,304}{10,933} = 21.1\%$$

The other three probabilities can be found in a similar fashion. The final answer is that the posterior probabilities of the manager being an underperformer, an in-line performer, a star, or a superstar are 21.1%, 28.6%, 31.6%, and 18.7%, respectively. Interestingly, even though the manager beat the market 60% of the time, the manager is almost as likely to be an underperformer or an in-line performer (49.7% probability) as a star or a superstar (50.3% probability).

7. 10%. You are given the following:

$$P[+ \mid Bull] = 75\%$$
$$P[+] = 50\%$$
$$P[Bull] = 60\%$$

You are asked to find $P[Bear \mid +]$. A direct application of Bayes' theorem will not work. Instead we need to use the fact that the Federal Reserve's statement must be either bearish or bullish, no matter what the market does; therefore:

$$P[Bear \mid +] = 1 - P[Bull \mid +] = 1 - \frac{P[+ \mid Bull]P[Bull]}{P[+]}$$

$$P[Bear \mid +] = 1 - \frac{75\% \cdot 60\%}{50\%} = 1 - \frac{\frac{3}{4}\frac{3}{5}}{\frac{1}{2}}$$

$$P[Bear \mid +] = 1 - \frac{9}{10} = 10\%$$

8. Because the prior distribution is a beta distribution and the likelihood can be described by a binomial distribution, we know the posterior distribution must also be a beta distribution. Further, we know that the parameters of the posterior distribution can be found by adding the number of successes to the first parameter, and the number of failures to the second. In this problem the initial distribution was $\beta(4,4)$ and there were 60 successes (up days), and $100 - 60 = 40$ failures. Therefore, the final distribution is $\beta(64,44)$. The mean of a beta distribution, $\beta(a,b)$, is simply $a/(a + b)$. The mean of our posterior distribution is then:

$$\mu = \frac{a}{a+b} = \frac{64}{64+44} = \frac{64}{108} = 59.26\%$$

We therefore believe there is a 59.26% probability that the strategy will be up tomorrow.

9. There are 27 possible states for the network: $3^3 = 27$. The minimum number of probabilities needed to define the network is 22. As an example, we could define $P[A = \text{up}]$, and $P[A = \text{unchanged}]$ for node A, which would allow us to calculate $P[A = \text{down}] = 1 - P[A = \text{up}] - P[A = \text{unchanged}]$. Similarly, we could define two probabilities for node B. For node C, there are nine possible input combinations (each of three possible states for A can be combined with three possible states from B). For each combination, we can define two conditional probabilities

and infer the third. For example, we could define $P[C = up \mid A = up, B = up]$ and $P[C = \text{unchanged} \mid A = up, B = up]$, which would allow us to calculate $P[C = down \mid A = up, B = up] = 1 - P[C = up \mid A = up, B = up] - P[C = \text{unchanged} \mid A = up, B = up]$. This gives us a total of 22 probabilities that we need to define: $2 + 2 + 9 \times 2 = 22$.

10. The correlation matrix for the first network is:

Network 1

|    | E | S1 | S2 |
|----|------|------|------|
| E  | 100% | 49% | 20% |
| S1 | 49% | 100% | 10% |
| S2 | 20% | 10% | 100% |

11. The correlation matrix for the second network is:

Network 2

|    | E | S1 | S2 |
|----|------|------|------|
| E  | 100% | 49% | 7% |
| S1 | 49% | 100% | 15% |
| S2 | 7% | 15% | 100% |

# CHAPTER 7

1. Mean = 45.0; standard deviation = 29.3; standard deviation of mean = 9.3. For the hypothesis that the mean is greater than 40, the appropriate $t$-statistic has a value of 0.54. For a one-sided $t$-test with 9 degrees of freedom, the associated probability is 70%. There is a 30% chance that the true mean is found below 40, and a 70% chance that it is greater than 40.

2. The mean is 6.9% and the standard deviation of the returns is 23.5%, giving a standard deviation of the mean of 7.4%. The $t$-statistic is 0.93. With 9 degrees of freedom, a one-sided $t$-test produces a probability of 81%. In other words, even though the sample mean is positive, there is a 19% chance that the true mean is negative.

3. A negative return would be greater than two standard deviations below the mean. For a normal distribution, the probability (one-tailed) is approximately 2.28%. If we do not know the distribution, then, by Chebyshev's inequality, the probability of a negative return could be as high as $12.5\% = 1/2 \times 1/(2^2)$. There could be a 25% probability of a +/−2 standard deviation event, but we're interested only in the negative tail, so we multiply by ½. We can perform this last step only because we were told the distribution is symmetrical.

4. The expected return is +10%. The 95% VaR is 35% (i.e., 5% of the returns are expected to be worse than −35%). The expected shortfall is 37.5% (again the negative is implied).

5. For a normal distribution, 5% of the weight is less than –1.64 standard deviations from the mean. The 95% VaR can be found as: 0.40% – 1.64 • 2.30% = –3.38%. Because of our quoting convention for VaR, the final answer is VaR = 3.38%.

6. We can use Equation 7.4 to calculate the expected variance of the sample variances. Because we are told the underlying distribution is normal, the excess kurtosis can be assumed to equal zero and $n = 33$; therefore:

$$E[(\hat{\sigma}^2 - \sigma^2)^2] = \sigma^4 \left( \frac{2}{n-1} + \frac{\kappa_{ex}}{n} \right) = 0.40^4 \left( \frac{2}{32} \right) = \frac{0.16^2}{4^2} = 0.04^2$$

The standard deviation of the sample variances is then 4.0%.

7. An appropriate null hypothesis would be: $H_0$: $\sigma = 40\%$. The appropriate test statistic is:

$$(33-1)\frac{0.50^2}{0.40^2} = 50$$

Using a spreadsheet or other program, we calculate the corresponding probability for a chi-squared distribution with 32 degrees of freedom. Only 2.23% of the distribution is greater than 50. At a 95% confidence level, we would reject the null hypothesis.

8. The answer is 12.5%. This is a –2 standard deviation event. According to Chebyshev's inequality, the probability of being more than two standard deviations from the mean is less than or equal to 25%.

$$P[|X - \mu| \geq n\sigma] \leq \frac{1}{n^2}$$

$$P[|X - 15\%| \geq 2 \cdot 10\%] \leq \frac{1}{2^2} = 25\%$$

Because the distribution of returns is symmetrical, half of these extreme returns are greater than +2 standard deviations, and half are less than –2 standard deviations. This leads to the final result, 12.5%.

9. The standard deviation of the mean is 2%:

$$\sigma_\mu = \frac{12\%}{\sqrt{36}} = 2\%$$

This makes the difference between the average fund return and the benchmark, 18% – 14% = 4%, a +2 standard deviation event. For a $t$ distribution with 35 degrees of freedom, the probability of being more than +2 standard deviations is just 2.67%. We can reject the null hypothesis, $H_0$: $\mu = 14\%$, at the 95% confidence level. The difference between the average return and the benchmark return is statistically significant.

10. To find the 95% VaR, we need to find $v$, such that:

$$\int_{-100}^{v} p\, d\pi = 0.05$$

Solving, we have:

$$\int_{-100}^{v} \frac{1}{200} d\pi = \left[ \frac{\pi}{200} \right]_{-100}^{v} = \frac{v+100}{200} = 0.05$$

$$v = -90$$

The VaR is a loss of 90. Alternatively, we could have used geometric arguments to arrive at the same conclusion. In this problem, the PDF describes a rectangle whose base is 200 units and whose height is 1/200. As required, the total area under the PDF, base multiplied by height, is equal to one. The leftmost fraction of the rectangle, from –100 to –90, is also a rectangle, with a base of 10 units and the same height, giving an area of 1/20, or 5% of the total area. The edge of this area is our VaR, as previously found by integration.

11. In the previous question we found that the VaR, $v$, was equal to –90. To find the expected shortfall, we need to solve the following equation:

$$ES = \frac{1}{0.05} \int_{-100}^{-90} \pi p d\pi$$

Solving, we find:

$$ES = \frac{1}{0.05} \int_{-100}^{-90} \pi \frac{1}{200} d\pi = \frac{1}{20} \int_{-100}^{-90} 2\pi d\pi = \frac{1}{20} [\pi^2]_{-100}^{-90}$$

$$= \frac{1}{20} ((-90)^2 - (-100)^2) = -95$$

The final answer, a loss of 95 for the expected shortfall, makes sense. The PDF in this problem is a uniform distribution, with a minimum at –100. Because it is a uniform distribution, all losses between the (negative) VaR, –90, and the minimum, –100, are equally likely; therefore, the average loss, given a VaR exceedance, is halfway between –90 and –100.

12. To find the 95% VaR, we need to find $v$, such that:

$$\int_{-15}^{v} p d\pi = 0.05$$

By inspection, half the distribution is below 5, so we need only bother with the first half of the function:

$$\int_{-15}^{v} \left( \frac{3}{80} + \frac{1}{400} \pi \right) d\pi = \left[ \frac{3}{80} \pi + \frac{1}{800} \pi^2 \right]_{-15}^{v}$$

$$= \frac{3}{80} (v+15) + \frac{1}{800} (v^2 - 225) = 0.05$$

$$v^2 + 30v + 185 = 0$$

We can use the solution to the quadratic equation:

$$v = \frac{-30 \pm \sqrt{900 - 4 \cdot 185}}{2} = -15 \pm 2\sqrt{10}$$

Because the distribution is not defined for $\pi < -15$, we can ignore the negative, giving us the final answer:

$$v = -15 + 2\sqrt{10} = -8.68$$

The one-day 95% VaR for Pyramid Asset Management is approximately 8.68.

## CHAPTER 8

**1.** $\mathbf{A} + \mathbf{B} = \begin{bmatrix} -10 & 9 \\ 8 & 7 \end{bmatrix} + \begin{bmatrix} 2 & 9 \\ 1 & 1 \end{bmatrix} = \begin{bmatrix} -8 & 18 \\ 9 & 8 \end{bmatrix}$

$\mathbf{BC} = \begin{bmatrix} 2 & 9 \\ 1 & 1 \end{bmatrix} \begin{bmatrix} -5 & 7 \\ -10 & 7 \end{bmatrix} = \begin{bmatrix} -100 & 77 \\ -15 & 14 \end{bmatrix}$

$\mathbf{CB} = \begin{bmatrix} -5 & 7 \\ -10 & 7 \end{bmatrix} \begin{bmatrix} 2 & 9 \\ 1 & 1 \end{bmatrix} = \begin{bmatrix} -3 & -38 \\ -13 & -83 \end{bmatrix}$

**2.** For the first part of the question, because matrix addition is commutative and associative, the order in which we perform the operations does not matter:

$$\mathbf{B} + (\mathbf{A} + \mathbf{C}) = \mathbf{A} + \mathbf{B} + \mathbf{C}$$

$$= \begin{bmatrix} -10 & 9 \\ 8 & 7 \end{bmatrix} + \begin{bmatrix} 2 & 9 \\ 1 & 1 \end{bmatrix} + \begin{bmatrix} -5 & 7 \\ -10 & 7 \end{bmatrix}$$

$$= \begin{bmatrix} -13 & 25 \\ -1 & 15 \end{bmatrix}$$

$$\mathbf{B}(\mathbf{A} - \mathbf{C}) = \begin{bmatrix} 2 & 9 \\ 1 & 1 \end{bmatrix} \left( \begin{bmatrix} -10 & 9 \\ 8 & 7 \end{bmatrix} - \begin{bmatrix} -5 & 7 \\ -10 & 7 \end{bmatrix} \right)$$

$$= \begin{bmatrix} 2 & 9 \\ 1 & 1 \end{bmatrix} \begin{bmatrix} -5 & 2 \\ 18 & 0 \end{bmatrix} = \begin{bmatrix} 152 & 4 \\ 13 & 2 \end{bmatrix}$$

**3.** $\mathbf{A}' = \begin{bmatrix} -10 & 8 \\ 9 & 7 \end{bmatrix}$  $\mathbf{C}' = \begin{bmatrix} -5 & -10 \\ 7 & 7 \end{bmatrix}$

4. $F + G = \begin{bmatrix} -6 & 1 \\ -8 & 2 \\ -6 & -3 \end{bmatrix} + \begin{bmatrix} 5 & 0 \\ 0 & -1 \\ -8 & -7 \end{bmatrix} = \begin{bmatrix} -1 & 1 \\ -8 & 1 \\ -14 & -10 \end{bmatrix}$

$FG' = \begin{bmatrix} -6 & 1 \\ -8 & 2 \\ -6 & -3 \end{bmatrix} \begin{bmatrix} 5 & 0 & -8 \\ 0 & -1 & -7 \end{bmatrix} = \begin{bmatrix} -30 & -1 & 41 \\ -40 & -2 & 50 \\ -30 & 3 & 69 \end{bmatrix}$

$F'G = \begin{bmatrix} -6 & -8 & -6 \\ 1 & 2 & -3 \end{bmatrix} \begin{bmatrix} 5 & 0 \\ 0 & -1 \\ -8 & -7 \end{bmatrix} = \begin{bmatrix} 18 & 50 \\ 29 & 19 \end{bmatrix}$

5. A matrix multiplied by an appropriately sized identity matrix is itself.

$$UI = U = \begin{bmatrix} 1 & 1 \\ 1 & 1 \end{bmatrix}$$

This is true when the identity matrix is multiplied by itself, too.

$$I^2 = II = I = \begin{bmatrix} 1 & 0 \\ 0 & 1 \end{bmatrix}$$

For $U^2$:

$$U^2 = \begin{bmatrix} 1 & 1 \\ 1 & 1 \end{bmatrix} \begin{bmatrix} 1 & 1 \\ 1 & 1 \end{bmatrix} = \begin{bmatrix} 2 & 2 \\ 2 & 2 \end{bmatrix}$$

For $AU$:

$$AU = \begin{bmatrix} -10 & 9 \\ 8 & 7 \end{bmatrix} \begin{bmatrix} 1 & 1 \\ 1 & 1 \end{bmatrix} = \begin{bmatrix} -1 & -1 \\ 15 & 15 \end{bmatrix}$$

6. To prove that **J** is the inverse of **K,** we need to show that the two matrices multiplied together produce an identity matrix.

$$JK = \begin{bmatrix} 4 & 1 \\ 9 & 2 \end{bmatrix} \begin{bmatrix} -2 & 1 \\ 9 & -4 \end{bmatrix} = \begin{bmatrix} 1 & 0 \\ 0 & 1 \end{bmatrix}$$

7. To solve this problem, we could multiply **M** by itself five times. Alternatively, we can reexpress **M** as the product of a constant and an identity matrix:

$$M^5 = \left( \begin{bmatrix} 2 & 0 \\ 0 & 2 \end{bmatrix} \right)^5 = \left( 2 \begin{bmatrix} 1 & 0 \\ 0 & 1 \end{bmatrix} \right)^5 = 2^5 \left( \begin{bmatrix} 1 & 0 \\ 0 & 1 \end{bmatrix} \right)^5 = 32 \begin{bmatrix} 1 & 0 \\ 0 & 1 \end{bmatrix}$$

$$= \begin{bmatrix} 32 & 0 \\ 0 & 32 \end{bmatrix}$$

8. At the end of the year, it is expected that 61% of the bonds will have an A rating, 36.4% B, 2.2% C, and 0.4% D. To get the answer, we can proceed one rating at a time. Of the 60% of bonds that are rated A at the start of the year, we expect 95% will still be rated A at the end of the year. Of the 40% of bonds that are rated B at the start of the year, we expect 10% to have been upgraded to A by the end of the year. Putting the two together, we have:

$$60\% \times 95\% + 40\% \times 10\% = 57\% + 4\% = 61\%$$

We can calculate the other three ratings similarly:

$$60\% \times 4\% + 40\% \times 85\% = 2.4\% + 34\% = 36.4\%$$

$$60\% \times 1\% + 40\% \times 4\% = 0.6\% + 1.6\% = 2.2\%$$

$$60\% \times 0\% + 40\% \times 1\% = 0\% + 0.4\% = 0.4\%$$

We can check our answer by noting that the sum of the answers is 100%. At the end of the year each bond must be either A, B, C, or D; therefore, the sum of the expected values must be 100%.

9. To calculate the two-year transition matrix, we simply square the one-year matrix. Using $T_1$ and $T_2$ to denote our one-year and two-year matrices, respectively, we have:

$$T_2 = T_1 T_1 = \begin{bmatrix} 0.95 & 0.04 & 0.01 & 0.00 \\ 0.10 & 0.85 & 0.04 & 0.01 \\ 0.00 & 0.20 & 0.65 & 0.15 \\ 0.00 & 0.00 & 0.00 & 1.00 \end{bmatrix} \begin{bmatrix} 0.95 & 0.04 & 0.01 & 0.00 \\ 0.10 & 0.85 & 0.04 & 0.01 \\ 0.00 & 0.20 & 0.65 & 0.15 \\ 0.00 & 0.00 & 0.00 & 1.00 \end{bmatrix}$$

$$T_2 = \begin{bmatrix} 0.9065 & 0.0740 & 0.0176 & 0.0019 \\ 0.1800 & 0.7345 & 0.0610 & 0.0245 \\ 0.0200 & 0.3000 & 0.4305 & 0.2495 \\ 0.0000 & 0.0000 & 0.0000 & 1.0000 \end{bmatrix}$$

Though not necessary, we can reformat this to match the original one-year matrix:

| 2-year | | To | | | |
|---|---|---|---|---|---|
| | | **A** | **B** | **C** | **D** |
| | **A** | 90.65% | 7.40% | 1.76% | 0.19% |
| | **B** | 18.00% | 73.45% | 6.10% | 2.45% |
| **From** | **C** | 2.00% | 30.00% | 43.05% | 24.95% |
| | **D** | 0.00% | 0.00% | 0.00% | 100.00% |

10. We can use our Cholesky algorithm to find the elements of the matrix:

$$l_{1,1} = \sqrt{\sigma_{11}} = \sqrt{4} = 2$$

$$l_{2,1} = \frac{1}{l_{11}}\sigma_{21} = \frac{1}{2}(14) = 7$$

$$l_{2,2} = \sqrt{\sigma_{22} - l_{2,1}^2} = \sqrt{50 - 7^2} = 1$$

$$l_{3,1} = \frac{1}{l_{1,1}}(\sigma_{3,1}) = \frac{1}{2}(16) = 8$$

$$l_{3,2} = \frac{1}{l_{2,2}}(\sigma_{3,2} - l_{3,1}l_{2,1}) = \frac{1}{1}(58 - 8\cdot 7) = 2$$

$$l_{3,3} = \sqrt{\sigma_{33} - l_{3,1}^2 - l_{3,2}^2} = \sqrt{132 - 8^2 - 2^2} = 8$$

We can express the full lower triangular matrix as:

$$L = \begin{bmatrix} 2 & 0 & 0 \\ 7 & 1 & 0 \\ 8 & 2 & 8 \end{bmatrix}$$

We can verify this answer by noting that $LL'$ is indeed equal to our original covariance matrix, $\Sigma$.

# CHAPTER 9

1. Vectors **a** and **b** are not orthogonal, but **b** and **c** are orthogonal. We know this from their inner products, which we can calculate as follows:

$$\mathbf{a}\cdot\mathbf{b} = \begin{bmatrix} 10 \\ -5 \\ 4 \end{bmatrix}\cdot\begin{bmatrix} 6 \\ 2 \\ -4 \end{bmatrix} = 10\cdot 6 + (-5)\cdot 2 + 4\cdot(-4) = 60 - 10 - 16 = 34 \neq 0$$

$$\mathbf{b}\cdot\mathbf{c} = \begin{bmatrix} 6 \\ 2 \\ -4 \end{bmatrix}\cdot\begin{bmatrix} 5 \\ 5 \\ 10 \end{bmatrix} = 6\cdot 5 + 2\cdot 5 + (-4)\cdot 10 = 30 + 10 - 40 = 0$$

2. In order for **A** to be an orthonormal basis, we require that the column vectors are orthogonal and have a magnitude of one. For the two column vectors to be orthogonal, we require that their inner product is zero:

$$\mathbf{a_1}\cdot\mathbf{a_2} = \begin{bmatrix} x \\ 1 \\ \frac{1}{3} \end{bmatrix}\cdot\begin{bmatrix} \frac{1}{3} \\ \frac{2\sqrt{2}}{3} \end{bmatrix} = x\cdot\frac{1}{3} + \frac{1}{3}\cdot\frac{2\sqrt{2}}{3} = 0$$

$$x = -\frac{2\sqrt{2}}{3}$$

We next check that the column vectors have a magnitude of one:

$$\| a_1 \| = \sqrt{a_1 \cdot a_1} = \sqrt{\begin{bmatrix} -\dfrac{2\sqrt{2}}{3} \\ \dfrac{1}{3} \end{bmatrix} \cdot \begin{bmatrix} -\dfrac{2\sqrt{2}}{3} \\ \dfrac{1}{3} \end{bmatrix}} = \sqrt{\dfrac{8}{9} + \dfrac{1}{9}} = 1$$

$$\| a_2 \| = \sqrt{a_2 \cdot a_2} = \sqrt{\begin{bmatrix} \dfrac{1}{3} \\ \dfrac{2\sqrt{2}}{3} \end{bmatrix} \cdot \begin{bmatrix} \dfrac{1}{3} \\ \dfrac{2\sqrt{2}}{3} \end{bmatrix}} = \sqrt{\dfrac{1}{9} + \dfrac{8}{9}} = 1$$

Both vectors are normal; therefore, the solution,

$$x = -\frac{2\sqrt{2}}{3}$$

makes **A** an orthonormal basis.

3. In order for **B** to be an orthonormal basis, we require that the column vectors are orthogonal and have a magnitude of one. For the two column vectors to be orthogonal, we require that their inner product is zero:

$$b_1 \cdot b_2 = \begin{bmatrix} x \\ y \end{bmatrix} \cdot \begin{bmatrix} \dfrac{1}{5} \\ \dfrac{2\sqrt{6}}{5} \end{bmatrix} = x \cdot \frac{1}{5} + y \cdot \frac{2\sqrt{6}}{5} = 0$$

$$x = -2\sqrt{6}y$$

Using the fact that the magnitude of the first column vector must be one:

$$\| b_1 \| = \sqrt{b_1 \cdot b_1} = \sqrt{x^2 + y^2} = 1$$

$$x^2 + y^2 = 1$$

Substituting in our previous result:

$$\left(-2\sqrt{6}y\right)^2 + y^2 = 24y^2 + y^2 = 1$$

$$y^2 = \frac{1}{25}$$

$$y = \pm\frac{1}{5}$$

Both the positive root and the negative root are legitimate solutions. There are actually two possible final answers.

$$\text{Solution 1: } y = +\frac{1}{5}; \; x = -\frac{2\sqrt{6}}{5}$$

$$\text{Solution 2: } y = -\frac{1}{5}; \; x = +\frac{2\sqrt{6}}{5}$$

4. Because **B** is an orthonormal basis, we can find the coordinate vector for **x**:

$$\mathbf{c} = \mathbf{B}'\mathbf{x} = \begin{bmatrix} \dfrac{1}{\sqrt{2}} & \dfrac{1}{\sqrt{2}} \\ -\dfrac{1}{\sqrt{2}} & \dfrac{1}{\sqrt{2}} \end{bmatrix} \begin{bmatrix} 6 \\ 4 \end{bmatrix} = \begin{bmatrix} \dfrac{10}{\sqrt{2}} \\ -\dfrac{2}{\sqrt{2}} \end{bmatrix}$$

5. A coordinate vector, **c**, for **x** should satisfy the following equation:

$$c_1 \begin{bmatrix} 4 \\ 1 \\ 5 \end{bmatrix} + c_2 \begin{bmatrix} 2 \\ -18 \\ 2 \end{bmatrix} + c_3 \begin{bmatrix} -46 \\ -1 \\ 37 \end{bmatrix} = \begin{bmatrix} -170 \\ -19 \\ 165 \end{bmatrix}$$

Working through produces three simultaneous equations:

$$4c_1 + 2c_2 - 46c_3 = -170$$
$$c_1 - 18c_2 - c_3 = 19$$
$$5c_1 + 2c_2 + 37c_3 = 165$$

By solving and substituting in, we arrive at the final answer: $c_1 = 3$, $c_2 = 1$, $c_3 = 4$.

# CHAPTER 10

1. The expected return of XYZ is 6.01%:

$$E[r_{XYZ}|r_{index}] = E[(\alpha + \beta r_{index} + \varepsilon)|r_{index}]$$
$$= E[\alpha|r_{index}] + \beta E[r_{index}|r_{index}] + E[\varepsilon|r_{index}]$$
$$E[r_{XYZ}|r_{index}] = \alpha + \beta r_{index} = 0.01\% + 1.20 \cdot 5.0\% = 6.01\%$$

2. The expected value of $r_{XYZ}$ is 0.07%:

$$E[r_{XYZ}] = E[\alpha + \beta r_{index} + \varepsilon] = E[\alpha] + \beta E[r_{index}] + E[\varepsilon]$$
$$E[r_{XYZ}] = \alpha + \beta E[r_{index}] = 0.01\% + 1.20 \cdot 0.05\% = 0.07\%$$

The variance of $r_{XYZ}$ is:

$$\text{Var}[r_{XYZ}] = E[(r_{XYZ} - E[r_{XYZ}])^2] = E[(\beta(r_{index} - E[r_{index}]) + \varepsilon)^2]$$
$$\text{Var}[r_{XYZ}] = E[\beta^2(r_{index} - E[r_{index}])^2 + 2\beta\varepsilon(r_{index} - E[r_{index}]) + \varepsilon^2]$$
$$\text{Var}[r_{XYZ}] = \beta^2 E[(r_{index} - E[r_{index}])^2] + 2\beta E[\varepsilon r_{index}]$$
$$\qquad - 2\beta E[\varepsilon]E[r_{index}] + E[\varepsilon^2]$$
$$\text{Var}[r_{XYZ}] = \beta^2 \text{Var}[r_{index}] + \text{Var}[\varepsilon^2] = 0.000424$$

To get to the last line, we use the fact that the covariance between the regressor and the disturbance term is zero in a linear regression, which implies:

$$\text{Cov}[\varepsilon, r_{\text{index}}] = E[\varepsilon r_{\text{index}}] - E[\varepsilon]E[r_{\text{index}}] = E[\varepsilon r_{\text{index}}] = 0$$

Taking the square root of the variance, we get a standard deviation of 2.06%.

3. We start by calculating the covariance:

$$\text{Cov}[r_{\text{XYZ}}, r_{\text{index}}] = E[(r_{\text{XYZ}} - E[r_{\text{XYZ}}])(r_{\text{index}} - E[r_{\text{index}}])]$$
$$= E[(\beta(r_{\text{index}} - E[r_{\text{index}}]) + \varepsilon)(r_{\text{index}} - E[r_{\text{index}}])]$$
$$\text{Cov}[r_{\text{XYZ}}, r_{\text{index}}] = E[\beta(r_{\text{index}} - E[r_{\text{index}}])^2 + \varepsilon r_{\text{index}} - \varepsilon E[r_{\text{index}}]]$$
$$\text{Cov}[r_{\text{XYZ}}, r_{\text{index}}] = E[\beta(r_{\text{index}} - E[r_{\text{index}}])^2] + E[\varepsilon r_{\text{index}}] - E[r_{\text{index}}]E[\varepsilon]$$
$$= \beta E[(r_{\text{index}} - E[r_{\text{index}}])^2]$$
$$\text{Cov}[r_{\text{XYZ}}, r_{\text{index}}] = \beta \text{Var}[r_{\text{index}}]$$

The correlation is then:

$$\rho = \frac{\text{Cov}[r_{\text{XYZ}}, r_{\text{index}}]}{\sqrt{\text{Var}[r_{\text{index}}]\text{Var}[r_{\text{XYZ}}]}} = \frac{\beta\text{Var}[r_{\text{index}}]}{\sqrt{\text{Var}[r_{\text{index}}]\text{Var}[r_{\text{XYZ}}]}} = \beta\frac{\sqrt{\text{Var}[r_{\text{index}}]}}{\sqrt{\text{Var}[r_{\text{XYZ}}]}}$$
$$= 1.20\frac{1.50\%}{2.06\%} = 87.42\%$$

4. The $R^2$ is 20%:

$$R^2 = 1 - \frac{\text{RSS}}{\text{TSS}} = 1 - \frac{10.80\%}{13.50\%} = 20\%$$

5. The corresponding $F$-statistic is 12:

$$\frac{R^2 / (n-1)}{(1-R^2)/(t-n)} = \frac{20\% / (2-1)}{(1-20\%)/(50-2)} = 12$$

   Using a spreadsheet or other program, we see that the probability associated with this $F$-statistic is 0.11%; that is, there is only a 0.11% chance that an $F$-statistic of this magnitude (or greater) would have happened by chance. The $F$-statistic is significant at the 95% confidence level.

6. We compute the adjusted $R^2$ for each model. The univariate model has two regressors, including the constant. The second model has four:

$$\bar{R}_2^2 = 1 - (1-0.60)\frac{20-1}{20-2} = 57.78\%$$
$$\bar{R}_4^2 = 1 - (1-0.64)\frac{20-1}{20-4} = 57.25\%$$

On this basis, the original univariate model is slightly better.

7. 30.5%:

$$E[r_{ABC} \mid r_A, r_B] = E[0.01 + 1.25r_A + 0.34r_B + \varepsilon \mid r_A, r_B]$$
$$= 0.01 + 1.25r_A + 0.34r_B$$
$$E[r_{ABC} \mid r_A, r_B] = 0.01 + 1.25 \cdot 10\% + 0.34 \cdot 50\%$$
$$= 0.01 + 0.125 + 0.17 = 30.5\%$$

8. One possible solution is to drop $X_3$ from the model:

$$r = \beta_1 + \beta_2 X_2 + \varepsilon_1$$

Another possibility, if the spread between $X_2$ and $X_3$ is of interest, is:

$$r = \beta_6 + \beta_7 X_2 + \beta_8 (X_3 - \beta_5 X_2) + \varepsilon$$

where $\beta_5$ is taken from the regression of $X_2$ on $X_3$. Based on the assumption of the OLS model, the term in parentheses will be uncorrelated with $X_2$.

9. We start by writing the equation for the covariance of $X$ and $Y$:

$$\text{Cov}[X, Y] = E[(X - E[X])(Y - E[Y])]$$

Using our linear regression equation and making use of the OLS assumptions, we see that the second term can be expressed in terms of $X$, $\beta$, and $\varepsilon$:

$$Y - E[Y] = (\alpha + \beta X + \varepsilon) - (\alpha + \beta E[X] + E[\varepsilon])$$
$$Y - E[Y] = \beta(X - E[X]) + (\varepsilon - E[\varepsilon])$$

Substituting this into our covariance equation:

$$\text{Cov}[X, Y] = E[(X - E[X])(\beta(X - E[X]) + (\varepsilon - E[\varepsilon]))]$$
$$\text{Cov}[X, Y] = E[\beta(X - E[X])^2 + (X - E[X])(\varepsilon - E[\varepsilon])]$$
$$\text{Cov}[X, Y] = \beta E[(X - E[X])^2] + E[(X - E[X])(\varepsilon - E[\varepsilon])]$$
$$\text{Cov}[X, Y] = \beta \sigma_X^2 + \text{Cov}[X, \varepsilon] = \beta \sigma_X^2$$

All that remains is to divide both sides by the variance of $X$, and to expand the correlation term:

$$\beta = \frac{\text{Cov}[X, Y]}{\sigma_X^2} = \frac{\rho_{XY} \sigma_X \sigma_Y}{\sigma_X^2} = \rho_{XY} \frac{\sigma_Y}{\sigma_X}$$

10. First, we find the optimal value of $\alpha$, $\alpha^*$:

$$\frac{\partial \text{RSS}}{d\alpha} = -2 \sum_{i=1}^{n} (y_i - \alpha - \beta x_i)$$

$$\sum_{i=1}^{n} (y_i - \alpha^* - \beta x_i) = 0$$

$$\sum_{i=1}^{n}(y_i - \beta x_i) = \sum_{i=1}^{n}\alpha^* = n\alpha^*$$

$$\alpha^* = \frac{1}{n}\sum_{i=1}^{n}(y_i - \beta x_i) = \frac{1}{n}\sum_{i=1}^{n}y_i - \beta\frac{1}{n}\sum_{i=1}^{n}x_i$$

$$\alpha^* = \overline{Y} - \beta\overline{X}$$

Next, we solve for $\beta$:

$$\frac{\partial \text{RSS}}{d\beta} = -2\sum_{i=1}^{n}x_i(y_i - \alpha - \beta x_i)$$

$$\sum_{i=1}^{n}x_i(y_i - \alpha - \beta^* x_i) = 0$$

$$\sum_{i=1}^{n}x_iy_i - \alpha\sum_{i=1}^{n}x_i = \beta^*\sum_{i=1}^{n}x_i^2$$

At this point we substitute in our optimal value of $\alpha$, $\alpha^*$:

$$\sum_{i=1}^{n}x_iy_i - (\overline{Y} - \beta^* \overline{X})n\overline{X} = \beta^*\sum_{i=1}^{n}x_i^2$$

$$\beta^* = \frac{\displaystyle\sum_{i=1}^{n}x_iy_i - n\overline{Y}\overline{X}}{\displaystyle\sum_{i=1}^{n}x_i^2 - n\overline{X}^2}$$

# CHAPTER 11

1. The models are:
   a. AR(2)
   b. AR(1)
   c. ARMA(2,1)
   d. Drift-diffusion

2. $E[r_t] = \dfrac{1}{1-\lambda}\alpha = \dfrac{1}{1-0.8}0.02 = 0.10$

3. The expected value of $r_t$ is 0.80% the next period, and 0.84% the following period:

$$E[r_t | r_{t-1}, r_{t-2}] = 0.01 + 0.30r_{t-1} - 0.20r_{t-2}$$
$$= 0.01 + 0.30\cdot0.02 - 0.20\cdot0.04 = 0.0080$$

To get the two-period-ahead forecast, we can use the previous result:

$$E[r_t|r_{t-1},r_{t-2}] = 0.01 + 0.30 \cdot 0.0080 - 0.20 \cdot 0.02 = 0.0084$$

Alternatively, we can substitute the original equation into itself to get $r_t$ in terms of $r_{t-2}$ and $r_{t-3}$:

$$r_t = 0.01 + 0.30r_{t-1} - 0.20r_{t-2} + \varepsilon_t$$

$$r_t = 0.01 + 0.30(0.01 + 0.30r_{t-2} - 0.20r_{t-3} + \varepsilon_{t-1}) - 0.20r_{t-2} + \varepsilon_t$$

$$r_t = 0.013 - 0.11r_{t-2} - 0.06r_{t-3} + \varepsilon_t + 030\varepsilon_{t-1}$$

$$E[r_t|r_{t-2},r_{t-3}] = 0.013 - 0.11r_{t-2} - 0.06r_{t-3}$$

$$= 0.013 - 0.11 \cdot 0.02 - 0.06 \cdot 0.04 = 0.0084$$

4. The expected log return over one year is 0.0%. The standard deviation of the annual log return is 24%.

   We can get this result by recognizing the annual return as a collection of i.i.d. variables, and using our square root rule to calculate the standard deviation. More formally, we can construct the annual return series (remember, log returns are additive):

$$r_{256,t} = \sum_{i=0}^{255} r_{t-i} = \sum_{i=0}^{255} \varepsilon_{t-i}$$

where $r_{256,t}$ is our 256-day annual return. We can find the expected value as follows:

$$E[r_{256,t}] = E\left[\sum_{i=0}^{255} \varepsilon_{t-i}\right] = \sum_{i=0}^{255} E[\varepsilon_{t-i}] = \sum_{i=0}^{255} 0 = 0$$

We can then calculate the variance as follows:

$$\text{Var}[r_{256,t}] = E\left[(r_{256,t} - E[r_{256,t}])^2\right] = E[r_{256,t}^2]$$

$$\text{Var}[r_{256,t}] = E\left[\left(\sum_{i=0}^{255} \varepsilon_{t-i}\right)^2\right] = E\left[\sum_{i=0}^{255}\sum_{j=0}^{255} \varepsilon_{t-i}\varepsilon_{t-j}\right]$$

$$\text{Var}[r_{256,t}] = E\left[\sum_{i=0}^{255}\sum_{j\neq i}^{255} \varepsilon_{t-i}\varepsilon_{t-j} + \sum_{i=0}^{255} \varepsilon_{t-i}^2\right]$$

$$\text{Var}[r_{256,t}] = \sum_{i=0}^{255}\sum_{j\neq i}^{255} E[\varepsilon_{t-i}\varepsilon_{t-j}] + \sum_{i=0}^{255} E[\varepsilon_{t-i}^2]$$

For each term in the final summation, we can determine the value by noting the following:

$$\text{Var}[\varepsilon_t] = E[(\varepsilon_t - E[\varepsilon_t])^2] = E[\varepsilon_t^2]$$

$$\text{Cov}[\varepsilon_s, \varepsilon_t] = E[(\varepsilon_s - E[\varepsilon_s])(\varepsilon_t - E[\varepsilon_t])] = E[\varepsilon_s \varepsilon_t] = 0 \ \forall \ s \neq t$$

Now we have:

$$\text{Var}[r_{256,t}] = \sum_{i=0}^{255}\sum_{j \neq i}^{255} 0 + \sum_{i=0}^{255} \text{Var}[\varepsilon_t] = 256 \cdot \text{Var}[\varepsilon_t]$$

The variance of the annual returns is 256 times as great as the variance of the daily returns. To get the standard deviation, we just take the square root of both sides:

$$\sigma_{256} = \sqrt{256 \cdot \text{Var}[\varepsilon_t]} = 16\sigma_\varepsilon = 16 \cdot 1.5\% = 24\%$$

5. The expected log return over one year is 25.6%. The standard deviation of the annual log return is 24%.

   As before, we can get this result by recognizing the annual return as a collection of i.i.d. variables, and using our square root rule to calculate the standard deviation. More formally, we can construct the annual return series (remember, log returns are additive):

$$r_{256,t} = \sum_{i=0}^{255} r_{t-i} = \sum_{i=0}^{255} (\alpha + \varepsilon_{t-i}) = 256\alpha + \sum_{i=0}^{255} \varepsilon_{t-i}$$

where $r_{256,t}$ is our 256-day annual return. We can find the expected value as follows:

$$E[r_{256,t}] = E\left[256\alpha + \sum_{i=0}^{255} \varepsilon_{t-i}\right] = 256\alpha + \sum_{i=0}^{255} (E[\varepsilon_{t-i}])$$

$$= 256\alpha + \sum_{i=0}^{255} 0 = 256\alpha = 25.6\%$$

Using this result, we can then calculate the variance as follows:

$$\text{Var}[r_{256,t}] = E[(r_{256,t} - E[r_{256,t}])^2] = E\left[\left(256\alpha + \sum_{i=0}^{255} \varepsilon_{t-i} - 256\alpha\right)^2\right]$$

$$\text{Var}[r_{256,t}] = E\left[\left(\sum_{i=0}^{255} \varepsilon_{t-i}\right)^2\right]$$

This is exactly the same as what we had in the previous question. The addition of the drift term does not impact the variance or standard deviation. The final result is the same as before:

$$\sigma_{256} = \sqrt{256 \cdot \text{Var}[\varepsilon_t]} = 16\sigma_\varepsilon = 16 \cdot 1.5\% = 24\%$$

6. The expected log return over two days is 0.40%. The standard deviation of the two returns is 3.0%. For the case where $\lambda$ equals $-0.50$, the mean of the two-day return would be approximately 0.13%, and the standard deviation would be approximately 1.73%.

We start by expressing the original AR(1) equation as an infinite sum of lags of the disturbance term:

$$r_t = \alpha + \lambda r_{t-1} + \varepsilon_{t-1} = \alpha \sum_{i=0}^{n-1} \lambda^i + \lambda^n r_{t-n} + \sum_{i=0}^{n-1} \lambda^i \varepsilon_{t-i}$$

$$r_t = \alpha \frac{1}{1-\lambda} + \sum_{i=0}^{\infty} \lambda^i \varepsilon_{t-i}$$

Constructing the two-period return is fairly straightforward. Paying careful attention to the time subscripts, we can group the disturbance terms into one summation:

$$r_{2,t} = r_t + r_{t-1} = 2\alpha \frac{1}{1-\lambda} + \varepsilon_t + (1+\lambda) \sum_{i=0}^{\infty} \lambda^i \varepsilon_{t-i-1}$$

where $r_{2,t}$ is our two-day return. We can find the expected value as follows:

$$\mu_2 = E[r_{2,t}] = 2\alpha \frac{1}{1-\lambda} + E[\varepsilon_t] + (1+\lambda) \sum_{i=0}^{\infty} \lambda^i E[\varepsilon_{t-i-1}] = 2\alpha \frac{1}{1-\lambda}$$

We then proceed to find the variance:

$$\text{Var}[r_{2,t}] = E[r_{2,t}^2] - E[r_{2,t}]^2$$

$$\text{Var}[r_{2,t}] = E\left[ \mu_2^2 + \varepsilon_t^2 + (1+\lambda)^2 \left( \sum_{i=0}^{\infty} \lambda^i \varepsilon_{t-i-1} \right)^2 + 2\mu\varepsilon_t \right.$$

$$\left. + 2\mu(1+\lambda) \sum_{i=0}^{\infty} \lambda^i \varepsilon_{t-i-1} + 2\varepsilon_t(1+\lambda) \sum_{i=0}^{\infty} \lambda^i \varepsilon_{t-i-1} \right] - \mu_2^2$$

$$\text{Var}[r_{2,t}] = E[\varepsilon_t^2] + (1+\lambda)^2 E\left[ \left( \sum_{i=0}^{\infty} \lambda^i \varepsilon_{t-i-1} \right)^2 \right] + 2(1-\lambda) \sum_{i=0}^{\infty} \lambda^i E[\varepsilon_t \varepsilon_{t-i-1}]$$

$$\text{Var}[r_{2,t}] = \sigma_\varepsilon^2 + (1+\lambda)^2 E\left[ \sum_{i=0}^{\infty} \lambda^{2i} \varepsilon_{t-i-1}^2 + \sum_{i=0}^{\infty} \sum_{j \neq i} \lambda^i \lambda^j \varepsilon_{t-i-1} \varepsilon_{t-j-1} \right] + 0$$

$$\text{Var}[r_{2,t}] = \sigma_\varepsilon^2 \left[ 1 + (1+\lambda)^2 \sum_{i=0}^{\infty} \lambda^{2i} \right] = 2\sigma_\varepsilon^2 \frac{1}{1-\lambda}$$

The standard deviation of the two-day return is then:

$$\sigma_2 = \sqrt{2\sigma_\varepsilon^2 \frac{1}{1-\lambda}} = \sigma_\varepsilon \sqrt{\frac{2}{1-\lambda}}$$

7. The unconditional mean of the model is equal to $\theta$, 4%. If interest rates start out at 6%, then we would expect interest rates to be 5.00%, then 4.50%, and then 4.25% over the next three periods. This result is obtained by noting that the conditional expectation for the next period's interest rate is, in this case, simply the average of the previous period's rate and the long-term mean of 4%:

$$E[r_t \mid r_{t-1}] = 0.5r_{t-1} + (1-0.5) \cdot 4\% + \sigma E[\varepsilon_t]$$
$$E[r_t \mid r_{t-1}] = 0.5(r_{t-1} + 4\%)$$

8. By iteratively substituting the equation into itself, we see that this process can be written as an infinite moving average:

$$r_t = \rho r_{t-1} + \varepsilon_t = \rho^2 r_{t-2} + \rho\varepsilon_t + \varepsilon_t = \rho^n r_{t-n} + \sum_{i=0}^{n-1} \rho^i \varepsilon_{t-i} = \sum_{i=0}^{\infty} \rho^i \varepsilon_{t-i}$$

The unconditional mean is 0:

$$E[r_t] = E\left[\sum_{i=0}^{\infty} \rho^i \varepsilon_{t-i}\right] = \sum_{i=0}^{\infty} \rho^i E[\varepsilon_{t-i}] = \sum_{i=0}^{\infty} \rho^i \cdot 0 = 0$$

Similarly, we can find the unconditional variance. First we note that, because the covariance between different disturbance terms is zero and the expected value of any individual disturbance terms is zero, we have the following:

$$\text{Cov}[\varepsilon_{t-i}, \varepsilon_{t-j}] = E[\varepsilon_{t-i}\varepsilon_{t-j}] + E[\varepsilon_{t-i}]E[\varepsilon_{t-j}] = E[\varepsilon_{t-i}\varepsilon_{t-j}] = 0 \ \forall i \neq j$$

Using this and the fact that the unconditional mean is also zero:

$$\text{Var}[r_t] = E[r_t^2] + E[r_t]^2 = E[r_t^2] = E\left[\sum_{i=0}^{\infty}\sum_{j=0}^{\infty} \rho^i \rho^j \varepsilon_{t-i}\varepsilon_{t-j}\right]$$

$$\text{Var}[r_t] = \sum_{i=0}^{\infty} \rho^{2i} E[\varepsilon_{t-i}^2] + \sum_{i=0}^{\infty}\sum_{j\neq i}^{\infty} \rho^i \rho^j E[\varepsilon_{t-i}\varepsilon_{t-j}] = \sigma^2 \sum_{i=0}^{\infty} \rho^{2i}$$

$$= \sigma^2 \frac{1}{1-\rho^2}$$

9. Using the results from the previous question, we first derive an expression for the covariance:

$$\text{Cov}[r_t, r_{t-n}] = E[r_t r_{t-n}] + E[r_t]E[r_{t-n}] = E[r_t r_{t-n}]$$

$$= E\left[\sum_{i=0}^{\infty} \rho^i \varepsilon_{t-i} \sum_{j=0}^{\infty} \rho^j \varepsilon_{t-j-n}\right]$$

$$\text{Cov}[r_t, r_{t-n}] = E\left[\left(\sum_{i=0}^{n-1}\rho^i\varepsilon_{t-i} + \sum_{i=n}^{\infty}\rho^i\varepsilon_{t-i}\right)\sum_{j=0}^{\infty}\rho^j\varepsilon_{t-j-n}\right]$$

$$\text{Cov}[r_t, r_{t-n}] = E\left[\left(\sum_{i=0}^{n-1}\rho^i\varepsilon_{t-i} + \rho^n\sum_{i=0}^{\infty}\rho^i\varepsilon_{t-i-n}\right)\sum_{j=0}^{\infty}\rho^j\varepsilon_{t-j-n}\right]$$

$$\text{Cov}[r_t, r_{t-n}] = E\left[\sum_{i=0}^{n-1}\rho^i\varepsilon_{t-i}\sum_{j=0}^{\infty}\rho^j\varepsilon_{t-j-n} + \rho^n\sum_{i=0}^{\infty}\sum_{j=0}^{\infty}\rho^i\rho^j\varepsilon_{t-i-n}\varepsilon_{t-j-n}\right]$$

$$\text{Cov}[r_t, r_{t-n}] = \rho^n E\left[\sum_{i=0}^{\infty}\sum_{j=0}^{\infty}\rho^i\rho^j\varepsilon_{t-i-n}\varepsilon_{t-j-n}\right] = \rho^n\text{Var}[r_t]$$

For the last line we were able to eliminate the first term in the expectations by noting that all the products contained different disturbance terms. From the preceding problem we know that the expected value of these cross products is zero. Because the unconditional variance is the same for both $r_t$ and $r_{t-n}$, finding the correlation is just a matter of dividing $\text{Var}[r_t]$:

$$\text{Corr}[r_t, r_{t-n}] = \frac{\rho^n\text{Var}[r_t]}{\sqrt{\text{Var}[r_t]}\sqrt{\text{Var}[r_t]}} = \frac{\rho^n\text{Var}[r_t]}{\text{Var}[r_t]} = \rho^n$$

10. We start by expressing both $r_t$, and $r_{t-1}$ as infinite series:

$$r_t = \frac{\alpha}{1-\lambda} + \sum_{i=0}^{\infty}\lambda^i\varepsilon_{t-i} = \frac{\alpha}{1-\lambda} + \varepsilon_t + \lambda\sum_{i=0}^{\infty}\lambda^i\varepsilon_{t-i-1}$$

$$r_{t-1} = \frac{\alpha}{1-\lambda} + \sum_{i=0}^{\infty}\lambda^i\varepsilon_{t-i-1}$$

Next we find the mean of both series:

$$E[r_t] = E[r_{t-1}] = \frac{\alpha}{1-\lambda}$$

Because the error terms are uncorrelated, we know that:

$$E[\varepsilon_s\varepsilon_t] = 0 \ \ \forall \ s \neq t$$

Using this and the previous results, we calculate the variances and covariance:

$$\text{Var}[r_t] = E\left[\left(\sum_{i=0}^{\infty}\lambda^i\varepsilon_{t-i}\right)^2\right] = \frac{\sigma_\varepsilon^2}{1-\lambda^2}$$

$$\text{Var}[r_{t-1}] = E\left[\left(\sum_{i=0}^{\infty}\lambda^i\varepsilon_{t-i-1}\right)^2\right] = \frac{\sigma_\varepsilon^2}{1-\lambda^2}$$

$$\text{Cov}[r_t, r_{t-1}] = E\left[\left(\varepsilon_t + \lambda\sum_{i=0}^{\infty}\lambda^i\varepsilon_{t-i-1}\right)\left(\sum_{i=0}^{\infty}\lambda^i\varepsilon_{t-i-1}\right)\right] = \frac{\lambda\sigma_\varepsilon^2}{1-\lambda^2}$$

Finally, the correlation is:

$$\text{Corr}[r_t, r_{t-1}] = \frac{\text{Cov}[r_t, r_{t-1}]}{\sqrt{\text{Var}[r_t]\text{Var}[r_{t-1}]}} = \lambda$$

11. To annualize the log return, we simply multiply by the number of months in a year, 12. To get the annualized standard deviation, we multiply by the square root of the number of periods. For skewness and kurtosis, we divide by the square root of 12 and 12, respectively. This gives: mean = 24%; standard deviation = 5.20%; skewness = −0.29; kurtosis = 0.20.

## CHAPTER 12

1. We need to find $h$, such that:

$$\sum_{i=0}^{h-1} \delta^i = \frac{1}{2}\sum_{i=0}^{n-1}\delta^i = \frac{1}{2}\frac{1-\delta^n}{1-\delta} = \frac{1-\delta^h}{1-\delta}$$

Solving, we find:

$$0.5(1-\delta^n) = 1-\delta^h$$
$$\delta^h = 0.5(\delta^n + 1)$$
$$h\ln(\delta) = \ln(0.5 + 0.5\delta^n)$$
$$h = \frac{\ln(0.5 + 0.5\delta^n)}{\ln(\delta)}$$

Alternatively, the formula for the half-life can be expressed as:

$$h = \frac{\ln(0.5) + \ln(1+\delta^n)}{\ln(\delta)}$$

2. We start by computing decay factors and values for $x^2$:

| $t$ | 0 | 1 | 2 | 3 | 4 | 5 | 6 | 7 |
|-----|-----|-----|-----|-----|-----|-----|-----|-----|
| $x$ | 11 | 84 | 30 | 73 | 56 | 58 | 52 | 35 |
| $\delta$ | 0.6983 | 0.7351 | 0.7738 | 0.8145 | 0.8574 | 0.9025 | 0.9500 | 1.0000 |
| $x^2$ | 121 | 7,056 | 900 | 5,329 | 3,136 | 3,364 | 2,704 | 1,225 |

For the mean, using Equation 12.2, we have:

$$\hat{\mu}_t = \frac{1-\delta}{1-\delta^n}\sum_{i=0}^{n-1}\delta^i x_{t-i} = 0.15 \times 336.86 = 50.04$$

For the variance, using Equation 12.12, we have:

$$\hat{\sigma}_t^2 = A \sum_{i=0}^{n-1} \delta^i x_{t-i}^2 - B \hat{\mu}_t^2 = 0.17 \times 19826.75 - 1.15 \times 50.04^2 = 505.18$$

Finally, we can take the square root of our answer for the variance, to get the standard deviation, 22.48.

3. We start by calculating the following values:

| $t$ | 0 | 1 | 2 | 3 | 4 | 5 |
|---|---|---|---|---|---|---|
| $x$ | 0.04 | 0.84 | 0.28 | 0.62 | 0.42 | 0.46 |
| $\delta_1$ | 1.0000 | 1.0000 | 1.0000 | 1.0000 | 1.0000 | 1.0000 |
| $\delta_2$ | 0.9044 | 0.9135 | 0.9227 | 0.9321 | 0.9415 | 0.9510 |
| $\delta_3$ | 0.3487 | 0.3874 | 0.4305 | 0.4783 | 0.5314 | 0.5905 |

| $t$ | 6 | 7 | 8 | 9 | 10 |
|---|---|---|---|---|---|
| $x$ | 0.66 | 0.69 | 0.39 | 0.99 | 0.37 |
| $\delta_1$ | 1.0000 | 1.0000 | 1.0000 | 1.0000 | 1.0000 |
| $\delta_2$ | 0.9606 | 0.9703 | 0.9801 | 0.9900 | 1.0000 |
| $\delta_3$ | 0.6561 | 0.7290 | 0.8100 | 0.9000 | 1.0000 |

We then use Equation 12.2 to calculate our estimates of the mean: mean (no decay) = 0.5236; mean (decay = 0.99) = 0.5263; mean (decay = 0.90) = 0.5486.

4. We start by expanding the table from our answer to question 3:

| $t$ | 0 | 1 | 2 | 3 | 4 | 5 |
|---|---|---|---|---|---|---|
| $x$ | 0.04 | 0.84 | 0.28 | 0.62 | 0.42 | 0.46 |
| $\delta_1$ | 1.0000 | 1.0000 | 1.0000 | 1.0000 | 1.0000 | 1.0000 |
| $\delta_2$ | 0.9044 | 0.9135 | 0.9227 | 0.9321 | 0.9415 | 0.9510 |
| $\delta_3$ | 0.3487 | 0.3874 | 0.4305 | 0.4783 | 0.5314 | 0.5905 |
| $x^2$ | 0.0016 | 0.7056 | 0.0784 | 0.3844 | 0.1764 | 0.2116 |
| $(x - E[x_1])^2$ | 0.233904 | 0.100086 | 0.059359 | 0.009286 | 0.01074 | 0.00405 |

| $t$ | 6 | 7 | 8 | 9 | 10 |
|---|---|---|---|---|---|
| $x$ | 0.66 | 0.69 | 0.39 | 0.99 | 0.37 |
| $\delta_1$ | 1.0000 | 1.0000 | 1.0000 | 1.0000 | 1.0000 |
| $\delta_2$ | 0.9606 | 0.9703 | 0.9801 | 0.9900 | 1.0000 |
| $\delta_3$ | 0.6561 | 0.7290 | 0.8100 | 0.9000 | 1.0000 |
| $x^2$ | 0.4356 | 0.4761 | 0.1521 | 0.9801 | 0.1369 |
| $(x - E[x_1])^2$ | 0.018595 | 0.027677 | 0.017859 | 0.217495 | 0.023604 |

In the last line, we have used our estimate of the mean (no decay) from the previous problem.

For the first estimator with no decay factor, we can use Equation 3.19 to calculate the variance:

$$\hat{\sigma}_1^2 \frac{1}{n-1}\sum_{i=1}^{n}(x_i - \hat{\mu}_x)^2 = \frac{0.7227}{11-1} = 0.0723$$

For the second and third estimators, we use Equation 12.12 and our estimates of the mean from the previous question:

$$\hat{\sigma}_2^2 = A\sum_{i=0}^{n-1}\delta^i x_{t-i}^2 - B\hat{\mu}_t^2 = 0.11\times10.47 - 1.10\times0.5263^2 = 0.0716$$

$$\hat{\sigma}_3^2 = A\sum_{i=0}^{n-1}\delta^i x_{t-i}^2 - B\hat{\mu}_t^2 = 0.16\times6.86 - 1.11\times0.5486^2 = 0.2610$$

Taking the square root of the variances, we arrive at our final answers: standard deviation (no decay) = 0.2688; standard deviation (decay = 0.99) = 0.2676; standard deviation (decay = 0.90) = 0.2610.

5. The new estimates are 10.10%, 9.82%, and finally 9.78%. These can be found as follows:

$$\hat{\mu}_t = 0.02x_t + 0.98\hat{\mu}_{t-1}$$
$$\hat{\mu}_1 = 0.02\cdot15\% + 0.98\cdot10\% = 10.10\%$$
$$\hat{\mu}_2 = 0.02\cdot-4\% + 0.98\cdot12.8\% = 9.82\%$$
$$\hat{\mu}_3 = 0.02\cdot8\% + 0.98\cdot11.744\% = 9.78\%$$

6. The half-lives are:

$$h_{200} = \frac{\ln(0.5 + 0.5\times0.95^{200})}{\ln(0.95)} = 13.5127$$

$$h_{1,000} = \frac{\ln(0.5 + 0.5\times0.95^{1,000})}{\ln(0.95)} = 13.5134$$

7. The half-life of the EWMA estimator is approximately 11.11 days. A rectangular window with 22 days would have the most similar half-life, 11 days.

$$h_{32} = \frac{\ln(0.5 + 0.5\times0.96^{32})}{\ln(0.96)} = 11.11$$

8. $1 - 0.96^{50} = 87\%$

9. Approximately 19.72%. We first update our estimate of the variance, and then take the square root:

$$\hat{\sigma}_t^2 = (1-\delta)(r_t - \mu)^2 + \delta\hat{\sigma}_{t-1}^2$$
$$\hat{\sigma}_t^2 = (1-0.97)(15\% - 10\%)^2 + 0.97\cdot20\%^2$$
$$\hat{\sigma}_t^2 = 0.038875$$
$$\hat{\sigma}_t = 19.72\%$$

**10.** Approximately 10.25%. We can use our updating rule,

$$\hat{\sigma}_t^2 = (1 - \delta)r_t^2 + \delta\hat{\sigma}_{t-1}^2$$

to calculate successive estimates of the variance. The estimate of the standard deviation is just the square root of the variance estimator:

| $t$ | 0 | 1 | 2 | 3 | 4 | 5 | 6 |
|---|---|---|---|---|---|---|---|
| $r$ | | –5% | 18% | 16% | –2% | 5% | –10% |
| $E[\sigma_2]$ | 0.010000 | 0.009625 | 0.010764 | 0.011506 | 0.010950 | 0.010528 | 0.010501 |
| $E[\sigma]$ | 10% | 9.81% | 10.37% | 10.73% | 10.46% | 10.26% | 10.25% |

# References

Allen, Linda, Jacob Boudoukh, and Anthony Saunders. 2004. *Understanding Market, Credit, and Operational Risk: The Value at Risk Approach*. Malden, MA: Blackwell Publishing.

Artzner, Philippe, Freddy Delbaen, Jean-Marc Eber, and David Heath. 1999. "Coherent Measures of Risk." *Mathematical Finance* 9 (3): 203–228.

Campbell, John, Andrew Lo, and A. Craig MacKinlay. 1996. *The Econometrics of Financial Markets*. Princeton, NJ: Princeton University Press.

Gigerenzer, Gerd, and Adrian Edwards. 2003. "Simple Tools for Understanding Risks: From Innumeracy to Insight." *BMJ* 327: 74a–744.

Hendry, David. 1980. "Econometrics—Alchemy or Science?" *Economica* 47 (188): 387–406.

Hua, Philip, and Paul Wilmott. 1997. "Crash Courses." *Risk* 10 (June): 64–67.

Kritzman, Mark, Yuanzhen Li, Sebastien Page, and Roberto Rigobon. 2010. "Principal Components as a Measure of Systemic Risk." *MIT Sloan Research* Paper No. 4785–10 (June 30).

Meucci, Attilio. 2009. "Managing Diversification." *Risk* 22 (May): 74–79.

# About the Author

**M**ichael B. Miller studied economics at the American University of Paris and the University of Oxford before starting a career in finance. He is currently the CEO of Northstar Risk Corp. Before that he was the Chief Risk Officer for Tremblant Capital, and prior to that Head of Quantitative Risk Management at Fortress Investment Group. Mr. Miller is also a certified FRM and an adjunct professor at Rutgers Business School.

# About the Companion Website

**M**any of the topics in this book are accompanied by an icon, as shown here. The icon indicates that Excel examples can be found on this book's companion website, www.wiley.com/go/millerfinance2e. Enter password: mathstats159 to access the site.

# Index